MODERN LANGUAGES
FOR MUSICIANS

Julie Yarbrough

MODERN LANGUAGES FOR MUSICIANS

by

Julie Yarbrough

PENDRAGON PRESS

STUYVESANT, NY

To

The Mixsons

The Library of Congress Cataloging-in-Publication Data
Yarbrough, Julie.
  Modern languages for musician / by Julie Yarbrough. p. cm.
  English, French, German, and Italian.
  ISBN 0-945193-06-8 :
  1. Languages, Modern--Study and teaching. 2. Musicians--Education--Languages.
I. Title.
  PB36.Y37 1992   92-3451
  418--dc20   CIP
                                                                         MN

TABLE OF CONTENTS

Foreword   xv

ENGLISH   1

International Phonetic Alphabet   3
    Consonants ● Vowels ● Neutrals ● Diphthongs

GERMAN   5

Chapter One
International Phonetic Alphabet   7
    General Principles of Pronunciation ● Specifics of Pronuncia-
    tion (Vowels, Diphthongs, Umlauts, Consonants)
      Exercises: Supplementary Pronunciation,15; Alphabet,16;
      Pitch Names, 17; Opera Titles, 18

Chapter Two
I. Nouns   21
    Specific Characteristics of Nouns in German (Capitalization,
    Functions, Gender, Characteristic of Gender, Gender Deter-
    mination, Plurals—Nominative Case, Plural Forms, Sum-
    mary—Noun Plurals
      Exercises: Instrument Names, 22, 23; Song Titles, 24, 25;
      Country Names/Languages, 30; Cardinal Numbers, 31;
      Ordinal Numbers, 31; Days of the Week, Months of the Year,
      32; Directions, Seasons, Nouns in Vocal Literature,33
II. Pronouns   36
    Pronoun Substitution ● Cases (Nominative Case, Accusative
    Case, Dative Case, Genitive Case) ● Demonstrative Pronouns
    ● Indefinite Pronouns ● Possessive Pronouns
      Exercises: Common terms, 46; Compositions, 48

Chapter Three

I. Verbs   49

Terminology (Tense, Conjugation, Auxiliary Verb) • Conjugations • Auxiliary Verbs • Principle Parts (Infinitive, Simple
Past Tense, Strong and Weak Verbs , Simple Past Tense Endings—Strong Verbs, Simple Past Tense Endings—Weak
Verbs, Simple Past Tense—Translation, Verbs Ending in
-ieren, Simple Past Tense—Auxiliary Verbs, Past Participle,
Translation Guidelines, Past Participle—Verbs Ending in
-ieren, Past Participle—Strong Verbs, Compound Past Tense)
• Voice (Transitive [active], Intransitive [passive]) • Imperative • Prefixes (Inseparable, Separable, Variables) • Modal
Auxiliary Verbs • Special Meanings

II. Reflexive Verbs   69

III. Tenses   70

Past Perfect Tense • Future Tense • Future Perfect Tense

IV. Summary   72

Categories of Verbs • Principle Parts • Auxiliary Verbs •
Conjugation • Prefixes • Tenses

Principle Parts of Strong and Weak Verbs   73

Reflexive Verbs   82

Verbs with Separable Prefixes   83

Idiomatic Verbs   86

Verbs Frequently Encountered in Music Scores, Texts on   86
Music, and Musicological Essays

Verbs Frequently Encountered in Vocal Literature   87

Musical Exercises, 88

Chapter Four

I. Adjectives   89

Demonstrative Adjectives • Possessive Adjectives • Predicate
Nominative • Predicate Adjectives • Unpreceded Adjectives •
Preceded Adjectives • Numerical Adjectives • Past Participle
• Present Participle

II. Comparative and Superlative   95

Research Questions, 98

III. Adverbs   99

   Degrees (Positive, Comparative) ● Forms of Adverb Superlatives (Relative Superlative, Absolute Superlative)

   Exercises, 103; Musical Vocabulary Building, 103;
   Adjectives and Adverbs, 109; Expressions, 114

Chapter Five

   I. Sentence Structure   113

   II. Prepositions   114

   Cases ● Special Uses

   III. Conjunctions   119

   Coordinating Conjunctions ● Subordinating Conjunctions

   IV. Particles   122

   Preposition Supplement (Time of Day, 124; Definite Time,
   Indefinite Time, 125); Abbreviations, Idiomatic Expressions,
   125; Translation Exercises, 126

Chapter Six

   I. Word Order In Sentence Structure   129

   Normal Word Order ● Inverted Word Order

   II. Interrogative Pronouns   130

   III. Relative Pronouns   132

   Translation Exercises, 136

Chapter Seven

   I. Additional Characteristics of Verbs   139

   II. Subjunctive Mood   141

   Forms ● Summary

   III. Conditional Mood   145

   Present Tense ● Past Tense ● Summary ● Conditions

   IV. Direct and Indirect Discourse   148

   Direct Discourse ● Indirect Discourse

   V. Passive Voice   149

   Translation Exercises, 150

FRENCH 153

Chapter One

I. International Phonetic Alphabet 155

General Principles of Pronunciation (Stress, Intonation) • Punctuation and Capitalization • Specifics of Pronunciation (Vowels, Nasal vowels, Semivowels, Consonants)

II. Pronunciation Guidelines 162

Symbols Exclusive to French (Accents, Diaresis) • Pronunciation of Final Consonants • Elision • Liaison • Cognates

Exercises, 164; Supplementary Pronunciation, Alphabet, Pitch Names, 165; Opera Titles, 166

Chapter Two

I. Nouns 171

Specific Characteristics of Nouns in French (Gender, Definite Article, Indefinite Article, Characteristics of Gender, Gender Determination, Plurals)

Exercises; Instrument Names, 172, 174; Song Titles, 175; Country Names/Languages, 176; Cardinal Numbers, 177; Ordinal Numbers, 178; Days of the Week, Months of the Year, 179; Directions, Seasons , Nouns in Vocal Literature, 180

II. Pronouns 184

Subject Pronouns • Meaning of Subject Pronouns

III. Prepositions 185

Musical Exercises, 187-188

Chapter Three

I. Verbs 189

Terminology • Categories of Verbs • Imperative • Compound Past Tense • Reflexive Verbs • Irregular Verb Spellings

II. Indicative Mood 204

Present Tense • Compound Past Tense • Simple Past Tense • Imperfect Tense • Future Tense • Future Perfect Tense • Pluperfect Tense

III. Prefixes 209

Forms • Translation principles

IV. Summary210

Categories of Verbs ● Auxiliary Verbs ● Stem Spelling ● Indicative Mood ● Tenses

Principle Parts of Regular and Irregular Verbs212

Reflexive Verbs226

Idiomatic Verbs227

Verbs Frequently Encountered in Music Scores, Texts on Music, and Musicological Essays229

Verbs Frequently Encountered in Vocal Literature230

Musical Exercises, 231

Chapter Four

I. Adjectives233

Demonstrative Adjectives ● Predicate Nominative ● Possessive Adjectives ● Adjective Word Order ● Descriptive Adjectives ● Past Participle ● Present Participle ● Liaison

Musical Exercises, 239

II. Comparative and Superlative241

Regular Adjectives ● Superlative Construction

III. Adverbs243

Forms ● Irregular Comparative and Superlative Forms ● Special Meanings ● Adverbs Used in Music

Research Questions, 245; Musical Vocabulary Building,247; Adjectives and Adverbs Encountered in Music, 253; Adjectives and Adverbs, 258; Expressions, 268

Chapter Five

I. Sentence Structure269

II. Partitive272

Partitive Forms ● Use of the Partitive ● Summary of Partitive Forms

III. Prepositions273

IV. Conjunctions279

V. Additional Pronoun Forms281

Direct Object Pronouns ● Indirect Object Pronouns ● Pronoun Word Order

VI. Stressed Form of Pronouns287

VII. Possessive Pronouns   289

VIII. Demonstrative Pronouns   290

Prepositions That Give Directions in Music, Abbreviations, 291; Idiomatic Expressions, 292; Preposition Supplement (Time of Day) 292; Translation Exercises, 294

Chapter Six

I. Word Order in Sentence Structure   297
Normal Word Order ● Inverted Word Order

II. Interrogative Adjectives   300

III. Interrogative Pronouns   301
Subject ● Direct Object ● Special Uses

IV. Relative Pronouns   302

V. Indirect Interrogative Pronouns   305

VI. Demonstrative Pronouns   306

VII. Indefinite Adjectives and Pronouns   306

VIII. Exceptions to Partitive Usage   309

Translation Example, 310; Translation Exercises, 312

Chapter Seven   315

I. Additional Characteristics of Verbs   315

II. Subjunctive Mood   320

III. Conditional Mood   324
Present Tense ● Uses ● Compound Past Tense
Translation Exercises, 327

ITALIAN 329

Chapter One

I. International Phonetic Alphabet   331
General Principles of Pronunciation (Stress, Punctuation, Capitalization, Syllabication) ● Specifics of Pronunciation (Vowels, Close and Open Vowels, Diphthongs, Consonants)

II. Pronunciation Guidelines   340
Symbols Exclusive to Italian ● Cognates
Exercises: Supplementary Pronunciation, 341; Alphabet, 342; Pitch Names, 343; Opera Titles, 344

Chapter Two

I. Nouns   349

Specific Characteristics of Nouns in Italian (Gender, Definite Article, Indefinite Article, Characteristic of Gender, Gender Determination, Noun Plurals)

Exercises: Instrument Names, 350, 352, Country Names/Languages, 357; Cardinal Numbers, 358; Ordinal Numbers, 359; Days of the Week, Months of the Year, 360; Directions, Seasons , Nouns in Vocal Literature, 361

II. Pronouns   364

III. Prepositions   366

Musical Exercises, 368

Chapter Three

I. Verbs   371

Terminology (Tense, Conjugation, Auxiliary Verbs, Principle Parts) ● Categories of Verbs (Regular Verbs, Irregular Verbs) ● Imperative ● Compound Past Tense ● Reflexive Verbs ● Irregular Verb Spellings

II. Indicative Mood   385

Present Tense ● Compound Past Tense ● Simple Past Tense ● Imperfect Tense ● Future Tense ● Future Perfect Tense ● Past Perfect Tense

III. Prefixes   391

Forms ● Cognates

IV. Summary   392

Categories of Verbs ● Auxiliary Verbs ● Stem Spelling ● Indicative Mood ● Tenses

Principle Parts of Regular and Irregular Verbs   394

Reflexive Verbs   403

Idiomatic Verbs   404

Verbs Frequently Encountered in Music Scores, Texts on Music, and Musicological Essays   406

Verbs Frequently Encountered in Vocal Literature   407

Musical Exercises, 408

Chapter Four

I. Adjectives 411

Demonstrative Adjectives ● Predicate Nominative ● Possessive Adjectives ● Adjective Word Order ● Descriptive Adjectives ● Past Participle ● Present Participle

Musical Exercises, 419

II. Comparative and Superlative 421

Regular Adjectives ● Relative Superlative ● Irregular Forms

III. Adverbs

Forms ● Irregular Comparative and Superlative Forms ● Adverbs Used in Music ● Suffixes ● Special Uses

*Research Questions, 428; Musical Vocabulary Building, 429;
Adjectives and Adverbs Encountered in Music, 439;
Adjectives and Adverbs, 453; Expressions, 459*

Chapter Five

I. Sentence Structure 461

II. Partitive 462

III. Prepositions 463

IV. Conjunctions 465

Coordinating Conjunctions ● Subordinating Conjunctions

V. Interjections 468

VI. Additional Pronoun Forms 469

Direct Object Pronouns ● Indirect Object Pronouns ● Position
of Conjunctive Pronouns

VII. Disjunctive Form 473

VIII. Possessive Pronouns 473

IX. Demonstrative Pronouns 474

*Prepositions That Give Directions in Music, 475; Preposition
Supplement (Time of Day, Dates), 476; Abbreviations Found
in Music, 477; Translation Exercises, 478*

Chapter Six

I. Word Order in Sentence Structure 481

Normal Word Order ● Inverted Word Order

II. Interrogative Adjectives and Pronouns 482

Forms of Interrogative Adjectives ● Interrogative Pronouns

III. Relative Pronouns 483

IV. Indefinite Adjectives and Pronouns   485
    Indefinite Adjectives • Indefinite Pronouns • Indefinite Adjectives or Pronouns
        Exercise, 486

Chapter Seven
    I. Additional Characteristics of Verbs   487
    II. Subjunctive Mood   489
    III. Conditional Mood   494
        Present Tense • Compound Past Tense • Uses
        Translation Exercises, 496

FOREWORD

The significance of modern languages as essential professional knowledge in the field of music has been somewhat obscured by the emphasis which has traditionally been placed on the study of classical languages. *MODERN LANGUAGES FOR MUSICIANS* is a unique synthesis of these two related subjects, designed to make languages both practical and applicable for musicians by transforming the symbols and sounds of language through relevant music terminology into a functional skill.

In approaching foreign languages there are some facts which should be systematically learned and others which are primarily for reference. Logically, it is more important to learn to recognize a verb stem and immediately associate its meaning than to memorize the conjugation of the verb in each tense and case. Because those whose native tongue is the English language presumably understand its grammatical construction and the meaning of words, the following study of English is devoted solely to the introduction and illustration of the International Phonetic Alphabet (IPA) symbols, as the phonetic reference for subsequent sections on German, French, and Italian.

Exercises and work lists appear throughout the book, usually at the end of the chapter. However, when they occur in the middle of text, they will be set within a box for clarity.

MODERN LANGUAGES FOR MUSICIANS is intended for performing musicians and for those seeking a reading and speaking acquaintance with modern languages; it thereby provides a practical approach to languages and a broader knowledge of music, so that the musician in turn might reflect the integration of the art of music and the craft of modern languages.

ENGLISH

As stated in the Foreword, this section on the English language is designed to establish through the study of the International Phonetic Alphabet a standard reference which may be applied to the subsequent study of German, French, and Italian.

The alphabet symbols of the English language represent sounds; since there are only twenty-six such symbols and more than forty different sounds incorporated into the pronunciation of the English language, an obvious discrepancy exists. In English, as well as in German, French, and Italian, selected symbols from the International Phonetic Alphabet (IPA) are used to differentiate each characteristic sound. In applying the IPA symbols it should thus be possible to recognize sounds and the manner of phonetic production implied by each symbol, regardless of the language.

The following list of IPA equivalents should not be memorized, but should be learned through repeated reference. The conversion of these symbols into knowledge is a fundamental skill necessary for the study of foreign languages.

INTERNATIONAL PHONETIC ALPHABET

A. Consonants

	Phonetic Name	Dictionary Symbol[1]	Composer's Name Illustrating Sound	IPA Symbol
1.	initial **b**	b	**B**ull	[b]
2.	initial **c**	k	**C**avendish	[k]
3.	initial **c**	ch	**C**hanler	[tʃ]
4.	initial **d**	d	**D**ibdin	[d]
5	initial **f**	f	**F**ord	[f]
6.	initial **g**	g	**G**ibbons	[g]
7.	initial **h**	h	**H**opkinson	[h]
8.	initial **j**	j	**J**ackson	[dʒ]
9.	initial **k**	k	**K**eel	[k]
10.	initial **l**	l	**L**inley	[l]
11.	initial **m**	m	**M**orley	[m]
12.	initial **n**	n	**N**ares	[n]
13.	internal **n**	ng	**P**ilki**ng**ton	[ŋ]
14.	initial **p**	p	**P**arry	[p]
15.	initial **r**	r	**R**osseter	[r]
16.	initial **s**	s	**S**tevens	[s]
17.	internal **s**	zh	**S**essions	[ʒ]
18.	initial **sh**	sh	**Sh**ield	[ʃ]
19.	initial **t**	t	**T**allis	[t]
20.	**th** (thin)	th	**Th**eobald	[θ]
21.	**th** (then)	th	Bli**th**eman	[ð]
22.	initial **v**	v	**V**aughan Williams	[v]
23.	initial **w**	w	**W**ilbye	[w]
24.	**wh**	hw	**Wh**elpley	[ʌ] or [hw]
25.	initial **y**	y	**Y**oung	[j]
26.	initial **z**	z	**Z**offany	[z]

[1]Webster's *Third New International Dictionary* (Springfield, Massachusetts: G. and C. Merriam Company, 1961).

B. Vowels

Phonetic Name	Dictionary Symbol	Composer's Name Illustrating Sound	IPA Symbol
1. long **a**	ā	Taylor	[e]
2. short **a**	ă	Campion	[æ] or [a]
3. **ah**	ä	Arne	[ɑ]
4. **aw**	ô	Lawes	[ɔ]
5. long **e**	ē	Weelkes	[i]
6. short **e**	ĕ	Leveridge	[ɛ]
7. short **i**	ĭ	Bishop	[ɪ]
8. long **o**	ō	Storace	[o]
9. short **u**	ŭ	Humfrey	[ʌ]
10. double long **o**	ōō	Goossens	[u]
11. double short **o**	ŏŏ	Hook	[ʊ]

C. Neutrals

Phonetic Name	Dictionary Symbol	Composer's Name Illustrating Sound	IPA Symbol
1. **uh**	ă, ĕ, ĭ, ŏ, ŭ	Wilson	[ə]
2. **er**	ēr	Purcell	[ɚ]
3. **ir**	ûr	Byrd	[ɝ]

D. Diphthongs

Phonetic Name	Dictionary Symbol	Composer's Name Illustrating Sound	IPA Symbol
1. **ah-e or i**	ĭ	Ives	[ɑɪ]
2. **a-e or i**	ā	Bacon	[ɛɪ]
3. **o-oo**	ō	Blow	[ou]
4. **ah-oo**	ou	Dowland	[ɑʊ]
5. **aw-i**	oi	Boyce	[ɔɪ]

GERMAN

The study of the German language is the most logical sequel to that of English because there are many German words that sound and/or look like words in the English language. The reference to cognates may be helpful in synthesizing the visual and aural skills of a foreign language by relating them to the familiar. The German language appears to be more complex than it actually is because of the multifarious grammatical forms; this study concentrates on reducing the German language to its most practical form for use by musicians in reading, speaking, translating, and performing.

Chapter One

INTERNATIONAL PHONETIC ALPHABET

The value of a standardized set of symbols representing sounds becomes immediately apparent when the same alphabet letters used in a different sequence create a foreign language. It is thus necessary only to supplement the IPA symbols introduced in the preceding study of English and explain the aural connotation of each symbol within the context of the German language. When the following guidelines are carefully followed it should be possible to correctly pronounce most words in the German language.

A. General Principles of Pronunciation

1. The stress or accent on most words in German is on the first syllable.

a) Exception: When the word begins with an unaccented prefix (be-, emp-, ent-, er-, ge-, ver-, zer-)(Chapter Three).

b) Most words of foreign derivation are stressed on the last syllable.

2. Most German words are spelled exactly as pronounced and, conversely, are pronounced exactly as spelled.

a) All nouns in German are capitalized.

3. Most punctuation marks in German are used as in English; the exceptions in the case of the comma and the exclamation point will be mentioned in the course of this study.

4. In German, individual words are spoken as distinct units; words are seldom elided. Accordingly, in spoken German the air flow is stopped long enough to separate the final consonant of a word from the initial vowel of the following word. This interrupting action is accomplished by means of a glottal stop, indicated by the IPA symbol [ʔ]. A glottal stop occurs when the air flow that produces sound is momentarily interrupted by a brief closure of the vocal chords, or glottis.

B. Specifics of Pronunciation

1. Vowels

a) The letters *a, e, i, o, u* each represent one pure sound pronounced without the diphthonic inflection often indigenous to these letters in English.

b) The words "long" and "short" as they apply to vowel sounds in German generally refer to the duration of the basic sound represented by the vowel letter.

(1) Vowels are "long" or prolonged

    (a) when final

    (b) when followed by a single consonant that ends the word or syllable

    (c) when followed by *h*

    (d) when doubled.

(2) Vowels are short

    (a) when followed by more than one consonant

    (b) when followed by a doubled consonant.

c) Specific sounds

(1) The basic vowel sound represented by the letter *a* in German is [ɑ]. The [ɑ] sound is frequently spelled *a, aa, ah* and is either long or short according to the foregoing rules.

LONG	SHORT
Brahms	Bach
Mahler	Franz
Stamitz	Gassmann
Wagner	Pachelbel

(2) The letter *a* also spells the [æ] sound; this sound occurs frequently in German but is illustrated in order to distinguish it from [ɑ].

        Cannabich

        Hammerschmidt

        Matthison

(3) The basic long vowel sound represented by the letter *e* in German is [eː].[1] This is a pure vowel sound with none of the characteristics of the [eɪ] diphthong.

> Beethoven
>
> Reger
>
> Sweelinck
>
> Weber
>
> Webern

(4) The letter *e* is also used to represent the [ɛ] sound.

> Albert
>
> Albrechtsberger
>
> Berg
>
> Schenk
>
> Schmelzer
>
> Schrecker

(5) When the letter *e* occurs in German in the final, unstressed position of a word the neutral [ə] sound is implied; the [ə] sound is generally pronounced

(a) in the prefixes ge- and be-

(b) when final in an *unstressed* syllable

> Buxtehud*e*
>
> Hen*ze*

(c) before the following consonants in final un- stressed syllables:

l (ln, lnd, lst, lt) – Händ*el*

m - von Ein*em*

n (nd, ns) - Beethov*en*

r (rs, rst, rt) - Bung*ert*

s

st

t

---

[1]Two vertical dots following an IPA symbol indicate the long vowel sound.

(d) in compound words where the first part of the compound ends in unstressed *e* or in unstressed *e* followed by any of the consonants listed above: Mendelssohn.

(6) The long vowel sound represented in German by the letter *i* is [ɪː]: B*i*ber

(a) The vowel combination *ie* is always pronounced [ɪː].

> Nietsche
>
> van Swieten
>
> Tieck
>
> Wieck

(7) The letter *i* is most frequently pronounced in German, however as [ɪ].

> Ditters von Dittersdorf
>
> Hiller
>
> Rilke
>
> Schiller

(8) The [o] sound is generally represented by the letter *o* in German spelling:

> Froberger
>
> Mozart
>
> Schobert

(9) The IPA symbol [ɔ] represents the short pronunciation of the letter *o* in German; the [ɔ] sound is pronounced more open than [o].

> Gombert
>
> Hoffmann
>
> Lortzing
>
> Monn
>
> Ofterdinger
>
> Wolf

(10) The long vowel sound of the letter *u* is [uː].

> Kuhlau
>
> Kuhnau
>
> Rubinstein

Schubert

Schumann

(11) The short vowel sound of the letter *u* is [ʊ].

Bruch

von Bruck

Bruckner

Fux

Gluck

Zumsteeg

2. Diphthongs

a) Diphthongs in German follow the same pattern as those in English: a stressed vowel immediately followed by an unstressed vowel sound.

(1) The diphthong [aɪ] has the following spellings in German:

ai (ay)	*ei (ey)*
Hofhaimer	Reichardt
Nicolai	Scheidemann
	Scheidt
	Schein
	Wagenseil

(2) The diphthong [aʊ] is spelled *au*:

Graun

Graupner

Schopenhauer

Strauss

(3) The diphthong [ɔɪ] is generally spelled in German *eu, äu*:

Kreutzer

Bäumler

3. Umlauts

a) The umlaut, two dots placed horizontally over a vowel, indicates that the pure vowel sound is modified in pronunciation.

b) Like pure vowels, those that are pronounced with umlauts can be either short or long.

(1) The long *ä* is pronounced [ɛː]: Schäfer

(2) The short *ä* is pronounced [ɛ]: Schäffer

(3) The long *ö* [øː] is pronounced as [e] with the lips rounded and protruded: Mörike

(4) The short *ö* [ø] is pronounced as [ɛ] with the lips rounded and protruded: von Köchel

(5) The long *ü* [yː] is pronounced as [ɪː] with the lips rounded and protruded: von Bülow, Grünewald

(6) The short *ü* [y] is pronounced as [ɪ] with the lips rounded and protruded: Büchner, Müller, Rückert, Schütz

   c) Although some German words pronounced with an umlaut vowel do not use the symbol (Schoenberg), frequently the two dots that constitute the umlaut symbol are not available for printing in English. In this case, the vowel letter that is pronounced with an umlaut is immediately followed by the letter *e* to so indicate this pronunciation: Mae*terlinck, Loewe, Loeffler.

  4. Consonants

   a) Many consonants in German correspond in sound to those used in English.

    (1) [b] is spelled *b* (*bb*): Böttcher

At the end of a word and before *t*, the letter *b* is pronounced [p].

    (2) The [ç] ("ich") sound is almost exclusive to the German language. It is always spelled *ch* and is produced by putting the top of the tongue close to the palate in the position for the vowel [ɪː], then expelling the breath very sharply between the tongue and the palate. This sound is clearly distinguished from the consonant [ʃ] in that the point of approximation between the tongue and the palate is farther back and the lips are spread rather than round.

      (a) The [ç] ("ich") sound occurs after *i, e, ä, ö, ü, eu, äu* and after consonants: Cannabich

      (b) The combination *ig* at the end of a word or syllable is pronounced [ç] as in "ich": Seelig

12

(3) The [x] ("ach") sound is exclusive to the German language and is pronounced by moving the back of the tongue up toward the soft palate so that the air passing between them causes a sound of friction. The [k] sound should be avoided in the production of the [x] sound.

(a) The "ach" sound is spelled: *ch* after *a, o, u,* and *au*: Bach

(4) [d] is spelled *d* (*dd*): Dessauer

At the end of a word or syllable and before the letter *t*, the letter *d* is pronounced [t] : Scheidt, Medtner

(5) [f] is spelled *f, ff,* and *ph*: Fortner

The letter *v* is generally pronounced [f] except in some foreign words: Vogler

(6) [g] is spelled *g* (*gg*): Gluck

At the end of a word or syllable and before *t*, the letter *g* is pronounced [k] : Wagner

(7) When the letter *h* occurs in the initial position of a word, it is pronounced [h] : Hiller, Himmel.

The letter *h* after a vowel lengthens the vowel, although the *h* is silent: Mahler. The letter *h* is part of a new sound when it occurs in combination with these consonants:

c - Bru*ch*

p - *Ph*ilipp

sc - *Sch*oeck

t - *Th*alberg

(8) [j] is the symbol used to represent the letter *y* in English. This sound is spelled exclusively *j* in German, and is pronounced more sharply than the [j] sound in English, so that a slight sound of friction is heard: Jahn, Joachim.

(9) The sound represented by the [k] symbol is spelled in the following ways in German:

k, kk: Keiser

ch: in some words of Greek derivation –*Ch*or

ch: before s=ks: Sa*ch*s, Dre*ch*sler

q: Quantze

g: at the end of a word or syllable in a final consonant cluster (except after *i* or *n*): Vogrich, Wagner

(10) The [l] sound in German is spelled *l* and *ll:* Lachner, Lassen

(11) The [m] sound in German is spelled *m and mm:* Marx, Marschner

(12) The [n] sound in German is spelled *n* and *nn:* Neefe, Neumeister

(13) Except for a few foreign words, the letters *ng* in German imply the [ŋ] sound: Spiering

(14) The [p] sound is spelled *p* and *pp:* Pranter, Prehl, Proch. The letter *b* has the sound of [p]:

   (a) at the end of a word or syllable: Abheiter

   (b) in a final combination: Abt

(15) The combination of [p] and [f] is treated in German as a single combined sound [pf]: Pfitzner

(16) The letter *q* is pronounced [k]. Since this letter is always followed by *u*, which implies the [v] sound in this sequence, the sound of *qu* in German is [kv] : Quantz

(17) The [r] sound in German is spelled *r:* Reger, Reissiger.

(18) The letter *s* has the following pronunciations:

   (a) *s* = [z] before a vowel: Hensel

   (b) *sp* and *st* at the end of a syllable or in the middle of a word = [s] : Rust

   (c) *ss* = [s] : Pressel. *ss* is printed with the symbol *ß* (es-zet) after a long vowel, at the end of a word, and after a short vowel at the end of a syllable.

   (d) *s* = [s] at the end of a word or syllable: Ries

(19) The [ʃ] sound in German is spelled in the following ways:

   (a) *sch:* Schubert, Schumann

   (b) *st, sp* at the beginning of a word: Stamitz, Spohr

(20) The [t] sound is spelled *t, tt,* and *th:* Tausig, Telemann. The letter *d* implies [t] :

   (a) at the end of a word or syllable : Schmid

   (b) in a final consonant cluster : Bezold

(21) Although *v* is pronounced [v] in some foreign words, the letter *v* is pronounced [f] in most German words: Lev.

(22) The letter *w* is pronounced [v]: Wagenseil

(23) The letter *z* and combination *tz* is pronounced [ts]: Pilz, Platz, Mozart. In the combination *-tion, t* also has the sound [ts].

MUSICAL EXERCISES

1. Look up the first name(s) of each composer cited in the pronunciation illustrations.

(a) Write out the full names of each composer using IPA symbols.

(b) List the birth and death dates of each composer.

SUPPLEMENTARY PRONUNCIATION EXERCISES

1. Just as the written symbol of each alphabet letter in English has a name (although the symbol may represent more than one sound) likewise in German each alphabet letter has a name and should be used when spelling any German word aloud. Further, the German language uses not only Roman type in printing, but also a distinctive style known as Fraktur, German, or Gothic type. Although for practical reasons this type is seldom printed today, the student interested in translating should become familiar with this printing style for easy reading access to older editions and periodicals.

a) Notes on Fraktur type

(1) Roman type *s* = ſ

ẞ at the end of a word or syllable

(2) *ss* is printed both ſſ and ß and pronounced the same

(3) capital letters *I* and *J* have the same form ℑ

(4) vowels with umlauts (*ä, ö, ü*) may be printed *ae, oe,* and *ue.*

ALPHABET

Roman type			*Fraktur type*	
A	a	[ɑ]	𝕬	𝖆
B	b	[be:]	𝕭	𝖇
C	c	[tse:]	𝕮	𝖈
D	d	[de:]	𝕯	𝖉
E	e	[e:]	𝕰	𝖊
F	f	[ɛf]	𝕱	𝖋
G	g	[ge]	𝕲	𝖌
H	h	[hɑ]	𝕳	𝖍
I	i	[ɪ:]	𝕴	𝖎
J	j	[jot]	𝕵	𝖏
K	k	[kɑ]	𝕶	𝖐
L	l	[ɛl]	𝕷	𝖑
M	m	[ɛm]	𝕸	𝖒
N	n	[ɛn]	𝕹	𝖓
O	o	[o]	𝕺	𝖔
P	p	[pe:]	𝕻	𝖕
Q	q	[kʊ:]	𝕼	𝖖
R	r	[ɛr]	𝕽	𝖗
S	s	[ɛs]	𝕾	𝖘
T	t	[te:]	𝕿	𝖙
U	u	[ʊ:]	𝖀	𝖚
V	v	[fɑu]	𝖁	𝖛
W	w	[ve:]	𝖂	𝖜
X	x	[ɪ:ks]	𝖃	𝖝
Y	y	üpsilon	𝖄	𝖞
Z	z	[tsɛt]	𝖅	ʒ

2. Just as alphabet letters are used to spell words, so the same symbols are used to designate the pitch names of the modern diatonic scale. The following are the German letter names and pronunciation of each scale degree:

English	German
English	*German*
C	C [tseː]
C flat	ces [tsɛs]
C sharp	cis [tsɪːs]
D	D [deː]
D flat	des [dɛs]
D sharp	dis [dɪːs]
E	E [eː]
E flat	es [ɛs]
E sharp	eis [ɛɪs]
F	F [ɛf]
F flat	fes [fɛs]
F sharp	fis [fɪːs]
G	G [geː]
G flat	ges [gɛs]
G sharp	gis [gɪːs]
A	A [ɑ]
A flat	as [ɑs]
A sharp	ais [ɑɪs]
B	H [hɑ]
B flat	b [beː]
B sharp	bis [bɪːs]
♭♭ = eses	
✕ = isis	

17

3. Opera titles in German

(a) Say each of the following opera titles aloud.

Die Abreise	Hänsel und Gretel
Die ägyptische Helena	Hans Heiling
Agnes von Hohenstaufen	Hans Sachs
Alfonso und Estrella	Hin und Zurück
Alpenkönig und Menschenfeind	Die Hochzeit des Camacho
Ariadne auf Naxos	Der junge Siegfried
Aschenbrödel	Die Kreuzfahrer
Bärenhäuter	Die Liebe auf dem Lande
Die Bergknappen	Das Liebesverbot
Der Bergsee	Lohengrin
Der Bergwerke zu Falun	Die Loreley
Der Bettelstudent	Die lustigen Weiber von Windsor
Die Bluthochzeit	Die Massnahme
Die Bürgschaft	Mathis der Maler
Der Corregidor	Die Meistersinger von Nürnberg
Doktor und Apotheker	Moses und Aron
Das Donauweibchen	Neues vom Tage
Der Dorfbarbier	Oberon
Die Dreigroschenoper	Parsifal
Die Entführung aus dem Serail	Peter Schmoll und seine Nachbarn
Erwartung	Die Räuber
Euryanthe	Das Rheingold
Faust	Der Ring des Nibelungen
Fidelio	Der Rosenkavalier
Die Fledermaus	Salome
Der fliegende Holländer	Der Schauspieldirektor
Die Frau ohne Schatten	Die Schweigsame Frau
Der Freischütz	Siegfried
Die Geisterinsel	Siegfrieds Tod
Die glückliche Hand	Das Stumme Waldmädchen
Die Götterdämmerung	

Tannhäuser

Von Heute auf Morgen

Der Teufel ist los

Die Walküre

Thamos, König in Ägypten

Die Zauberflöte

Tristan und Isolde

Zar und Zimmermann

Undine

(b) Identify the composer of each work and cite the date of the first performance of each.

(c) Write out each title phonetically using IPA symbols.

Chapter Two

In Chapter One German phonetics are so presented, that it should now be possible to pronounce most words in German correctly. With this chapter begins the simplified grammatical approach to German which will ultimately enable musicians to read and translate for professional purposes, perform with understanding, and command the basic language skills of conversation and comprehension. When this is accomplished, German is indeed a practical modern language and a necessary tool for professional musicians.

I. NOUNS

A noun is the name of a person, place, or thing.

Specific Characteristics of Nouns in German

1. As stated in chapter 1, all nouns in German are capitalized. Accordingly, when translating from German into English, the first step should be to pick out the nouns in the sentence.

2. Nouns have two main functions:

   a) to simply name persons, places, or things

   b) to participate in sentence construction

   (1) The simplest function of a noun in a sentence occurs when the noun is the subject of the sentence (subject: the word or word group performing the action or on whom the action is performed). When a noun functions as the subject of a sentence in German it is said to be in the *Nominative Case*, the first of four cases (how the word functions in the sentences) of nouns in the German language.

3. All nouns in German have a *gender*, with the grammatical designation of masculine, feminine, or neuter.

   a) A definite article is a word modifying a noun that points out a particular person, place, or thing. In English the definite article used to distinguish nouns of all genders is *the*; in German there is a separate definite article for each gender. In the nominative case the definite articles are:

21

der [der] – masculine

die [di:] – feminine

das [dɑs] – neuter

EXERCISES

1. Consult the pronunciation guide at the end of Chapter One; list all opera titles that contain the definite articles *der, die, das*, and classify the modified nouns accordingly:

Masculine   *Feminine*   *Neuter*

2. For further pronunciation practice read the following list of instrument names aloud:

English	*German*
piccolo	die kleine Flöte
flute	die Flöte
oboe	die Oboe
English horn	das englisch Horn
clarinet	die Klarinette
bass clarinet	die Bassklarinette
bassoon	das Fagott
contrabassoon	das Kontrafagott
horn	das Horn
trumpet	die Trompete
trombone	die Posaune
tuba	die Tuba
timpani	die Pauken
bass drum	die grosse Trommel
cymbals	die Becken
snare drum	die kleine Trommel
tenor drum	die Rührtrommel
triangle	der Triangel
tambourine	die Schellentrommel
gong	der Tam-tam
castanets	die Kastagnetten
xylophone	das Xylophon
glockenspiel	das Glockenspiel
bells or chimes	die Glocken
celesta	die Celesta
harp	die Harfe

violin	die Violine (Geige)
viola	die Bratsche
violoncello	das Violoncello
double bass	der Kontrabass

It should be clear from the foregoing exercises that every noun in German possesses a gender, which is indicated by the preceding article.

b) As in English, there also exists in German the indefinite article, a word modifying a noun that does not indicate a *particular* person, place, or thing. The indefinite articles in English are *a* and *an*; in German the indefinite articles in the nominative case are:

ein [aɪn] = masculine

eine [aɪnɛ] = feminine

ein [aɪn] = neuter

EXERCISE

Substitute the correct indefinite article for the definite article in the preceding list of instrument names; write out each name phonetically.

---

4. The primary difference between nouns in English and German, then, is the characteristic of gender. In English

the tone

the music

the piano

must be learned in German as

der Ton

die Musik

das Klavier[1]

a) Because nouns in German do not exist independently of their gender, it is necessary to learn the gender of each noun along with the meaning of the word and thereby associate the appropriate definite or indefinite article with each word. It is essential to learn noun genders for the purpose of accurate translating and reading in German and most especially for effective conversation, as much

---

[1]In German-speaking countries a distinction is made between *das Klavier* which designates an upright, or practice-type piano, and *der Flügel*, which designates a grand piano.

German grammar is founded upon noun genders.

EXERCISE

Say the following song titles from *Die Winterreise* (The Winter Journey) by Schubert:

die Krähe

der Leiermann

der Lindenbaum

der Wegweiser

die Wetterfahne

das Wirtshaus

Note that five titles are compound nouns, that is, a new word formed by joining two simple nouns; the gender of the final noun determines the gender of the compound noun. Each simple noun is pronounced distinctly, with no elision of internal consonants: das Wirts-haus.

---

5. The gender of many nouns can be determined by the word meaning or ending. The following general rules are applicable:

a) Masculine gender

(1) male beings

(2) names of seasons, days, months

(3) names of professional activities generally associated with men: der Violinist; der Pianist

b) Feminine gender

(1) female beings

(2) nouns ending in *-in*: die Violinistin; die Pianistin

(3) most nouns ending in *-e*

(4) all nouns ending in *-heit, -keit, - schaft, -ung*

(5) all nouns ending in *-ie, -ion, - tät*

c) Neuter gender

    (1) all nouns ending in *-chen* and *- lein*[2]

    (2) verb infinitives used as nouns: das Singen

    (3) names of continents, countries and cities

EXERCISE

From the foregoing guidelines determine the gender of each of the following Schubert song titles:

> Erlkönig
>
> Erstarrung
>
> Einsamkeit
>
> Heidenröslein
>
> Hoffnung
>
> Liebesbotschaft
>
> Seligkeit
>
> Zügenglöcklein

---

6. Just as nouns in English have a plural form designating more than one person, place, or thing, nouns in German may also be pluralized. German noun plurals, however, are not as easily formed as in English, where either *s* or *es* is generally added to the singular noun form. In the nominative case in German all plural nouns of all three genders take the definite article *die*. Although plural nouns can not take the word *ein* as an indefinite article, it is possible to modify plural German nouns with a group of indefinite articles known as "ein"-words, because they take the same forms as the word *ein*. Similarly there exists a group of definite articles *der, die, das,* and are known accordingly as "der"-words.

---

[2]The endings *-chen* and *- lein* are known as *diminuitives* because when they are suffixed to German nouns the word assumes a different, generally diminished meaning, either (1) literal: die Frau (lady), das Fräulein (young lady), or (2) a charming, personal meaning for which there is no accurate equivalent in English: die Rose— "O Röschen rot" (Mahler, Second Symphony).

"ein"-words
Nominative Case

	Singular			Plural (all cases)
	M	F	N	
kein —no, not any	keine	kein	kein	keine
mein—my	meine	mein	mein	meine
dein—your	deine	dein	dein	deine
sein—his	seine	sein	sein	seine
unser—our	unser	unsere	unser	unsere
euer— your	euer	euere	euer	euere
Ihr—your	Ihr	Ihre	Ihr	Ihre

" ... *kein* Schlaf ..."
(Wolf, "In der Frühe")

"der"-words
Nominative Case

	Singular			Plural (all cases)
	M	F	N	
aller—all	aller	alle	alles	alle
dieser—this	dieser	diese	dieses	diese
jeder—each, every	jeder	jede	jedes	–
jener—that, those	jener	jene	jenes	–
mancher—many a	mancher	manche	manches	manche
solcher—such a	solcher	solche	solches	–
welcher—which, what	welcher	welche	welches	welche

" ... hell und herrlich, *jener* Stern ..."
(Schumann, *Frauenliebe und Leben*–2)

A thorough acquaintance with the "der"-words and "ein"-words greatly facilitates translation, as these are the small critical words that generally help determine sentence meaning. In subsequent reference to case and definite/indefinite articles it should be understood that the "der"-words and "ein"- words are included.

7. Although German nouns are generally not as simple to pluralize as those in English, it is possible to determine the plural of most nouns from their form and gender. Most important to musicians is correct pronunciation in performance and the ability to recognize a noun in print as plural, indicated either by the definite or indefinite article and/or the change in the noun (always capitalized) itself. It is advisable to learn the plural form along with the noun gender and singular word meaning.

    a) The plural forms of German nouns may be divided into the following categories:

        (1) those nouns whose spelling remains exactly the same in the plural:

            (a) neuter nous ending in *-el, -er, - chen, -lein*

das Theater	die Theater	the theater(s)
das Mädchen	die Mädchen	the girl(s)
das Fräulein	die Fräulein	the young lady(s)

            (b) masculine nouns ending in *-el, -en, - er* that add no ending in the plural

der Dämpfer	die Dämpfer	the mute(s)
der Musiklehrer	die Musiklehrer	the music teacher
der Dichter	die Dichter	the poet(s)
der Musiker	die Musiker	the musician(s)

        (2) those nouns whose spelling remains the same except that an umlaut is added to the vowel:

            (a) masculine nouns ending in *-el, -en, -er* that take an umlaut

der Garten	die Gärten (Pfitzner, "Der Gärtner")	The garden(s)
der Vater	die Väter (Schubert, "Erlkönig")	the father(s)

        (3) those nouns (generally one-syllable words that appear both singly and as the last part in a compound noun) which add the ending *-e* to the singular form:

(a) masculine nouns that add only -*e* to the singular to form the plural

| der Berg | die Berge | the mountain(s) |

(Beethoven, "An die ferne Geliebte")

| der Fisch | die Fische | the fish |

(Mahler, "Phantasie")

| der Ring | die Ringe | the ring(s) |

(Schumann, *Frauenliebe und Leben*–4)

(b) masculine nouns that umlaut the vowels a = ä, o = ö, u = ü and au = äu and add -*e* to the singular to form the plural

| der Fluss | die Flüsse | the river(s) |

(Schubert, *Die Winterreise*–7)

| der Traum | die Träume | the dream(s) |

(Schubert, *Die Winterreise*–11)

(c) masculine nouns that add -*e* to the singular to form the plural but do not umlaut the vowels *a, o, u*

| der Hund | die Hunde | the dog(s) |
| der Tag | die Tage | the day(s) |

(Mahler, *Kindertotenlieder*–4)

(d) feminine nouns that add -*e* to the singular to form the plural and always umlaut the vowel (*a, o, u, au*)

| die Hand | die Hände | the hand(s) |

(Schubert, "Der Tod und das Mädchen")

| die Nacht | die Nächte | the night(s) |

(Schubert, "Nacht und Träume")

(e) neuter nouns that add -*e* to the singular to form the plural and never umlaut the vowel

das Pult	die Pulte	the stand(s)
das Klavier	die Klaviere	the piano(s)
das Werk	die Werke	the work(s)
das Gedicht	die Gedichte	the poem(s)

(4) those nouns which always umlaut *a, o, u,* and *au* and add the ending -*er* (generally one-syllable words) to the singular to form the plural:

der Mann	die Männer	the man (men)
das Dorf	die Dörfer	the village(s)
der Wald	die Wälder	the wood(s)
das Feld	die Felder	the field(s)
das Lied	die Lieder	the song(s)

(5) those nouns which add the ending *-n* or *- en* to the singular to form the plural (these nouns never umlaut the vowel)

(a) masculine nouns ending in *-e* that add *- n* in the plural

der Deutsche	die Deutschen	the German(s)
der Franzose	die Franzosen	the French
der Russe	die Russen	the Russian(s)

(Schumann, "Die beiden Grenadiere")

(b) masculine nouns (denoting male beings) with the last syllable accented or ending in *-or* that add *- en* in the plural

der Komponist	die Komponisten	the composer(s)
der Professor	die Professoren	the professor(s)

(c) feminine nouns that end in *-e, -el, -er* that add *-n* in the plural

die Saite	die Saiten	the string(s)
die Symphonie	die Symphonien	the orchestra(s)
die Orgel	die Orgeln	the organ(s)
die Oper	die Opern	the opera(s)

(d) feminine nouns that add *-en* to form the plural

die Kultur	die Kulturen	the culture(s)
die Komposition	die Kompositionen	the composition(s)

(e) feminine nouns that end in *-in* add the ending *-nen* to form the plural

die Flötistin	die Flötistinnen	the flutist(s)
die Geigerin	die Geigerinnen	the violinist(s)

8. In summarizing noun plurals the following points should be reiterated:

    a) It is possible to determine the plural of most nouns from their form and gender.

    b) It is important to learn to recognize noun plurals for understanding and practical application in text translation and pronunciation.

EXERCISES

1. Practice the pronunciation of the following country names, inhabitants, and languages.

America	das	Amerika	die	Amerikaner(n)	das Englisch
			die	Amerikanerin(nen)	
Germany	das	Deutschland	der	Deutsche(n)	das Deutsch
			die	Deutsche	
England	das	England	der	Engländer(n)	das Englisch
			die	Engländerin(nen)	
France	das	Frankreich	der	Franzose(n)	das Französisch
			die	Französin	
Greece	das	Griechenland	der	Grieche(n)	das Griechisch
			die	Grieche	
Italy	das	Italien	der	Italiener(n)	das Italienisch
			die	Italienerin(nen)	
Austria	das	Österreich	der	Österreicher(n)	das Deutsch
			die	Österreicherin(nen)	
Russia	das	Russland	der	Russe(n)	das Russisch
			die	Russe	
Spain	das	Spanien	der	Spanier(n)	das Spanisch
			die	Spanierin(nen)	
Switzer-land	die	Schweiz	der	Schweizer(n)	das Deutsch
			die	Schweizerin(nen)	

2. As with alphabet letters, the written symbols that represent numbers also have names for spoken use in German. The cardinal numbers (a numeral which answers the question "how many?") are:

0	– null	21	– einundzwanzig
1	– eins	22	– zweiundzwanzig
2	– zwei	30	– dreissig
3	– drei	33	– dreiunddreissig
4	– vier	40	– vierzig
5	– fünf	44	– vierundvierzig
6	– sechs	50	– fünfzig
7	– sieben	55	– fünfundfünfzig
8	– acht	60	– sechzig
9	– neun	66	– sechsundsechzig
10	– zehn	70	– siebzig
11	– elf	77	– siebenundsiebzig
12	– zwölf	80	– achtzig
13	– dreizehn	88	– achtundachtzig
14	– vierzehn	90	– neunzig
15	– fünfzehn	99	– neunundneunzig
16	– sechzehn	100	– hundert
17	– siebzeh	105	– hundertfünf
18	– achtzehn	285	– zweihundertfünfundachtzig
19	– neunzehn	500	– fünfhundert
20	– zwanzig	1000	– tausend

3. The ordinal numbers (a numeral expressing the order of a number in a series) are:

1st	der erste
2nd	der zweite
3rd	der dritte
4th	der vierte
5th	der fünfte
6th	der sechste
7th	der siebente
8th	der achte
9th	der neunte
10th	der zehnte

11th	der elfte
12th	der zwölfte
13th	der dreizehnte
14th	der vierzehnte
15th	der fünfzehnte
20th	der zwanzigste
30th	der dreissigste
40th	der vierzigste
50th	der fünfzigste
60th	der sechzigste
70th	der siebzigste
80th	der achtzigste
90th	der neunzigste
100th	der hundertste

4. Names of the days of the week:

Sunday	der Sonntag
Monday	der Montag
Tuesday	der Dienstag
Wednesday	der Mittwoch
Thursday	der Donnerstag
Friday	der Freitag
Saturday	der Sonnabend (Samstag)

5. Names of the months of the year:

January	der Januar
February	der Februar
March	der März
April	der April
May	der Mai
June	der Juni
July	der Juli
August	der August
September	der September

October	der Oktober
November	der November
December	der Dezember

6. Names of directions:

north	der Norden
south	der Süden
east	der Osten
west	der Westen

7. Names of the seasons of the year (die Jahreszeiten):

winter	der Winter
spring	der Frühling
summer	der Sommer
autumn	der Herbst

a) Describe in detail the composition entitled *Die Jahreszeiten* by Joseph Haydn, including historical background, instrumentation, and concept.

8. Survey the symphonies by Beethoven; write out in German the name and number of instruments used in each work.

9. The following are nouns frequently encountered in vocal literature:

der Abend	evening
der Arm	arm
die Augen	eyes
der Bach	brook
das Bächlein	brooklet, stream
der Berg	mountain
das Bild	picture, image
die Blätter	leaves
die Blume	flower
die Brust	breast, bosom
das Dorf	village
das Eis	ice
die Erde	earth

das Fenster	window
der Fluss	river, stream
die Freude	joy
der Friede	peace
der Garten	garden
das Gesicht	face
der Gipfel	summit, peak
das Grab	grave
das Gras	grass
das Haar	hair
die Hand	hand
das Haus	house
das Herz	heart
der Himmel	heaven
das Kind	child
der Knabe	boy
der Kopf	head
das Leben	life
das Leid	wrong, suffering
die Liebe	love
das Lied	song
die Lilie	lily
die Lippen	lips
die Luft	air
das Mädchen	girl
der Mann	man
das Meer	sea, ocean
die Mühe	trouble
die Mutter	mother
die Nacht	night
die Nachtigall	nightingale
die Not	need
der Ort	place, spot

34

die Quelle	spring, fountain
der Regen	rain
die Rose	rose
die Ruhe	rest
der Schatten	shadow
der Schmerz	pain
der Schnee	snow
der See	lake
die See	sea, ocean
der Sohn	son
die Sonne	sun
die Stadt	city, town
die Strasse	street
der Tag	day
die Taube	dove
die Tochter	daughter
das Tor	gate
die Träne	tear
der Traum	dream
der Vater	father
das Veilchen	violet
der Vogel	bird
die Wangen	cheeks
der Weg	way
die Welt	world
das Wetter	weather
der Wind	wind
der Winter	winter

a) For each noun substitute the correct indefinite article for the definite article.

b) Form the plural of each noun.

10. Survey each song of the cycle by Schumann entitled *Dichterliebe.*

a) List all of the nouns in each song and indicate the gender of each.

11. From the lieder repertoire by Hugo Wolf

a) List the names of all songs whose title contains a noun and indicate the gender of each noun.

12. In any article from the *Neue Zeitschrift für Musik* list all of the nouns and indicate the gender of each.

II. PRONOUNS

A pronoun is a word used in place of a noun. The following are the pronouns in German used in the nominative case:

Singular	Plural
ich – I	wir – we
du – you	ihr – you
er – he	sie – they
sie – she	
es – it	
Sie– you	Sie – you

A. Pronoun Substitution

When a pronoun is substituted in sentence structure for the name of a person, place, or thing, it must agree in gender (masculine, feminine or neuter), number (singular or plural), and case (the function of the word in the sentence) with the noun it replaces.

1. In the nominative case the forms *du*, *ihr*, and *Sie* all mean "you."

a) The pronoun *Sie* (always capitalized) is the polite or conventional form of the word "you" , and can refer to one or more persons. It replaces the names of persons in German addressed as "Herr" (Mr.), "Frau" (Mrs.), or "Fräulein" (Miss). When one addresses a person in conversational German, the pronoun *Sie* is always used, unless the person addressed is a family member, an intimate friend, or a child up to the age of 13 or 14, in which case *du* is used. However, in German-speaking countries friends may continue to address one another as "Herr" and "Frau" and use the pronoun *Sie* for long associations. The suggestion to use the *du* form is usually initiated by the elder friend, indicating hope for a lasting close personal contact; students generally address each other as *du*. Whereas *Sie* may refer to one or more persons, *du* is the singular form of the familiar "you"; *ihr* is the plural form of *du*. When a pronoun is substituted for a noun in the nominative case, *er* must replace a masculine noun, *sie* must replace a feminine noun, and *es* must replace a neuter noun. The plural form of *er*, *sie*, and *es* is the pronoun *sie*, meaning "they." Because the word *sie* is used in German to denote three different pronoun meanings (you, she, they), there are two important guidelines for these pronouns in translating:

(1) When *Sie* is capitalized it is always the polite form of the word *you*, either singular or plural.

(2) The verb form in sentence structure will always indicate whether *sie* means "she" or "they."

B. Cases

To this point, all nouns and pronouns have been in reference to the nominative case, indicating the subject of the sentence. The four cases (case: the form of a noun, pronoun, or adjective which indicates its relationship to other words) in German determine the forms for definite and indefinite articles, which change in order to properly modify the noun or pronoun.

1. *Nominative Case* (see page 21)

2. The *Accusative Case* is that case of a noun, pronoun, or adjective which indicates the *direct object* of the sentence. The direct object is the word towards which the action of the verb is directed. The forms for the definite and indefinite articles in the accusative case are:

Singular
Masculine: Definite: *den*

" ...du...gibst mir *den* Strauss ..."
(Schumann, *Liederkreis*–14)

"Er hat *den* Knaben ..."
(Schubert, "Erlkönig")

Indefinite: *einen*

"... hast du *einen* Freund ..."
(Schumann, *Liederkreis*–10)

"Ich hör' *meinen* Schatz, *den* Hammer er schwinget, ..."
(Brahms, "Der Schmied")

Feminine: Definite: *die*

" ...ich liebe...*die* Kleine, *die* Feine, *die* Reine."
(Schumann, *Dichterliebe*–3)

Indefinite: *eine*

"Ich frage *keine* Blume ..."
(Schubert, *Die schöne Müllerin*–6)

Neuter: Definite: *das*

"... hör ich *das* Liedchen klingen ..."
(Schumann, *Dichterliebe*, 10)

Indefinite: *ein*

"Ein Jüngling liebt *ein* Mädchen ..."
(Schumann, *Dichterliebe*–11)

Plural:

All genders: Definite: *die*

"... schenk ich dir *die* Blumen all ..."
(Schumann, *Dichterliebe*–2)

The foregoing examples indicate that only masculine nouns in the accusative case change the nominative case article from *der* to *den* and from *ein* to *einen*.

When a pronoun is substituted for a noun in the accusative case the following changes in the nominative forms should be made:

Singular

Nominative:	ich	du	er (man)[1]	sie	es	Sie
Accusative:	mich	dich	ihn	sie	es	Sie

[1]The indefinite pronoun *man* may be translated *one, people, we, they, you*; it is singular and takes the third person singular verb.

"Ich liebe *dich*, mich reizt deine schöne Gestalt; ..."
(Schubert, "Erlkönig")

"Die Post bringt keinen Brief für *dich* ..."
(Schubert, *Die Winterreise*–13)

"Er fasst *ihn* sicher, er hält *ihn* warm"
(Schubert, "Erlkönig")

"Ich finde *sie* nimmer ..."
(Schubert, "Gretchen am Spinnrade")

"Ich sah *es* an einem Sonntag ..."
(Brahms, "Sonntag")

For the purpose of translating it is important to recognize that *ihn* is the direct object (accusative case) for a masculine person, place or thing.

Plural

Nominative:	wir	ihr	sie	Sie
Accusative:	uns	euch	sie	Sie

"... *euch* soll man legen ..."
(Schubert, *Die schöne Müllerin*–1)

"Ihr führt ins Leben *uns* hinein ..."
(Wolf, *Harfenspieler-Lieder*–3)

3. When a noun occurs in a sentence as the *indirect object*, it is in the *Dative Case*. The indirect object indicates *to* or *for whom* the action of the verb is done. As in the accusative case, the definite and indefinite articles change to indicate the dative case, and to properly modify the noun or pronoun.

   a) In the dative case, the forms for the definite and indefinite articles are:

Singular

Masculine: Definite: *dem*
           Indefinite: *einem*

" ...doch plötzlich ward *dem* Diebe die Zeit zu lang ..."
(Schubert, "Die Forelle")

Feminine: Definite: *der*
          Indefinite: *einer*

"... die Blumen einst pflanzt' er *der* Liebe zum Strauss ..."
(Schumann, "Wanderlied")

39

Neuter: Definite: *dem*

               Indefinite: *einem*

"..ach, nur *dem* halbgetrockneten Auge...wie tot die Welt ihm erscheint!"
(Beethoven, "Wonne der Wehmut")

Plural

All genders: Definite: *den*

             Indefinite: *keinen*

"..und bläst *den* Kindern schöne Tänz und Lieder vor ..."
(Schubert, *Die schöne Müllerin*–16)

b) In contrast to the accusative case, the definite and indefinite article forms in the dative case are dissimilar to the nominative and accusative case forms. The dative case, however, is relatively easy to identify in text translation ; the article *dem* (*einem*), for example, always indicates the masculine singular definite article in the nominative case, the article *der* (*einer*) clearly indicates the feminine singular in the dative case when the noun is feminine. Likewise, the article *den* also indicates the masculine singular of the accusative case; when the noun is clearly plural (all genders), however, and receives the action of the verb indirectly, the article *den* clearly indicates the plural form of the dative case. Learning to recognize what words indicate, as in the four case forms, rather than memorizing single unrelated words is important for translation; this process of word association simplifies the application of modern languages.

c) When a pronoun is substituted for a noun and its definite or indefinite article in the dative case, the following changes in the pronoun forms are made:

Singular

Nominative:	ich	du	er	sie	es	Sie
Dative:	mir	dir	ihm	ihr	ihm	Ihnen
Accusative:	mich	dich	ihn	sie	es	Sie

"... O zeigt *mir* doch den Weg zurück ..."
(Brahms, "O wüsst ich doch den Weg zurück")

" ...was hat man *dir*...getan?"
(Wolf, *Mignon I*)

"... sie sucht nur zu verkünden *ihm* die nächste süsse Stunde ..."
(Schubert, "Geheimes")

" ...da hab' ich *ihr* gestanden ..."
(Schumann, *Dichterliebe*–1)

Plural

Nominative:	wir	ihr	sie	Sie
Dative:	uns	euch	ihnen	Ihnen
Accusative:	uns	euch	sie	Sie

(1) Note the similarity in the article and pronoun forms in the dative case; this comparison should help in recognizing the dative case:

Singular			*Pronoun*
Masculine:	Definite:	dem	ihm
	Indefinite:	einem	
Feminine:	Definite:	der	ihr
	Indefinite:	einer	
Neuter:	Definite:	dem	ihm
	Indefinite:	einem	
	Plural		
All genders:	Definite:	den	ihnen
	Indefinite:	keinen	

4. The fourth noun case is the *Genitive Case*, that case denoting a possessive relationship or a "belonging to each other" between nouns. The genitive case is also indicated by distinct forms of the definite and indefinite article:

Singular

Masculine:	Definite:	des
	Indefinite:	eines

Des Knabens Wunderhorn

Auf Flügeln *des* Gesanges

Feminine:	Definite:	der
	Indefinite:	einer

Die Harmonie *der* Welt

Die Kunstwerk *der* Zukunft

Die Kunst *der* Fuge

Denkmäler *der* Tonkunst

Neuter: Definite   des

         Indefinite: eines

         Ahle – Der Tag *des* Weltgerichts

Plural

All genders: Definite: der

         Indefinite: keiner

         Schubert, Lob *der* Thränen

a) Two important distinctions of the genitive case are:

(1) In English the possessive is often indicated by the addition of *'s* or *s'* to a word ending; in German, masculine and neuter nouns add the ending -*s*. Monosyllabic nouns add the ending -*es*: Schubert, Bach*es* Wiegenlied. Feminine nouns remain unchanged.

(2) The definite or indefinite article modifies the *possessor*, not the possession.

Des Knabens Wunderhorn = Das Wunderhorn des Knabens

the boy's wonderhorn = the wonderhorn possessed by the *boy*

(a) Note the abbreviated form of the genitive here, which is approximately equivalent to the English *'s*; this form is encountered frequently in poetic texts.

b) The pronouns in the genitive case are:

Singular

Nominative:	ich	du	er	sie	es	Sie
Genitive:	meiner	deiner	seiner	ihrer	seiner	Ihrer
Dative:	mir	dir	ihm	ihr	ihm	Ihnen
Accusative:	mich	dich	ihn	sie	es	Sie

Plural

Nominative:	wir	ihr	sie		Sie
Genitive:	unser	euer	ihrer		Ihrer

Dative:	uns	euch	ihnen	Ihnen
Accusative:	uns	euch	sie	Sie

c) All forms of genitive pronouns end in -r; when these pronouns stand alone they indicate the genitive case.

C. Demonstrative Pronouns

A *demonstrative pronoun* is a word that points out or indicates used in place of a noun. Demonstrative pronouns are mentioned in relationship to simple pronouns because they also stand alone in sentence structure. The grammatical significance of demonstative pronouns in sentence structure will be further clarified in Chapter Six. The most important pronouns are:

1. *der, die, das*— that, that one, that man, that woman, or emphatic he, she, it.

	Singular			*Plural*
Nominative:	der	die	das	die
Genitive:	dessen	deren	dessen	deren
Dative:	dem	der	dem	denen
Accusative:	den	die	das	die

Krieger – *Der* hat gesiegt, *den* Gott vergnügt

"... *der* kennt euch nicht, ihr himmlischen Mächte ..."
(Wolf, *Harfenspieler Lieder*–3)

"... *die* hat einen andern erwählt; ..."
(Schumann, *Dichterliebe*–11)

"... der Mond, *der* ist ihr Buhle ..."
(Schumann, "Die Lotosblume")

" ...*das* seh ich oft im Traum... "
(Schumann, *Dichterliebe*–15)

2. *dieser, diese, dieses* - this, this one, the latter

3. *jener, jene, jenes* - that, that one, the former

" ..ich liebe *diesen* und nicht etwa *den* and *jenen* ..."
(Schubert, "Geheimes")

4. *solcher, solche, solches* - such, such a one, such people

5. *derselbe, dieselbe, dasselbe* - the same; he, she, it, they

This word is most frequently used as an adjective (Chapter Four), meaning "the same". In the case of this pronoun, both *der* and *selb* are declined.

	Singular			*Plural*
	m.	*f.*	*n.*	*all genders*
Nominative:	derselbe	dieselbe	dasselbe	dieselben
Genitive:	desselben	derselben	desselben	derselben
Dative:	demselben	derselben	demselben	denselben
Accusative:	denselben	dieselben	dasselbe	dieselben

6. *derjenige, diejenige, dasjenige* - the one; he, she, etc. is declined like *derselbe; derjenige* is usually followed by a relative clause (Chapter Six).

D. Indefinite Pronouns

Indefinite pronouns are used to replace nouns and are general in meaning:

alles - everything, everyone

etwas - something

nichts - nothing

jedermann - everybody, everyone

jeder - each, every, others

jemand - somebody, someone

niemand - nobody, no one

man - one, people, they, you

kein - no one

"... *alles* nimmt sie ..."
(Strauss, "Die Nacht")

"... denn *alles* ist wie damals noch ..."
(Schubert, "Im Frühling")

1. When used as the subject of a sentence (nominative case), these pronouns are considered singular and take the verb in the third person singular (Chapter Three); Exception: *alle* is considered plural.

"... *alle* sind ins Tal gezogen ..."
(Schumann, *Liederkreis*–7)

2. *kein* and *jeder* are declined like the definite articles *der, die*, and *das* when used as indefinite pronouns.

"... ein *jeder* sucht ..."
(Wolf, *Mignon-Lieder*–2)

"... ein *jeder* lebt, ein *jeder* liebt ..."
(Wolf, *Harfenspieler-Lieder*–1)

"... *jeder* wird sich glücklich scheinen ..."
(Wolf, *Harfenspieler-Lieder*–2)

"... es kennt mich dort *keiner* mehr ..."
(Schumann, *Liederkreis*–1)

"... doch *keiner* fühlt die Schmerzen ..."
(Schumann, *Liederkreis*–9)

3. "ein"-words (see p. 25) used alone as pronouns have the endings of "der"-words:

"... gib mir nur *einen* deiner süssen Blicke ..."
(Strauss, "Allerseelen")

"... nur *Eine* kennt meinen Schmerz ..."
(Schumann, *Dichterliebe*–8)

"... will ja nur *Eines* wissen ..."
(Schubert , *Die schöne Müllerin*–6)

E. Possessive Pronouns

Possessive pronouns are used to replace nouns and indicate the possessor, or to whom the possession belongs. Possessive pronouns are declined regularly and can be used in all cases; the following declensions are all in the nominative case. Possessive pronouns in German have three distinct forms.

1. Possessive pronouns may be declined like "der"-words:

meiner	meine	meines	mine
deiner	deine	deines	yours
seiner	seine	seines	his
ihrer	ihre	ihres	hers
unserer	unsere	unseres	ours
eurer	eure	eures	yours
ihrer	ihre	ihres	theirs
Ihrer	Ihre	Ihres	yours

2. Possessive pronouns may be composed of the definite article *der, die, das* plus the possessive adjective declined according to the pattern for adjectives preceded by a definite article (Chapter Four).

der meine	die meine	das meine	mine
der deine	die deine	das deine	yours
der seine	die seine	das seine	his
der ihre	die ihre	das ihre	hers
der unsere	die unsere	das unsere	ours
der eure	die eure	das eure	yours
der ihre	die ihre	das ihre	theirs
der Ihre	die Ihre	das Ihre	yours

3. Possessive pronouns may also be expressed:

der meinige	die meinige	das meinige	mine
der deinige	die deinige	das deinige	yours
der seinige	die seinige	das seinige	his
der ihrige	die ihrige	das ihrige	hers
der unsrige	die unsrige	das unsrige	ours
der eurige	die eurige	das eurige	yours
der ihrige	die ihrige	das ihrige	theirs
der Ihrige	die Ihrige	das Ihrige	yours

"... vergleich ich ihn *dem deinigen?*"
(Brahms, "Wie bist du, meine Königin")

MUSICAL EXERCISES

1. Identify each of the following:

a) Des Knabens Wunderhorn

b) Die Harmonie der Welt

c) Die Kunstwerk der Zukunft

d) Die Kunst der Fuge

e) Denkmäler der Tonkunst

2. Define the following terms, all of which are nouns:

Abendmusik

Feldmusik

Festschrift

Festspiel

Gebrauchmusik

Generalpause

Gesellschaftslied

Hammerklavier

Handstück

Hausmusik

Heldentenor

Hoflied

Hoftanz

Kammersymphonie

Kapelle

Kirchenlied

Klangfarbenmelodie

Liebeslieder

Liederkreis

Musikwissenschaft

Nachtmusik

Nachtstück

Nachschlag

Schlummerlied

Singspiel

Spieloper

Sprechgesang

Sprechstimme

Stimmtausch

Strophenlied

Tafelmusik

Tondichtung

Tonfarbe

Tonwort

Versett
Volkslied
Vorimitation
Vorschlag
Walze
Wechselnote

3. Define historically *Minnelieder* and *Minnesinger; Meistersinger.*

4. Define the term *Leitmotiv.*

5. Define the term *Klangideal.*

6. Define

a) Sturm und Drang

b) Oper und Drama

7. Define the terms *Urlinie* and *Ursatz* in reference to the Schenker System.

8. Identify the following compositions (composer, form, and style):

Das Augenlicht
Bauernkantate
Die Davidsbundlertänze
Der Erlkönig
Frauenliebe und Leben
Geisslerlieder
Gurrelieder
Kaffeekantate
Kaiserquartett
Kindertotenlieder
Das Marienleben
Nänie
Orgelbüchlein
Schicksalslied
Die Schöpfung
Schwanengesang
Sonnenquartett
Tod und Verklärung

Chapter Three

I. VERBS

The following study of verbs demonstrates how the theory of noun construction (noun genders, plurals, cases, and pronoun substitution) is transformed into practical knowledge, especially as it relates to text translation.

A *verb* is that part of speech which expresses an action or state of being. German verbs appear complicated because of the number of different forms and the seemingly complex word order in sentence structure; it is therefore desirable to reduce the study of verbs to its simplest and most practical form in order to facilitate translation, comprehension, and conversation.

A. Terminology

The terminology used in reference to verbs should be defined before actually beginning with German verbs; although other terms will be subsequently defined, an understanding of these terms is essential:

1. *Tense* is the form of the verb showing the time of an action or of a state or condition. The two forms of tense are:

   a) *Simple* - verb form that requires no auxiliary verb to express the time.

   b) *Compound* - verb form that requires an auxiliary verb to express the time.

2. *Conjugation* - the inflections or changes of form in verbs showing:

   a) *Tense* - (simple or compound)

   b) *Mood* - the form of the verb showing the speaker's attitude toward what he says (indicative, subjunctive, conditional).

   (1) *Attitudes*: ability, permission, compulsion, desire, obligation.

   c) *Voice* - the form of the verb indicating whether the subject acts (Active Voice) or is acted upon (Passive Voice).

   d) *Person*

   e) *Number* - the form of a verb indicating one (singular) or more than one (plural).

3. *Auxiliary Verb* - a verb which helps in the conjugation of another verb.

B. Conjugations

The following verbs refer specifically to music:

singen - to sing

spielen - to play

klingen - to sound

musizieren - play, or have music

The *infinitive* is the verb form which expresses general meaning without the distinction of grammatical person or number. The foregoing examples indicate that the *infinitive* form of German verbs usually ends in *-en*. In order to conjugate verbs, that is, assign person and number, a common denominator derived from the verb infinitive is necessary. This common denominator is known as the *verb stem* and is obtained by dropping the final *-en* of the infinitive.

singen (sing-) - to sing   spielen (spiel-) - to play

In conjugating verbs in German (assigning person and number) it is necessary to add an ending to the *verb stem*.

1. In the *present tense* only the third person singular form in English has an ending; in German, the verb has an ending for *each* person in the present tense. The following endings are added to the verb stem to form the present tense in German:

singen - to sing

Singular		*Plural*	
ich	singe	wir	singen
du	singst	ihr	singt
er	singt	sie	singen
sie	singt		
es	singt		
Sie	singen	Sie	singen

spielen - to play

Singular		*Plural*	
ich	spiele	wir	spielen
du	spielst	ihr	spielt
er	spielt	sie	spielen

sie	spiel*t*		
es	spiel*t*		
Sie	spiel*en*	Sie	spiel*en*

Depending on the context, the present tense in German may be equivalent in English to:

a) the simple verb form: ich singe - I sing

b) the progressive form: ich singe - I am singing

c) the emphatic form: ich singe - I do sing

d) the future tense, when used with an adverb of time: ich singe bald - I will sing soon

2. In the present tense some German verbs change the stem vowel *a* to *ä* or the stem vowel *e* to *i* or *ie* in the second (du) and third (er, sie, es) persons singular:

fahren - to go (drive)

Singular		*Plural*	
ich	fahre	wir	fahren
du	fährst	ihr	fahrt
er	fährt	sie	fahren
sie	fährt		
es	fährt		
Sie	fahren	Sie	fahren

"...du schläfst...den Todesschlaf..."
(Schumann, *Frauenliebe und Leben*–8)

sprechen - to speak

ich	spreche	wir	sprechen
du	sprichst	ihr	sprecht
er	spricht	sie	sprechen
sie	spricht		
es	spricht		
Sie	sprechen	Sie	sprechen

lesen - to read

lesen -to read

ich	lese		wir	lesen
du	liest		ihr	lest
er	liest		sie	lesen
sie	liest			
es	liest			
Sie	lesen		Sie	lesen

sehen -to see

ich	sehe		wir	sehen
du	siehst		ihr	seht
er	sieht		sie	sehen
sie	sieht			
es	sieht			
Sie	sehen		Sie	sehen

C. Auxiliary Verbs

Three important verbs in German are:

sein - to be

haben - to have

werden - to become

Besides being independent verbs, these three verbs are the *auxiliary verbs* in German; one is always present in the conjugation of verbs in compound tenses. These verbs are conjugated in the present tense:

sein -to be

Singular		*Plural*	
ich bin	I am	wir sind	we are
du bist	you are	ihr sind	you are
er ist	he is	sie sind	they are
sie ist	she is		
es ist	it is		
Sie sind	you are	Sie sind	you are

haben -to have

ich habe	I have	wir haben	we have
du hast	you have	ihr habt	you have
er hat	he has	sie haben	they have
sie hat	she has		
es hat	it has		
Sie haben	you have	Sie haben	you have

werden -to become

ich werde	I become	wir werden	we become
du wirst	you become	ihr werdet	you become
er wird	he becomes	sie werden	they become
sie wird	she becomes		
es wird	it becomes		
Sie werden	you become	Sie werden	you become

D. Principle Parts

It is desirable to learn the *principle parts* of German verbs because they are the basis of verb structure; it is practical for this study to be able to recognize verb forms in texts. German verbs have three principle parts from which the six tenses are formed: the *infinitive*, the first person singular of the *simple past tense*, and the *past participle*.

1. The meaning and significance of the *infinitive* has been discussed.

2. The *simple past tense* refers to the second tense formed from the infinitive requiring no auxiliary verb used:

    a) to express progressive, continued, customary, or repeated action in the past

    b) to describe or narrate a series of related events in the past (especially important for translation)

3. Before explaining further the *simple past tense* it should be noted that there are two categories of verbs in German:

    a) *Strong* (irregular) verbs

    b) *Weak* (regular) verbs

Strong verbs form the *simple past tense* by changing the vowel or diphthong of the stem:

klingen - klang

singen - sang

The most frequently encountered vowel changes are:

a= ie	blasen, blies
a= u	fahren, fuhr
all= iel	fallen, fiel
au= ie	laufen, lief
e= a	lesen, las
e= i	gehen, ging
ei= ie	bleiben, blieb
ie= a	liegen, lag
ie= o	bieten, bot
im= a	schwimmen, schwamm
in= a	singen, sang
itz= aß	sitzen, saß
o= a	kommen, kam
u= a	tun, tat

4. To conjugate the simple past tense of strong (irregular) verbs the following endings are added to the first person singular form of the simple past tense:

singen - to sing

Singular		*Plural*	
ich	sang	wir	sang*en*
du	sang*st*	ihr	sang*t*
er	sang	sie	sang*en*
sie	sang		
es	sang		
Sie	sang*en*	Sie	sang*en*

"...als alle Vögel *sangen*..."
(Schumann, *Dichterliebe*–1)

klingen - to sound

ich	klang	wir	klang*en*
du	klang*st*	ihr	klang*t*
er	klang	sie	klang*en*
sie	klang		
es	klang		
Sie	klang*en*	Sie	klang*en*

Note that the first and third person singular forms are the same when conjugating strong verbs in the simple past tense. When the second person endings -*st* and -*t* are not easily pronounced when joined directly to the stem, an *e* may be inserted between the stem and the ending.

> "*Sah* ein Knab' ein Röslein stehn..."
> (Schubert, "Heidenröslein")

> "...auf seinem Bette weinend *sass*..."
> (Wolf, *Harfenspieler-Lieder*–3)

> "Wer nie sein Brot mit Tränen *ass*..."
> (Wolf, *Harfenspieler-Lieder*–3)

> "...es *sank* und *starb*..."
> (Mozart, "Das Veilchen")

> "...er *schuf* die Schönheit..."
> (Wolf, "Gesegnet sei, durch den die Welt entstund")

> "...wir *sassen* stumm...der Nebel *stieg*,
> das Wasser *schwoll*...die Möwe *flog*...
> *fielen* die Tränen nieder..."
> (Schubert, *Schwanengesang*–12)

5. Weak verbs, the larger number of German verbs, form the simple past tense by adding the following endings (approximately equivalent to -*ed* in English) to the verb stem, with no change in the stem vowel:

spielen - to play

Singular		*Plural*	
ich	spiel*te*	wir	spiel*ten*
du	spiel*test*	ihr	spiel*tet*

er	spiel*te*	sie	spiel*ten*
sie	spiel*te*		
es	spiel*te*		
Sie	spiel*ten*	Sie	spiel*ten*

"...da *blitzten* viel Reiter..."
(Schumann, *Liederkreis*, 11)

"...und meine Seele *spannte*..."
(Schumann, *Liederkreis*, 5)

If the verb stem ends in *t, d, m*, or *n*, preceded by a consonant other than *l* or *r*, an *e* is inserted between the final consonant of the stem and the *t* of the ending.

beobachten -to observe

ich	beobachtete	wir	beobachteten
du	beobachtetest	ihr	beobachtetet
er	beobachtete	sie	beobachteten
sie	beobachtete		
es	beobachtete		
Sie	beobachteten	Sie	beobachteten

6. The simple form of the past tense in German may be translated:

a) simply - ich spielte - I played

b) progressively - ich spielte - I was playing

c) emphatically - ich spielte - I did play

d) showing customary action - I used to play

7. Verbs that end in *-ieren* are usually derived from French or Latin verbs and almost always have an English cognate:

musizieren -to make music

komponieren -to compose

vokalisieren -to vocalise

These verbs are weak verbs and are conjugated accordingly.

8. The verbs *sein, haben*, and *werden* do not conform to the conjugation rules for either strong or weak verbs in the simple past tense.

sein -to be

Singular		Plural	
ich	war	wir	waren
du	warst	ihr	wart
er	war	sie	waren
sie	war		
es	war		
Sie	waren	Sie	waren

haben -to have

ich	hatte	wir	hatten
du	hattest	ihr	hattet
er	hatte	sie	hatten
sie	hatte		
es	hatte		
Sie	hatten	Sie	hatten

werden -to become

ich	wurde	wir	wurden
du	wurdest	ihr	wurdet
er	wurde	sie	wurden
sie	wurde		
es	wurde		
Sie	wurden	Sie	wurden

9. The third member of the three principle parts of the verb is the *past participle*, the verb form used as part of a compound tense. The word *compound* implies more than one part; a compound verb structure requires some form of an auxiliary verb (sein, haben, and/or werden), plus the past participle of the verb. The past participle of weak (regular) verbs is formed by adding the prefix *ge-* and the ending *-t* to the verb stem. The *compound past tense*, which can be compared in meaning to the simple past tense, is formed with the present tense of the appropriate auxiliary verb plus the past participle of the verb. The compound past tense of most verbs consists of the present tense of the auxiliary verb *haben* and the past participle of the verb. The verb *sein* is used as the auxiliary in compound tenses of verbs which cannot take an accusative object and which also express a change of position or condition.

spielen - spielte - *gespielt*

Singular			*Plural*		
ich habe	gespielt		wir	haben	gespielt
du hast	gespielt		ihr	habt	gespielt
er hat	gespielt		sie	haben	gespielt
sie hat	gespielt				
es hat	gespielt				
Sie haben gespielt			Sie	haben	gespielt

10. The study of structure is the obvious tool of translation; the following guidelines for efficient translation should be cultivated:

a) Determine the subject of the sentence: who or what performs the action expressed by the verb, or on whom the action is performed.

b) Determine the verb meaning by dissecting the form. When one of the three verbs that can be used as auxiliary verbs is encountered this should indicate the possibility of compound verb structure; the past participle stands last in a simple sentence with compound verb structure and in all main sentence clauses. Having determined the meaning of the verb from the past participle, it should be possible to translate the tense of the verb form. Verb placement in sentence structure is an unaccustomed aspect of German grammar; it is important in translating to develop the practice of first consulting the end of the sentence (or clause) to determine the verb meaning and tense.

c) Determine the direct object and/or the indirect object. Nouns and pronouns in the accusative and dative cases occur in sentence structure between the auxiliary verb and the past participle when the verb is in a compound tense, and after the verb if the tense is simple.

11. Weak verbs ending in *-ieren* do not have the prefix *ge-* in the past participle.

musizieren - musizierte - *musiziert*

12. The past participle of strong (irregular) verbs has the prefix *ge-*, in many cases a stem vowel different from that of the infinitive, and the ending *-en*.

singen - sang - gesungen

klingen - klang - geklungen

sein -to be

Singular			*Plural*		
ich bin	gewesen		wir	sind	gewesen
du bist	gewesen		ihr	seid	gewesen
er ist	gewesen		sie	sind	gewesen
sie ist	gewesen				
es ist	gewesen				
Sie sind	gewesen		Sie	sind	gewesen

werden -to become

Singular			*Plural*		
ich bin	geworden		wir	sind	geworden
du bist	geworden		ihr	seid	geworden
er ist	geworden		sie	sind	geworden
sie ist	geworden				
es ist	geworden				
Sie sind	geworden		Sie	sind	geworden

Since the vowel changes of strong (irregular) verbs follow no regular pattern, the principle parts of verbs should be systematically learned. For translation it is necessary to identify verbs as strong or weak, indicated by the past participle ending of *-t* or *-en*. When the past participle ends in *-en* the verb is strong (irregular), implying the possibility or probability that the stem vowel of the verb has been changed.

13. The compound past tense is generally used in conversation to express a single event completed in the past or a condition that existed in the past. Such an action or condition is normally reported in English in the simple past tense; such an action or condition is reported in German in the compound past tense.

E. Voice

Strong and weak verbs can function in two ways:

1. *Transitive* (active) - a verb that takes a direct object.

2. *Intransitive* (passive) - a verb expressing an action, change of position, or state of being that does not require a direct object. In order to determine whether a verb is transitive or intransitive, the question "who or what does the action of the verb affect?" should be asked. If the

question can be answered, the verb is transitive, or the action is performed upon a direct object; if the question can not be answered, the verb is intransitive or passive. Determining whether a verb is transitive or intransitive simplifies the formation of compound tenses: most transitive verbs take *haben* as the auxiliary verb, most intransitive verbs take *sein* as the auxiliary verb.

> "...*hab'* Obdach ich gefunden..."
> (Schubert, *Die Winterreise*–19)

F. Imperative

The *imperative* is the mood of a verb expressing a command. Since there are three ways of expressing "you" in German, there are three ways of giving commands; direct commands may be given to persons addressed as *du*, *ihr*, and *Sie*. The *du* or familiar singular form of the imperative ends in *-e* in most cases (the *-e* is frequently dropped in colloquial speech):

> "...*kehre* wieder, heil'ge Nacht!"
> (Schubert, "Nacht und Träume")

> "...*bleib'* an meinem Herzen..."
> (Schumann, *Frauenliebe und Leben*–6)

> "...*geh'*, wilder Knochenmann!"
> (Schubert, "Der Tod und das Mädchen")

> "...*hüte...dich*, bleib wach und munter!"
> (Schumann, *Liederkreis*–10)

The *ihr* or familiar plural form of the imperative is exactly the same as the *ihr* form of the present tense.

> "...so *lebt* denn wohl, Hereon!"
> (Schubert, "An die Leier")

> "...*streuet* ihm...*bringt* ihm...*helft* mir...*dient*...*windet* geschäftig..."
> (Schumann, *Frauenliebe und Leben*–5)

> "...ihr heil'gen Engel, *stillet* die Wipfel!"
> (Wolf, "Die ihr schwebet")

The polite or *Sie* form of the imperative is the infinitive plus *Sie* (Exception: the imperative of *sein*, "Seien Sie!"). German imperatives are generally followed by an exclamation point. Verbs that change the stem vowel *e* to *ie* or *i* in the second and third person singular form of the present tense also use the changed vowel in the *du* form of the imperative without a final -*e*:

> "*...brich*, o Herz, was liegt daran!"
> (Schumann, *Frauenliebe und Leben*–2)

Verbs which change the stem vowel *a* to *ä* keep *a* in all imperative forms:
> "*Schlafe*, mein Liebster!"
> (Bach, *Weihnachtsoratorium*)

G. Prefixes

Two additional points should be made before examining a large number of verbs.

1. A large number of German verbs begin with an unaccented prefix known as *inseparable* prefixes: *be-, emp-, ent-, er-, ge-, ver-, zer-*. Verbs composed of a simple verb (a verb which may also function independently of the prefix) plus an inseparable prefix have the following characteristics:

a) The inseparable prefix is never accented.

> bekommen -to receive
>
> bestellen -to order
>
> gebrauchen -to use
>
> vergessen -to forget
>
> verkaufen -to sell
>
> verstehen -to understand

b) Verbs with inseparable prefixes are conjugated exactly like verbs without a prefix, except that the past participle does not have the prefix *ge-*.

c) Inseparable prefixes generally do not suggest the meaning of the verb.

> (1) The prefix *zer-*, however, always indicates a destructive force:
>
> > zerbrechen -to break to pieces
> >
> > zerfallen -to fall to pieces
> >
> > zerstören -to destroy

An important principle to remember in translating is that many verbs are formed by the union of two (or more) verbs, by adding an inseparable prefix to the main verb, or by joining a separable prefix (see below) to the main or basic verb. In this process the new verb formed may be directly related in meaning to the basic verb or altogether unrelated in

61

meaning. In the listing of verbs at the end of this chapter, when a new verb originates from a basic verb, the basic verb within the new verb is italicized. It is an asset to efficient translation to recognize the basic verb and rely on the knowledge of the basic verb form for correct grammatical structure.

stehen - to stand

bestehen - to exist

gestehen - to confess

entstehen - to arise, originate

2. Another group of verbs in German consist of a *separable* prefix and a simple verb. A separable prefix is one that may, under certain conditions, be separated from the verb stem and stand alone in sentence structure. Separable prefixes are accented when they are attached to the main verb. When separable prefixes are separated from the verb in the present tense, simple past tense and imperative they stand last in the sentence or clause.

Present tense

anklopfen

"...ans Fenster *klopfe* leise *an*..."
(Brahms, "Verrat")

eintreten

"...unangeklopft ein Herr *tritt* abends bei mir *ein*..."
(Wolf, "Abschied")

Simple past tense

einschlafen

"...*schlief* mir mein Geliebter *ein*..."
(Wolf, "In dem Schatten meiner Locken")

Imperative

aufstehen

"...*steh auf*!"
(Mahler, "Frühlingsmorgen")

anrühren

"...und *rühre* mich nicht *an*!"
(Schubert, "Der Tod und das Mädchen")

A separable prefix can stand alone in a sentence with the function of an adverb (Chapter Four); in this function, when the separable prefix is joined to a simple verb it usually denotes the direction of the action. The most frequently encountered separable prefixes are:

ab - away

an - at, to

auf - up, upon

aus - out

ein - in

fort - away

her- here

heraus - out (there)

herein - in (here)

hin - away

hinaus - out (there)

hinein - in (there)

mit - with, along

vor - before

weg - away

wieder - again

zu - to

zurück - back

zusammen - together

"...ich *lass* die reine Hülle...und den Kranz *zurück*."
(Wolf, *Mignon-Lieder*–4)

"...der harte Fels *schliesst* seinen Busen *auf*..."
(Wolf, *Mignon-Lieder*–1)

"...der Wahnsinn *fasst* mich *an*!"
(Wolf, "Benedeit die sel'ge Mutter")

"...ich *schau'* dich *an*..."
(Schumann, "Du bist wie eine Blume")

a) *hin* and *her* are used as prefixes of direction with verbs of motion: *hin* denotes motion away from the speaker; *her* denotes motion toward the speaker.

herab - hinab

heraus - hinaus

herein - hinein

"...ich *eile* von der schönen Erde *hinab*..."
(Wolf, *Mignon-Lieder*–4)

b) The separable prefix is attached to the past participle when the verb is expressed in a tense requiring the past participle.

"...ich hatt' ihn aus*ge*träumet..."
(Schumann, *Frauenliebe und Leben*–4)

Separable prefixes can be summarized:

(1) The separable prefix is separated from the verb in the present tense, in the simple past tense, and in imperative sentences.

(2) In simple tenses the separable prefix must always stand at the end of the sentence or clause.

(3) In compound tenses the separable prefix is attached to the past participle of the simple verb.

3. The group of prefixes known as *variables* include only a small number of prefixes which may be used as either separable or inseparable prefixes.

über

durch

hinter

um

unter

wieder

When a verb with a variable prefix is pronounced with the stress on the prefix, the prefix separates as with separable prefix verbs. When a verb with a variable prefix is pronounced without stress on the prefix, it is inseparable from its verb and does not take *ge*- in the past participle.

	über*setzen*	- to translate
Separable:	*über*setzen	- to ferry across
	über*fallen*	- to attack

Separable: *über*fallen - to fall over
               wieder*holen* - to repeat
Separable: *wieder*holen - to bring again

H. Modal Auxiliary Verbs

German has six *modal auxiliary verbs* which express the manner (mode) in which an action takes place. The German verbs which describe a state of mind or mood and help to convey the idea expressed by any complementary infinitive called modal auxiliaries are:

dürfen - expresses permission - to be allowed, be permitted to, may

können - expresses ability and possibility - can, to be able to, may

mögen - expresses liking or preference - to like (to)

müssen - expresses necessity, compulsion - to have to, must

sollen - expresses obligation - to be supposed to

wollen - expresses desire or wishing - to want to

Principle parts

dürfen	durfte	gedurft/dürfen
können	konnte	gekonnt/können
mögen	mochte	gemocht/mögen
müssen	musste	gemusst/müssen
sollen	sollte	gesollt/sollen
wollen	wollte	gewollt/wollen

The present tense of the modal auxiliary verbs:

	dürfen	können	mögen	müssen	sollen	wollen
ich	darf	kann	mag	muss	soll	will
du	darfst	kannst	magst	musst	sollst	willst
er, sie, es	darf	kann	mag	muss	soll	will
wir	dürfen	können	mögen	müssen	sollen	wollen
ihr	dürft	könnt	mögt	müsst	sollt	wollt
Sie	dürfen	können	mögen	müssen	sollen	wollen

Although the *Sie* form is slightly abbreviated, it is understood that the *Sie* form is the same for the singular and plural and also the same as the *sie* (plural - "they") form.

Modal auxiliaries have no endings in the first and third persons singular of the present tense. The simple past tense of modal auxiliary verbs is conjugated regularly:

ich	durfte	konnte	mochte	musste	sollte	wollte
du	durftest	konntest	mochtest	musstest	solltest	wolltest
er, sie, es	durfte	konnte	mochte	musste	sollte	wollte
wir	durften	konnten	mochten	mussten	sollten	wollten
ihr	durftet	konntet	mochtet	musstet	solltet	wolltet
Sie	durften	konnten	mochten	mussten	sollten	wollten

1. In sentence structure modal auxiliary verbs are generally followed by an infinitive to complete their meaning (complementary infinitive); the infinitive always stands at the end of the sentence or clause:

"...ich *kann* wohl manchmal *singen*..."
(Schumann, *Liederkreis*–9)

"Ich *will* meine Seele *tauchen*..."
(Schumann, *Dichterliebe*–5)

"...dort *will* ich dich dann *erwarten*..."
(Strauss, "Heimliche Aufforderung")

"...in Grün *will* ich mich *kleiden*..."
(Schubert, *Die schöne Müllerin*–18)

"...*muss* selbst den Weg mir *weisen*..."
(Schubert, *Die Winterreise*–1)

"...*sollte* mir das Herz auch *brechen*..."
(Schumann, *Frauenliebe und Leben*–2)

"...*darfst* mich...nicht *kennen*..."
(Schumann, *Frauenliebe und Leben*–2)

"...*sollt'* ihrer Macht *entrauschen*!...
ich *will*...*singen*!...
die Leier *möcht'* ich *tauschen*!"
(Schubert, "An die Leier")

"...*will* in's Ohr dir *flüstern*..."
(Schumann, *Frauenliebe und Leben*–6)

"Auch kleine Dinge *können* uns *entzücken*..."
(Wolf, "Auch kleine Dinge")

a) Note that modal auxiliary verbs have two forms of the past participle, one beginning with *ge-*, the other the same as the infinitive. The infinitive form of the past participle is used when a modal auxiliary in any compound tense has a complementary infinitive. This is sometimes referred to as "double infinitive construction". Since modal auxiliary verbs are usually accompanied by a complementary infinitive, the *ge-* form of the past participle is used infrequently. All six modal auxiliary verbs use *haben* in the *compound past tense.*

I. Special Meanings

The three verbs which express "to know" merit special consideration:

1. "to know"

a) *kennen* - to know or be acquainted with persons, books, places, etc.
Principle parts: kennen - kannte - gekannt
"*Kennst* du das Land...?"
(Schumann, *Mignon*–1)

b) *wissen* - to know, followed by a dependent clause

Principle parts: wissen - wusste - gewusst
"...ihr *wisst* ja, was ich meine."
(Schubert, *Die schöne Müllerin*–10)

"...dann *weiss* ich, wo die Liebe thront.."
(Schubert, *Die schöne Müllerin*–14)

"...ich *weiss* nicht, wo ich bin..."
(Schumann, *Liederkreis*–8)

"...*weiss* nicht, wo ich abends ruh'..."
(Wolf, "Der Musikant")

c) *können* - to know how to do something; to know a language.

Principle parts: können - konnte - gekonnt

2. An *impersonal* verb makes a general statement rather than referring to any particular person or thing. Impersonal verbs take the subject *es* and can therefore be used only in the third person singular. The use of impersonal verbs especially in idiomatic expressions, is more frequently encountered in German than in English.

a) Those verbs which describe the weather are impersonal verbs:

blitzen	blitzte	geblitzt	to lighten
donnern	gedonnert	donnerte	to thunder
frieren	fror	gefroren	to freeze
regnen	regnete	geregnet	to rain
schneien	schneite	geschneit	to snow

b) The verbs *gelingen* (to succeed) and *geschehen* (to happen) are used impersonally in German; both take *sein* as the auxiliary. The verb *gelingen* takes the dative case.

3. The verb *leid tun* (to be sorry) is idiomatic and is conjugated according to the verb *tun* (auxiliary verb: *haben*). Literally this verb means "to cause pain or suffering to" and accordingly always takes the dative case. The verb *leid tun* is used in all tenses and may refer to any person or persons.

"...Erlkönig *hat* mir ein *Leids getan!*"
(Schubert, "Erlkönig")

4. The verb *gehen* is idiomatic when used with the dative case.

Wie geht es Ihnen?

Mir geht's gut.[1]

5. The generalities "there is" and "there are" may be expressed:

a) *es gibt* - followed by the accusative case

b) *es ist, es sind* - followed by the nominative case; "es gibt" is used in a general sense; "es ist" is used specifically and definitely. Both expressions can be used in all tenses.

"...*es ist* der Vater mit seinem Kind..."
(Schubert, "Erlkönig")

6. When the impersonal *es* is followed by the verb and the real subject, *es* serves to emphasize the statement.

"...*es* kennt mich dort keiner mehr..."
(Schumann, *Liederkreis*–1)

"...*es* hat ein Traum mich berückt..."
(Schumann, *Frauenliebe und Leben*–3)

"*es* bellen die Hunde, *es* rasseln die Ketten..."
(Schubert, *Die Winterreise*–17)

---

[1]*geht's* is a contraction for *geht es*; contractions occur frequently in German, especially in poetic texts.

"...*es* klirren die Balken, *es* zittert das Haus!

es rollet der Donner, *es* leuchtet der Blitz..."
(Schubert, "Die junge Nonne")

II. REFLEXIVE VERBS

A *reflexive verb* is a verb whose subject reflects or reacts upon itself; its object is always a pronoun corresponding to the subject. The *reflexive pronouns* in German are:

Singular	*Plural*
ich - mich	wir - uns
du - dich	ihr - euch
er - sich	sie - sich
sie - sich	
es - sich	
Sie - sich	Sie - sich

Reflexive verbs take the auxiliary verb *haben*; almost all transitive verbs may be used reflexively. Reflexive construction occurs more frequently in German than in English. The most frequently encountered reflexive verbs include:

sich amüsieren - to have a good time, amuse oneself

sich befinden - to be located; to be, feel

sich erinnern - to remember

sich erkälten - to catch cold

sich freuen - to be glad, be pleased with, rejoice at, look forward to

sich fürchten - to be afraid of

sich setzen - to seat oneself, sit down

Present Tense		*Simple Past Tense*		*Imperative*
ich setze	mich	ich setzte	mich	
du setzest	dich	du setztest	dich	Setze dich!
er setzt	sich	er setzte	sich	
wir setzen	uns	wir setzten	uns	
ihr setzt	euch	ihr setztet	euch	Setzt euch!
Sie setzen	sich	Sie setzten	ich	Setzen Sie sich!

69

In simple tenses the reflexive pronoun follows the verb; in compound tenses the reflexive pronoun follows the auxiliary verb in sentence structure.

A. Some reflexive verbs require an indirect object (dative case) reflexive pronoun.

sich ansehen	- to look at
sich denken	- to imagine
sich Sorgen machen	- to worry

The dative reflexive pronouns are:

Singular		*Plural*	
ich	- mir	wir	- uns
du	- dir	ihr	- euch
er	- sich	sie	- sich
sie	- sich		
es	- sich		
Sie	- sich	Sie	- sich

Verbs with dative reflexive pronouns will be noted in the listing at the end of this chapter.

III. TENSES

There are six tenses in German. The three tenses directly related to the principle parts of the verb are the present tense, simple past tense, and the compound past tense. The three remaining tenses are:

A. Past Perfect Tense

The *past perfect tense* is a compound tense composed of the simple past tense of the auxiliary verb (*haben* or *sein*) plus the past participle of the main verb.

spielen		singen	
ich	hatte gespielt	ich	hatte gesungen
du	hattest gespielt	du	hattest gesungen
er	hatte gespielt	er	hatte gesungen
wir	hatten gespielt	wir	hatten gesungen
ihr	hattet gespielt	ihr	hattet gesungen
Sie	hatten gespielt	Sie	hatten gesungen

haben	sein	werden
ich hatte gehabt	ich war gewesen	ich war geworden
du hattest gehabt	du warst gewesen	du warst geworden
er hatte gehabt	er war gewesen	er war geworden
wir hatten gehabt	wir waren gewesen	wir waren geworden
ihr hattet gehabt	ihr wart gewesen	ihr wart geworden
Sie hatten gehabt	Sie waren gewesen	Sie waren geworden

The past perfect tense is translated according to the union of the auxiliary verb and the past participle:

"...der Mai *war* mir *gewogen*..."
(Schubert, *Die Winterreise*–1)

It is important to learn to recognize the past perfect tense, as this tense is encountered frequently in translating.

B. Future Tense

The *future tense* is a compound tense composed of the present tense of the verb *werden* plus the verb infinitive, which is always placed at the end of the sentence or clause. The future tense is formed regularly and according to the same pattern for all verbs:

spielen	singen
ich werde spielen	ich werde singen
du wirst spielen	du wirst singen
er wird spielen	er wird singen
wir werden spielen	wir werden singen
ihr werdet spielen	ihr werdet singen
Sie werden spielen	Sie werden singen

sein	haben	werden
ich werde sein	ich werde haben	ich werde werden
du wirst sein	du wirst haben	du wirst werden
er wird sein	er wird haben	er wird werden
wir werden sein	wir werden haben	wir werden werden
ihr werdet sein	ihr werdet haben	ihr werdet werden
Sie werden sein	Sie werden haben	Sie werden werden

"...du *wirst* nicht *weinen,* leise, leise *wirst* du *lächeln*..."
(Strauss, "Befreit")

C. Future Perfect Tense

The *future perfect tense* completes the six tenses in German. The future perfect tense consists of the future tense of the auxiliary verb (see p. 71) plus the past participle of the verb, and may express probability, that is, something that probably happened in the past.

spielen		singen	
ich werde	gespielt haben	ich werde	gesungen haben
du wirst	gespielt haben	du wirst	gesungen haben
er wird	gespielt haben	er wird	gesungen haben
wir werden	gespielt haben	wir werden	gesungen haben
ihr werdet	gespielt haben	ihr werdet	gesungen haben
Sie werden	gespielt haben	Sie werden	gesungen haben

IV. SUMMARY

A. Categories of Verbs

All verbs in German are either

1. Strong (irregular) or
2. Weak (regular)

Strong and weak verbs are either

1. Transitive - take a direct object
2. Intransitive - do not take a direct object

B. Principle Parts

All verb forms can be derived from the three principle parts of any verb.

C. Auxiliary Verbs

All verbs in German have an auxiliary verb.

D. Conjugation

Some verbs change the stem vowel in conjugation.

E. Prefixes

Three types of prefixes occur in German verb structure:

1. Inseparable
2. Separable
3. Variable

F. Tenses

There are six tenses in German:

1. present tense: verb stem (infinitive) + endings

2. simple past tense: verb stem (first person singular of the simple past tense) + endings

3. compound past tense: present tense of auxiliary verb (*haben* or *sein*) + past participle

4. past perfect tense: simple past tense of auxiliary verb + past participle

5. future tense: present tense of *werden* + infinitive

6. future perfect tense: future tense of auxiliary verb + past participle

PRINCIPLE PARTS OF STRONG AND WEAK VERBS

R = Regular
I = Irregular
h = haben:auxiliary
s = sein:auxiliary

infinitive	*first person simple past*	*past participle*		
addieren	addierte	addiert	(R-h)	to add
ändern	änderte	geändert	(R-h)	to change
antworten	antwortete	geantwortet	(R-h)	to answer
arbeiten	arbeitete	gearbeitet	(R-h)	to work
baden	badete	gebadet	(R-h)	to bathe
balancieren	balancierte	balanciert	(R-h)	to balance
bauen	baute	gebaut	(R-h)	to build
beabsichtigen	beabsichtigte	beabsichtigt	(R-h)	to intend
be*antworten*				to answer
beeindrucken	beeindruckte	beeindruckt	(R-h)	to impress
beeinflussen	beeinflusste	beeinflusst	(R-h)	to influence
beenden	beendete	beendet	(R-h)	to finish
be*fehlen*				to order
begegnen	begegnete	begegnet	(R-h)	to meet
begeistern	begeisterte	begeistert	(R-h)	to inspire

73

beginnen	begann	begonnen	(I-h)	to begin
be*greifen*				to understand
be*grüssen*				to greet
be*halten*				to retain
be*handeln*				to treat
behaupten	behauptete	behauptet	(R-h)	to assert
be*herrschen*				to control
be*kommen*				to receive
belagern	belagerte	belagert	(R-h)	to besiege
belästigen	belästigte	belästigt	(R-h)	to annoy
be*merken*				to notice
benachrichtigen	benachrichtigte	benachrichtigt	(R-h)	to inform
beneiden	beneidete	beneidet	(R-h)	to use
beobachten	beobachtete	beobachtet	(R-h)	to prepare
beschädigen	beschädigte	beschädigt	(R-h)	to damage
be*schreiben*				to describe
be*schützen*				to protect
besichtigen	besichtigte	besichtigt	(R-h)	to view
be*sitzen*				to possess, win
besorgen	besorgte	besorgt	(R-h)	to take care
be*sprechen*				to discuss
be*stehen*				to consist
be*steigen*				to get on
be*suchen*				to visit
beten	betete	gebetet	(R-h)	to pray
betrachten	betrachte	betrachtet	(R-h)	to consider
be*tragen*				to amount to
be*treten*				to step into
be*wohnen*				to occupy
be*wundern*				to admire
bezeichnen	bezeichnete	bezeichnet	(R-h)	to denote
bieten	bot	geboten	(I-h)	to offer
binden	band	gebunden	(I-h)	to bind
bitten	bat	gebeten	(I-h)	to request
blasen	blies	geblasen	(I-h)	to blow
blättern	blätterte	geblättert	(R-h)	to turn over
blicken	blickte	geblickt	(R-h)	to look
blinken	blinkte	geblinkt	(R-h)	to blink

74

borgen	borgte	geborgt	(R-h)	to borrow
brauchen	brauchte	gebraucht	(R-h)	to need
brauen	braute	gebraut	(R-h)	to brew
brechen	brach	gebrochen	(I-h)	to break
brennen	brannte	gebrannt	(I-h)	to burn
bringen	brachte	gebracht	(I-h)	to bring
dämpfen	dämpfte	gedämpft	(R-h)	to mute
danken	dankte	gedankt	(R-h)	to thank
dauern	dauerte	gedauert	(R-h)	to last
decken	deckte	gedeckt	(R-h)	to cover
definieren	definierte	definiert	(R-h)	to define
denken	dachte	gedacht	(I-h)	to think
deprimieren	deprimierte	deprimiert	(R-h)	to depress
dienen	diente	gedient	(R-h)	to serve
diskutieren	diskutierte	diskutiert	(R-h)	to discuss
doppeln	doppelte	gedoppelt	(R-h)	to double
dringen	drang	gedrungen	(I-h)	to urge
drücken	drückte	gedrückt	(R-h)	to press
dürfen	durfte	gedurft/dürfen	(I-h)	may
ehren	ehrte	geehrt	(R-h)	to honor
eilen	eilte	geeilt	(R-h)	to hurry
empfangen	empfing	empfangen	(I-h)	to receive
empfehlen	empfahl	empfohlen	(I-h)	to recommend
ent*decken*				to discover
ent*fliehen*				to escape
ent*stehen*				to originate
er*fahren*				to learn
er*finden*				to invent
er*füllen*				to fulfill
ergänzen	ergänzte	ergänzt	(R-h)	to complete
er*greifen*				to seize
er*halten*				to receive
er*kennen*				to notice
erklären	erklärte	erklärt	(R-h)	to explain
erlauben	erlaubte	erlaubt	(R-h)	to allow
er*leben*				to experience
erledigen	erledigte	erledigt	(R-h)	to take care of
er*lernen*				to learn

erleuchten	erleuchtete	erleuchtet	(R-h)	to illuminate
erobern	eroberte	erobert	(R-h)	to conquer
erreichen				to reach
erscheinen				to appear
erschrecken	erschrak	erschrocken	(I-s)	to frighten
erschüttern	erschütterte	erschüttert	(R-s)	to shake
ersetzen				to replace
erwähnen	erwähnte	erwähnt	(R-h)	to mention
erwarten				to expect
erwidern	erwiderte	erwidert	(R-h)	to answer
erzählen				to tell
essen	aß	gegessen	(I-h)	to eat
existieren	existierte	existiert	(R-h)	to exist
fahren	fuhr	gefahren	(I-s)	to go, ride
fallen	fiel	gefallen	(I-s)	to fall
fangen	fing	gefangen	(I-h)	to catch
fehlen	fehlte	gefehlt	(R-h)	to be missing
feiern	feierte	gefeiert	(R-h)	to celebrate
finden	fand	gefunden	(I-h)	to find
fliegen	flog	geflogen	(I-s)	to fly
fliehen	flohen	geflohen	(I-s)	to flee
fliessen	floß	geflossen	(I-s)	to flow
flüstern	flüsterte	geflüstert	(R-h)	to whisper
folgen	folgte	gefolgt	(R-s)	to follow
fragen	fragte	gefragt	(R-h)	to ask
fühlen	fühlte	gefühlt	(R-h)	to feel
füllen	füllte	gefüllt	(R-h)	to fill
fürchten	fürchtete	gefürchtet	(R-h)	to fear
geben	gab	gegeben	(I-h)	to give
gebrauchen				to use
gefallen				to like
gehen	ging	gegangen	(I-s)	to go
gehören				to belong to
gelingen	gelang	gelungen	(I-s)	to succeed
gelten	galt	gegolten	(I-h)	to mean
geschehen	geschah	geschehen	(I-s)	to happen
geniessen	genoß	genossen	(I-h)	to enjoy
gestehen				to confess

gewinnen	gewann	gewonnen	(I-h)	to win
giessen	goß	gegossen	(I-h)	to water
glauben	glaubte	geglaubt	(R-h)	to believe
gleichen	glich	geglichen	(I-h)	to be like
gratulieren	gratulierte	gratuliert	(R-h)	to congratulate
greifen	griff	gegriffen	(I-h)	to seize
grüssen	grüsste	gegrüsst	(R-h)	to greet
haben	hatte	gehabt	(I-h)	to have
halten	hielt	gehalten	(I-h)	to stop
handeln	handelte	gehandelt	(R-h)	to deal with
hängen	hängte	gehängt	(R-h)	to hand
hassen	hasste	gehasst	(R-h)	to hate
heben	hob	gehoben	(I-h)	to lift
heiraten	heiratete	geheiratet	(R-h)	to marry
heissen	hieß	geheißen	(I-h)	to be called
herrschen	herrschte	geherrscht	(R-h)	to prevail
hoffen	hoffte	gehofft	(R-h)	to hope
holen	holte	geholt	(R-h)	to pick up
hören	hörte	gehört	(R-h)	to hear
imponieren	imponierte	imponiert	(R-h)	to impress
inspirieren	inspirierte	inspiriert	(R-h)	to inspire
kämpfen	kämpfte	gekämpft	(R-h)	to struggle
kaufen	kaufte	gekauft	(R-h)	to buy
kennen	kannte	gekannt	(I-h)	to know
kennen *lernen*				to get to know
klagen	klagte	geklagt	(R-h)	to complain
klären	klärte	geklärt	(R-h)	to clear
kleiden	kleidete	gekleidet	(R-h)	to clothe
klingen	klang	geklungen	(I-h)	to sound
klingeln	klingelte	geklingelt	(R-h)	to ring (a bell)
klopfen	klopfte	geklopft	(R-h)	to knock
kommen	kam	gekommen	(I-s)	to come
komponieren	komponierte	komponiert	(R-h)	to compose
können	konnte	gekonnt/können	(I-h)	to be able
kritisieren	kritisierte	kritisiert	(R-h)	to criticize
küssen	küsste	geküsst	(R-h)	to kiss
lächeln	lächelte	gelächelt	(R-h)	to smile
lachen	lachte	gelacht	(R-h)	to laugh

77

laden	lud	geladen	(I-h)	to invite
lassen	ließ	gelassen	(I-h)	to leave
laufen	lief	gelaufen	(I-s)	to run
leben	lebte	gelebt	(R-h)	to live
legen	legte	gelegt	(R-h)	to put, lay
lehren	lehrte	gelehrt	(R-h)	to teach
leiden	litt	gelitten	(I-h)	to suffer
leihen	lieh	geliehen	(I-h)	to loan
leisten	leistete	geleistet	(R-h)	to achieve
lernen	lernte	gelernt	(R-h)	to learn
lesen	las	gelesen	(I-h)	to read
lieben	liebte	geliebt	(R-h)	to love
liegen	lag	gelegen	(I-h)	to lie
loben	lobte	gelobt	(R-h)	to praise
machen	machte	gemacht	(R-h)	to do, make
malen	malte	gemalt	(R-h)	to paint
meinen	meinte	gemeint	(R-h)	to mean
merken	merkte	gemerkt	(R-h)	to notice
mieten	mietete	gemietet	(R-h)	to rent
miss*verstehen*				to misunderstand
mögen	mochte	gemocht/mögen	(I-h)	to like
musizieren	musizierte	musiziert	(R-h)	to make music
müssen	musste	gemusst/müssen	(I-h)	to have to, must
nehmen	nahm	genommen	(I-h)	to take
nennen	nannte	genannt	(I-h)	to name
nicken	nickte	genickt	(R-h)	to nod
nützen	nützte	genützt	(R-h)	to use
öffnen	öffnete	geöffnet	(R-h)	to open
packen	packte	gepackt	(R-h)	to pack
pflegen	pflegte	gepflegt	(R-h)	to cultivate
plagen	plagte	geplagt	(R-h)	to bother
plaudern	plauderte	geplaudert	(R-h)	to chat
preisen	pries	gepriesen	(I-h)	to praise
prüfen	prüfte	geprüft	(R-h)	to test
quälen	quälte	gequält	(R-h)	to torment
quellen	quoll	gequollen	(I-s)	to gush
raten	riet	geraten	(I-h)	to advise
rasen	raste	gerast	(R-h)	to rush

rauschen	rauschte	gerauscht	(R-h)	to rustle
rechnen	rechnete	gerechnet	(R-h)	to figure
reden	redete	geredet	(R-h)	to talk
regnen	regnete	geregnet	(R-h)	to rain
reichen	reichte	gereicht	(R-h)	to hand
reisen	reiste	gereist	(R-h)	to travel
rennen	rannte	gerannt	(I-s)	to run
reservieren	reservierte	reserviert	(R-h)	to reserve
riechen	roch	gerochen	(I-h)	to smell
rufen	rief	gerufen	(I-h)	to call
ruhen	ruhte	geruht	(R-h)	to rest
sammeln	sammelte	gesammelt	(R-h)	to gather
sagen	sagte	gesagt	(R-h)	to say
schaffen	schuf	geschaffen	(I-h)	to create
schallen	schallte	geschallt	(R-h)	to sound
schätzen	schätzte	geschätzt	(R-h)	to appreciate
schauen	schaute	geschaut	(R-h)	to look at
scheiden	schied	geschieden	(I-h)	to separate
scheinen	schien	geschienen	(I-h)	to seem
schenken	schenkte	geschenkt	(R-h)	to present
scherzen	scherzte	gescherzt	(R-h)	to joke
schicken	schickte	geschickt	(R-h)	to send
schieben	schob	geschoben	(I-h)	to push
schlafen	schlief	geschlafen	(I-h)	to sleep
schlagen	schlug	geschlagen	(I-h)	to hit, beat
schliessen	schloss	geschlossen	(I-h)	to close
schlummern	schlummerte	geschlummert	(R-h)	to slumber
schmecken	schmeckte	geschmeckt	(R-h)	to taste
schneiden	schnitt	geschnitten	(I-h)	to cut
schneien	schneite	geschneit	(R-h)	to snow
schreiben	schrieb	geschrieben	(I-h)	to write
schreien	schrie	geschrieen	(I-h)	to shout
schütteln	schüttelte	geschüttelt	(R-h)	to shake
schützen	schützte	geschützt	(R-h)	to protect
schweigen	schwieg	geschwiegen	(I-h)	to be silent
schwimmen	schwamm	geschwommen	(I-s)	to swim
sehen	sah	gesehen	(I-h)	to see
sein	war	gewesen	(I-s)	to be

senden	sandte	gesandt	(I-h)	to send
setzen	setzte	gesetzt	(R-h)	to place, put
singen	sang	gesungen	(I-h)	to sing
sinken	sank	gesunken	(I-h)	to sink
sitzen	saß	gesessen	(I-h)	to sit
sollen	sollte	gesollt/sollen	(I-h)	ought to
sorgen	sorgte	gesorgt	(R-h)	to look after
speisen	speiste	gespeist	(R-h)	to eat
spielen	spielte	gespielt	(R-h)	to play
sprechen	sprach	gesprochen	(I-h)	to speak
springen	sprang	gesprungen	(I-h)	to jump
spüren	spürte	gespürt	(R-h)	to feel
stammen	stammte	gestammt	(R-s)	to originate
stärken	stärkte	gestärkt	(R-h)	to strengthen
starren	starrte	gestarrt	(R-h)	to start
staunen	staunte	gestaunt	(R-h)	to be astonished
stechen	stach	gestochen	(I-h)	to sting
stehen	stand	gestanden	(I-s)	to stand
steigen	stieg	gestiegen	(I-s)	to climb
stellen	stellte	gestellt	(R-h)	to put
sterben	starb	gestorben	(I-s)	to die
stimmen	stimmte	gestimmt	(R-h)	to tune
stoßen	stieß	gestoßen	(I-h)	to push
strecken	streckte	gestreckt	(R-h)	to stretch
strömen	strömte	geströmt	(R-s)	to stream
studieren	studierte	studiert	(R-h)	to study
suchen	suchte	gesucht	(R-h)	to look for
tanzen	tanzte	getanzt	(R-h)	to dance
tauschen	tauschte	getauscht	(R-h)	to change
teilen	teilte	geteilt	(R-h)	to divide
telefonieren	telefonierte	telefoniert	(R-h)	to telephone
tragen	trug	getragen	(I-h)	to carry
treten	trat	getreten	(I-h)	to step
trinken	trank	getrunken	(I-h)	to drink
treffen	traf	getroffen	(I-h)	to meet
tun	tat	getan	(I-h)	to do
üben	übte	geübt	(R-h)	to practice

überraschen	überraschte	überrascht	(R-h)	to surprise
übertreiben	übertrieb	übertrieben	(I-h)	to exaggerate
überzeugen	überzeugte	überzeugt	(R-h)	to convince
umarmen	umarmte	umarmt	(R-h)	to embrace
unterbrechen				to interrupt
unterrichten	unterrichtete	unterrichtet	(R-h)	to teach
unterscheiden				to distinguish
verbringen				to spend (time)
vergehen				to pass
vergessen	vergaß	vergessen	(I-h)	to forget
vergleichen				to compare
verlieren	verlor	verloren	(I-h)	to lose
vermissen	vermisste	vermisst	(R-h)	to miss
verschreiben				to prescribe
versehen				to provide
versichern	versicherte	versichert	(R-h)	to assure
versprechen				to promise
verstehen				to understand
versuchen				to try
verurteilen	verurteilte	verurteilt	(R-h)	to condemn
verzeihen	verzieh	verziehen	(I-h)	to forgive
wachen	wachte	gewacht	(R-h)	to awake
wachsen	wuchs	gewachsen	(I-s)	to grow up
wählen	wählte	gewählt	(R-h)	to elect
wandern	wanderte	gewandert	(R-s)	to wander
warten	wartete	gewartet	(R-h)	to wait
wechseln	wechselte	gewechselt	(R-h)	to change
wenden	wandte	gewandt	(R-h)	to turn
werden	wurde	geworden	(I-s)	to become
werfen	warf	geworfen	(I-h)	to throw
wiederholen	wiederholte	wiederholt	(R-h)	to repeat
wiegen	wog	gewogen	(I-h)	to weigh
winken	winkte	gewinkt	(R-h)	to beckon
wissen	wusste	gewusst	(I-h)	to know
wohnen	wohnte	gewohnt	(R-h)	to live
wollen	wollte	gewollt/wollen	(I-h)	to want
wundern	wunderte	gewundert	(R-h)	to wonder
wünschen	wünschte	gewünscht	(R-h)	to wish

zahlen	zahlte	gezahlt	(R-h)	to pay
zählen	zählte	gezählt	(R-h)	to count
zeigen	zeigte	gezeigt	(R-h)	to show
ziehen	zog	gezogen	(I-h)	to draw
zwingen	zwang	gezwungen	(I-h)	to force

REFLEXIVE VERBS

sich ab*schliessen*				to seclude oneself
sich amüsieren	amüsierte	amüsiert	(R-h)	to amuse oneself
sich an*sehen*				to look at oneself
sich *anziehen*				to dress oneself
sich ärgern	ärgerte	geärgert	(R-h)	to get angry
sich aufregen	aufregte	aufgeregt	(R-h)	to get excited
sich be*eilen*				to hurry
sich be*finden*				to be located
sich bemühen	bemühte	bemüht	(R-h)	to trouble oneself
sich bewegen	bewegte	bewegt	(R-s)	to move
sich drehen	drehte	gedreht	(R-h)	to turn
sich entwickeln	entwickelte	entwickelt	(R-h)	to develop
sich er*heben*				to rise
sich erinnern	erinnerte	erinnert	(R-h)	to remember
sich erkälten	erkältete	erkältet	(R-h)	to catch cold
sich freuen	freute	gefreut	(R-h)	to be glad
sich fürchten	fürchtet	gefürchtet	(R-h)	to be afraid of
sich genieren	genierte	geniert	(R-h)	to feel embarrassed
sich hin*geben*				to devote oneself
sich hin*setzen*				to sit down
sich interess-ieren	interessierte	interessiert	(R-h)	to be interested
sich langweilen	langweilte	gelangweilt	(R-h)	to be bored
sich leisten	leistete	geleistet	(R-h)	to afford
sich Sorgen machen				to worry
sich um*kleiden*				to change clothes
sich ver*heiraten*				to get married
sich vor*stellen*				to imagine

sich wärmen	wärmte	gewärmt	(R-h)	to warm oneself
sich waschen	wusch	gewaschen	(I-h)	to wash oneself
sich zurück*ziehen*				to withdraw

VERBS WITH SEPARABLE PREFIXES

abbrechen	to break off
abfahren	to start, leave
abgehen	to leave, go off
abhalten	to hold
abhängen	to depend
abholen	to pick up, call for
abreisen	to set out
abziehen	to subtract
anbieten	to offer
anfangen	to begin
angeben	to mention, state
angreifen	to attack
anhaben	to wear
anhalten	to stop
ankämpfen	to struggle
anklingeln	to telephone
ankommen	to arrive
annehmen	to assume
anreden	to address
anrufen	to call up
anschreien	to cry out
anstarren	to stare at
aufbauen	to build up, rebuild
auffallen	to notice
auffliegen	to fly open
aufführen	to perform
aufgeben	to give up
aufgehen	to rise
aufhalten	to keep, detain
aufhören	to stop
aufklären	to explain, inform
aufmachen	to open
aufnehmen	to absorb

aufregen	to excite
aufschreiben	to write down
aufsein	to be up
aufspringen	to jump up
aufstehen	to get up
aufsteigen	to arise, get on
aufteilen	to divide up
aufwachen	to wake up
aufwachsen	to grow up
aufwärmen	to warm up
aufwarten	to serve, wait on
ausdrücken	to express
ausfüllen	to fill out, fill up
ausgeben	to spend
ausgehen	to go out
aushalten	to endure, stand
auspacken	to unpack
ausrechnen	to calculate
ausrufen	to call out
aussehen	to appear, seem, look
ausspielen	to finish playing
aussteigen	to get off
dasein	to be present
dahingehen	to go there
durchblättern	to leaf through
durchführen	to carry on, accomplish
durchschneiden	to cut across
einbauen	to build in
einfahren	to enter
einführen	to introduce, establish
eingiessen	to pour in
einladen	to invite
einkaufen	to buy, shop
einschenken	to serve
einschlafen	to fall asleep
einschliessen	to include
einsteigen	to get on
eintreten	to step into

einwandern	to immigrate
festsetzen	to set, fix, arrange
fortfahren	to leave
fortsetzen	to continue
haltmachen	to stop
herabnehmen	to take down
heranfahren	to ride up
hereinkommen	to come in
herreisen	to travel here
herstellen	to produce, manufacture
hinaufgehen	to go up
hinauftragen	to carry up
hinausschauen	to look out
hinaustreten	to step outside
hineingehen	to go in
hineintreten	to step inside
hinüberspringen	to jump across
hinuntergehen	to go downstairs
hinwegfahren	to ride along
mitteilen	to inform
nachdenken	to think, reflect
nachgeben	to give in
nachlesen	to read up
nahekommen	to approach, get close
nachprüfen	to check
nachschauen	to watch, look after
niederbrennen	to burn down
stattfinden	to take place
umherreisen	to travel about
umschauen	to arrange
umrechnen	to change, convert
unternehmen	to undertake
vorbeifahren	to ride past
vorlegen	to place before
vorschlagen	to suggest
vorstellen	to introduce
vorzeigen	to present
vorziehen	to prefer

weggehen	to go away
weitergehen	to continue
weitersprechen	to go on speaking
widerstehen	to resist
zuhören	to listen
zumachen	to close
zunehmen	to increase
zurückgeben	to give back
zurückgehen	to go back
zurücklegen	to put behind, cover

IDIOMATIC VERBS

Abschied nehmen	to say goodbye
eine Frage stellen	to ask a question
die Gelegenheit ergreifen	to seize the opportunity
im Begriff sein	to be about to
nach Hause gehen	to go home
Recht haben	to be right
zu Fuss gehen	to walk
zur Verfügung stehen	to be at the service of
zur Schule gehen	to go school

VERBS FREQUENTLY ENCOUNTERED IN MUSIC SCORES, TEXTS ON MUSIC, AND MUSICOLOGICAL ESSAYS

abdämpfen	to mute (especially kettle drums)
absetzen	to separate, either notes or phrases
abstossen	1) violin playing - detached bow
	2) organ playing - take off a stop
aufführen	to perform
ausdrücken	to express
aushalten	to sustain a note
ausspielen	to finish playing
dämpfen	to mute (horns and other instruments)
detonieren	to sing off pitch
dirigieren	to conduct
kolorieren	to introduce coloraturas
komponieren	to compose

schlagen	to beat, hit
schallen	to sound
schleppen	to drag
spielen	to play
stopfen	to stop up, as in horn playing
teilen	to divide, as in string parts
üben	to practice
überblasen	to overblow
übergreifen	to cross the hands in piano playing
überschlagen	to cross the hands in piano playing
umblättern	to turn pages
umstimmen	to change the tuning (of kettle drums)
unterrichten	to give lessons
untersetzen	to put under the thumb in piano playing
verdoppeln	to double, as in parts
verstärken	to reinforce the sound
vokalisieren	to vocalize
vorbereiten	to prepare in advance (organ stops)
zurückhalten	to hold back

VERBS FREQUENTLY ENCOUNTERED IN VOCAL LITERATURE

dienen	to serve
	(Reger, "An die Hoffnung")
fliessen	to flow
	(Schubert, *Schwanengesang*–5)
flüstern	to whisper
	(Brahms, "Das Mädchen spricht")
folgen	to follow
	(Bach, *Johannespassion*, "Ich folge dir")
fühlen	to feel
	(Wolf, *Italienisches Liederbuch*–35)
grüßen	to greet
	(Pfitzner, "Der Gärtner")
küssen	to kiss
	(Beethoven, "Der Kuss")
leiden	to suffer
	(Brahms, "Von ewiger Liebe")

lieben	to love
	(Beethoven, " Ich liebe dich")
rauschen	to rustle
	(Schubert, *Die schöne Müllerin–2*)
schlummern	to slumber
	(Bach, *Kantate BWV 72–2*)
schweigen	to be silent
	(Brahms, "Von ewiger Liebe")

MUSICAL EXERCISES

1. Survey the texts of the four Mignon-Lieder (Goethe) as set by Wolf, Schumann, or Schubert.

   a) List all verbs

   b) Translate each

   c) Indicate the tense in which each is used

   d) Indicate whether the verb has a separable or an inseparable prefix.

2. Survey one of the six choral motets by J. S. Bach.

   a) List all nouns and indicate the gender of each

   b) List all pronouns and indicate the noun for which each is substituted

   c) List all verbs, translate each, and state the tense and auxiliary verb of each.

3. Survey the song cycle *Die Schöne Müllerin* by Schubert.

   a) List and translate all verbs

   b) Indicate the auxiliary verb of each

   c) Cite the tense used.

Chapter Four

I. ADJECTIVES

An *adjective* is a word that describes or modifies a noun or pronoun and answers the question "which?", "which one?", or "what kind of?" a noun or pronoun.

A. Demonstrative Adjectives

Demonstrative adjectives point out or indicate the object spoken of; they do not describe. These adjectives are declined like the definite articles *der*, *die*, and *das* (see p. 26).

aller- all

dieser- this, these

jeder- each, every

jener- that, those

mancher- many (a), some

solcher- such

welcher- which, what

"...*dieses* weissen hauses..."
(Strauss, "Freundliche Vision")

B. Possessive Adjectives

Possessive adjectives indicate possession, or to whom something belongs; these adjectives are declined like the indefinite articles *ein*, *eine*, *ein* (see p. 26).

mein - my	unser - our
dein - your	euer - your
sein - his, its	ihr - their
ihr - her	
Ihr - your	Ihr - your
kein - no	kein - no

"...du kühlst den brennenden Durst *meines* Busens..."
(Schubert, "Ganymed")

"...lasset nur, ihr lieben Leute,
euer Wundern, *euer* Sehnen!"
(Schubert, "Geheimes")

89

Like definite and indefinite articles, demonstrative and possessive adjectives must agree with the noun they modify in gender (masculine, feminine, or neuter), number (singular or plural), and case (nominative, accusative, genitive, dative).

1. *ihr* may mean either "her" or "their"; context will determine which meaning is indicated.

2. The three forms of the possessive adjective "your" are:

    a) *dein* - a person addressed as *du*

    b) *euer* - persons addressed as *ihr*

    c) *Ihr* - persons addressed as *Sie*

3. When an ending is added to the adjective *euer*, the middle *e* is dropped.

4. The adjective *unser* may be spelled out, or the *e* of the stem may be dropped when an ending is added.

C. Predicate Nominative

The *predicate nominative* is a noun used as part of the subject to describe the subject; it is used with the verb *sein*.

    "...das Glück ist *die Liebe*, die lieb' is *das Glück* ..."
    (Schumann, Frauenliebe und Leben–7)

    "... du bist *die Hexe* Lorelei..."
    (Schumann, *Liederkreis*–3)

    "...ich bin ja auch *kein Gärtner*..."
    (Schubert, Der Neugierige)

    "...das Leben ist der *schwüle Tag*..."

(Brahms, "Der Tod, das ist die kühle Nacht")

D. Predicate Adjectives

A *predicate adjective* is an adjective used after the verbs *sein* or *werden*; an adjective which follows a verb has no ending. Some frequently encountered adjectives are:

alt	old
dunkel	dark
hart	hard
heiss	hot

hell	light
jung	young
kalt	cold
kühl	cool
leer	empty
leicht	light
mild	mild
neu	new
schön	beautiful
schwer	heavy, difficult
treu	true
voll	full
warm	warm
blau	blue
braun	brown
gelb	yellow
grau	gray
orange	orange
rot	red
schwarz	black
weiss	white

"...aber Vater und Mutter sind lange *tot*..."
(Schumann, *Liederkreis*–1)

"...zukunft ist...*leer*..."
(Brahms, *Magelone Romanzen*–3)

"...stürmend Herz...werde *mild*..."
(Brahms - "Auf dem See")

1. The names of all nationalities (Chapter Two) can be used as adjectives and are declined accordingly. Adjectives in German that are derived from geography are not capitalized.

E. Unpreceded Adjectives

When an adjective is not preceded by a "der"-word or an "ein"-word it is an *unpreceded adjective*. An unpreceded adjective has the same endings as "der"-words in all cases, both singular and plural:

Singular			*Plural*
N	-er, -e,	-es[1]	-e
G	-en, -er,	-en	-er
D	-em,-er,	-em	-en
A	-en, -e,	-es	-e

"...*holde* Lippen, *klares* Auge, *heller* Sinn und *fester* Mut..."
(Schumann, *Frauenliebe und Leben*–2)

"...mit *leichtem* Schritt und *munterm* Sinn..."
(Mozart, "Das Veilchen")

"...und bringen *neues* Gluck..."
(Brahms, "Alte Liebe")

"...*blauer* Himmel, *blaue* Wogen..."
(Brahms, "Auf dem See")

"...Lust ist nur *tieferer* Schmerz...Leben ist *dunkles* Gram..."
(Brahms, *Magelone Romanzen*–9)

"...*treue* Liebe...*schöne* Liebesphantasien...*zarte* Träume..."
(Brahms, *Magelone Romanzen*–9)

"...*einsamer* Wald...*einsame* Wälder..."
(Brahms, *Magelone Romanzen*–1)

F. Preceded Adjectives

Adjectives *preceded* by a definite article or "der"-word are declined with the following endings:

Singular			*Plural*
N	-e, -e,	-e	-en
G	-en, -en,	-en	-en
D	-en, -en,	-en	-en
A	-en, -e,	-e	-en

"...*den ersten besten* Mann..."
(Schumann, *Dichterliebe*–11)

"Die Himmel rühmen des *Ewigen* Ehre..."
(Beethoven, "Die Ehre Gottes aus der Natur")

"...*Tränen der ewigen* Liebe!"
(Beethoven, "Wonne der Wehmut")

---

[1]-*es* may be encountered occasionally in the genitive singular (masculine and neuter), but this form is rare. -*en* is generally used instead of -*es*.

Note that *preceded* adjectives all end in either *-e* or *-en*; *-en* is used exclusively in the plural.

"...die *dunkle* Schwalbe...die *frommen* Störche...den *alten* Liebe-
sharm..."
(Brahms, "Alte Liebe")

"...das *goldene* Haar...die *süssen* Worte..."
(Brahms, *Magelone Romanzen*–7)

"...den *Herrlichen* Lauf...das *edele* Blut..."
(Brahms, *Magelone Romanzen*–8)

"...das *grausame* Meer...den *stürmenden* Wettern..."
(Brahms, *Magelone Romanzen*–10)

"...die *trunkene, wonneklopfende* Brust...
die *liebliche, selige, himmlische* Lust..."
(Brahms, *Magelone Romanzen*–15)

Adjectives preceded by an indefinite article or an "ein"-word are declined with the following endings:

Singular			*Plural*
N -er,	-e,	-es	-en
G -en,	-en,	-en	-en
D -en,	-en,	-en	-en
A -en	-e,	-es	-en

"...ein *alter* Traum..."
(Brahms, "Alte Liebe")

"...ein *irdisches* Leben..."
(Brahms, *Magelone Romanzen*–7)

"...mein *köstliches* Gut..."
(Brahms, *Magelone Romanzen*–8)

"...kein *wahres* Leben..."
(Brahms, *Magelone Romanzen*–12)

"...dein *irrender* Fuß..."
(Brahms, *Magelone Romanzen*–13)

Note again that *-en* is used in all cases in the plural.

G. Numerical Adjectives

The following *numerical adjectives* are always plural in meaning:

alle- all

ander(e)- other, others

einige- some

etwas- some, somewhat

mehrere- several

etliche- some

beide- both

manche- many

viele- many

weinige- few

Numerical adjectives usually function like unpreceded adjectives and accordingly have the plural endings of "der"-words: *-e, -er, -en, -e*. When a descriptive adjective follows a numerical adjective, the descriptive adjective takes the same ending as the numerical adjective. After *alle, beide, manche* the descriptive adjective takes *-en* in all four cases.

"...so *manchen süssen* Traum..."
(Schubert, *Die Winterreise*–5)

H. Past Participle

The *past participle* of a verb can be used as an adjective with regular adjective endings:

"...du *geliebter* Mann..."
(Schumann, *Frauenliebe und Leben*–6)

I. Present Participle

The *present participle* of verbs is formed by adding *-d* to the verb infinitive. The present participle may be used as an adjective or adverb.

"...freudig *scheidend* aus eurer Schar."
(Schumann, *Frauenliebe und Leben*–5)

"...ich bin nicht *lebend* mehr..."
(Schumann, *Frauenliebe und Leben*–8)

"...erwartet sie *träumend* die Nacht..."
(Schumann, "Die Lotosblume")

Among the present participles most frequently encountered in music are:

drängend- pressing on
eilend- hurrying
erlöschend- fading away
ermattend- tiring, weakening
fliessend- flowing
gehend- moving
hinsterbend- dying away
klagend- lamenting
nachlassend- relaxing, slackening
schleppend- dragging, heavy
treibend- hurrying
singend- singing

II. COMPARATIVE AND SUPERLATIVE

The comparative and superlative of adjectives is formed in English either by adding *-er* and *-est* (bigger, biggest), or by using the modifiers *more* and *most* (more interesting, most interesting).

A. Forms

The comparative of all adjectives in German is formed by adding *-er* to the positive form of the adjective; the superlative is formed by adding *-st* to the positive form of the adjective. Adjectives ending in *-d, -t, -ß,* and *-z* in the positive form add *-est* to form the superlative.

reich	reicher	reichst
interessant	interessanter	interessantest

"...unsere Liebe ist *fester* noch mehr..."
(Brahms, "Von ewiger Liebe")

"...suche *dunklere* Schatten..."
(Brahms, "Die Mainacht")

"...bebt mir *heisser* die Wang' herab!"
(Brahms, "Die Mainacht")

"...*holder* klingt der Vogelsang..."
(Brahms, "Minnelied")

"...im Dunkel wird mir *wohler* sein."
(Schubert, *Die Winterreise*–23)

"Er, der *herrlichste* von allen..."
(Schumann, *Frauenliebe und Leben*–2)

1. The following one-syllable adjectives add an umlaut to the stem vowel in the comparative and superlative:

Positive	Comparative	Superlative
alt	älter	ältest
arm	ärmer	ärmst
jung	jünger	jügest
kalt	kälter	kältest
klug	klüger	klügest
krank	kränker	kränkst
kurz	kürzer	kürzest
lang	länger	lägnst
schwach	schwächer	schwächst
stark	stärker	stärkst
warm	wärmer	wärmst

2. A few adjectives are compared irregularly:

groß	größser	größt
gut	besser	best
hoch	höher	höchst
nah	näher	nächst
viel	mehr	meist

"...doch *besser*..."
(Schubert, *Die schöne Müllerin*–15)

3. The comparative and superlative forms of adjectives are declined in the same way and with the same endings as in the positive form; *mehr* is invariable and never takes an ending.

"...meiner Sehnsucht *allerheissesten* Schmerz..."
(Schubert, *Die schöne Müllerin*–13)

"Sonne, hast du keinen *hellern* Schein?"
(Schubert, *Die schöne Müllerin*–12)

"...dort weiss ich den *schönsten* Ort..."
(Mendelssohn, "Auf flügeln des Gesanges")

"...den *seligsten* Tod mich schlürfen..."
(Schumann, *Frauenliebe und Leben*–3)

"...taucht aus *tiefstem* Dunkel heller nur empor..."
(Schumann, *Frauenliebe und Leben*–1)

"...der *tiefsten* Nächte!"
(Wolf, "Zur Ruh', zur Ruh'!")

"...bis an sein *fernstes* Ende..."
(Wolf, "Dass doch gemalt all' deine Reize wären")

"...das *lieblichste2 Glück*..."
(Brahms, *Magelone Romanzen*–1)

"...den *seligsten* Ort..."
(Brahms, *Magelone Romanzen*–4)

"...das *tiefste* Verlangen..."
(Brahms, *Magelone Romanzen*–7)

"...die *süsseste* Ruh..."
(Brahms, *Magelone Romanzen*–9)

4. Predicate adjectives (adjectives used after the verbs *sein* or *werden*) do not take an ending in the positive and comparative; however, when the superlative is used as a predicate adjective, it always takes the following form:

> am besten
> am fleißigsten
> am interessantesten
> am reichsten
> am schönsten

5. Persons or things may be compared in the following ways:

a) Equality is expressed by *ebenso (so)...wie*

b) Inequality is expressed by the comparative form of the adjective and *als*

c) *The more...the more* is expressed by *je...je (desto)*
"...*je* weher *desto* besser!"
(Wolf, "Mausfallen-Sprüchlein")

6. In German, adjectives are frequently used as nouns. These nouns are capitalized; the definite article indicates the gender. Adjectives used as nouns are declined like adjectives; their endings are those of preceded adjectives.

"...wunderlicher *Alter*, soll ich mit dir gehn?"
(Schubert, *Die Winterreise*–24)

"...die klänge schleichen der *Schönsten*...'
(Brahms, "Ständchen")

"...nur die *Würdigste* von allen..."
(Schumann, *Frauenliebe und Leben*–2)

"...du die *Holdeste* der Erden..."
(Wolf, "Benedeit die sel'ge Mutter")

7. Abstract adjectives used as nouns are always neuter:

das Gute- the good

das Schöne- the beautiful

das Schlechte- the bad

das Interessante- the interesting

For translation it is important to become familiar with the positive form of all adjectives and be able to recognize the forms for comparative and superlative and adjectives compared irregularly.

RESEARCH QUESTIONS

1. Define the following terms:

bezifferter Bass

durchbrochene Arbeit

empfindsamer Stil

gebrochener Akkord

gebundener Stil

gehender Bass

neue Musik

neue Sachlichkeit

norddeutsche Schule

sinfonische Dichtung

vergleichende Musikwissenschaft

volkstümliches Lied

2. Identify: Lochamer Liederbuch; Glogauer Liederbuch

3. Describe historically *Die neue Zeitschrift für Musik*.

4. Identify each of the following (composer, style, etc.):

akademische Festouvertüre

ein deutsches Requiem

erste Walpurgisnacht

ein' feste Burg

fünfzig Lieder und Psalmen

geistliche Chormusik

grosse Fuge

Italienisches Liederbuch

kleine geistliche Konzerte

eine kleine Nachtmusik

ein musikalischer Spass

das musikalisches Opfer

die schöne Müllerin

Spanisches Liederbuch

Til Eulenspiegels lustige Streiche

verklärte Nacht

vier ernste Gesänge

das wohltemperierte Klavier

III. ADVERBS

An *adverb* is a word that modifies a verb, an adjective, or another adverb. Adverbs answer the questions "How?", "Where?", "When?", "In what manner?", and are among the most important words in German for giving directions in music. The following are adverbs frequently encountered in music literature:

bedächtig	deliberate
behaglich	with ease
behende	quickly
belebt	brisk, animated
bestimmt	with decision
betont	stressed, with emphasis
bewegt	animated, with motion
breit	broad, largo
deutlich	clear, distinct
doppel	double
durchkomponiert	through-composed
entschieden	determined, resolute

99

feierlich	solemn
flüssig	flowing
frei	free
fröhlich	joyful
gebunden	legato
gedämpft	muted
gedehnt	stretched out, slow
gefühlvoll	full of feeling
gehalten	held out, sustained
geistlich	sacred
gelassen	quiet, calm
gemächlich	comfortably, leisurely
gemässigt	moderate
gemessen	restrained
gesangvoll	songlike, cantabile
geschwind	quick, nimble
gesteigert	increased
geteilt	divided
getragen	sustained, slow
gleichmässig	even
gross	large, great
halb	half
hastig	with haste
haupt	chief, principal
heftig	violent
heiter	cheerful
innig	heartfelt, tender
kammer-	chamber
kirchen-	church
klar	clear, distinct
kräftig	strong, vigorous
kurz	short
langsam	slow
lebendig, lebhaft	lively
lustig	merry, cheerful
leidenschaftlich	passionate
markiert	marked, stressed
markig	vigorous
munter	merry, cheerful
nachdrücklich	emphatic, expressive

rasch	quick
sanft	soft, gentle
schnell	quick, fast
schrittmässig	measured
schwungvoll	animated, spirited
seelenvoll	soulful
sehr	very
traumerisch	dreamy
ungebunden	unrestrained, free
ungestüm	violent, raging
unmerklich	imperceptible
unruhig	restless
wuchtig	weighty, heavy
würdig	heavy, with dignity
wehmütig	sad, melancholy
zart	tender, soft
ziemlich	rather

A. Degrees

The positive degree of most adjectives may be used as positive adverbs:

	adjective	*adverb*
schön	beautiful	beautifully
leicht	easy	easily
genau	exact	exactly
langsam	slow	slowly

2. The comparative degree of adverbs is formed like the comparative of adjectives, by adding *-er* to the positive form.

Forms of Adverb Superlatives

There are two forms of adverb superlatives:

1. The *relative superlative* is the same form as the adjective superlative when comparison is expressed:

> am besten
> am schönsten
> am schnellsten

2. The *absolute superlative* is used when no comparison is implied, but rather a very high degree of something is expressed:

101

aufs beste
aufs schönste
aufs schnellste

3. The positive, comparative and superlative of adverbs have the following forms:

schön	schöner	am schönsten	(aufs schönste)
schnell	schneller	am schnellsten	(aufs schnellste)
leicht	leichter	am leichtesten	(aufs leichteste)

4. The adverb *gern* means "gladly"; used with a verb it expresses the idea "to like to". When used in the comparative the adverb *gern* is declined

gern	lieber	am liebsten

"...möchte *lieber* weinen..."
(Schumann, *Frauenliebe und Leben*–1)

5. The following types of words generally indicate adjectives and adverbs in translation:

a) the past participle of verbs, ending in -*t*

b) the present participle of verbs, ending in -*d*

c) words ending in -*ig*

d) words ending in -*lich*

e) words ending in -*voll*

MUSICAL EXERCISES

1. Survey the nine symphonies by Gustav Mahler.

a) list all adjectives and adverbs in German which give directions in music

b) translate each expression

2. Survey an opera by Richard Wagner. List, in German

a) instrumentation - number and names of instruments

b) all musical expressions in German; translate each

3. Survey a tone poem by Richard Strauss for musical expressions in German; translate each.

MUSICAL VOCABULARY BUILDING

Einleitung	introduction
Abschnitt	section
Themenaufstellung	exposition (sonata form)
Durchführung	development (sonata form)
Reprise	recapitulation (sonata form)
Hauptsatz	first theme (of a sonata)
Nebensatz	second theme (of a sonata)
Fuge	fugue
Durchführung	exposition (fugue)
Zwischenspiel	episode (fugue)
Eintritt	entrance of a fugal subject
Engführung	stretto of fugues
Gefährte	answer of a fugal subject
Gegenfuge	counter fugue
Gegenthema	countersubject
Spiegelfuge	mirror fugue
Antwort	answer (in fugues)
Doppelfuge	double fugue
Symphonie	symphony
Orchester	orchestra
Dirigent	conductor
Leiter	leader of an orchestra
Einsatz	1) attack 2) entrance of an orchestral part
Konzert	concerto
Oper	opera
Auftritt	scene of an opera
Aufzug	act of an opera
Bühne	stage
Generalprobe	dress rehearsal
Inszenierung	staging of an opera
Vortrag	interpretation, performance
Vorspiel	prelude, overture
Nachspiel	postlude
Tokkate	toccata
Kanon	canon
Veränderungen	variations
Durchimitation	through-imitation
Gegenbewegung	contrary motion

Nachahmung	imitation
Motiv	motive
Kontrapunkt	counterpoint
einstimmig	monophonic
vielstimmig	polyphonic
beschleunigt	accelerando
anschwellend	crescendo
abnehmend	diminuendo
Vergrösserung	augmentation
Verkleinerung	diminution
übermässig	augmented
vermindert	diminished
Zahlzeit	beat
Auftakt	up beat
Schwebungen	beats
Takt	beat; measure; meter, time
Zeitmass	tempo
Taktstrich	bar line
Taste	key (of piano, organ)
Untertaste	white key
Obertaste	black key
Klangboden	sounding board
Verschiebung	soft pedal
Anschlag	touch
Geläufigkeit	technical fluency
Gabelgriff	cross fingering
Fingerfertigkeit	agility of the fingers, virtuosity
Kadenz	cadenza
Begleitung	accompaniment
Auszug	keyboard arrangement of a score
Bearbeitung	arrangement
Füllstimme	"filling" part
Gesamtausgabe	complete edition
Stil	style
Stück	piece, composition
Streichinstrumente	stringed instruments
Sreichquartett	string quartet
Strich	bow stroke
Bogen, Streich	bow
Aufstrich	up bow

leere Saite	open string
Lage	positon, range
Doppelgriff	double stop
Dämpfer	mute
Abzug	scordatura
Wirbelkasten	peg box of a stringed instrument
Wirbel	peg of a stringed instrument
Obertöne	upper harmonics
Primgeiger	first violinist, concertmaster
Kammerton	pitch
Kammerkantate	chamber cantata
Kammermusik	chamber music
reine Stimmung	just intonation
Blechinstrument	brass instrument
Doppelzunge	double-tonguing
Luftpause	breathing rest
Ventil	valve
Zug	slide
Blasinstrument	wind instrument
Zunge	reed
Achtelnote	eighth note
Achtelpause	eighth rest
Viertelnote	quarter note
Viertelpause	quarter rest
Halbenote	half note
Halbepause	half rest
Punkt	dot of a note
Halbton	semitone
Viertelton	quarter tone
Tonschrift	notation
Hilfslinie	ledger line
Vorzeichnung	key and meter signatures
Baßschlüssel	f-clef
Altschlüssel	alto clef
Tonart	key
dur	major
moll	minor
Tonalität	tonality
dur Akkord	major chord
dur Dreiklang	major triad

Dreiklang	triad
Akkord	chord
Grundlage	root position
Grundton	root of a chord
Lage	position of chords (close or open)
Klangfolge	chord progression
Tonika	tonic
Oberdominante	dominant
Unterdominante	subdominant
Zwischendominante	secondary dominant
Wechseldominante	dominant of the dominant
Untermediante	dominant of the dominant
Klanggeschlecht	mode (major or minor)
Erhöhungszeichen	sharp
Erniedrigungszeichen	flat
Doppelkreuz	double sharp
Versetzungszeichen	accidental
Auflösungszeichen	natural sign
Auflösung	resolution, cancellation
Grundtonart	main key
Haupttonart	original key
Einklang	unison
Ausweichung	modulation
Versetzung	transposition
Schlüssel	cadence
Ganzschluss	full cadence
Halbschluss	half cadence
Trugschluss	deceptive cadence
Kadenz	cadence
Kirchenschluss	plagal cadence
Tonabstand	interval
Umkehrung	inversion of intervals, chords melodies
Triller	trill
Trillerkette	chain or series of trills
Vorhalt	suspension or appogiatura
Vorausnahme	anticipation
Durchgangsnote	passing note
Lauf	rapid passage (scales)
Fermate	hold

taktmässig	in strict time
schrittmässig	measured
dreitaktig	in phrases of three measures
Duole	duplet
Triole	triplet
Skala	scale
Stufe	degree of the scale
Akzent	accent
Bogen	phrase
Tonhöhe	tone pitch
Klangfarbe	tone color, timbre
Vortragszeichen	expression marks
Sopran	soprano
Alt	alto
Tenor	tenor
Bariton	baritone
Fistelstimme	falsetto
Kopfstimme	head voice
Lage	range
Umfang	compass, range of a voice
Atem	breath
Vokal	vowel
Vokalise	vocalisation
Gesang	song
Lied	song
Liederbuch	song book
Liedform	song form
Vers	verse
Domchor	cathedral choir
Doppelchor	double choir
gemischte Stimme	mixed voices
Unterstimme	lower or lowest part
Wechselgesang	antiphonal singing
Rollschweller	crescendo pedal of organ
Orgel	organ
Orgelpunkt	pedal point
Kirchensonate	church sonata
Kirchenmusik	church music
Kirchenkantate	church cantata

ADJECTIVES AND ADVERBS

abwesend	absent
ähnlich	similar
allein	alone
allerdings	to be sure
allgemein	general
allzu	too much, far too
alt	old
anders	otherwise
anfangs	originally
angeboren	inborn
angenehm	pleasant
ärgerlich	angry
auffällig	striking
aufgeregt	excited
aufmerksam	attentive
aufregend	exciting
ausführlich	detailed, circumstantial
ausgezeichnet	excellent
ausserdem	besides, moreover
ausserordentlich	extremely
auswärtig	foreign
bald	soon
behilflich	helpful
bekannt	known
breit	wide
bereit	ready
berühmt	famous
beschäftigt	busy
besetzt	occupied
besonders	especially
bequem	comfortable
böse	angry
beliebt	popular
bunt	colorful
dagegen	in comparison with
daneben	close by, beside
dankbar	thankful
dunkel	dark
dünn	thin

eigentlich	really, exactly
endlich	finally
entfernt	distant
erfolgreich	successful
ernst	serious
erst	first
erstaunlich	astonishing
erwartungsvoll	expectant
etwas	somewhat
fällig	due, scheduled
falsch	false, wrong
fast	almost
faul	lazy .
feinaussehend	good-looking
fertig	ready
fleissig	intelligent
fliessend	fluent
fortwährend	continually
frei	free
furchtbar	terrible
früh	early
ganz	whole
geistig	spiritual
geduldig	patient
gesund	well
gewaltig	powerful
gewöhnlich	usual, customary
glatt	smooth
gleichzeitig	simultaneously
grossartig	splendid
gründlich	thoroughly
gütig	good, kind
häufig	numerous, frequent
hell	light
hervorragend	outstanding
historisch	historical
hoffentlich	hopefully
höflich	polite
hübsch	pretty
idealisiert	idealized

immer	always
indessen	in the meantime
interessant	interesting
jetzt	now
jung	young
kaum	scarcely
klassisch	classical
klein	small
kompliziert	complicated
kräftig	strong
krank	sick
kühl	cool
kulturell	cultural
lang	long
langsam	slowly
leicht	easy
leider	unfortunately
letzt	last
liebenswürdig	likable
lyrisch	lyrical
mindestens	at least
modern	modern
möglich	possible
müde	tired
nah	near
nämlich	namely
nass	wet
natürlich	naturally
neugierig	curious
nie	never
niedrig	low
nimmer	never
noch	still, yet
nun	now
nur	only
nützlich	useful
offenbar	obviously
passend	suitable, fitting
plötzlich	suddenly
rasch	quickly

reich	rich
riesengroß	huge, gigantic
romantisch	romantic
rund	round
schliesslich	finally
schon	already
schön	beautiful
schrecklich	terrible
schwach	weak
schwer	heavy, difficult
schwierig	difficult
selten	seldom
sicherlich	surely
sofort	immediately
sogar	even
spät	late
stark	strong
stolz	proud
störend	disturbing
stürmig	stormy
tapfer	courageous
tatsächlich	actually
technisch	technical
traurig	sad
trocken	dry
tüchtig	able, diligent
üblich	usual
unbedingt	absolute
ungefähr	approximately
unmöglich	impossible
unterwegs	on the way
vergnüglich	pleasurable
viereckig	square
weit	far
wertvoll	valuable
wichtig	important
windig	windy
wirklich	really
wunderbar	wonderful
ziemlich	rather

zufrieden	content, pleased
zusammen	together
zuvorkommend	obliging
zweifellos	doubtlessly

EXPRESSIONS

1. Practice the following conversational expressions:

Guten Morgen	good morning
Guten Tag	good day
Guten Abend	good evening
Gute Nacht	good night
Danke	thank you
Danke schön	thank you very much
vielen Dank	many thanks
herzichen Dank	hearty thanks
schön Dank	thank you
bitte schön	you're welcome (please)
bitte sehr	you're very welcome
auf Wiedersehen	good-bye
bis Morgen	until tomorrow

2. The following are frequently used expressions of indefinite time:

gestern Morgen	yesterday morning
gestern Nachmittag	yesterday afternoon
gestern Abend	yesterday evening
heute Morgen	this morning
heute Nachmittag	this afternoon
heute Abend	this evening
morgen früh	tomorrow morning
morgen Abend	tomorrow evening
vorgestern	day before yesterday
morgens	in the morning
nachmittags	in the afternoon
abends	in the evening

Chapter Five

I. SENTENCE STRUCTURE

The study of sentence structure in the next three chapters should substantially facilitate the translation of texts and augment understanding of the basic elements of grammatical construction .

Negative Forms

1. The word *nein* is the negative answer to a question and means "no". The word *ja* is the positive answer to a question and means "yes". When *nein* or *ja* occurs in sentence structure and does not function as the answer to a question, it is a *particle*. Used as a particle *ja* serves to give the sentence an affirmative emphasis.

"...ich sah dich *ja* im Traum..."
(Schumann, *Dichterliebe*–7)

"...du hast es *ja* gewollt!"
(Schubert, "Der Atlas")

"...bin ich selber Fürstin *ja*.-"
(Schumann, "Die Kartenlegerin")

"...Frühling, *ja* du bist's!"
(Wolf, "Er ist's")

The use of particles is a characteristic feature of German; for the purpose of translation it is especially valuable to learn to recognize these words and realize that many such particles are intended for sentence emphasis rather than specific word meaning.

2. The word *nicht* in German means "not"; *nicht* is most often used to negate a whole clause. When negating a whole clause, *nicht* stands at the end of the clause.

"...so fängt er die Forelle mit seiner Angel *nicht*."
(Schubert, "Die Forelle")

In sentence structure *nicht* precedes

a) a predicate adjective
"...ich bin *nicht* wild!"
(Schubert, "Der Tod und das Mädchen")

b) a predicate nominative
> "...ach, meine Sonnen seid ihr *nicht*!"
> (Schubert, *Die Winterreise*–20)

c) an adverb
> "...so still ist's *nicht* draussen im Schnee..."
> (Schumann, *Liederkreis*–4)

> "...ich gehe *nicht* schnell, ich eile *nicht*..."
> (Strauss, "Traum durch die Dämmerung")

> "...ich lieb' sie *nicht* mehr..."
> (Schumann, *Dichterliebe*–3)

d) a prepositional phrase
> "...'s ist *nicht* für Mädchenbusen..."
> (Schubert, *Die schöne Müllerin*–20)

When negating a particular word for the sake of emphasis, *nicht* stands immediately before that word.
> "...*nicht* im Schlafe hab' ich das geträumt..."
> (Strauss, "Freundliche Vision")

When *nicht* negates a whole clause and the verb is in the compound past or past perfect tense, *nicht* precedes the past participle.
> "So hab' ich doch...mein feines Liebchen *nicht* gesehen..."
> (Brahms, "Sonntag")

When *nicht* negates a whole clause, the verb of which has a separable prefix, *nicht* precedes the separable prefix (see p. 62).
> "...ich lass dich *nicht* ein..."
> (Brahms, "Vergebliches Ständchen")

II. PREPOSITIONS

A *preposition* shows the grammatical relationship of a noun or pronoun to some other element in the sentence. The accusative, dative, or genitive case is required after certain prepositions.

A. Cases

1. The following prepositions always take the accusative case:

bis - till, until, as far as

durch - through

für - for

gegen - against

ohne - without

um - around

"...wie dein Licht *durch* diese Bäume..."
(Schubert, "Nachtfeier")

"...*für* dich, mit dir..."
(Brahms, "Nicht mehr zu dir zu gehen")

"...alles *um* mich her..."
(Schumann, *Frauenliebe und Leben*–1)

The prepositions *an* (of), *auf* (for), *über* (about), require the accusative when they are used in a figurative, rather than a literal sense.

"...*an* dich hab' ich gedacht..."
(Schubert, *Die Winterreise*–1)

"...*auf* einen Totenacker hat mich mein Weg gebracht..."
(Schubert, *Die Winterreise*–17)

"...*übern* Garten durch die Lüfte..."
(Schumann, *Liederkreis*–12)

2 The following prepositions always take the dative case:

aus - out of, from

ausser - except, besides

bei - by, near; with, at (the house of)

mit - with

nach - after, to; according to

seit - since

von - from, of, off; by

zu - to

"...*aus* meinen Tränen spriessen..."
(Schumann, *Dichterliebe*–2)

"...*mit* seinem grossen Dome..."
(Schumann, *Dichterliebe*–6)

Das Leiden unseres Herrn Jesu Christi *nach* dem Evangelisten
Matthäus
(Bach, *Matthäuspassion*)

"...nun geh ich *zu* der schönsten Frau..."
(Strauss, "Traum durch die Dämmerung")

"...was sprichst du...*zu* mir...?
(Schumann, *Liederkreis*–6)

3. The following prepositions can take either the accusative or the
dative case:

an - at, on, up against

auf - on, upon, on top of

hinter - behind

in - in

neben - next to, near

über - over, above

unter - under, among

vor - before, in front of

zwischen - between

a) The use of the accusative case with these prepositions expresses
   motion to a place, which can be affirmed by asking the question
   "where to?".

"...ich drücke dich...*an* die Lippen...*an* das Herze..."
(Schumann, *Frauenliebe und Leben*–4)

"...stell *auf* den Tisch..."
(Strauss, "Allerseelen")

b) The use of the dative case with these prepositions expresses a fixed
   position or locality which can be affirmed by asking the question
   "where?".

"...*meinen* Schatten an der Wand..."
(Wolf, "Abschied")

"Du Ring *an* meinem Finger..."
(Schumann, *Frauenliebe und Leben*–4)

"...*auf* goldenem Leder gemalt..."
(Schumann, *Dichterliebe*–6)

"Aus der Heimat *hinter* den Blitzen rot..."
(Schumann, *Liederkreis*–1)

"...ich sing' ihn *in* der Weite..."
(Schubert, "Der Musensohn")

"...und *über* mir rauschet die schöne Waldeinsamkeit..."
(Schumann, *Liederkreis*–1)

"...hell am Tage sah ichs schön *vor* mir..."
(Strauss, "Freundliche Vision")

Although the definite or indefinite article generally indicates the case, it is important to learn the exact meaning of prepositions for translation; these words are critical in determining sentence meaning.

4. The following prepositions always take the genitive case:

während - during

wegen - on account of

anstatt - instead of

trotz - in spite of

B. Special Uses

1. Four prepositions all mean "to" with verbs of motion:

a) in the sense of "up to" the preposition *an* is required

b) meaning "into" (a building) the preposition *in* is required and takes the accusative case

c) with names of cities and countries the preposition *nach* is required

d) with persons, buildings, and proper nouns the preposition *zu* is required

2. The following contractions of prepositions with the definite article occur frequently:

an dem= am

an das= ans

auf das= aufs

bei dem= beim

für das= fürs

in dem= im

in das= ins

117

von dem = vom

zu dem = zum

zu der = zur

"...seh' ich *ans* Firmament..."
(Wolf, *Mignon-Lieder*–3)

"...*im* hohen grünen Gras...*durchs* tiefe Blau..."
(Brahms, "Feldeinsamkeit")

"...*im* öden, unendlichen Raum..."
(Schumann, *Frauenliebe und Leben*–4)

3. Prepositions are seldom used with "it" or "them" (referring to things) in the dative and accusative cases. When a pronoun refers to one or more objects or ideas, the pronoun is replaced by the prefix *da-* (*dar-* before a vowel) and attached to the required preposition:

dadurch = through it (them)

dafür = for it (them)

damit = with it (them)

daraus = out of it (them)

darin = in it (them)

darüber = over it (them)

danach = after it (them)

darauf = on it (them)

davon = from it (them)

dazu = to it (them)

"...ich danke dir *dafür*..."
(Schubert, "An die Musik")

"...so liebevoll umarmst du mich *darauf*..."
(Wolf, "Wenn du, mein Liebster, steigst zum Himmel auf")

"...und *daraus* dein Bildnis mir entgegen lacht."
(Schumann, *Frauenliebe und Leben*–6)

"...*damit* seine Tränen die Menschen nicht sehn."
(Schubert, *Die schöne Müllerin*–22)

"...mein Himmel du, *darein* ich schwebe..."
(Schumann, "Widmung")

"...ich durfte nichts *dazu* sagen!"
(Mahler, *Kindertotenlieder*–5)

III. CONJUNCTIONS

A *conjunction* is a word used to connect words, phrases, or clauses; a *clause* is a group of words containing a subject and a verb. A *main* (independent) clause can form a sentence in itself; a *subordinate* (dependent) clause can function only with an independent clause.

A. Coordinating Conjunctions

Coordinating conjunctions connect expressions of equal value. The following coordinating conjunctions do not affect the word order of a clause.

aber	- but
denn	- for
oder	- or
sondern	- but
und	- and

"...*denn* alles ist wie damals noch..."
(Schubert, "Im Frühling")

When *aber* is used as a conjunction, it always stands first in the clause.
"...*aber* ich wende mich...und die einsame Träne rinnt."
(Brahms, "Die Mainacht")

When *aber* is not the first word in the clause, it is an adverb meaning "however".
"...ich *aber* wandle stumm."
(Schumann, *Dichterliebe*–12)

The conjunction *sondern* is used after a negative clause to introduce an idea contradictory to that of the foregoing clause.
"...fällt auf ihr Gesicht erst der Blick mir nicht,
sondern auf die Stelle...wo würde dein lieb Gesichtchen sein..."
(Mahler, *Kindertotenlieder*–3)

B. Subordinating Conjunctions

Subordinating conjunctions introduce dependent clauses and connect them with main clauses. The most frequently encountered subordinating conjunctions are:

als - when

bevor - before

bis - until

da - since (reason)

damit - in order that

dass - that

ehe - before

falls - in case

nachdem - after

ob - whether

obgleich - although

seitdem - since (time)

sobald - as soon as

während - while

wann - when

weil - because

wenn - if, when

wie - how

"...ich bin vergnügt, *daß* beides aus deinen Händen quillt..."
(Wolf, "Gebet")

"...ich steche dich, *daß* du ewig denkst an mich..."
(Mozart, "Heidenröslein")

"...dann denk ich es ganz, *daß* du ewig mich schufst..."
(Schubert, "Dem Unendlichen")

"Ja, du weisst es...*daß* ich fern von dir mich quäle..."
(Strauss, "Zueignung")

"...komm an mein Herz, *daß* ich dich wieder habe..."
(Strauss, "Allerseelen")

1. *als*, *wann*, and *wenn*, all mean "when":

a) *als* is equivalent to "when" if it introduces a single definite past action, but not if "when" can be replaced by "whenever".
"...*als* alle Vögel sangen..."
(Schumann, *Dichterliebe*–1)

b) *wann* is used to introduce a direct or indirect question.
"*Wann* ruh' ich ihr am Busen endlich wieder aus?"
(Schubert, "Der Musensohn")

c) *wenn* is used with all verb tenses if "when" can be replaced by "whenever".
"...mir graust es, *wenn* ich sein Antlitz sehe..."
(Schubert, *Schwanengesang*–13)

"...*wenn* ich in deine Augen seh'..."
(Schumann, *Dichterliebe*–4)

"...rufen, *wenn* der Tag erwacht..."
(Schubert, "Nacht und Träume")

"...*wenn* mein Bild vor ihm erscheint..."
(Wolf, *Harfenspieler-Lieder*–2)

2. When the conjunction *dass* (daß) "that" is implied but is omitted in German, the dependent clause is in normal word order. When the conjunction *wenn* (if) is implied but omitted, inverted word order is required.

"...damit du mögest sehen, an dich hab' ich gedacht..."
(Schubert, *Die Winterreise*–1)

3. Conjunctive expressions

weder...noch	=	neither ...nor
entweder...oder	=	either ...or
ob...oder nicht	=	whether ...or not
nicht nur...sondern auch	=	not only ...but also
um...zu	=	in order to; so as to

IV. PARTICLES

Forms

1. Used as an adjectival pronoun the word *selbst* means "self", "myself", "himself", "yourself", "itself". As an adverb *selbst* means "even", "very", and is used in sentence structure primarily for emphasis.

> "...muss *selbst* den Weg mir weisen..."
> (Schubert, *Die Winterreise*–1)

2. The adverb *sonst* literally means "else", "otherwise", "besides", "moreover", "as a rule", "usually" and is used frequently to give authority in sentence context.

> "...kein Mensch es *sonst* wissen soll!"
> (Schumann, *Liederkreis*–4)

3. The word *doch* can function as an adverb or as a conjunction; it is translated "yet", "however", "nevertheless", "at least", "though", "surely", "anyway".

> "...und bist *doch,* wo du bist, zu Haus!...
> *doch* bin ich nirgend - ach! zu Haus!"
> (Schubert, "Der Wanderer an den Mond")

The particle *doch* can be used:

a) to strengthen an imperative

b) to strengthen an implication without giving additional meaning.
> "...*doch* auf der Heimat Boden steht!"
> (Schubert, "Der Wanderer an den Mond")

c) to emphasize a particular point in a statement, in which case *doch* means "surely".

d) to contradict a negative statement, in which case *doch* means "on the contrary".

4. The adverb *mal* (time) is frequently used as an emphatic particle; it is also used in combination:

vorigesmal	- last time
nächtesmal	- next time
diesmal	- this time
einmal	- one time

122

5. The adverb *schon* (already) is often used as a particle with the present tense to express an action begun in the past and continuing in the present.

6. The adverb *überhaupt,* used as a particle, serves to express feelings without attaching a definite meaning to the particle itself.

7. When *wohl* is used as a particle, it means "I dare say", "indeed", "to be sure", "no doubt", "perhaps".

"...es singen *wohl* die Nixen..."
(Schubert, *Die schöne Müllerin*–2)

"...manche Schöne macht *wohl* Augen..."
(Wolf, "Der Musikant")

"...kennst du es *wohl*?-"
(Wolf, *Mignon-Lieder*–1)

8. When set off by a comma the particle *nun* means "well"; otherwise it is an adverb meaning "now".

"...je *nun,* sie haben ihr Teil genossen..."
(Schubert, *Die Winterreise*–13)

"...*nun* seh' ich wohl..."
(Mahler, *Kindertotenlieder*–2)

9. When the adverb *nur* (only) is used as a particle, it imparts a typically German inflection to the sentence which defies literal translation.

"...womit *nur* deck' ich des Kindleins Glieder!"
(Wolf, "Die ihr schwebet")

10. The adverb *noch* (still) functions as a particle to reinforce another word, such as *auch,* with an implied meaning of "in addition".

noch ein - another

noch einmal - once more

noch nicht - not yet

"...gelt, du bist wohl auch *noch nicht* lange braut?"
(Brahms, "Das Mädchen spricht")

"...möcht ich *noch* einmal rückwärts sehn..."
(Schubert, *Die Winterreise*–9)

PREPOSITION SUPPLEMENT
A. Time of day

1. Wieviel Uhr ist es?, Wie spät ist es? What time is it?

2. Es ist ein Uhr. It is one o'clock.

3. The half hour is expressed:

   (a) Es ist halb zehn. (9:30)

   (b) Es ist neun Uhr dreißig.

4. The quarter after the hour may be expressed:

   (a) Es ist acht Uhr fünfzehn. (8:15)

   (b) Es ist ein Viertel nach acht. (8:15)

   (c) Es ist ein Viertel neun. (8:15)

   (d) Es ist ein Viertel auf neun. (8:15)

5. The quarter to the hour may be expressed:

   (a) Es ist ein Viertel vor zwölf. (11:45)

   (b) Es ist zwölf Uhr fünfundvierzig. (11:45)

   (c) Es ist drei Viertel zwölf. (11:45)

   (d) Es ist drei Viertel auf zwölf. (11:45)

6. Odd minutes are expressed by nach (after) and vor (to).

7. Two factors are important in telling time in German:

   a) The 24-hour clock is widely used, especially for travel; after noon 1:00 p.m. is 13:00 Uhr, and so forth.

   b) To express the time 8:15 "ein Viertel neun", means that a quarter of the ninth hour has passed.

8. To express time passed the preposition *vor* plus the dative case is used:

vor fünfzehn minuten	fifteen minutes ago
vor Jahren	years ago
vor langer Zeit	a long time ago

9. An expression of time precedes an expression of place in German.

B. Definite Time

To denote definite time, the accusative case is used:

den ganzen Tag	all day
die ganze Woche	all week
das ganze Jahr	the whole year
jeden Tag	every day
jede Woche	every week
jedes Jahr	every year

C. Indefinite Time

To denote indefinite time, the genitive case is used; its application is limited to the following expressions:

eines Tages	one day
eines Morgens	one morning
eines Abends	one evening

ABBREVIATIONS

b.w.	bitte, wenden	please turn the page
bzw.	beziehungsweise	respectively
d.h.	daß heisst	that is to say
u.a.m.	und andere mehr	and other things
u.s.w.	und so weiter	and so forth
z.B.	zum Beispiel	for example

IDIOMATIC EXPRESSIONS

beliebt bei	a favorite with
das versteht sich	that goes without saying
ein bißchen	a little, a little bit
ein paar	a few, a pair
eine Weile	a while
entzückt von	delighted with
gar nicht	not at all
im Alter von	at the age of
im Gegenteil	on the contrary
im Jahre	in the year
in Bezug auf	in respect to, in the matter of

in der nächsten Zeit = bald	soon
mit Recht	rightly
mit Vergnügen	with pleasure
nacheinander	one after the other, in succession
gewiss = sicher	sure, surely
ohne Zweifel	doubtless
stimmt	that's correct
viel wert	worth a great deal
vor allem	above all, first of all
zwar = es ist wahr	it is true
Nun also?	well then?
nicht wahr?	isn't it true?

TRANSLATION EXERCISES

1. The following is an excerpt from Hugo Riemann's Musik Lexikon (Elfte Auflage, bearbeitet von Alfred Einstein, Berlin: Max Hesse Verlag, 1929) entitled "Berliner Schule". This is a typical example of a short entry in a comprehensive dictionary and illustrates the grammar studied to this point:

Man spricht von einer konservativen Berliner Schule oder Norddeutschen Schule im 18. Jahrhundert, besonders im Gegensatz zu der neuen Stilrichtung der Mannheimer oder Süddeutschen Schule.

2. The following is a definition in the *Handbuch der Musikgeschichte* by Guido Adler:

CHORAL: Entweder katholischer (Gregorianischer) Kirchengesang oder protestantisches (evangelisches) Kirchenlied.

3. Translate the following from the article "Musikwissenschaft" from the *Handbuch der Musikgeschichte by Guido Adler*:

Guido Adler hat 1885 die "Vierteljahrsschrift für Musikwissenschaft" mit der Studie "Umfang, Methode und Ziele der Musikwissenschaft" eröffnet, worin dieser Erkenntniszweig folgendermaßen abgegrenzt wird:

I. Historischer Teil:

    A. Notenschriftwesen.

    B. Kunstform (in modern wissenschaftlicher Erfassung).

    C. Theorie des Tonsatzes (in zeitgenössischer Formulierung).

    D. Instrumente.

    Hilfswissenschaften: Paläographie, Chronologie, Diplomatik, Literaturgeschichte, Biographistik.

II. Systematischer Teil:

    A. Spekulative Theorie (Harmonik, Rhythmik, Metrik)

    B. Ästhetik

    C. Pädagogik (Elementarlehre, Harmonielehre, Kontrapunkt, Komposition, Instrumentation, Methodik).

    D. Musikologie (musikalische Ethnographie). Hilfswissenschaften: Akustik, Mathematik, Physiologie, Psychologie, Logik, Grammatik, allgemeine Pädagogik, allgemeine Ästhetik.

4. Translate the following excerpt from the article "Musikwissenschaft" in the *Handbuch der Musikgeschichte* by Guido Adler:

...von historischen Werken gibt es allgemeine Musikgeschichten (Originalarbeiten und Kompendien), Spezialarbeiten (nach Kompositionsgattungen, Zeitabschnitten und Territorien gesondert), Biographien einzelner Meister, ferner Neudrucke von Musikwerken und theoretischen Schriften älterer Epochen, endlich erkenntnistheoretische Werke (wie Guido Adlers "Stil in der Musik" und "Methode der Musikgeschichte").

1710 begründete Dr. Johann Christoph Pepusch in London die "Academy of ancient music"; und 1776 erschienen "A general history of the science and practice of music" von John Hawkins (1719-1789) und der erste Band von "A general history of music" der Dr. Charles Burney (1726-1814, letzter Band 1781). Vorher (1756) hatte freilich schon das Werk eines Italieners zu erscheinen begonnen, die "Storia della musica" von Padre Giambattista Martini (1706-84, letzter Band 1781), doch kam dieser über griechische Musik nicht hinaus, während die beiden englischen Musikgeschichten den gesamten Stoff erledigten. 1780 folgte dann der "Essay sur la musique ancienne et moderne" von Jean Benjamin de Laborde und 1788-1801 das erste deutsche Werk dieser Art, die "Allgemeine Geschichte der Musik" von Johann Nikolaus Forkel (1749-1818), die leider mit dem Jahre 1500 abschließt. Ein ähnliches Schicksal hatten die späteren Werke von August Wilhelm Ambros (1816-76) "Geschichte der Musik" (1862-82 erschienen, geht bis zum Beginn des 17. Jahrhunderts) und François Joseph Fétis (1784-1871), "Histoire générale de la musique" (erschienen 1869-75, reicht bis 1500). Die überfülle des Materials erforderte eben Spezialisierung der Forschungsarbeit und so ist es erklärlich, daß selbst das "Handbuch der Musikgeschichte" von Hugo Riemann (1905-13 erschienen) trotz des Versuches der Zusammenfassung nur als eine Folge von Spezialstudien über einzelne Probleme erscheint, die den Autor besonders fesselten. Die englische "Oxford history of music" (1901-05 erschienen) suchte die Aufgabe durch Zuweisung der einzelnen großen Epochen an verschiedene Bearbeiter zu erfüllen (H. Ollis Wooldridge, Hubert H. Parry, John Alexander Fuller-Maitland, William Harry Hadow, Edward Dannreuther), während die von Hermann Kretzschmar herausgegebenen "Kleinen Handbücher der Musikgeschichte" den Stoff in seine Einzelgebiete (Instrumentalkonzert, Oratorium, Motette, Messe, Lied, usw.) auflösen, die von Spezialisten arbeitet werden.

Mit einem Teile der eben angeführten Namen ist auch die Aufstellung und Inswerksetzung der modernen Musikwissenschaft verbunden. Chrysander ließ 1863 und 1867 "Jahrbücher für musikalische Wissenschaft" erscheinen, deren 1. Band eine knappe programmatische Einleitung enthält. 1884 begründete Adler mit Chrysander und Philipp Spitta die "Vierteljahrsschrift für Musikwissenschaft", deren Programm die eingangs zitierte Studie Adlers über "Umfang, Methode und Ziele der Musikwissenschaft" festlegte.

Chapter Six

I. WORD ORDER IN SENTENCE STRUCTURE

A. Normal Word Order

1. Subject and its modifiers
2. Verb
3. Verbal modifiers

   a) An adverb in German is never put between the subject and the verb.

   > "... ich gehe nicht *schnell*, ich eile nicht ..."
   > (Strauss, "Traum durch die Dämmerung")

B. Inverted Word Order

For stylistic variety or in order to emphasize a particular element, a sentence in German may begin with an element other than the subject; this is known as *inverted word order*. If the independent clause begins with any word (*hier, da, heute, gestern, bald*, etc.), or group of related words other than the subject, such as a prepositional phrase, the second element in the sentence must be the verb.

1. In inverted word order a sentence is composed of:

   a) any word or group of words other than the subject

   b) the verb

   c) the subject

   d) other modifiers

   > "Auf Flügeln des Gesanges ... trag' ich dich fort ..."
   > (Mendelssohn, "Auf Flügeln des Gesanges")

   > "Nun hast du mir den ersten Schmerz getan ..."
   > (Schumann, *Frauenliebe und Leben*–8)

   > "Aus dem Walde tritt die Nacht ..."
   > (Strauss, "Die Nacht")

   > "...wie im wachen Traume, schwebt sein Bild mir vor ..."
   > (Schumann, *Frauenliebe und Leben*–1)

Word order is the same in a dependent clause whether it follows or precedes the main (independent) clause: the verb stands last. If the showing person, number, and tense) is the last word in the clause or sentence. When the dependent clause begins the sentence, the main clause is in *inverted word order*.

2. Another form of inverted word order is the question. Questions are usually formed in German by inverting the subject and verb; this form is known as a direct question.

"Kennst du das Land?"
(Wolf, *Mignon-Lieder*–1)

"Ist das denn meine Straße?"
Schubert, *Die Schöne Müllerin*–2)

"Schlief die Mutter endlich ein ..."
(Schumann, "Die Kartenlegerin")

"Giebst du, Sonne, mir deinen Schein?"
(Schumann, *Frauenliebe und Leben*–5)

"Siehst, Vater, du den Erlkönig nicht?"
(Schubert, "Erlkönig")

a) When a question is subordinated to a question or statement, it is an indirect question; dependent word order is used in indirect questions (the verb stands last).

b) Some idiomatic expressions of question are

Seit wann? - since when

Wie lange? - how long

Was kostet? - how much does ...cost?

The interrogative "was für ein?" (what kind of a) is a frequently used idiomatic expression in German. In this phrase, the preposition *für* is part of the idiom and therefore does not dictate the case of the following noun.

II. INTERROGATIVE PRONOUNS

Forms

1. A question may also be formed by using an *interrogative prounoun*. The two most frequently encounted interrogative pronouns, *wer* (who) and *was* (what), are declined:

Masculine and Feminine	Neuter
N wer (who)	was (what)
G wessen (whose)	-
D wem (to whom)	-
A wen (whom)	was (what)

"*Was* mag der Unterschied wohl sein?"
(Schubert, "Der Wanderer an den Mond")

"*Was* sag' ich denn von Rauschen?"
(Schubert, *Die Schöne Müllerin*–2)

"*Was* treibt mich jeden Morgen ...?"
(Schubert, *Die schöne Müllerin*–20)

"*Was* will dieses Graun bedeuten?"
(Schumann, *Liederkreis*–10)

"*Was* reitst du einsam durch den Wald?"
(Schumann, *Liederkreis*–3)

"Ei, *was* hab' ich zu erwarten? ... Ei, *was* wird das Ende sein?"
(Schumann, "Die Kartenlegerin")

"Herr, *was* trägt der Boden hier ...?"
(Wolf, "Herr, was trägt der Boden hier")

"*Wer* reitet so spät durch Nacht und Wind?"
(Schubert, "Erlkönig")

"*Wer* trägt der Himmel unzählbare Sterne?"
(Beethoven, "Die Ehre Gottes aus der Natur")

"*Wer* mag sie erraten, *wer* holte sie ein?"
(Wolf, "Verschwiegene Liebe")

"... durch *wen* ist alles?"
(Beethoven, "Die Ehre Gottes aus der Natur")

"... zu *wessen* Zier ...?"
(Wolf, "Herr, was trägt der Boden hier")

2. *Was* is used only as the subject and direct object of verbs. When *was* is implied in the genitive, dative, and accusative cases as the object of a preposition, it is generally represented by a compound of *wo* (before vowels, *wor-*) and the preposition:

131

worin= in what

worauf= on what

wozu= to what

womit= with what

wofür= for what

woraus= out of what

"*... womit* nur deck' ich des Kindleins Glieder!"
(Wolf, "Die ihr schwebet")

"*... wovon* so nass?"
(Schubert, *Die schöne Müllerin*–21)

3. The adverb *wo* also asks the question "where?". The combination *woher* asks the question "where from?", *wohin* asks the question "where to?".

"O Bächlein, sprich, *wohin?*"
(Schubert, *Die Schöne Müllerin*–2)

"*Wohin?* Ach, *wohin?*"
(Schubert, "Ganymed")

4. The adverb *wie* asks the question "how?", *warum* asks the question "why?".

"*... wie* hätt' er doch unter allen mich Arme erhöht und beglückt?"
(Schumann, *Frauenliebe und Leben*–3)

"O *warum* sucht' ich nach dem Glück ...?"
(Brahms, "O wüsst ich doch den Weg zurück")

III. RELATIVE PRONOUNS

A *relative pronoun* is used to connect a dependent (relative) clause to a main clause; the relative pronoun refers to a noun in the main clause. The accurate identification of relative pronouns is a key to efficient translation.

Forms

1. English uses three relative pronouns: *who* refers to a person; *which*, *that* refer to a thing.

2. In German only one word is used to refer to either a person or a thing; this word is similar to the definite article *der, die, das*. In order to distinguish relative pronouns from articles when translating, note the

punctuation of the sentence; relative pronouns introduce dependent clauses, which are always set off by a comma. The relative pronoun *der, die, das* is declined:

	Singular			*Plural*	
N der	die	das		die	who, which, that
G dessen	deren	dessen		dessen	of whom, of which, whose
D dem	der	dem		denen	to whom, to which
A den	die	das		die	whom, which, that

Note that *der, die, das* the article, and *der, die, das* the relative pronoun, are declined alike except in the genitive forms and in the dative plural.

"... den ersten besten Mann, *der* ihr in den Weg gelaufen ..."
(Schumann, *Dichterliebe*–11)

"... Tau, *der* mich nässte ..."
(Brahms, "Sapphische Ode")

"... träume ... von dem Himmel, *der* die Blumen bringt ..."
(Strauss, "Wiegenlied")

"... ach! von des Knaben, *der* mir so lieb war ..."
(Brahms, "An eine Aeolsharfe")

"... Gott ist es, *den* ihr preist!"
(Schubert, "Dem Unendlichen")

"... zeigt sich Einer, *den* ich meine ..."
(Schumann, "Die Kartenlegerin")

"... und auf dem Wege, *den* ich gehen werde ..."
(Strauss, "Morgen")

"... ich hab'... nur ihn geliebt ... *dem* jetzt man den Tod doch giebt."
(Schumann, "Der Soldat")

"... und meinen Herd, um *dessen* Glut du mich beneidest."
(Wolf, "Prometheus")

"... und meine Hütte, *die* du nicht gebaut ..."
(Wolf, "Prometheus")

Die Rose, die Lilie... *die* liebt' ich einst alle ..."
(Schumann, *Dichterliebe*–3)

"... und ich geh mit Einer, *die* mich lieb hat ..."
(Strauss, "Freundliche Vision")

"... ihr Blümlein alle, *die* sie mir gab ..."
(Schubert, *Die schöne Müllerin*–21)

"... du meine Welt, in *der* ich lebe ..."
(Schumann, "Widmung")

"... ein Geschlecht, *das* mir gleich sei ..."
(Wolf, "Prometheus")

"... das Liedchen,... *das* einst die Liebste sang ..."
(Schumann, *Dichterliebe*–3)

"... von dem Lied, *das* deine Mutter singt."
(Strauss, "Wiegenlied")

"... das Kind, *dem* sie die Nahrung gibt ..."
(Schumann, *Frauenliebe und Leben*–7)

"... weisst du nun die Tränen, *die* ich weinen kann ..."
(Schumann, *Frauenliebe und Leben*–6)

"... diese Lieder, *die* ich dir, Geliebte, sang ..."
(Beethoven, *An die ferne Geliebte*–6)

3. Relative pronouns have the following characteristics:

a) They agree in gender and number with the noun to which they refer.

b) The case of the relative pronoun is determined by its function within the relative clause.

c) Since the relative clause is a dependent clause, the verb always stands at the end.

d) The relative pronoun must always be expressed in German.

4. Another frequently encountered relative pronoun is *welcher, welche, welches*. It can be used wherever *der, die, das* is used, except in the genitive case, and is declined:

	Singular		*Plural*		
N welcher	welche	welches	welche		who, which, that
D welchem	welcher	welchem	welchen		to whom, to which
A welchen	welche	welches	welche		whom, which, that

134

"... o, lächelndes Bild, *welches*... durch die Seele mir strahlt ..."
(Brahms, "Die Mainacht")

"... von dem Zweig, von *welchem* sie gepflückt!"
(Schubert, "Im Frühling")

To express "of whom" and "whose", *dessen* and *deren* are used.

5. *wer* and *was* may be used as *indefinite relative pronouns* and are declined:

	Who	*What*
N	wer	was
G	wessen	-
D	wem	-
A	wen	was

After *alles* (all, everything), *nichts* (nothing), *etwas* (something), and *viel* (much), the relative pronoun *was* is always used.

Because it is general in meaning, the relative pronoun *wer* (he who, whoever, who) never has an antecedent.

"*Wer* sich der Einsamkeit ergibt ..."
(Wolf, *Harfenspieler-Lieder*–1)

"... ich weiss nicht... *wer* den Rat mir gab ..."
(Schubert, *Die schöne Müllerin*–2)

"... du weisst nicht, *wer* ich bin ..."
(Schumann, *Liederkreis*–3)

"... um zu erfahren, *was* du gedacht in jenem Fall."
(Brahms, "Wir wandelten")

"... und ich weiss nicht, *was* er weint ..."
(Wolf, *Harfenspieler-Lieder*–1)

"... ich... weiss recht gut, *was* das bedeutet ..."
(Schubert, "Geheimes")

"... Hörest du nicht, *was* Erlenkönig mir leise verspricht?-"
(Schubert, "Erlkönig")

"... ich weiss nicht, *was* soll es bedeuten ..."
(Liszt, "Die Lorelei")

"... nur eine Mutter weiss allein, *was* Lieben heisst ..."
(Schumann, *Frauenliebe und Leben*–7)

TRANSLATION EXERCISES

1. Translate the following excerpts from the article entitled "Symphonie" from *Musik in Geschichte und Gegenwart*:

> B. Die Entwicklung der Symphonie im 18. Jahrhundert. I. Italien. 1. Die Ouvertüre. Die Entwicklung der Opern-Sinfonia erstreckt sich auf das gesamte 18. Jh., aber gegen 1730 zweigt die Konzert-Symphonie davon ab und verfolgt ihren eigenen Weg.
>
> 2. Die Konzert-Symphonie. Verhältnismäßig wenige Italiener zeigten größeres Interesse für die Konzert-Symphonie, aber diese wenigen zählten zu den fähigsten Komp. ihrer Zeit. Obwohl Pergolesi, Vivaldi und Porpora bereits Symphonien schrieben, trugen sie kaum zur Entwicklung bei;... Wichtig ist dagegen das frühe Werk von G. B. Sammartini, das heute auf die Zeit um 1730 datiert werden kann: eine dreisätzige Konzert-Symphonie in bereits fortgeschrittener Sonatenform, die vom B. Churgin (Phil. Diss. Harvard 1963) als Tl. der Oper *Memet* (1732) identifiziert wurde und die Stellung Sammartinis als des ersten wirklichen Symphonikers noch vor einem Monn und Stamitz erheblich stärkt.

2. Translate the following excerpts from the article entitled "Streichquartett" from *Musik in Geschichte und Gegenwart*:

> I. Definition, Terminologie und Theorie des Streichquartetts. Streichquartett ist im weitesten Sprachgebrauch jede Kompos. für vier solistische Streichinstr., im eingebürgerten engeren Sinne ein mehrsätziges Werk für zwei V., Va. und Vc. Die modernen Bezeichnungen "Streichquartett", "String Quartet", "Quatour à cordes", "Quartetto d'archi" haben sich erst im 19. Jh. ganz eingebürgert.
>
> II. Vorgeschichte des Streichquartetts. Das klass. StrQu. hat eine ungewöhnlich komplizierte und bisher kaum in den Grundzügen überschaubare Vorgeschichte, die hier nur angedeutet werden kann.

3. Translate the following excerpt from the article entitled "Berliner Schule", which appears in the Sachenteil of the *Musik Lexikon* by Hugo Riemann:

Berliner Schule oder Norddeutsche Schule ist ein Sammel-
name für die in der 2. Hälfte des 18. Jh. in Berlin wirkenden
Komponisten, die zum großen Teil mit dem Hof Friedrichs
des Großen (1740-86) verbunden waren, so an erster Stelle
C.Ph.E. Bach (ab 1767 in Hamburg) und J.J. Quantz, ferner
J.G. Graun, C.H. Graun und Fr. Benda, Chr. Nichelmann,
Fr.W. Marpurg, J.Ph. Kirnberger, J.Fr. Agricola, Chr.Fr.
Fasch u.A. Die mit versehenen Komponisten waren Schüler
von J.S. Bach, dessen Andenken hier besonders im Kreis um
Kirnberger und die Prinzessin Anna Amalia von Preußen
gepflegt wurde. Am bedeutendsten ist die B. Sch. auf dem
Gebiet der Instrumentalmusik (Symphonien, Konzerte,
Klavier- und Kammermusik) und dem des Liedes. Kenn-
zeichen der norddeutschen Instrumentalmusik sind der
kontrapunktisch "gearbeitete", gebundene, strenge Stil und
die "galante", freie, melodisch gefällige (zärtliche, rührende,
empfindsame) Schreibart.

Chapter Seven

I. ADDITIONAL CHARACTERISTICS OF VERBS

Special Uses

1. The following verbs in German always require the dative case:

antworten - to answer

danken - to thank

fehlen - to be missing

gefallen - to please

glauben - to believe

helfen - to help

sagen - to say

verzeihen - to pardon

> "... sag *mir,* wohin geht dein Lauf?"
> (Schubert, *Die Winterreise*–6)

> "Helft *mir*, ihr Schwestern ..."
> (Schumann, *Frauenliebe und Leben*–5)

2. Any infinitive may be used as a noun. These verbal nouns are neuter:

das Singen

das Spielen

das Hören

das Dirigieren

> "*Das Wandern* ist des Müllers Lust ..."
> (Schubert, *Die Schöne Müllerin*–1)

> "... Höre nicht *mein* stilles *Beten* ..."
> (Schumann, *Frauenliebe und Leben*–2)

3. The word *zu* is a particle that connects verb infinitives; when verbs take a complementary infinitive the dependent infinitive is preceded by *zu*. In sentence structure *zu* is translated approximately "for to".

> "... glaub ich blind *zu* sein ..."
> (Schumann, *Frauenliebe und Leben*–1)

> "... *zu* leiden, *zu* weinen, *zu* geniessen, und *zu* freuen sich ..."
> (Wolf, "Prometheus")

"Nicht mehr zu dir *zu* gehen ..."
(Brahms, "Nicht mehr zu dir zu gehen")

a) When the infinitive of a verb with a separable prefix is used with *zu*, *zu* stands between the prefix and the infinitive and the three parts become one word.

"... durch Feld und Wald zu schweifen, mein Liedchen *wegzu-pfeifen* ..."
(Schubert, "Der Musensohn")

4. *Modal auxiliary verbs* have two forms of the past participle:

a) one beginning with the prefix *ge-*

b) one the same as the infinitive

The infinitive form of the past participle is used when a modal auxiliary in any compound tense has a complementary infinitive. This construction is called a "double infinitive".

"Ja, ich werde *sterben müssen* ..."
(Brahms, "Lied")

"... und willst du deinen Liebsten *sterben sehen* ..."
(Wolf, "Und willst du deinen Liebsten sterben sehen")

When the double infinitive construction is used in a dependent clause, the auxiliary *haben* does not occur at the end of the sentence, but stands immediately before the two infinitives.

5. Like modals, the verbs *helfen, hören, lassen, lehren, lernen, sehen* have two past participles and take a complementary infinitive without *zu*, thus forming a double infinitive.

6. The verb *lassen* has the following meanings:

a) to leave

"... *lass* der feuchten Perlen... in den Wimpern mir ..."
(Schumann, *Frauenliebe und Leben*–6)

b) to let

"... O *lass* im Traum mich sterben ..."
(Schumann, *Frauenliebe und Leben*–3)

c) to have something done, make someone do something; used in this sense *lassen* is a causative verb because the doer causes something to be done.

140

It is most important to become familiar with the following information on the subjunctive and conditional moods and the passive voice in order to facilitate efficient translation.

II. SUBJUNCTIVE MOOD

A. Forms

The *subjunctive* is the mood (form of the verb showing the speaker's attitude toward what he says) which expresses conditions contrary to fact, wishes (a wish is not a factual statement because it contains an element of unreality), doubts, or what is possible, rather than certain. The six verb tenses studied in Chapter Three are all in the *indicative mood*, that is, all of these tenses express fact, rather than probability. Modern English has only a few genuine subjunctive forms and, consequently, uses substitute words like *may, let, should,* and *would*; German has distinct subjunctive forms which are used frequently. The subjunctive mood has the following characteristics:

1. Six tenses, each one similar to the corresponding tense in the indicative mood.

2. German subjunctive forms (with the exception of *sein*) have the following endings:

$$
\begin{array}{rl}
\text{ich} & \text{- e} \\
\text{du} & \text{- est} \\
\text{er, sie, es} & \text{- e} \\
\text{Sie} & \text{- en} \\
\text{wir} & \text{- en} \\
\text{ihr} & \text{- et} \\
\text{sie} & \text{- en} \\
\text{Sie} & \text{- en}
\end{array}
$$

These endings are added to the infinitive verb stem, which remains unchanged; the stem vowel changes in the indicative mood verb forms do *not* occur in the subjunctive.

3. The *present tense* of the subjunctive mood always consists of the verb stem plus the subjunctive endings:

	spielen	singen	haben	werden	EXCEPTION: sein
ich	spiele	singe	habe	werde	sei
du	spielest	singest	habest	werdest	seiest
er	spiele	singe	habe	werde	sei
wir	spielen	singen	haben	werden	seien
ihr	spielet	singet	habet	werdet	seiet
sie	spielen	singen	haben	werden	seien
Sie	spielen	singen	haben	werden	seien

"... als ob ich fröhlich *sei* ..."
(Schumann, *Liederkreis*–9)

"... mir war's er *habe* gesprochen ..."
(Schumann, *Frauenliebe und Leben*–3)

"... damit du *mögest* sehen ..."
(Schubert, *Die Winterreise*–1)

The present tense of the subjunctive mood is encountered frequently in texts; when the verb is in the subjunctive mood, the context of the sentence will determine whether the meaning of the verb is equivalent to one of the English subjunctive substitutes (should, could, let, may) or whether an English indicative form is implied.

4. The *simple past tense* of the subjunctive mood has the same endings as the present tense (subjunctive mood). These endings are added to the stem of the simple past tense in the indicative mood (first person singular—see principle parts pp. 73-83). The simple past tense of irregular verbs in the subjunctive mood is basically the same as the simple past tense form in the indicative mood. However, all irregular verbs with a vowel that can be modified (a,o,u) and the modal auxiliaries (except *sollen* and *wollen*) take an umlaut:

	haben	sein	werden	können	singen
ich	hätte	wäre	würde	könnte	sänge
du	hättest	wärest	würdest	könntest	sängest
er	hätte	wäre	würde	könnte	sänge
wir	hätten	wären	würden	könnten	sängen
ihr	hättet	wäret	würdet	könntet	sänget
sie	hätten	wären	würden	könnten	sängen

"... ich *gäbe* viel, um zu erfahren ..."
(Brahms, "Wir wandelten")

"... wollte Gott, ich *wär'* heute bei ihr ..."
(Brahms, "Sonntag")

"... *hätt'* ich tausend... *könnt'* ich brausend ..."
(Schubert, *Die schöne Müllerin*–5)

"... du *fändest* Ruhe dort!"
(Schubert, *Die Winterreise*–5)

"... jauchzen *möcht* ich, *möchte* weinen ..."
(Schumann, *Liederkreis*–12)

"... dann *säng* er hell ..."
(Schubert, *Die schöne Müllerin*–8)

"... und *wüssten's* die Nachtigallen... sie *liessen* fröhlich erschallen...
"... und *wüssten* sie mein Wehe... sie *kämen*... *und sprächen*
Trost mir ein ..."
(Schumann, *Dichterliebe*–8)

"... ich *möchte* dir mein ganzes Innre zeigen ..."
(Wolf, *Mignon-Lieder*–2)

The simple past tense of the subjunctive mood is used to express a condition contrary to fact (or unlikely to be fulfilled) at the present time or in the future; the simple past tense of the subjunctive mood is encountered frequently in poetic texts:

"Ach, denkt das Veilchen, *wär'* ich nur die schönste Blume ..."
(Mozart, "Das Veilchen")

"Ich *wünsch'*, ich *wäre* ein Vöglein und *zöge* über das Meer ..."
(Schumann, *Liederkreis*–4)

"Es war, als *hätt* der Himmel ..."
(Schumann, *Liederkreis*–5)

"Ich *wollt'*, ich *wär'* ein Fisch ..."
(Schubert, "Liebhaber in allen Gestalten")

"O *wüsst* ich doch den Weg zurück ..."
(Brahms, "O wüsst ich doch den Weg zurück")

5. The compound tenses of the subjunctive mood are formed in the same way as in the indicative mood, except that the subjunctive forms of the auxiliary verbs *haben, sein,* and *werden* are used. The *compound past*

143

tense of the subjunctive mood is formed from the present tense of the auxiliary verb in the subjunctive mood plus the past participle.

singen			gehen		
ich	habe	gesungen	ich	sei	gegangen
du	habest	gesungen	du	seiest	gegangen
er	habe	gesungen	er	sei	gegangen
wir	haben	gesungen	wir	seien	gegangen
ihr	habet	gesungen	ihr	seiet	gegangen
sie	haben	gesungen	sie	seien	gegangen
Sie	haben	gesungen	Sie	seien	gegangen

6. The *past perfect tense* of the subjunctive mood is a compound tense consisting of the simple past tense of the auxiliary verb in the subjunctive mood, plus the past participle of the verb.

singen			gehen		
ich	hätte	gesungen	ich	wäre	gegangen
du	hättest	gesungen	du	wärest	gegangen
er	hätte	gesungen	er	wäre	gegangen
wir	hätten	gesungen	wir	wären	gegangen
ihr	hättet	gesungen	ihr	wäret	gegangen
sie	hätten	gesungen	sie	wären	gegangen
Sie	hätten	gesungen	Sie	wären	gegangen

7. The *future tense* of the subjunctive mood is a compound tense composed of the present tense of the auxiliary verb *werden* in the subjunctive mood plus the verb infinitive.

singen			spielen		
ich	werde	singen	ich	werde	spielen
du	werdest	singen	du	werdest	spielen
er	werde	singen	er	werde	spielen
wir	werden	singen	wir	werden	spielen
ihr	werdet	singen	ihr	werdet	spielen
sie	werden	singen	sie	werden	spielen
Sie	werden	singen	Sie	werden	spielen

8. The *future perfect tense* of the subjunctive mood consists of the present tense of the auxiliary verb *werden* in the subjunctive mood plus the past participle of the finite verb, plus *haben* or *sein*.

spielen			gehen		
ich werde	gespielt haben		ich werde	gegangen sein	
du werdest	gespielt haben		du werdest	gegangen sein	
er werde	gespielt haben		er werde	gegangen sein	
wir werden	gespielt haben		wir werden	gegangen sein	
ihr werdet	gespielt haben		ihr werdet	gegangen sein	
sie werden	gespielt haben		sie werden	gegangen sein	
Sie werden	gespielt haben		Sie werden	gegangen sein	

B. Summary

Summary of the subjunctive mood

1. present tense: verb stem + endings

2. simple past tense: stem (first person singular of the simple past tense in the indicative mood) + endings

3. compound past tense: present tense subjunctive of the auxiliary verb + past participle

4. past perfect tense: simple past tense subjunctive of the auxiliary verb + past participle

5. future tense: present tense subjunctive of *werden* + infinitive

6. future perfect tense: present tense subjunctive of *werden* + past participle + *haben* or *sein*

III. CONDITIONAL MOOD

The *conditional mood* is used to state what "would be" or "would have been". The fulfillment of the chain of actions is contingent on the occurrence of some basic action; the basic action is always a condition, expressed or understood. There are two tenses in the *conditional mood*: present and past.

A. Present Tense

The *present tense* of the conditional mood tells what "would happen" and consists of the simple past tense of *werden* in the subjunctive mood plus the infinitive.

haben	sein	studieren
ich würde haben	ich würde sein	ich würde studieren
du würdest haben	du würdest sein	du würdest studieren
er würde haben	er würde sein	er würde studieren
wir würden haben	wir würden sein	wir würden studieren
ihr würdet haben	ihr würdet sein	ihr würdet studieren
Sie würden haben	Sie würden sein	Sie würden studieren

"... er *würde* dir ein gross Geschenk *verehren* ..."
(Wolf, "Dass doch gemalt all' deine Reize wären")

"... Sie *würden* mit mir *weinen* ..."
(Schumann, *Dichterliebe*–8)

B. Past Tense

The *past tense* of the conditional mood tells what "would have happened" and consists of the simple past tense of *werden* in the subjunctive mood plus the past participle plus *haben* or *sein*.

singen	gehen
ich würde gesungen haben	ich würde gegangen sein
du würdest gesungen haben	du würdest gegangen sein
er würde gesungen haben	er würde gegangen sein
wir würden gesungen haben	wir würden gegangen sein
ihr würdet gesungen haben	ihr würdet gegangen sein
Sie würden gesungen haben	Sie würden gegangen sein

C. Summary

Summary of the conditional mood

1. present tense: simple past tense subjunctive of *werden* + infinitive

2. past tense: simple past tense subjunctive of *werden* + past participle + *haben* or *sein*

D. Conditions

A conditional sentence consists of a subordinate clause with the conjunction *wenn*, called the *conditional clause*, and a main clause, called the *conclusion*. The conjunction *wenn* may be omitted from conditional sentence structure; the conditional clause must then have inverted word order.

146

1. A *simple* or real condition implies nothing as to fulfillment; the *wenn* ("if") clause of a simple condition assumes something which may or may not be true. Both clauses of simple conditions are in the *indicative mood*.

> "... *wenn* ich in deine Augen seh' so schwindet all mein Leid
> und Weh ..."
> (Schumann, *Dichterliebe*–4)

> "... *wenn* ich küsse deinen Mund, so werde' ich ganz und gar gesund."
> (Schumann, *Dichterliebe*–4)

2. Unreal conditions may be divided into two categories:

   a) *Contrary-to-fact* conditions denoting *present* or *future* time. This type of condition implies that the *"if" clause* (conditional clause) is now unfulfilled or that the possibility of its fulfillment is remote. A sentence expressing a *contrary-to-fact* condition requires the simple past tense of the subjunctive mood in the *"if" clause* and the simple past tense of the subjunctive mood or the present tense of the conditional mood in the conclusion; the conditional mood is never used in the *"if" clause*.

   > "... *wenn* du es wüsstest... was träumen heisst... du kämst zu mir."
   > (Strauss, "Wenn du es wüsstest")

   b) *Contrary-to-fact* conditions denoting *past* time. This type of sentence implies that the condition was not fulfilled and requires the past perfect tense of the subjunctive mood in the *"if" clause* and the past perfect tense of the subjunctive in the conclusion.

3. Summary of *conditional* sentence structure

	conditional *"if" clause*	*conclusion*
simple condition	indicative mood	indicative mood
Contrary-to-fact condition		
a) present or future	simple past subj.	present conditional
b) past	past perfect subj.	past perfect subj.

IV. DIRECT AND INDIRECT DISCOURSE

A. Direct Discourse

A statement or question is in *direct discourse* when the exact words or thoughts of a person are reported directly, that is, quoted after verbs of saying, telling, relating, thinking, asking, etc.; direct statements are in quotation marks.

" ...'Ach,' denkt das Veilchen, *'wär* ich nur die schönste Blume ...' "
(Mozart, "Das Veilchen")

B. Indirect Discourse

A statement or question is in *indirect discourse* when the statement or question is merely reported, but not in the exact words of the speaker or thinker. Statements in indirect discourse usually occur after verbs of saying and thinking, such as *denken, erzählen, fragen, glauben, hoffen, sagen, schreiben.* The conjunction *dass* may be omitted in indirect discourse. In quoting indirectly what a person has said, thought, or asked, the subjunctive mood is generally used to emphasize the idea of uncertainty. The use of the indicative mood in indirect discourse indicates that the speaker fully endorses the statement quoted. The same tense of the verb is generally used in the indirect statement (subjunctive or conditional mood) as in the direct statement; the present, future, and compound past tense are encountered most frequently in indirect discourse.

PATTERN OF TENSES IN DIRECT AND INDIRECT DISCOURSE

Direct Discourse	*Indirect Discourse*
present	present subjunctive
	or
	simple past subjunctive
simple past	compound past subjunctive
compound past	or
past perfect	past perfect subjunctive
future	future subjunctive
	or
	present conditional

future perfect

future perfect subjunctive

or

past conditional

V. PASSIVE VOICE

As stated in Chapter Three, there are two voices of German verbs: active and passive. In the active voice, the subject performs some act; in the *passive voice* the subject is acted upon. The meaning of a statement in either the active or the passive voice is generally the same. The passive voice is used less frequently in German than in English; it is generally preferable and easier to use the active voice. An active sentence with the indefinite pronoun *man* is often used to avoid the passive voice. In the passive voice the person "by whom" or the thing "by which" an act is performed is called the *agent*; the agent, when expressed, is indicated by *von*. The passive voice is often introduced by *es* when no particular subject is stated, or when some indefinite word like *etwas, nichts, alles*, is the subject.

Tenses

The passive voice has exactly the same number of tenses as the active voice: 6-indicative mood, 6-subjunctive mood, 2-conditional mood, and is expressed by the auxiliary verb *werden*, which tells the time of the action, plus the past participle of the verb. In the passive voice, the past participle *geworden* is shortened to *worden*.

SYNOPSIS of *es wird gespielt*

INDICATIVE

Present	es	wird	gespielt
Simple past	es	wurde	gespielt
Compound past	es	ist	gespielt worden
Past perfect	es	war	gespielt worden
Future	es	wird	gespielt werden
Future perfect	es	wird	gespielt worden sein

SUBJUNCTIVE

Present	es	werde	gespielt
Simple past	es	würde	gespielt
Compound past	es	sei	gespielt worden

Past perfect	es	wäre	gespielt worden
Future	es	werde	gespielt worden
Future perfect	es	werde	gespielt worden sein

CONDITIONAL

| Present | es | würde | gespielt werden |
| Past | es | würde | gespielt worden sein |

TRANSLATION EXERCISES

1. Translate the following excerpts from the article entitled "Deutsche Musik" from the Sachenteil of the *Musik Lexikon* by Hugo Riemann:

Der 1911 geborene Fr. Liszt begann als Klaviervirtuose, unterrichtet vom Beethoven-Schüler C. Czerny, und entwickelte in Paris einen persönlichen Vortragsstil. Seit der Klavierübertragung der *Symphonie fantastique* von Berlioz 1833 wirkte Liszt, durchaus revolutionär, im Sinne eines neuen Subjektivismus der Musik.

Die Wende zum Heutigen brachte der 1874 geborene A. Schönberg. Nach langer Vorbereitung schritt er 1921 in Wien zur Kompositionsmethode "mit 12 nur aufeinander bezogenen Tönen", ermöglicht durch Wagners *Tristan*. Schönberg hatte in Wien mehrere hervorragende Schüler. A. Berg schrieb außer Kammer- und Orchesterwerken, teils mit Gesang, die Oper *Wozzeck*, die seit 1925 ungewöhnlichen Erfolg hatte. Weniger beachtet wurde zu Lebzeiten A. Webern, trotz seiner alles überbietenden Ausdrucksintensität und Knappheit der Form. Die seit 1900 geborenen Komponisten hatten die Wahl, die Zwölftontechnik abzulehnen oder aufzugreifen. An ihrer Spitze steht der 1900 geborene E. Krenek; nach Versuchen übernahn er diese Methode seit 1938 und bereicherte sie durch Kenntnis spätmittelalterlicher Polyphonie. Ablehnend verhielten sich 2 Altersgenossen mit Theaterinteresse. Von H. Reutter gibt es oratorienhafte Opern, Ballette und Oratorien; der Schwerpunkt des übrigen Schaffens liegt in der Orchester- und Kammermusik, auch mit Gesang. Der Bayer W. Egk hatte dank seinem Theatersinn seit 1933 mit Opern vielfach Erfolg und wirkte ungewöhnlich in die Breite;

das gilt auch für Egks Ballette seit 1940. Anders bei W. Fortner, der seit 1929 Instrumental- und Gesangsmusik tonal in persönlichem Stil schrieb; die Zwölftontechnik entwickelte er jedoch seit 1948 weiter, bedachte nun auch Oper und Ballet. Die erst nach 1945 bekannten Komponisten, frühestens 1926 geboren, bilden eine Gruppe für sich. H.W. Henze beherrscht die Zwölftontechnik und alles Neue ebenso wie das spätromantische Orchester; angesichts der Farbigkeit seiner Musik stehen Oper und Ballett voran, doch hat er außerdem fast alle Gattungen bedacht, die Instrumentalmusik gern mit außermusikalischen Anregungen. Der um 2 Jahre jüngere K. Stockhausen schrieb vielbeachtete Klaviermusik und andere Instrumentalwerke; besonders verdient machte er sich bei der Einführung elektronischer Musik. Beim Blick auf Europa zeigt sich, daß neben die D.M. seit Wagners Tod eine von ihr unabhängig ausländische Kunst gewesen war (Verdi, Puccini, Debussy, Mussorgskij). Doch anderseits hat sich Schönbergs Zwölftontechnik seit 1921 international verbreitet.

FRENCH

French and Italian, two of the five so-called "Romance Languages" (Spanish, Portuguese, and Rumanian constitute the other three), have a common linguistic heritage and are thus semantically related languages.

Historically, it is interesting that not a single modern language existed at the beginning of the Middle Ages; similarly, relatively little is known of music literature and music practice before the beginning of the Middle Ages. By contrast, however, modern music, as it has evolved to the present, developed deliberately over several centuries, whereas almost all modern languages, as they have survived to the present, had fully emerged by the end of the Middle Ages.

Although Latin was preserved throughout the Middle Ages as a means of international communication, as evident in music in the extant examples of Gregorian Chant, the vocabulary and grammatical structure of modern languages had developed from Latin and Germanic roots by the beginning of the Modern Age (1492). The term "Romance Language" derives from the fact that Latin was the vernacular tongue of ancient Rome; accordingly, it significantly influenced the evolution of modern languages. A knowledge of Latin is an invaluable frame of reference for the linguistic concepts of French and Italian, especially in word recognition and vocabulary building.

Chapter One

I. INTERNATIONAL PHONETIC ALPHABET

The value of a standardized set of symbols representing sounds becomes immediately apparent when the same alphabet letters used in a different sequence create a foreign language. It is thus necessary only to supplement the IPA symbols introduced in the foregoing study of English with those symbols exclusive to French and explain the aural connotation of each within the context of the French language. When the following guidelines are carefully followed it should be possible to correctly pronounce most words in French.

A. General Principles of Pronunciation

1. Every syllable in French receives approximately the same degree of *stress*; the last syllable in a phrase group receives a slightly stronger stress.

2. *Intonation* is the rise and fall of the pitch in the speaking voice.

a) The intonation pattern for short declarative sentences in French (those sentences which make a statement) usually consists of a rising and a falling group, that is, the voice rises in pitch with each syllable of the rising group and descends with each syllable of the falling group.

(1) In long declarative sentences, there may be several rising groups until the high point in the sentence (generally the next to the last word group) is reached; the rest of the sentence then falls in pitch progressively.

b) Intonation patterns for questions

(1) If the question is to be answered by "yes" or "no", the intonation pattern starts at a low pitch and rises to a high pitch.

(2) If the question is to be answered by a statement other than "yes" or "no", the intonation pattern starts on a high pitch and descends in pitch.

c) Intonation pattern in commands

(1) In commands or imperative statements the intonation pattern starts on a high pitch and descends in pitch with each syllable.

155

B. Punctuation and Capitalization

Most punctuation and capitalization is the same in French as in English; the special use of the hyphen in French numbers is noted in Chapter Two.

C. Specifics of Pronunciation

1. Vowels

a) The French [a] sound is a combination of the [æ], the "short a" sound, and [ɑ], the broad "ah" sound with no suggestion of diphthong. The [a] sound is produced with the lips opened wide and the tongue arched toward the front of the mouth; it is generally spelled in French:

a, à: Adam, Attaignant, Cambert, Campra, Catel, Chabrier, Charpentier, Franck, Racine, Ravel, Satie

i after *o*: Boieldieu

b) The [ɑ] sound is spelled in French:

a, â[1]: de la Hale

a before [s] when it is spelled *ss*: Massenet

a before [z] when it is spelled *z* or *s*: Bazin

a before a final silent *s*: Dukas, Thomas

i after *o* before a final silent consonant: Bunois

c) The pure vowel sound [e] in French is formed with the lips spread apart and tensed; the front of the tongue is arched high in the front of the mouth and the tip of the tongue touches the back of the lower front teeth. The [e] sound is spelled in French:

final *ai*: primarily in verb forms (Chapter Three)

e before a final silent consonant except *s*: Messager

é: Carré, Dupré, Méhul

d) The [ɔ] sound in French is pronounced with the jaws open, the lips rounded, and the back of the tongue arched toward the middle of the mouth. The [ɔ] sound is spelled in French:

o: Prudhomme, Chambonnières

au before *r*: Fauré

---

[1]The ^ sign over a vowel is a circumflex accent (accent circonflexe) and is used to indicate a lengthening of the vowel; the circumflex is used with all vowels.

e) The pure vowel sound [i] in French is formed with the lips apart and the tip of the tongue touching the back of the lower front teeth; the [i] sound is spelled in French:

i, î: Ibert, Isouard, Scribe

ie at the end of a word or syllable: Satie

y: Debussy, Grétry, Lully

f) The pure vowel sound [ɛ] in French must be clearly distinguished from [e]; the [ɛ] sound is spelled in French:

ê, è: Molière, Dezède

e before a pronounced final consonant: Gossec, Claudel

e before two or more consonants: Honegger

e before silent *t*: Collet, Bizet

ai, aî: Baudelaire, Beaumarchais

aie, aient in verb forms (Chapter Three)

ei, ey: Reyer

g) The pure vowel sound [o] is spelled in French:

ô, o, (final sound in a word): Gounod, Lalo, Verdelot

o before [z]: Berlioz

au: Auber, Audran, Milhaud, Clérambault

eau: Bruneau, Cocteau, Mocquereau, Rameau

h) The pure vowel sound [u] is produced with the lips rounded and protruded, the tip of the tongue down, and the back of the tongue arched up. The [u] sound is generally spelled in French:

ou, oû, où: Boulanger, Couperin, Leroux, Poulenc, Rousseau, Roussel

i) The [y] sound in French is produced with the lips in the position for [u] while the tongue is in the position for [i]. The French [y] is spelled:

u, û: Duparc, Dupont, Grabu, Lully

j) The [ø] sound is exclusive to French; [ø] is a vowel sound combination of [e] and [o] produced with the tongue in position for [e] and the lips in position for [o]. The [ø] sound is spelled in French:

eu, eû, or *oeu* as the final sound in a word: Beaujoyeulx, Beaulieu, Boieldieu

k) The French vowel [œ] is produced with the lips in position for [ɔ] and the tongue in position for [ɛ]. The [œ] sound is spelled in French:

eu or *oeu* when this vowel combination is not final:

Coeur-de-Lion

oe: Boesset

l) The neutral [ə] sound in French is approximately the unstressed equivalent of the [ø] vowel sound. The neutral [ə] sound is pronounced:

(1) In many words whose first syllable is spelled *e*: Debussy

(2) In many monosyllables spelled with *e*. Many words in French are spelled with a final *e* which is silent in spoken French.

2. Nasal Vowels

Most vowels are produced while air flows unobstructed through the mouth only; a vowel is nasal when air is allowed to rush through both the mouth and the nose for the duration of the vowel. Nasal vowels are an important characteristic of spoken French. In general, nasal vowels occur in French whenever an *n* or *m* is final or is followed by another consonant; the *n* or *m* is not pronounced as a separate consonant but causes the preceding vowel to assume a nasal quality. The addition of [˜] over a phonetic symbol indicates nasality; the phonetic symbols otherwise imply standard vowel sounds.

a) The nasal vowel sound [ɑ̃] should be open in order to distinguish it from [ɑ̃]. The nasal vowel [ɑ̃] is spelled in French:

am: Cambert, Lambert

an: Bannville, Maupassant

em, en: Messiaen

b) The nasal vowel sound [ɔ̃] (sometimes indicated by the symbol [õ]) is spelled in French:

om, on: Berton, Certon, Chausson, Créquillon, Demonte, Dupont, Monsigny

c) The nasal vowel [ɛ̃] sounds more like [æ] than the vowel [ɛ], and is spelled in French:

aim, ain, eim, ein: Alain

im, in, ym, yn: Bazin, Couperin, D'Indy, Daquin, Fevin

d) The nasal vowel sound [œ̃] is a combination of [ɛ̃] and [ɔ]; the tongue is placed in position for [ɛ̃] and the lips are rounded as for [ɔ]. The nasal vowel sound [œ̃] is spelled in French:

um, un: Kartun

3. Semivowels

Semivowels are vowels used as consonants. The three semivowels [j] [ɥ] and [w] are actually the vowels [i] [y] and [u] used as consonants. Whenever *i, u,* or *ou* appears in French before another vowel, the first vowel is shortened to become a consonant or semivowel. The French semivowel is a short transition sound rather than a separate syllable.

a) The french semivowel [j] is pronounced [y] or [i] when used as a consonant; the semivowel [j] is spelled in French:

i before another vowel: Angiers, Chabrier, Pierné, Soulier

ille final when preceded by a vowel; Corneille

ill: Bouilly

b) The French semivowel [ɥ] is produced with the lips, jaws, and tongue in a position for [y]; the [ɥ] sound is the vowel [y] shortened to form a consonant. The semivowel [ɥ] is spelled in French:

u before another vowel: Dup*u*is, Pers*u*is

c) The French semivowel [w] implies the vowel sound [u]; the semivowel sound [w] is characterized by lip-rounding and is spelled in French:

oi; Boieldieu

4. Consonants

a) Voiceless consonants are those which are produced without vocalization and have no pitch. The slight aspiration after the voiceless consonants [p] [t] and [k] in English should not be articulated in French; no expulsion of air should accompany the articulation of voiceless consonants in French.

(1) The voiceless consonant sound [ʃ] is spelled in French:

ch: Charpentier

(2) The voiceless consonant sound [f] is spelled in French:

f, ff: Févin, Fauré

ph: Danican-Philidor

(3) The [h] sound does not exist as such in French. When the letter *h* occurs in spelling, though normally silent (Honegger, Halévy), it is usually classified as either a "mute *h*" or an "aspirate *h*". Words beginning with an aspirate *h* are usually indicated in dictionaries.

(4) The voiceless consonant sound [k] is spelled in French:

c or *cc* before *a, o, u* or a consonant: Delacroix

final *c*: Bar-le-Duc

qu: Créquillon, Planquette, Quinault

final *q*: Lecocq

k: Kartun

the first of a double *c* (*cc*) before *e, i,* or *y*: (infrequent)

ch in words of Greek derivation: choeur

(5) The voiceless consonant sound [p] is spelled in French:

p, pp: Poulenc

(6) The voiceless consonant sound [s] is spelled in French:

initial *s*: Sauguet, Scribe

s before or after a consonant: Ronsard

final *d* (not elided): Saint-Saëns

ss: Colasse, Coussemaker, Gossec, Massenet, Terrasse

c, ç ²: before *e, i,* or *y*: Racine

(7) The voiceless consonant sound [t] is pronounced in French with the tongue behind the upper front teeth (rather than on the alveolar ridge as in English); the [t] sound is spelled in French:

t, tt: Marmontel

th: Thomas

b) Voiced consonants are those which are produced with vocalization and have fractional initial pitch.

---

²The cedilla (ــ) cédille, under c indicates that it is pronounced [s].

(1) The voiced consonant sound [b] is spelled in French:

b, bb: Berlioz, Bizet, Blondel, Bouffons

(2) The voiced consonant sound [d] is pronounced in French not with the tongue on the alveolar ridge as in English, but with the tongue further forward, behind the upper front teeth. The [d] sound is spelled in French:

d, dd: Daudet, Delacroix, Delibes

(3) The voiced consonant sound [g] is spelled in French:

g, gg followed by *a, o, u,* or a consonant: Gualtier, Gossec, Grabu, Grétry

gu before *e, i,* or *y*: Guy, Nogues

the first of a double *g* (*gg*) before *e, i,* or *y*: Honegger

(4) The voiced consonant sound [ʒ] is spelled in French:

j: jongleurs

before *e, i,* or *y - g*: *G*eorges

before another vowel - *ge* or *je*: *Je*an-Baptiste Lully

(5) The voiced consonant sound [v] is spelled in French:

v: Véron

w: Widor

(Note: the letter *w* occurs infrequently in French)

(6) The voiced consonant sound [z] is spelled in French:

s between two vowels within the same word or in liaison: Lesueur

z: Bizet

c) Liquid consonants are those which are produced with vocalization and have full pitch.

(1) The liquid consonant sound [l] in French is produced with the tip of the tongue down and placed between the upper front teeth; the [l] sound is produced in French the same in the initial and final positions. In the final position the [l] sound in English is pronounced with the back of the tongue raised; this should be avoided in French. The liquid consonant sound [l] is spelled in French:

l, ll: Lully

(2) The liquid consonant sound [m] is spelled in French:

m, mm: Murger, de Muris, Thomas

(3) The liquid consonant sound [n] is spelled in French:

n, nn: Gounod, Chambonnières, Delannoy

(4) The liquid consonant sound [ɲ] is produced when the tongue moves in a single motion directly to the hard palate while the nasal passages are simultaneously opened. The liquid consonant sound [ɲ] is spelled in French:

gn: Attaignant, Guignon, Monsigny

(5) The liquid consonant [r] in French is pronounced in two ways. In standard conversation the so-called "uvular r" is phonetically correct. The "uvular r," denoted [R] in the International Phonetic Alphabet in order to distinguish its physiological production from [r], is produced when air rushes through the uvula, the small opening at the back of the mouth between the tongue and the back of the roof of the mouth. The uvular [R] is a voiced sound and has no counterpart in English. The flipped or rolled [r] sound indigenous to other modern languages (English, German, Italian) is standard practice for singing in French. The liquid consonant sound [r] ([R]) is spelled in French:

r, rr: Herold, Rabaud, Rameau

II. GUIDELINES FOR EFFICIENT PRONUNCIATION IN SYNTAX

A. Symbols Exclusive to French

1. Accents are used in French primarily to indicate the correct pronunciation of a letter. Accents on capital letters are usually not written or printed in French (exception: É). Accents indicate that a syllable is pronounced according to the foregoing guidelines, and do not affect the stress of the syllable.

a) The acute accent (´), *accent aigu*, is used only on the letter *e*. The *é* is pronounced [e] in French: Duruflé, Levadé.

b) The grave accent (`), *accent grave*, is used primarily on the letter *e* followed by a final *s* or *-re*: Glière. The *è* is always pronounced [ɛ] in French: Dezède. The *accent grave* is also used to distinguish monosyllabic adverbs from other parts of speech.

2. Two dots placed over the second of two consecutive vowels is a diaresis (¨) or tréma in French. The diaresis indicates that the vowel begins a new syllable: Paër

    Exception: Saint-Saëns

B. Pronunciation of Final Consonants

1. The following consonants are generally silent when final:

    d, g, p: Gounod, Herold, Isouard, Milhaud, Ronsard

    m: Adam

    n: Berton, Couperin

    s: Delibes, Marais, Thomas, Dupuis

    t: Aubert, Benoit, Bizet, Collet, Ibert, Lambert, Maillart, Sauguet

    x: Gaveaux, Leroux, Françaix, Croix

    z: Ropartz

Exception: Berlioz = [z]

    a) When a final *s* is added to a word after a consonant, the *s* does not alter the pronunciation of the word; the consonant preceding the final *s* is therefore regarded as the final consonant of the word.

2. The following consonants are generally pronounced when final:

    c ([k]): Bar-le-Duc, Dalayrac, Gossec, Séverac, Auric

Exception: Final *c* preceded by *n* is usually silent, although the final *c* is sometimes pronounced for emphasis: Poulenc

    f: Baïf

    l: Méhul, Marmontel, Ravel, Roussel

    q ([k]): Lecocq

    r: Auber

Although *r* is generally pronounced when final, many words ending in *-er* have a final silent *r*:

    a) verb infinitives ending in *-er* (Chapter Three)

    b) nouns ending in *-ier* which connote occupation or function.

C. Elision

1. Elision occurs when a vowel is dropped and replaced by an apostrophe before a word beginning with a vowel or mute *h*; not all final vowels, however, are elided before all initial vowels. Elision does not occur before a word beginning with an aspirate *h* (see p. 160).

D. Liason

1. Liason or linking occurs when a final consonant which is normally silent is pronounced with the initial vowel sound of the following word. However, liason does not automatically occur before all words that begin with a vowel sound. There are certain cases where liason always takes place, other cases where it is optional, and still other instances where liason should never occur. The principles of liason will be clarified further in following chapters.

E. Cognates

French and English cognates include:

1. words spelled alike, especially those ending in *-able, -al, -ance, -ible, -ion, -ude*

2. words spelled differently but easily recognized, especially those ending in *-ain, -aire, -ance, -eur, -eux, -ien, -ique, -iste, -té*

3. recognizable words which cannot be classified according to any system

4. scientific and technical terms

5. The circumflex accent on a French vowel often indicates that an *s* follows the vowel in the English cognate of the word.

6. Not all words that look alike, however, are true cognates. Many words look alike in French and English but have widely different meanings; these words are known as false cognates.

MUSICAL EXERCISES

1. Look up the first name(s) of each composer cited in the pronunciation illustrations.

a) Write out the full names of each composer using IPA symbols.

b) List the birth and death dates of each composer.

SUPPLEMENTARY PRONUNCIATION EXERCISES

1. Just as the written symbol of each alphabet letter in English has a name (although the symbol may represent more than one sound) likewise in French each alphabet letter has a name which should be used when spelling any French word aloud.

ALPHABET

A	a	[ɑ]	N	n	[ɛn]
B	b	[be]	O	o	[o]
C	c	[se]	P	p	[pe]
D	d	[de]	Q	q	[ky]
E	e	[ə]	R	r	[eːr]³
F	f	[ɛf]	S	s	[ɛs]
G	g	[ʒe]	T	t	[te]
H	h	[aʃ]	U	u	[y]
I	i	[i]	V	v	[ve]
J	j	[ʒi]	W	w	[dublə ve]
K	k	[kɑ]	X	x	[iks]
L	l	[ɛl]	Y	y	[i grɛk]
M	m	[ɛm]	Z	z	[zed]

2. Just as alphabet letters are used to spell words, so the same symbols are used to designate the pitch names of the modern diatonic scale. The following are the French letter names and pronunciation of each scale degree:

English	*French*	
C	ut	[yt]
C flat	ut bémol	[yt bemɔl]
C sharp	ut dièse	[yt djɛːz]
D	ré	[re]
D flat	ré bémol	[re bemɔl]
D sharp	ré dièse	[re djɛːz]
E	mi	[mi]
E flat	mi bémol	[mi bemɔl]
E sharp	mi dièse	[mi djɛːz]

³: indicates that the vowel is long in relative duration.

165

F	fa	[fa]
F flat	fa bémol	[fa bemɔl]
F sharp	fa dièse	[fa djɛːz]
G	sol	[sɔl]
G flat	sol bémol	[sɔl bemɔl]
G sharp	sol dièse	[sɔl djɛːz]
A	la	[lɑ]
A flat	la bémol	[lɑ bemɔl]
A sharp	la dièse	[lɑ djɛːz]
B	si	[si]
B flat	si bémol	[si bemɔl]
B sharp	si dièse	[si djɛːz]

♭♭ = double bémol

✗ = double dièse

3. Opera titles in French

a) Say each of the following opera titles aloud.

b) Identify the composer of each work; cite the date of the first performance of each.

c) Write out each title phonetically using IPA symbols.

Acanthe et Céphise	La Belle Hélène
L'Africaine	Bellérophon
Aline, reine de Golconde	Le Bon Roi Dagobert
Les Amants Magnifiques	Le Bourgeois Gentilhomme
Angélique	La Brebis égarée
Antar	Cadmus et Hermione
Ariane ou le mariage de Bacchus	La Caïd
Ariodant	Carmen
Armide et Renaud	Castor et Pollux
L'Attacque du Moulin	La Caverne
Atys	Cendrillon
Les Aventures du Roi Pausole	Le Chant de la Cloche
Barbe-Bleue	Charlotte Corday
Le Barosse du Saint-Sacrement	La Chartreuse de Parme
Béatrice et Bénédict	Le Chemineau

Chilpéric
Les Choéphores
Le Cid
Les Cloches de Corneville
La Comtesse d'Escarbagnas
Continuation des Amours
Coppélia
Cris du monde
La Dame blanche
La damnation de Faust
Dardanus
David
Le Délire
Le Désert
Le Déserteur
Les deux Journées
Les Deux Petits Savoyards
Le Devin du village
Les Diologues des Carmélites
Dinorah
Djamileh
Le Domino noir
La Double Echelle
Les Dragons de Villars
L'Eclair
Elisa ou Le Voyage au Mont-Ber-
nard
Emile
L'Enfant et les sortilèges
L'Enfant prodigue
L'Enfant roi
Esclarmonde
Esmeralda
L'Etoile du nord
L'Etranger
Les Eumenides
L'Europe galante
La Fanchonette

Faust
La Fée Urgèle
Fervaal
Les Festes venitiennes
Les Fêtes de Thalie
Fêtes d'Hébé
Les Fêtes grecques et romaines
La Fille de Madame Angot
La Fille de Tabarin
Une Folie
La Forêt bleue
Fra Diavolo
La Gageure imprévue
Galatée
Georges Dandin
Guillaume Tell
Gwendoline
Hamlet
Henri III et sa cour
Henri VIII
Hippolyte et Aricie
Les Huguenots
Hulda
Les Indes galantes
Iphigénie en Aulide
Iphigénie en Tauride
Isis
L'Isle des Foux
Issé
Jean de Nivelle
Jean de Paris
Jeanne d'Arc au bûcher
Jeannot et Colin
Jephté
Jérusalem délivrée
Le Jeu de Robin et Marion
Joconde
Le Jongleur de Notre Dame

Joseph
Judith
La Juive
Lakmé
La Légende de St. Christophe
Léonore, ou l'Amour conjugale
Louise
Le Macon
Le Maître de Chapelle
Maître Pathelin
Le Malade imaginaire
Les Malheurs d'Orphée
Les Mamelles de Tirésias
Manon
Mârouf, savetier du Caire
Le Martyre de Saint-Sébastien
La Mascotte
Maximilien
Médée
Mélidor et Phrosine
Mignon
Mireille
Monsieur Beaucaire
Monsieur de la Palisse
Monsieur de Pourceaugnac
Les Mousquetaires au couvent
Nadeshda
La Naissance de la lyre
Namouna
La Navarraise
Nicolas de Flue
Les Noces de Jeannette
Notre-Dame-de-Paris
Nouvelle Héloïse
L'Oeil crevé
On ne s'avise jamais de tout
Orfeo ed Euridice
Orphée aux enfers

Ossian, ou Les Bardes
L'Ouragon
Padmâvati
Le Pardon de Ploermel
Paride et Elena
La Partie de chasse de Henri IV
La Passion
Paul et Virginie
Le Pauvre Matelot
Le Pays
La Peau de chagrin
Les Pêcheurs de perles
Pelléas et Mélisande
Pénélope
La Périchole
La Perle du Brésil
Persée
Le Petit Chaperon rouge
Les Petites Cardinal
Le Petit Faust
Phaëton
Philémon et Baucis
Phryné
Platée
Le Plumet du Colonel
Le poirier de misère
Pomone
Postillon de Longjumeau
Le Pré aux clercs
La Princesse d'Elide
La Prise de Troie
Prométhée
Le Prophète
Proserpine
Psyché
La Reine de Chypre
La Rencontre imprévue
Le Rendez-vous bourgeois

Le Rêve

Richard Coeur-de-Lion

Robert le Diable

Le Roi Arthus

Le Roi David

Le Roi de Lahore

Le Roi des Aulnes

Le Roi d'Ys

Le Roi d'Yvetot

Le Roi et le fermier

Le Roi l'a dit

Le Roi malgré lui

Le Roi s'amuse

Roland

Roméo et Juliette

La Rôtisserie de la Reine Pédauqze

La Route d'Emeraude

Samson et Dalila

Scènes de la vie de Bohême

Le Siège de Corinthe

Sigurd

Le Sire de Vargy

Songe d'une nuit d'été

Le Tableau parlant

Télémaque

Thaïs

Thérèse

Thétis et Pélée

La Tragédie de Salomé

Les Trois Fermiers

Les Troyens à Carthage

Uthal

La Vie Parisienne

Les Visitandines

La Voix humaine

Le Voyage en Chine

Werther

Zaïs

Chapter Two

In Chapter One French phonetics are so presented, that it should now be possible to pronounce correctly most words in French. With this chapter begins the simplified grammatical approach to French which will ultimately enable musicians to read and translate for professional purposes, perform with understanding, and command the basic language skills of conversation and comprehension. When this is accomplished, French is indeed a practical modern language and a necessary tool for professional musicians.

I. NOUNS

A *noun* is the name of a person, place, or thing.

Specific Characteristics of Nouns in French

1. All nouns in French have a gender, with the grammatical designation of masculine or feminine. It is important to learn the gender of each noun in French along with the word meaning; the form of articles, adjectives, pronouns and some verbs must conform to the gender of the noun to which it refers.

2. A *definite article* is a word modifying a noun which points out a particular person, place, or thing. In English the definite article used to distinguish nouns of all genders is *the*; in French there are four forms of the definite article:

a) *le* [lə] is used before masculine singular nouns that begin with a consonant other than a mute *h*.

b) *la* [lɑ] is used before feminine singular nouns that begin with a consonant other than a mute *h*.

c) *l'* [l] is used before masculine or feminine singular nouns that begin with a vowel or mute *h*; *l'* is the elided form of the definite articles *le, la.*

d) *les* [le] is used before masculine or feminine plural nouns. When the definite article *les* modifies a noun beginning with a vowel or mute *h*, the definite article *les* is linked to the noun; in this liason the *s* of *les* is pronounced [z].

EXERCISES

1. Consult the pronunciation guide at the end of Chapter One; list all opera titles that contain the definite articles *le, la, l', les,* and classify the modified nouns:

Masculine   *Feminine*

2. Identify the following instruments; note the gender of each.

almérie	cornet
bombarde	crécelle
carillon	crotales
cervelas	éoliphone
chalumeau	épinette
clairon	fifre
clavessin	mirliton
clavicorde	quinton
clavier	tympanon
cloches	viole d'amour

3. For further pronunciation practice, read the following list of instrument names aloud:

English	*French*
piccolo	la petite flûte
flute	la flûte (traversière)
oboe	le hautbois
English horn	le cor Anglais
clarinet	la clarinette
bass clarinet	la clarinette basse
bassoon	le basson
contrabassoon	la contre-basson
horn	le cor
trumpet	la trompette
trombone	le trombone
tuba	le tuba
timpani	les timbales (f.)
bass drum	la grosse caisse

cymbals	les cymbales (f.)
snare drum	le tambour
tenor drum	la caisse roulante
triangle	le triangle
tambourine	le tambour de Basque
gong	le tam-tam
castanets	les castagnettes (f.)
xylophone	le xylophone le claquebois
glockenspiel	le jeu de timbres
bells or chimes	les cloches (f.)
celesta	le célesta
harp	la harpe
violin	le violon
viola	le alto (l'alto)
violoncello	le violoncelle
double bass	le contrebasse
f. = feminine	
m. = masculine	

3. It should be clear from the foregoing exercises that every noun in French possesses a gender, which is indicated by the preceding article.

As in English, there also exists in French the *indefinite article*, a word modifying a noun that does not indicate a *particular* person, place, or thing. The indefinite articles in English are *a* and *an*; in French the indefinite articles are:

a) *un* [œ̃] is used with masculine singular nouns.

b) *une* [yn] is used with feminine singular nouns.

EXERCISES

1. Substitute the correct indefinite article for the definite article in the preceding list of instrument names; write out each name phonetically.

2. Identify the following musical terms; indicate whether each noun is masculine or feminine.

173

agréments	carole	doublé	ouvert
amener	carrure	écossaise	pavane
anglaise	chanterelle	ensemble	pincé
arpège	charivari	entremet	plainte
badinage	chase	entrée	prélude
barcarolle	chifonie	enté	prose
basse	chute	envoi	récit
battement	clos	expression	réjouissance
berceuse	comédie	fantaisie	ritournelle
boutade	concertant	flatté	rondeau
branle	conservatoire	fricassée	sanglot
broderie	contredanse	intermède	solfège
brunette	cortège	machicotage	style
brusque	coulé	menuet	tirade
canarie	courante	messe	valse
cantique	déchant	noël	vaudeville
caprice	déploration	nuances	verset
		ordre	vocalise

3. Define historically the term *chansonnier*.

4. The primary difference between nouns in English and French, then, is the characteristic of gender. In English

> the music
> the piano

must he learned in French as

> la musique
> le piano[1]

a) Because nouns in French do not exist independently of their gender, it is necessary to learn the gender of each noun with the meaning of the word and thereby associate the appropriate definite or indefinite article with each word. Although nouns often occur in French, especially in musical titles, without a definite or indefinite

---

[1] In French a distinction is made between an upright piano, *piano droit*, and a grand piano, *piano à queue*.

article to indicate the gender, it is essential to learn noun genders for the purpose of accurate translating and reading in French and most especially for effective conversation.

EXERCISES

1. Say the following song titles from *Trois Chansons de Bilitis* by Dubussy:

> La Flûte
>
> La Chevelure
>
> Le Tombeau des naïdes

2. Substitute the correct indefinite article for the definite article and spell out the noun which it modifies phonetically.

---

5. The gender of many nouns can be determined by the word meaning or ending; the following general guidelines are applicable:

a) The gender of those nouns that refer to persons usually corresponds to their sex.

b) The gender of the vast majority of nouns, those that refer to things, places, activities, abstractions, materials, measurements, etc., must be learned by repeated correct usuage.

c) Nouns of nationality have the following characteristics:

(1) The masculine form becomes feminine by adding *-e* to the masculine form: *un Français, une Française*

(2) Nouns ending in *-e* in the masculine form do not change in the feminine: un Russe, une Russe

(3) Nouns ending in *-ien* in the masculine form become *-ienne* in the feminine form: un Italien, une Italienne

(4) Nouns of nationality are capitalized only when they refer to people.

6. Just as nouns in English have a plural form designating more than one person, place, or thing, nouns in French may also be pluralized.

a) The plural of most French nouns is formed by adding *-s* to the singular form; this *s* is silent in pronunciation.

b) Nouns ending in *-s* in the singular are the same in the plural: le Français, les Français

c) In spoken French the plural of most nouns is distinguished from the singular by the article used:

Singular: le, la, l'

Plural: les

d) The plural form of the indefinite articles *un* and *une* is *des*; it is pronounced [de] before a noun beginning with a consonant, [dez] before a noun beginning with a vowel or mute *h*.

e) Most nouns which end in *-al* in the singular drop this ending and add *-aux* to form the plural.

f) All nouns ending in *-eau* are pluralized by adding *-x*.

g) Some masculine nouns ending in *-ou* are pluralized by adding *-x* to the singular form.

h) Nouns ending in *-er* in the masculine end in *-ère* in the feminine.

i) The plural article *les* is used before the name of a family used in the plural sense; *-s* is not added to the name.

EXERCISES

1. Practice the pronunciation of the following country names, inhabitants, and languages.

America	l'Amérique	l'Américain(s) l'anglais
		l'Américaine(s)
Germany	l'Allemand	l'Allemande(s) l'allemand
		l'Allemande(s)
England	l'Angleterre	l'Anglais l'anglais
		l'Anglaise(s)
France	la France	le Français le français
		la Française(s)
Greece	la Grèce	le Grec(s) le grec
		la Grecque(s)
Italy	l'Italie	l'Italien(s) l'italien
		l'Italienne(s)
Austria	l'Autriche	l'Autrichien(s) l'allemand
		l'Autrichienne(s)

Russia	la Russie	le Russe(s)	le russe
		la Russe(s)	
Switzerland	la Suisse	le Suisse(s)	l'allemand
		la Suissesse(s)	
Spain	l'Espagne	l'Espagnol(s)	l'espagnol
		l'Espagnole(s)	

2. As with alphabet letters, the written symbols that represent numbers have names for spoken use in French. The cardinal numbers (a numeral that answers the question "how many?") are:

0 - zéro, rien

1 - un, une[2]

2 - deux

3 - trois

4 - quatre

5 - cinq

6 - six

7 - sept

8 - huit

9 - neuf

11 - onze

12 - douze

13 - treize

14 - quatorze

15 - quinze

16 - seize

17 - dix-sept

18 - dix-huit

19 - dix-neuf

20 - vingt

21 - vingt et un

22 - vingt-deux

30 - trente

33 - trente-trois

44 - quarante

44 - quarante-quatre

50 - cinquante

55 - cinquante-cinq

60 - soixante

66 - soixante-six

77 - soixante-dix-sept

80 - quatre-vingt

88 - quatre-vingt-huit

90 - quatre-vingt dix

99 - quatre-vingt-dix-neuf

100 - cent

105 - cent cinq

285 - deux cents quatre-vingt cinq

500 - cinq cents

1000 - mille

a) The final consonant of all numbers are pronounced when the number is followed by a word beginning with a vowel or mute *h*. The

---

[2]*une* is used before feminine nouns; the other cardinal numbers have only one form.

177

final consonants of *deux, trois, six, dix* are pronounced [z]; the *f* in *neuf* is pronounced [v].

b) The final consonants of the following cardinal numbers are pronounced when these numbers stand alone:

> cinq
> six
> sept
> huit
> neuf
> dix
> dix-huit

When used before a word beginning with a consonant sound, the final consonant of these numbers are silent. The final *t* is pronounced in *vingt-cinq, vingt-six,* etc., however.

c) The numbers 21, 31, 41, 51, and 61 use the word *et* ("and") in the expression of the word "one"; hyphens are used in number combinations that do not include the word *et*. The multiples of 100, 1000, and 1,000,000 are not hyphenated.

d) In French, decimal places are set off by a comma and thousands are shown by a period, the reverse of English.

3. The ordinal numbers (a numeral expressing the order of a number in a series) are:

1st	premier, première
2nd	second, seconde, deuxième
3rd	troisième
4th	quatrième
5th	cinquième
6th	sixième
7th	septième
8th	huitième
9th	neuvième
10th	dixième
11th	onzième
12th	douzième
13th	treizième

14th	quatorzième
15th	quinzième
16th	seizième
17th	dix-septième
18th	dix-huitième
19th	dix-neuvième
20th	vingtième
30th	trentième
40th	quarantième
50th	cinquantième
60th	soixantième
70th	soixante-dixième
80th	quatre-vingtième
90th	quatre-vingt-dixième
100th	centième

a) The word *an* ("year") is used with *cardinal numbers*: trois ans. The word *année* ("year") is used with *ordinal numbers*: la trosième année

"...mes vingt ans..."
(Fauré, "Automne")

4. Names of the days of the week:

Sunday	dimanche
Monday	lundi
Tuesday	mardi
Wednesday	mercredi
Thursday	jeudi
Friday	vendredi
Saturday	samedi

5. Names of the months of the year:

January	janvier
February	fevrier
March	mars
April	avril

179

May	mai
June	juin
July	juillet
August	août
September	septembre
October	octobre
November	novembre
December	décembre

a) *Cardinal numbers* are used for all the days of the month except the first: le 15 septembre - le quinze septembre
le 1ᵉʳjuin - le premier juin

6. Names of directions:

north	le nord
south	le sud
east	l'est
west	l'ouest

7. Names of the seasons of the year (la saison):

winter	l'hiver
spring	le printemps
summer	l'été
autumn	l'automne

8. The following are nouns frequently encountered in vocal literature.

l'absence (f.)	absence
l'aile (f.)	wing
l'air (m.)	air
l'ame (f.)	soul
l'ami (m.)	friend
l'amour (m.)	love
l'arbre (m.)	tree
l'astre (m.)	star
l'aurore (f.)	dawn
le baiser	kiss
la beauté	beauty

la bien-aimée	beloved
le blé	wheat
le bonheur	happiness
la bouche	mouth
le bras	arm
le calme	stillness, calm
la chambre	room
la chanson	song
le charme	charm
le chemin	way, road
le cheval	horse
les cheveux	hair
le ciel	heaven, sky
la clarté	light, splendor
le coeur	heart
le col	neck
le cou	neck
la couche	bed, couch
le doigt	finger
l'eau (f.)	water
l'enfant (m.,f.)	infant, child
l'épaule (f.)	shoulder
l'esprit (m.)	spirit
l'étoile (f.)	star
l'extase (f.)	ecstasy
la fenêtre	window
le feu	fire
la flamme	flame
la fleur	flower
la flûte	flute
la fontaine	fountain
le foyer	hearth
la grenouille	frog

l'haleine (f.)	breath
l'herbe (f.)	grass
l'heure (f.)	hour
l'hyacinthe (f.)	hyacinth
l'image (f.)	image
l'infidélité (f.)	infidelity
le jardin	garden
la joie	joy
la jour	day
la larme	tear
la lèvre	lip
la lumière	light
la lune	moon
la main	hand
le matin	morning
la mer	sea
la mère	mother
le monde	world
la musique	music
la nature	nature
le nid	nest
la nuit	night
la nymphe	nymph
l'odeur (f.)	odor, smell
l'oiseau (m.)	bird
l'ombre (f.)	shadow, shade
l'or (m.)	gold
la paix	peace
le parc	park
le parfum	perfume
le pays	country, land
la perle	pearl
le pied	foot, track

le plaisir	pleasure
le pleur	tear
le poisson	fish
le rayon	ray, beam
le regard	look, glance
la rencontre	meeting, encounter
le rêve	dream
le rire	laughter
le rivage	shore, beach
le roi	king
la rose	rose
la route	road, way
le sang	blood
le silence	silence
la soeur	sister
le soir	evening, night
le soleil	sun
le sommeil	sleep
le soupir	sigh, breath
le sourire	smile
le temps	time, moment
la terre	earth, land
la tête	head
le tombeau	tomb, grave
le trépas	death
la tristesse	sadness
la vapeur	vapor, mist
le vent	wind, breeze
la vie	life
la voix	voice, tone
le vol	flying, flight
les yeux	eyes

a) For each noun substitute the correct indefinite article for the definite article.

b) Form the plural of each noun.

9. Survey each song of the cycle by Gabriel Fauré entitled "Mirages".

a) List all nouns in each song; indicate the gender of each.

10. From the song repertoire by Claude Debussy

a) List the names of those songs whose title contains a noun; indicate the gender of each noun.

11. In any article from *La Revue Musicale* list all nouns and indicate the gender of each.

II. PRONOUNS

A *pronoun* is a word used in place of a noun.

A. Subject Pronouns

The following are the *subject pronouns* in French:
Singular

before consonants		*before vowels*	
je	[ʒe]	j' [ʒ]	I
tu	[ty]	[ty]	you
il	[il]	[il]	he, it
elle	[ɛl]	[ɛl]	she, it

Plural

nous	[nu]	[nuz]	we
vous	[vu]	[vuz]	you
ils	[il]	[ilz]	they (m.)
elles	[ɛl]	[ɛlz]	they (f.)

All subject pronouns except *je* (*j'*) have only one written form. *Je, nous, vous, ils,* and *elles* have two spoken forms: when followed by a word beginning with a consonant sound, the final consonant of the subject pronoun is silent; when followed by a word beginning with a vowel sound or a mute *h*, the final consonant is pronounced, and thereby linked to the vowel sound (liaison).

When a pronoun is substituted in sentence structure for the name of a person, place, or thing, it must agree in gender (masculine or feminine) and number (singular or plural) with the noun it replaces.

B. Meaning of Subject Pronouns

1. The pronoun *vous* is the polite or conventional form of the word "you", and can refer to one or more persons. It replaces the names of persons in French addressed as "Monsieur" (Mr.), "Madame" (Mrs.), or "Mademoiselle" (Miss). When addressing a person in conversational French, the pronoun *vous* is used unless it is a family member, an intimate friend, or a child, in which case the pronoun *tu* is used. The use of the *tu* form has become more common in modern French usage, especially among young people; however, the *tu* form should never he used in speaking to a French person unless it has already been used in direct address.

2. The subject pronouns *il, elle, ils,* and *elles* are used to refer to persons or things that have already been definitely identified in sentence context: *ils* refers to groups in which all or some members are masculine, *elles* is used for groups in which all members are feminine.

3. The indefinite pronoun *on* may be translated "one", "people", "we", "they", "you"; the pronoun *on* is singular and takes the third person singular of verbs.

4. The pronoun *ce* (*c'*) is sometimes used as the subject instead of *il(s)* or *elle(s)* when referring to nationality, religion, or profession.

5. Since all nouns in French have a gender, when a subject pronoun is substituted for a noun, *il* must replace a masculine noun, and *elle* must replace a feminine noun.

III. PREPOSITIONS

A *preposition* shows the grammatical relationship of a noun or pronoun to some other element in the sentence.

Forms

1. The preposition *de* (of, from)

   a) When the preposition *de* is used with a noun whose definite article is *le*, the contracted preposition form *du* is used instead of *de le*:

      L'enfance *du* Christ

La Fille *du* Régiment

Le sacre *du* printemps

b) When the preposition *de* is used with a noun whose definite article is *la*, the form *de la* is used:

Gaspard *de la* nuit

Le spectre *de la* rose

c) When the preposition *de* is used with a noun whose definite article is *l'*, the form *de l'* is used:

Traité *de l'* harmonie

d) When the preposition *de* is used with a noun whose definite article is *les*, the contracted preposition form *des* is used:

Les Dialogues *des* Carmélites

L'Isle *des* foux

e) The preposition *de* (*d'* before a vowel sound) is used to indicate possession in French when *de* (*d'*) is followed by the name of the possessor without a definite article:

le jeu de cartes

clair de lune

Les contes d'Hoffmann

l'oiseau de feu

poème d'extase

le tombeau de Couperin

2. The preposition *à* (to, at, in)

a) When the preposition *à* is used with a noun whose definite article is *le*, the contracted preposition form *au* is used instead of *à le*:

Elisa ou le voyage *au* Mont-Bernard

L'invitation *au* voyage

Au cimitière

b) When the preposition *à* is used with a noun whose definite article is *là*, the form *à la* is used:

"...elle à la mer..."

(Debussy, "Beau Soir")

(1) When the preposition *à* is used with a noun whose definite article is *l'*, the form *à la* is used.

c) When the preposition *à* is used with a noun whose definite article is *les,* the form *aux* is used:

> Orphée *aux* enfers

MUSICAL EXERCISES

1. Identify each of the following:

> Académie de Poésie et de Musique
> Les adieux, l'absence, et le retour
> L'Après-midi d'un faune
> L'art de toucher le clavecin
> Le carnaval des animaux
> Guerre des bouffons
> L'histoire du soldat
> Livre d'airs de cour
> Les Six

2. Define the following terms, all of which are nouns:

allemande	bergerette	étude	ouverture
antienne	bouffons	humoresque	passepied
arabesque	bourdon	impromptu	pastourelle
ariette	chanson	légende	potpourri
aubade	chansonnier	livret	rondeau
bagatelle	clavecin	ménestrandise	soubrette
ballade	courante	musette	virelai

3. Define historically *troubadour* and *trouvère*; *jongleur*.

4. Compare and contrast the terms *mélodie* and *chanson*.

5. Define historically the term *fauxbourdon*.

6. Define historically

> a) Guerre des bouffons
> b) Traité de l'harmonie (Rameau)

7. Describe the *Chevé System*.

8. Identify the following compositions, including composer, form, and style:

L'Arlésienne

Les béatitudes

Clair de lune

Les contes d'Hoffmann

Daphnis et Chloé

L'enfance du Christ

La fille du régiment

Gaspard de la nuit

Images

Le jeu de cartes

La mer

Miroirs

l'oiseau de feu

Poème d'extase

Le sacre du printemps

Le tombeau de Couperin

Chapter Three

I. VERBS

The following study of verbs demonstrates how the theory of noun construction (noun genders, plurals, and article forms) is transformed into practical knowledge, especially as it relates to text translation.

A *verb* is that part of speech which expresses an action or state of being. French verbs appear to be complicated because of the number of different forms and the seemingly complex word order in sentence structure; it is therefore desirable to reduce the study of verbs to its simplest and most practical form in order to facilitate translation, comprehension, and conversation.

A. Terminology

The terminology used in reference to verbs should be defined before actually beginning with French verbs; although other terms will be subsequently defined, an understanding of these terms is essential:

1. Tense is the form of the verb showing the time of an action or of a state or condition. The two forms of tense are:

    a) *Simple*-verb form that requires no auxiliary verb to express the time

    b) *Compound*-verb form that requires an auxiliary verb to express the time

2. *Conjugation*-the inflections or changes of form in verbs showing:

    a) *Tense* -(simple or compound)

    b) *Mood* - the form of the verb showing the speaker's attitude toward what he says (indicative, subjunctive, conditional).

        (1) *Attitudes* - ability, permission, compulsion, desire, obligation

    c) *Voice* - the form of the verb indicating whether the subject acts (Active Voice) or is acted upon (Passive Voice)

    d) *Person*

    e) *Number* - the form of a verb indicating one (singular) or more than one (plural)

3. *Auxiliary verb* - a verb which helps in the conjugation of another verb

4. *Principle parts* - verb forms from which tenses are formed

a) *Infinitive* - the verb form which expresses general meaning without the distinction of grammatical person or number:

chanter - to sing

b) *Present participle* - the verb form ending in *-ant* equivalent to the verb form in English ending in *-ing:* chant*ant* - singing

c) *Past participle* - the verb form used as part of a compound tense. The word *compound* implies more than one part; a compound verb structure requires some form of an auxiliary verb plus the past participle of the verb.

It is desirable to learn the principle parts of French verbs because they are the basis of verb structure; it is practical for this study to be able to recognize verb forms in texts.

B. Categories of Verbs

Before explaining French verb tenses, it should be noted that certain large groups of verbs are conjugated in the same way. The two categories of verbs in French are:

1. *Regular verbs* - Verbs that follow the pattern of a particular conjugation group are regular verbs; all forms of regular verbs can be derived from certain key verb forms.

a) The following are verbs that refer specifically to music:

chanter - to sing

jouer - to play

sonner - to sound

The *infinitive* of the foregoing French verbs ends in *-er*. In order to conjugate verbs, that is, assign person and number, a common denominator derived from the verb infinitive known as the *verb stem* is necessary. The verb stem of the group of French verbs known as *regular "-er"* verbs is obtained by dropping the final *-er* of the infinitive. This is by far the largest group of French verbs. Regular verbs ending in *-ier* (étudier - to study) are conjugated like *regular "-er" verbs*.

chanter (chant-) - to sing

jouer (jou-) - to play

étudier (étud-) - to study

190

In conjugating verbs in French (assigning person and number) it is necessary to add an ending to the verb stem. In the *present tense* only the third person singular form in English has an ending; in French, the verb has an ending for *each* person in the present tense. The following endings are added to the verb stem to form the present tense of *regular "-er" verbs* in French:

chanter - to sing

Singular			Plural		
je chante		I sing	nous chantons		we sing
tu chantes	you	sing	vous chantez		you sing
il chante	he	sings	ils chantent		they sing
elle chante	she	sings	elles chantent		they sing

jouer - to play

je joue			nous jouons	
tu joues			vous jouez	
il joue			ils jouent	
elle joue			elles jouent	

There are five written forms, then of *regular "-er" verbs* in the present tense. Note that the following verb forms are all pronounced alike; the ending of each is silent:

je chante

tu chantes

il (elle) chante

ils (elles) chantent

b) Depending on the context, the present tense in French may be equivalent in English to:

(1) the simple verb form: je chante - I sing (all the time, as a habit)

(2) the progressive form: je chante - I am singing (right now)

c) The second group of regular French verbs are those know as *regular "-ir" verbs*; relatively few common verbs belong to this group. The verb stem of *regular "-ir" verbs* is obtained by dropping the final *-ir* of the infinitive. The following endings are added to the verb stem to form the present tense of *regular "-ir" verbs* in French:

applaudir - to applaude

Singular		*Plural*	
je applaud*is*	I applaude	nous applaud*issons*	we applaude
tu applaud*is*	you applaude	vous applaud*issez*	you applaude
il applaud*it*	he applaudes	ils applaud*issent*	they applaude
elle applaud*it*	she applaudes	elles applaud*issent*	they applaude

There are five written forms, then, of *regular "-ir" verbs* in the present tense. Note that there are four spoken forms for the present tense of verbs in this category: whereas the endings of the singular forms are all silent, the final [s] of the third person plural (ils, elles) is pronounced, thus distinguishing this form from the singular.

   d) The third group of regular French verbs are those known as *regular "-re" verbs*; relatively few common verbs belong to this group. The verb stem of *regular "-re" verbs* is obtained by dropping the final *-re* of the infinitive. The following endings are added to the verb stem to form the present tense of *regular "-re"* verbs in French:

entendre - to hear

Singular		*Plural*	
j'entend*s*	I hear	nous entend*ons*	we hear
tu entend*s*	you hear	vous entend*ez*	you hear
il entend	he hears	ils entend*ent*	they hear
elle entend	she hears	elles entend*ent*	they hear

There are five written forms, then, of *regular " -re" verbs* in the present tense. Note that there are four spoken forms for the present tense of verbs in this category. The final [d] of the third person plural (ils, elles) form is pronounced, thus distinguishing this form from the singular.

   2. *Irregular verbs* - those verbs which are dissimilar to other groups of verbs and which do not follow an established pattern of conjugation are known as *irregular verbs*.

   a) Almost all irregular verbs have the endings -*s, -s, -t, -ons, -ez, -ent* in the present tense; a few verbs have the singular endings -*e, -es, -e* in the present tense.

   b) Irregular verbs may have two spellings of the verb stem, one for the first and second persons plural, another for the other persons.

192

écrire - to write

Singular		*Plural*	
j'écris	I write	nous écrivons	we write
tu écris	you write	vous écrivez	you write
il écrit	he writes	ils écrivent	they write
elle écrit	she writes	elles écrivent	they write

aller - to go

je vais	nous allons
tu vas	vous allez
il va	ils vont
elle va	elles vont

envoyer - to send

j'envoie	nous envoyons
tu envoies	vous envoyez
il envoie	ils envoient
elle envoie	elles envoient

c) Three groups of *irregular verbs* end in *-ir:*

(1) Those which have two stems in the present tense and which are irregular only in the present tense:

	Stems
dormir- to sleep	dor-, dorm-
partir- to leave	par-, part-
sentir- to smell	sen-, sent-
servir- to serve	ser-, serv-
sortir- to go out	sor-, sort-

The *past participle* of these irregular verbs ends in *-i*:

dormi

parti

senti

servi

sorti

" ...je dors!"
(Ravel, "À son âme")

(2) Those which have two stems in the present tense, an irregular future tense, and a past participle which ends in *-u*.

tenir (tenu) - to hold up, keep

venir (venu) - to come

Singular	*Plural*
je viens	nous venons
tu viens	vous venez
il vient	ils viennent
elle vient	elles viennent

(3) Those which have a past participle that ends in *-ert*. The endings in the singular forms of the present tense of these irregular verbs are *-e, -es, -e.*

	past participle
couvrir - to cover	couvert
ouvrir - to open	ouvert
offrir - to offer	offert
souffrir - to suffer	souffert

d) Two groups of irregular verbs end in *-re*:

(1) Those which have two stems in the present tense and a past participle which ends in *-u*:

boire - to drink	bu
connaître - to know	connu
croire - to believe	cru
lire - to read	lu

(2) Those which have two stems in the present tense and have a past participle which ends in *-i, -is,* or *-it.*

mettre - to put (met-, mett-) mis

e) Two important irregular verbs in French are:

être - to be

avoir - to have

Besides being independent verbs, these two verbs are the auxiliary verbs in French; one is always present in the conjugation of verbs in compound tenses. These two verbs are conjugated in the present tense:

être - to be

Singular		*Plural*	
je suis	I am	nous sommes	we are
tu es	you are	vous êtes	you are
il est	he is	ils sont	they are
elle est	she is	elles sont	they are

avoir - to have

j'ai	I have	nous avons	we have
tu as	you have	vous avez	you have
il a	he has	ils ont	they have
elle a	she has	elles ont	they have

f) Since the spelling changes in the stems of irregular verbs follow no regular pattern, the various forms, especially for the purpose of conversation, should be systematically learned. For translation it is necessary to identify verbs as regular or irregular, indicated by the stem spelling and/or the past participle ending.

C. Imperative

The *imperative* is the mood of a verb expressing a command. Direct commands may be given to persons addressed as *tu, nous*, and *vous*. The command, or imperative form of verbs is the same form as the *tu, nous,* and *vous* forms of the present tense without the subject pronoun. The imperative forms of *être* and *avoir* are irregular:

être	avoir
sois	aie
soyons	ayons
soyez	ayez

"...*prends* un chevel...*pars, et suis* mon chemin..."
(Duparc, "Le manoir de Rosemonde")

"...*reviens*, ô nuit mystérieuse!"
(Fauré , "Après un rêve")

"...*rêvons*, c'est l'heure."
(Fauré, *La Bonne Chanson* - 3)

"...*laissez-* là, s'apaiser..."
(Debussy, "Green")

Some musical terms which give a command are:

cédez - slow down

mettez - draw (an organ stop)

pressez - press, hurry

remettez - take off (an organ stop)

D. Compound Past Tense

The *compound past tense*, or *passé composé*, is composed of the present tense of the appropriate auxiliary verb (avoir or être) plus the past participle of the verb. The compound past tense in French is used to express an event completed in the past or a condition that existed in the past, and corresponds in meaning to the present perfect tense and the simple past tense in English.

1. The compound past tense of most French verbs consists of the present tense of the auxiliary verb *avoir* and the past participle of the verb; most French verbs that take *avoir* as the auxiliary verb are *transitive* (active) verbs, that is, they can take a direct object. The verb *être* is used as the auxiliary verb in compound tenses of *intransitive* (passive) verbs, that is, verbs expressing an action, change of position, or state of being which do not require a direct object. In order to determine whether a verb is transitive or intransitive, the question "who or what does the action of the verb affect?" should be asked. If the question can be answered, the verb is transitive, or the action is performed upon the direct object; if the question can not be answered, the verb is intransitive or passive. Determining whether a verb is transitive or intransitive simplifies forming compound tenses; most transitive verbs take *avoir* as the auxiliary verb, most intransitive verbs take *être* as the auxiliary verb.

2. The past participle of regular verbs is formed:

a) For *regular "-er" verbs*: by adding *-é* to the stem of the verb:

chanter - to sing

j' ai chanté		nous avons	chanté
tu as chanté		vous avez	chanté
il a chanté		ils ont	chanté
elle a chanté		elles ont	chanté

b) For *regular "-ir" verbs*: by adding *-i* to the stem of the verb:

applaudir - to applaude

j' ai applaudi	nous avons	applaudi
tu a applaudi	vous avez	applaudi
il a applaudi	ils ont	applaudi
elle a applaudi	elles ont	applaudi

c) For *regular "-re" verbs*: by adding *-u* to the stem of the verb:

entendre - to hear

j' ai entendu	nous avons	entendu
tu a entendu	vous avez	entendu
il a entendu	ils ont	entendu
elle a entendu	elles ont	entendu

3. The past participle of irregular verbs are formed according to the patterns discussed on pp. 192-194.

4. The auxiliary verbs are conjugated in the compound past tense:

être

j' ai été	nous avons	été
tu a été	vous avez	été
il a été	ils ont	été
elle a été	elles ont	été

avoir

j' ai eu	nous avons	eu
tu as eu	vous avez	eu
il a eu	ils ont	eu
elle a eu	elles ont	eu

5. When *être* is used as the auxiliary verb in a compound tense, the past participle must agree in gender and number with the subject:

arriver

je suis	arrivée (f.)
il est	arrivé
elle est	arrivée
ils sont	arrivés
elles sont	arrivées

6. The study of structure is the obvious tool of translation; the following guidelines for efficient translation should be cultivated:

    a) Determine the subject of the sentence: who or what performs the action expressed by the verb, or on whom the action is performed, in the case of intransitive verbs.

    b) Determine the verb meaning by dissecting the form. When one of the verbs that can be used as an auxiliary verb is encountered, this should immediately indicate the possibility of a compound verb structure; the past participle is distinguished in French by its ending. Having determined the verb meaning from the past participle, it should be possible to translate the tense of the verb form. It is of primary importance in translating to develop the practice of first determining the verb meaning and tense.

    c) Determine the direct object and/or the indirect object.

E. Reflexive Verbs

A *reflexive verb* is a verb whose subject reflects or reacts upon itself; its object is always a pronoun corresponding to the subject. In reflexive verb construction, a *reflexive pronoun* is placed before the verb. The reflexive pronouns in French used accordingly are:

je - me	myself
tu - te	yourself
il, elle - se	himself, herself, itself
nous - nous	ourselves
vous - vous	yourself, yourselves
ils, elles - se	themselves

The pronouns *me*, *te*, and *se* are contracted to *m'*, *t'*, and *s'* before words beginning with a vowel sound. The reflexive pronoun must agree in gender and number with its corresponding subject. Among the most frequently encountered reflexive verbs in French are:

s'appeler	to be named
s'arrêter	to stop
se coucher	to go to bed
se débrouiller	to get along
se demander	to wonder
s'habiller	to get dressed

se lever	to get up
se reposer	to rest
se réveiller	to wake up
se retrouver	to meet each other
se trouver	to be located

1. Reflexive verbs are conjugated according to the type of verb (regular or irregular); the verb endings agree in gender and number with the subject and reflexive pronoun.

2. All reflexive verbs in French are conjugated with the auxiliary verb *être*; accordingly, the past participle of all compound tenses must agree in gender and number with the subject.

3. The imperative of reflexive verbs is formed regularly according to the type of verb; the reflexive pronoun is hyphenated to the inflected verb form in a command.

se laver - to wash oneself

Present tense

Singular			*Plural*		
je me	lave		nous	nous	lavons
tu te	laves		vous	vous	lavez
il se	lave		ils	se	lavent
elle se	lave		elles	se	lavent

Compound past tense

Singular			*Plural*		
je me suis	lavé		nous	nous	sommes lavé(e)s
tu t'es	lavé(e)		vous	vous	êtes lavé(e)(s)(es)
il s'est	lavé		ils	se	sont lavés
elle s'est	lavée		elles	se	sont lavées
on s'est	lavé				

"...le mond *s'endort*..."
(Duparc, "l'Invitation au Voyage")

"...ton extase *s'éveille*..."
(Fauré, "Rencontre")

"...que mon âme *s'arrache* et *se dépouille...*"
(Fauré, "Toujours")

"...nos bouches *s'unissent...*"
(Debussy, "La Flûte")

"...des jardins de la nuit *s'envolent* les étoiles..."
(Fauré, "Aurore")

F. Irregular Verb Spellings

The following irregularities in verb spellings should be noted:

1. Verbs that are regular in the present tense except for a slight variation in the stem spelling:

    a) The stem vowel of the following verbs is written *è* in the first, second, and third persons singular and the third person plural forms in the present tense. The stem vowel is changed to *è* in all persons of the future tense and in the conditional mood (Chapter Seven).

acheter	- to buy
crever	- to burst, crack
élever	- to raise
lever	- to raise
se lever	- to get up
mener	- to lead
se promener	- to take a walk

acheter - to buy

Singular	*Plural*
j' achète	nous achetons
tu achètes	vous achetez
il achète	ils achètent
elle achète	elles achètent

    b) In the following verbs, the final *l* or *t* of the stem is doubled in the first, second and third person singular and the third person plural form in the present tense. The final *l* or *t* is doubled in all persons of the future tense and in the conditional mood.

appeler	- to call
s'appeler	- to be named

jeter - to throw

projeter - to project

rappeler - to call back

se rappeler - to remember

s'appeler - to be named

Singular	*Plural*
je m'appe*lle*	nous nous appe*l*ons
tu t'appe*lles*	vous vous appe*l*ez
il s'appe*lle*	ils s'appe*ll*ent
elle s'appe*lle*	elles s'appe*ll*ent

c) In the following verbs the stem vowel *é* is written *è* and pronounced [ɛ] in the first, second, and third person singular and the third person plural form of the present tense, and in the present tense of the subjunctive mood (Chapter Seven). The stem vowel *é* remains unchanged in all other tenses.

célébrer - to celebrate

compléter - to complete

considérer - to consider

espérer - to hope

pénétrer - to penetrate

posséder - to possess

précéder - to precede

préférer - to prefer

régler - to regulate

regner - to reign

répéter - to repeat

suggérer - to suggest

préférer - to prefer

Singular	*Plural*
je préfère	nous préférons
tu préfères	vous préférez
il préfères	ils préfèrent
elle préfère	elles préfèrent

d) In the following verbs the final *c* of the stem is written ç whenever it is followed by an *a* or *o* in conjugation.

annoncer - to announce

avancer - to put forth

commencer - to begin

se fiancer - to become engaged

forcer - to force

influencer - to influence

lancer - to throw

menacer - to threaten

placer - to place, put

prononcer - to pronounce

recommencer - to begin again

remplacer - to take the place of

tracer - to trace

commencer - to begin

Singular	*Plural*
je commence	nous commençons
tu commences	vous commencez
il commence	ils commencent
elle commence	elles commencent

e) In the following verbs *ge* is substituted for *g* when followed by the vowel *a* or *o* in conjugation:

aménager - to arrange

changer - to change

diriger - to direct

encourager - to encourage

s'engager - to engage oneself

juger - to judge

manger - to eat

mélanger - to mix

nager - to swim

négliger - to neglect

neiger - to snow

voyager - to travel

manger - to eat

Singular	*Plural*
je mange	nous man*geons*
tu manges	vous mangez
il mange	ils mangent
elle mange	elles mangent

f) In verbs ending in *-oyer* and *-uyer*, *i* is substituted for *y* when the following verb ending is a silent *-e*.

appuyer - to hold up

employer - to use

ennuyer - to bother, annoy

employer - to use

j'empl*oie*	nous employons
tu empl*oies*	vous employez
il empl*oie*	ils empl*oient*
elle empl*oie*	elles empl*oient*

g) In verbs ending in *-ayer*, *y* may be retained in every person and tense, or *i* may be substituted for *y* when the verb ending is a silent *-e*.

essayer - to try

payer - to pay

j'essaie	j' essaye	nous essayons	
tu essaies	tu essayes	vous essayez	
il essaie	il essaye	ils essaient	ils essayent
elle essaie	elle essaye	elles essaient	elles essayent

II. INDICATIVE MOOD

There are seven tenses in the *indicative mood* (the mood of a verb expressing a fact) in French:

A. Present Tense

B. Compound Past Tense (passé composé)

C. Simple Past Tense (passé simple)

The names *passé composé* (compound past) and *passé simple* (simple, absolute, or literary past) are used to distinguish two tenses which generally have the same meaning; both tenses are used to express simple past actions. The compound past tense in French is most frequently used in conversation; the *simple past tense* is used almost exclusively in literary narrative style. This is especially important for translation. It is advisable that the musician interested in French translation become familiar with the simple past tense form, which is otherwise of relatively minor importance. The simple past tense is formed according to the following pattern:

1. The stem for the simple past tense of regular verbs is obtained by dropping the *-er, -ir,* and *-re* of the infinitive; the following endings are added to the verb stem to form the simple past tense:

a) Regular "-er" verbs

chanter - to sing

Singular	Plural
je chant*ai*	nous chant*âmes*
tu chant*as*	vous chant*âtes*
il chant*a*	ils chant*èrent*
elle chant*a*	elles chant*èrent*

b) Regular "-ir" and "-re" verbs

applaudir - to applaude

j' applaud*is*	nous applaud*îmes*
tu applaud*is*	vous applaud*îtes*
il applaud*it*	ils applaud*irent*
elle applaud*it*	elles applaudirent

entendre - to hear

j'entend*is*	nous entend*îmes*
tu entend*is*	vous entend*îtes*
il entend*it*	ils entend*irent*
elle entend*it*	elles entend*irent*

2. The stem for the simple past tense of most irregular verbs is the past participle, to which the following endings are added:

avoir - to have

j'eu*s*	nous eû*mes*
tu eu*s*	vous eû*tes*
il eu*t*	ils eu*rent*
elle eu*t*	elles eu*rent*

EXCEPTION

être - to be

je fus	nous fûmes
tu fus	vous fûtes
il fut	ils furent
elle fut	elles furent

D. Imperfect Tense

The *imperfect tense* in French generally expresses habitual actions in the past, a state of affairs in the past, or continuous past action. The imperfect tense is used to tell what used to be done, what was done in the past, or the way things were in the past, and is formed using the stem of the first person plural form of the present tense:

nous chantons	chant-
nous applaudissons	applaudiss-
nous entendons	entend-

The following endings are added to the stem to form the imperfect tense:

chanter	applaudir	entendre
je chant*ais*	je applaudiss*ais*	j'entend*ais*
tu chant*ais*	tu applaudiss*ais*	tu entend*ais*
il chant*ait*	il applaudiss*ait*	il entend*ait*
elle chant*ait*	elle applaudiss*ait*	elle entend*ait*

nous chant*ions*	nous applaudiss*ions*	nous entend*ions*
vous chant*iez*	vous applaudiss*iez*	vous entend*iez*
ils chant*aient*	ils applaudiss*aient*	ils entend*aient*
elles chant*aient*	elles applaudiss*aient*	elles entend*aient*

"...je *rêvais*,...tu *rayonnais*...et je *quittais*..."
(Fauré, "Après un rêve")

avoir	*EXCEPTION*: être
j' av*ais*	j' étais
tu av*ais*	tu étais
il av*ait*	il était
elle av*ait*	elle était
nous av*ions*	nous étions
vous av*iez*	vous étiez
ils av*aient*	ils étaient
elles av*aient*	elles étaient

There are three spoken forms for all verbs in the imperfect tense; the first, second, and third person singular and the third person plural forms of the imperfect tense are pronounced alike, except when liason occurs.

    1. The imperfect tense is used most often:

        a) to describe an habitual action in the past

        b) to describe what was going on when an action took place

        c) to describe a situation that existed in the past

        d) to describe one's impression, feeling, or appearance in the past.

E. Future Tense

The *future tense* in French is used to donote futurity. The following endings are added to the infinitive to form the future tense in French:

chanter	applaudir	entendre[1]
je chanter*ai*	je applaudir*ai*	j' entendr*ai*
tu chanter*as*	tu applaudir*as*	tu entendr*as*
il chanter*a*	il applaudir*a*	il entendr*a*

---

[1]The *-e* of infinitives ending in "-re" is dropped before the future tense endings are added.

elle chanter*a*	elle applaudir*a*	elle entendr*a*
nous chanter*ons*	nous applaudir*ons*	nous entendr*ons*
vous chanter*ez*	vous applaudir*ez*	vous entendr*ez*
ils chanter*ont*	ils applaudir*ont*	ils entendr*ont*
elles chanter*ont*	elles applaudir*ont*	elles entendr*ont*

"...je me *noierai* dans ta clarté..."
(Duparc, "Chanson triste")

The future tense of *être* and *avoir* is irregular:

avoir		être	
j' aur*ai*		je ser*ai*	
tu aur*as*		tu ser*as*	
il aur*a*		il ser*a*	
elle aur*a*		elle ser*a*	
nous aur*ons*		nous ser*ons*	
vous aur*ez*		vous ser*ez*	
ils aur*ont*		ils ser*ont*	
elles aur*ont*		elles ser*ont*	

1. Other verbs also form the future tense using irregular stems; in translating, the letter *r* before a future ending should indicate the future tense.

F. Future Perfect Tense

The *future perfect tense* (futur antérieur) is used to express an action that will take place in the future before another future action takes place. When the future perfect tense is used in a clause in sentence structure, the verb in the other clause is always in the future tense. The future perfect tense consists of the future tense of the auxiliary verb *avoir* or *être* and the past participle of the finite verb.

chanter

j' aurai	chanté	I	will have sung
tu auras	chanté	you	will have sung
il aura	chanté	he	will have sung
elle aura	chanté	she	will have sung
nous aurons	chanté	we	will have sung

vous aurez	chanté		you	will have sung
ils auront	chanté		they	will have sung
elles auront	chanté		they	will have sung

applaudir			entendre	
j' aurai	applaudi	j'	aurai	entendu
tu auras	applaudi	tu	auras	entendu
il aura	applaudi	il	aura	entendu
elle aura	applaudi	elle	aura	entendu
nous aurons	applaudi	nous	aurons	entendu
vous aurez	applaudi	vous	aurez	entendu
ils auront	applaudi	ils	auront	entendu
elles auront	applaudi	elles	entendu	auront

avoir			être	
j' aurai	eu	j'	aurai	été
tu auras	eu	tu	auras	été
il aura	eu	il	aura	été
elle aura	eu	elle	aura	été
nous aurons	eu	nous	aurons	été
vous aurez	eu	vous	aurez	été
ils auront	eu	ils	auront	été
elles auront	eu	elles	auront	été

G. Pluperfect Tense

The *pluperfect tense* expresses an action that had already taken place when another past action took place. The pluperfect tense consists of the imperfect tense of the auxiliary verb *avoir* or *être* and the past participle of the finite verb.

chanter			
j' avais	chanté	I	had sung (when they finally arrived)
tu avais	chanté	you	had sung
il avait	chanté	he	had sung
elle avait	chanté	she	had sung
nous avions	chanté	we	had sung

vous aviez	chanté	you	had sung
ils avaient	chanté	they	had sung
elles avaient	chanté	they	had sung

	applaudir			entendre	
j' avais	applaudi		j'	avais	entendu
tu avais	applaudi		tu	avais	entendu
il avait	applaudi		il	avait	entendu
elle avait	applaudi		elle	avait	entendu
nous avions	applaudi		nous	avions	entendu
vous aviez	applaudi		vous	aviez	entendu
ils avaient	applaudi		ils	avaient	entendu
elles avaient	applaudi		elles	avaient	entendu

	avoir			être	
j' avais	eu		j'	avais	été
tu avais	eu		tu	avais	été
il avait	eu		il	avait	été
elle avait	eu		elle	avait	été
nous avions	eu		nous	avions	été
vous aviez	eu		vous	aviez	été
ils avaient	eu		ils	avaient	été
elles avaient	eu		elles	avaient	été

III. PREFIXES

Two additional points should be made before examining a large number of verbs:

A. Forms

A number of French verbs begin with a prefix that is attached to a simple verb; such verbs are conjugated like the root verb without the prefix. In the listing of verbs that follow, when a new verb originates from a basic verb, the basic verb within the new verb is underlined. Although the prefix generally does not suggest the meaning of the new verb, the following may assist in translating verbs to which a prefix has been added:

1. The prefix *de-* generally has a negative connotation, approximately equivalent to the English prefix *un-*.

décevoir - to deceive (be *un*true to)

découvrir - to *un*cover

défaire - to *un*do

démentir - to deny

2. The prefix *dis-* is often equivalent to the prefix *dis-* in English:

discourir - to discourse

discuter - to discuss

disparaître - to disappear

distinguer - to distinguish

3. The prefix *pré-* is often equivalent to the prefix *pre-* in English:

prédire - to predict

préférer - to prefer

préparer - to prepare

prévenir - to precede

4. The prefix *re-* generally indicates a repetition of an action:

commencer - to begin   recommencer - to begin again

construire - to build   reconstruire - to rebuild

venir - to come   revenir - to come back

B. Translation Principles

An important principle in translating verb meanings is that many French verbs have English cognates, that is, counterparts that sound and/or are spelled alike. It is an asset to efficient translation to recognize the basic verb and rely on the knowledge of the basic verb form for correct grammatical structure.

IV. SUMMARY

A. Categories of Verbs

All verbs in French are either

1. Regular
2. Irregular

Regular and irregular verbs are either

1. Transitive - take a direct object
2. Intransitive - do not take a direct object

B. Auxiliary Verbs

All verbs in French have an auxiliary verb.

1. All reflexive verbs take the auxiliary verb *être.*

C. Stem Spelling

Some irregular verbs have two stems in conjugation.

1. Some regular verbs have a slight variation in the stem spelling.

D. Indicative Mood

There are seven tenses in French in the *Indicative Mood* (the mood of a verb expressing a fact):

1. Present tense
2. Compound past tense
3. Simple (literary) past tense
4. Imperfect tense
5. Future tense
6. Future perfect tense
7. Pluperfect tense

E. Tenses

The seven tenses are formed:

1. Present tense = verb stem plus endings
2. Simple past tense = verb stem plus endings
3. Imperfect tense = nous chant-(ons) plus endings
4. Future tense - infinitive plus endings
5. Compound past tense = present tense of auxiliary verb plus past participle
6. Future perfect tense = future tense of auxiliary verb plus past participle
7. Pluperfect tense = imperfect tense of auxiliary verb plus past participle

PRINCIPLE PARTS OF REGULAR AND IRREGULAR VERBS

R = Regular
I = Irregular
a = avoir: auxiliary
e = être: auxiliary

infinitive	*first person present tense*	*past participle*	
abandonner		abandonné	(a-R) to abandon
ab*attre*			(a-I) to throw down
abriter		abrité	(a-R) to shelter
abs*traire*			(a-I) to isolate
accepter		accepté	(a-R) to accept
accompagner		accompagné	(a-R) to accompany
ac*courir*			(e-I) to run up to
ac*cueillir*			(a-I) to welcome
accuser		accusé	(a-R) to accuse
acheter		acheté	(a-R) to buy
acquérir	j'acquiers nous acquerons	acquis	(a-I) to acquire
ad*mettre*			(a-I) to admit
admirer		admiré	(a-R) to admire
adopter		adopté	(a-R) to adopt
adorer		adoré	(a-R) to adore
affirmer		affirmé	(a-R) to affirm
agir		agi	(e-R) to act
agrandir		agrandi	(a-R) to enlarge
aider		aidé	(a-R) to aid, help
aimer		aimé	(a-R) to like, love
ajouter		ajouté	(a-R) to add
aller	je vais nous allons	allé	(e-I) to go
allumer		allumé	(a-R) to light
amener	j'amène nous amenons	amené	(a-I) to bring, lead

212

amuser		amusé	(a-R) to amuse
ancrer		ancré	(e-R) to anchor
annoncer		annoncé	(a-R) to announce
apercevoir	j'aperçois	aperçu	(a-I) to perceive
	nous apercevons		
apparaître		apparu	(e-I) to appear
appartenir	j'appartiens	appartenu	(e-I) to belong
	nous appartenons		
appeler	j'appelle	appelé	(a-I) to call
	nous appelons		
applaudir		applaudi	(a-R) to applaude
appliquer		appliqué	(a-R) to apply
apporter		apporté	(a-R) to bring
ap*prendre*			(a-I) to learn
appuyer		appuyé	(a-I) to press, push
arrêter		arrêté	(a-R) to stop
arriver		arrivé	(e-R) to arrive
assaillir	j'assaille	assailli	(a-I) to assault
	nous assaillons		
assister		assisté	(e-R) to attend
astreindre	j'astreins	astreint	(a-I) to oblige
	nous astreignons		
attaquer		attaqué	(a-R) to attack
atteindre	j'atteins	atteint	(a-I) to attain
	nous atteignons		
attendre		attendu	(a-R) to wait (for)
attirer		attiré	(a-R) to attract
attraper		attrapé	(a-R) to catch
avancer		avancé	(a-R) to put forth
avoir	j'ai	eu	(a-I) to have
	nous avons		
avouer		avoué	(a-R) to confess
battre	je bats	battu	(a-I) to beat
	nous battons		
blesser		blessé	(a-R) to wound

213

boire	je bois nous buvons	bu	(a-I) to drink
bouillir	je bous nous bouillons	bouilli	(e-I) to boil
briller		brillé	(e-R) to shine
brosser		brossé	(a-R) to brush
brûler		brûlé	(a-R) to burn
capter		capté	(a-R) to capture
causer		causé	(a-R) to cause
célébrer		célébré	(a-R) to celebrate
centraliser		centralisé	(a-R) to centralize
changer		changé	(a-R) to change
chanter		chanté	(a-R) to sing
chercher		cherché	(a-R) to look for
circuler		circulé	(e-R) to circulate
com*battre*			(a-I) to combat
commander		commandé	(a-R) to order-things
commencer		commencé	(a-R) to begin
com*mettre*			(a-I) to commit
comparer		comparé	(a-R) to compare
compléter		complété	(a-R) to complete
composer		composé	(a-R) to compose
com*prendre*			(a-I) to understand
compro*mettre*			(a-I) to compromise
compter		compté	(a-R) to count
conclure	je conclus nous concluons	conclu	(a-I) to conclude
condamner		condamné	(a-R) to condemn
conduire	je conduis nous conduisons	conduit	(a-I) to drive
conjuguer		conjugué	(a-R) to conjugate
connaître	je connais nous connaissons	connu	(a-I) to know

conquérir	je conquérs nous conquérons	conquis	(a-I)	to conquer
con*sentir*			(e-I)	to consent
conserver		conservé	(a-R)	to conserve
considérer	je considère nous considérons	considéré	(a-I)	to consider
consister		consisté	(e-R)	to consist
consterner		consterné	(a-R)	to dismay
construire	je construis nous construisons	construit	(a-I)	to build
consulter		consulté	(a-R)	to consult
contempler		contemplé	(a-R)	to contemplate
con*tenir*			(a-I)	to contain
continuer		continué	(a-R)	to continue
contraindre	je contrains nous contraignons	contraint	(a-I)	to constrain
contre*dire*			(a-I)	to contradict
contre*faire*			(a-I)	to imitate
con*vaincre*			(a-I)	to convince
con*venir*			(e-I)	to agree
convertir		converti	(a-R)	to convert
copier		copié	(a-R)	to copy
coudre	je couds nous cousons	cousu	(a-I)	to sew
courir	je cours nous courons	couru	(e-I)	to run
coûter		coûté	(e-R)	to cost
couvrir	je couvre nous couvrons	couvert	(a-1)	to cover
craindre	je crains nous craignons	craint	(a-1)	to fear
critiquer		critiqué	(a-R)	to criticize
croire	je crois nous croyons	cru	(a-I)	to believe

croître	je croîs	crû	(e-I) to grow
	nous croissons		
cueillir	je cueille	cueilli	(a-I) to pick
	nous cueillons		
cultiver		cultivé	(a-R) to cultivate
dater		daté	(a-R) to date
débarquer		débarqué	(a-R) to land
décevoir	je déçois	deçu	(a-1) to deceive
	nous décevons		
décider		décidé	(a-R) to decide
dé*couvrir*			(a-1) to uncover
dé*crire*			(a-I) to describe
déduire	je déduis	déduit	(a-1) to deduce
	nous déduisons		
dé*faire*			(a-I) to undo
défendre		défendu	(a-R) to defend
définir		défini	(a-R) to define
déjeuner		déjeuné	(e-R) to breakfast
délivrer		délivré	(a-R) to deliver
demander		demandé	(a-R) to ask, demand
dé*mentir*			(a-I) to deny
demeurer		demeuré	(e-R) to live, dwell
dépasser		dépassé	(a-R) to pass
de*plaire*			(e-I) to displease
déplorer		déploré	(a-R) to deplore
dériver		dérivé	(a-R) to derive
descendre		descendu	(a-R) to go down
désirer		désiré	(a-R) to want
dessiner		dessiné	(a-R) to draw
dé*tenir*			(a-1) to detain
détruire	je détruis	détruit	(a-1) to destroy
	nous détruisons		
dévaster		dévasté	(a-R) to devastate
de*venir*			(e-I) to become

devoir	je dois nous devons	dû	(a-I) to owe, have to
diminuer		diminué	(a-R) to diminish
dîner		diné	(e-R) to have dinner
dire	je dis nous disons	dit	(a-I) to say, tell
diriger		dirigé	(a-R) to conduct
dis*courir*			(e-I) to discourse
discuter		discuté	(a-R) to discuss
dis*paraître*			(e-I) to disappear
dispenser		dispensé	(a-R) to exempt
distinguer		distingué	(a-R) to distinguish
dis*traire*			(a-I) to separate
dominer		dominé	(e-R) to dominate
donner		donné	(a-R) to give
dormir	je dors nous dormons	dormi	(e-I) to sleep
douter		douté	(a-R) to doubt
durer		duré	(e-R) to endure, last
échouer		échoué	(e-R) to fail
éclairer		éclairé	(a-R) to light
écouter		écouté	(a-R) to listen to
écrire	j'écris nous écrivons	écrit	(a-I) to write
élever		élevé	(a-R) to raise
élire			(a-I) to elect
embellir		embelli	(a-R) to beautify
émettre			(a-I) to emit
emmener	j'emmène nous emmenons	emmené	(a-I) to take
émouvoir			(a-I) to move
employer	j'emploie nous employons	employé	(a-I) to use
emporter		emporté	(a-R) to take away

en*dormir*			(a-I) to put to sleep
enfreindre	j'enfreins	enfreint	(a-I) to infringe
	nous enfreignons		
enseigner		enseigné	(a-R) to teach
entendre		entendu	(a-R) to hear
entourer		entouré	(a-R) to surround
entre*prendre*			(a-I) to attempt
entrer		entré	(e-R) to enter
entre*tenir*			(a-I) to hold together
entre*voir*			(a-I) to glimpse
entr'*ouvrir*			(a-I) to half-open
envoyer	j'envoie	envoyé	(a-I) to send
	nous envoyons		
épouser		épousé	(a-R) to marry
équiper		équipé	(a-R) to equip
espérer		espéré	(a-R) to hope
essayer		essayé	(a-R) to try
éteindre	j'éteins	éteint	(a-I) to put out
	nous éteignons		
étonner		étonné	(a-R) to surprise
être	je suis	été	(a-I) to be
	nous sommes		
étudier		étudié	(a-R) to study
éviter		évité	(a-R) to avoid
exclure	j'exclus	exclu	(a-I) to exclude
	nous excluons		
exécuter		exécuté	(a-R) to execute
exister		existé	(e-R) to exist
expliquer		expliqué	(a-R) to explain
exposer		exposé	(a-R) to expose
exprimer		exprimé	(a-R) to express
ex*traire*			(a-I) to extract
fabriquer		fabriqué	(a-R) to manufacture
fâcher		fâché	(a-R) to anger

faire	je fais nous faisons	fait	(a-I) to do, make
falloir	il faut	fallu	(a-I) to be necessary
feindre	je feins nous feignons	feint	(a-I) to feign
fermer		fermé	(a-R) to close
finir		fini	(a-R) to finish, end
fixer		fixé	(a-R) to fasten
forcer		forcé	(a-R) to force
former		formé	(a-R) to form
frequenter		fréquenté	(a-R) to frequent
fuir	je fuis nous fuyons	fui	(e-I) to flee
fumer		fumé	(e-R) to smoke
gagner		gagné	(a-R) to win, earn
garantir		garanti	(a-R) to guarantee
garder		gardé	(a-R) to keep
geindre	je geins nous geignons	geint	(e-I) to whine, moan
goûter		goûté	(a-R) to taste
habiter		habité	(a-R) to live, dwell
hair	je haïs nous haïssons	haï	(a-I) to hate
ignorer		ignoré	(a-R) to ignore
importer		importé	(e-R) to matter
imposer		imposé	(a-R) to impose
indiquer		indiqué	(a-R) to indicate
inscrire	j'inscris nous inscrivons	inscrit	(a-I) to inscribe
inspirer		inspiré	(a-R) to inspire
inter*dire*			(a-j) to forbid
inter*venir*			(e-I) to intervene
introduire	j'introduis nous introduisons	introduit	(a-I) to introduce

inviter		invité	(a-R) to invite
jeter	je jette nous jetons	jeté	(a-I) to throw
joindre	je joins nous joignons	joint	(a-I) to join
jouer		joué	(a-R) to play
juger		jugé	(a-R) to judge
laisser		laissé	(a-R) to let, allow
laver		lavé	(a-R) to wash
lire	je lis nous lisons	lu	(a-I) to read
louer		loué	(a-R) to rent
main*tenir*			(a-I) to maintain
manger		mangé	(a-R) to eat
manquer		manqué	(a-R) to lack
marcher		marché	(e-R) to walk
mé*dire*			(e-I) to slander
mélanger		melange	(a-R) to mix
mener		mené	(a-R) to lead
mentir	je mens nous mentons	menti	(e-I) to lie
mériter		mérité	(a-R) to merit
mettre	je mets nous mettons	mis	(a-I) to put, place
monter		monté	(e-R) to go up
montrer		montré	(a-R) to show
mourir	je meurs nous mourons	mort	(e-I) to die
mouvoir	je meus nous mouvons	mû	(a-I) to move
nager		nagé	(e-R) to swim
naître	je nais nous naissons	né	(e-I) to be born
neiger	il neige	neigé	(a-I) to snow

noter		noté	(a-R) to note
ob*tenir*			(a-I) to obtain
occuper		occupé	(a-R) to occupy
offrir	j'offre	offert	(a-I) to offer
	nous offrons		
o*mettre*			(a-I) to omit
organiser		organisé	(a-R) to organize
oser		osé	(a-R) to dare
oublier		oublié	(a-R) to forget
ouvrir	j'ouvre	ouvert	(a-I) to open
	nous ouvrons		
paraître	je parais	parru	(e-I) to appear, seem
	nous paraissons		
par*courir*			(a-I) to travel
pardonner		pardonné	(a-R) to pardon
parler		parlé	(a-R) to speak
partir	je pars	parti	(e-I) to leave
	nous partons		
par*venir*			(e-I) to reach
passer		passé	(e-R) to pass
payer		payé	(a-R) to pay
peindre	je peins	peint	(a-I) to paint
	nous peignons		
penser		pensé	(a-R) to think
perdre		perdu	(a-R) to lose
per*mettre*			(a-I) to permit
piquer		piqué	(a-R) to arouse
placer		placé	(a-R) to place
plaindre	je plains	plaint	(a-I) to complain
	nous plaignons		
plaire	je plais	plu	(e-I) to please
	nous plaisons		
pleuvoir	il pleut	plu	(a-I) to rain
porter		porté	(a-R) to carry, wear
poser		posé	(a-R) to ask-question

pour*suivre*			(a-I) to pursue
pour*voir*			(e-I) to provide
pouvoir	je peux (puis)	pu	(a-I) to be able, can
	nous pouvons		
pratiquer		pratiqué	(a-R) to practice
pré*dire*			(a-I) to predict
préférer		préféré	(a-R) to prefer
prendre	je prends	pris	(a-I) to take
	nous prenons		
préparer		préparé	(a-R) to prepare
prescrire	je prescris	prescrit	(a-I) to prescribe
	nous prescrivons		
présenter		présenté	(a-R) to introduce
pré*venir*			(e-I) to precede
pré*voir*			(a-I) to foresee
produire	je produis	produit	(a-I) to produce
	nous produisons		
projeter	je projette	projeté	(a-I) to plan
	nous projetons		
pro*mettre*			(a-I) to promise
prononcer		prononcé	(a-R) to pronounce
raconter		raconté	(a-R) to tell, relate
recevoir	je reçois	reçu	(a-I) to receive
	nous recevons		
réciter		récité	(a-R) to recite
re*commander*			(a-R) to recommend
re*commencer*			(a-R) to begin again
re*conduire*			(a-I) to lead back
re*connaître*			(a-I) to recognize
re*cueillir*			(a-I) to gather
re*devenir*			(e-I) to become again
réduire	je réduis	réduit	(a-I) to reduce
	nous réduisons		
refuser		refusé	(a-R) to refuse
regarder		regardé	(a-R) to look at

regretter		regretté	(a-R) to be sorry
re*joindre*			(a-I) to rejoin
remarquer		remarqué	(a-R) to notice
re*mener*			(a-I) to take back
re*mettre*			(a-I) to postpone
rencontrer		rencontré	(a-R) to meet
rendre		rendu	(a-R) to give back
rentrer		rentré	(e-R) to go back in
re*nvoyer*			(a-I) to send again
re*partir*			(a-R) to answer
répéter	je répéte nous répétons	répété	(a-I) to repeat
répondre		répondu	(a-R) to answer
re*prendre*			(a-I) to retake
résoudre	je résous nous résolvons	résolu	(a-I) to resolve
respirer		respiré	(a-R) to breathe
res*sentir*			(a-I) to feel
rester		resté	(e-R) to remain
restreindre	je restreins nous restreignons	restreint	(a-I) to restrict
re*tenir*			(a-I) to reserve
retourner		retourné	(e-R) to return
re*trouver*			(a-R) to find again
réussir		réussi	(e-R) to succeed
re*venir*			(e-I) to come back
re*voir*			(a-I) to see again
rire	je ris nous rions	ri	(e-I) to laugh
rouler		roulé	(a-R) to roll
satis*faire*			(a-I) to satisfy
savoir	je sais nous savons	su	(a-I) to know (how)
se*courir*			(a-I) to assist

sembler		semblé	(e-R) to seem
sentir	**je sens**	senti	(a-I) to smell
	nous sentons		
servir	**je sers**	servi	(a-I) to serve
	nous servons		
sortir		sorti	(e-I) to go out
souffrir	**je souffre**	souffert	(a-I) to suffer
	nous souffrons		
sou*mettre*			(a-I) to subdue
sou*rire*			(e-I) to smile
souscrire	**je souscris**	souscrit	(a-I) to subscribe
	nous souscrivons		
sou*tenir*			(a-I) to hold up
sou*straire*			(a-I) to take away
suffire	**je suffis**	suffi	(e-I) to suffice
	nous suffisons		
suggérer	**je suggère**	suggéré	(a-I) to suggest
	nous suggerons		
suivre	**je suis**	suivi	(a-I) to follow
	nous suivons		
sur*prendre*			(a-I) to surprise
tâcher		tâché	(e-R) to try
teindre	**je teins**	teint	(a-I) to dye
	nous teignons		
tenir	**je tiens**	tenu	(a-I) to hold
	nous tenons		
terminer		terminé	(a-R) to end
tomber		tombé	(e-R) to fall
toucher		touché	(a-R) to touch
tourner		tourné	(a-R) to turn
traduire	**je traduis**	traduit	(a-I) to translate
	nous traduisons		
traire	**je trais**	trait	(a-I) to milk
	nous trayons		
trans*mettre*			(a-I) to transmit
travailler		travaillé	(a-R) to work

tressaillir	je tressaille nous tressaillons	tressailli	(e-I) to shudder
troubler		troublé	(a-R) to trouble
trouver		trouvé	(a-R) to find, think
tuer		tué	(a-R) to kill
utiliser		utilisé	(a-R) to use
vaincre	je vaincs nous vainquons	vaincu	(a-I) to conquer
valoir	je vaux nous valons	valu	(e-I) to be worth
vendre		vendu	(a-R) to sell
venir	je viens	venu	(e-I) to come
vêtir	je vêts nous vêtons	vêtu	(a-I) to clothe
visiter		visité	(a-R) to visit
vivre	je vis nous vivons	vécu	(e-I) to live
voir	je vois nous voyons	vu	(a-I) to see
vouloir	je veux nous voulons	voulu	(a-I) to want, to wish
voyager		voyagé	(a-R) to travel

REFLEXIVE VERBS

sabs*tenir*	(e-I) to abstain
s'addresser	(e-R) to speak to
s'allier	(e-R) to unite
s'amuser	(e-R) to have a good time
s'appeler	(e-I) to be named
s'asseoir	(e-I) to sit down
se contenter	(e-R) to be content
se coucher	(e-R) to go to bed
se débarrasser de	(e-R) to get rid of
se débattre	(e-I) to be debated
se débrouiller	(e-R) to get along
se depêcher	(e-R) to hurry
se dérouler	(e-R) to take place
s'efforcer	(e-R) to endeavor
s'élever	(e-R) to rise
s'endormir	(e-I) to fall asleep
s'enfuir	(e-I) to run away
s'engager dans	(e-R) to enter a street
s'établir	(e-R) to settle
s'exprimer	(e-I) to express oneself
se fâcher	(e-R) to get angry
s'habiller	(e-R) to get dressed
s'habituer à	(e-R) to get used to
s'harmoniser	(e-R) to harmonize
s'installer	(e-R) to settle
s'intéresser à	(e-R) to be interested in
se laver	(e-R) to wash oneself
se lever	(e-R) to get up
se marier	(e-R) to get married
se mettre à	(e-I) to begin
s'occuper de	(e-R) to take care of
se plaindre	(e-I) to complain

se promener			(e-R) to take a walk
se rappeler			(e-R) to remember
se reposer			(e-R) to rest
se retrouver			(e-R) to meet
se réveiller			(e-R) to wake up
se servir de			(e-I) to use
se souvenir de			(e-I) to remember
se taire	je me tais	tu	(e-I) to be quiet
	nous nous taisons		

IDIOMATIC VERBS

aller mal	to be sick
avoir...ans	to be...years old
avoir besoin de	to need
avoir chaud	to be warm (person)
avoir envie de	to feel like, to want to
avoir faim	to be hungry
avoir froid	to be cold (person)
avoir l'air	to seem, to look, to appear
avoir l'intention de	to intend to
avoir lieu	to take place
avoir mal à	to have a...ache
avoir mal au coeur	to be nauseated
avoir peur	to be afraid
avoir raison	to be right
avoir soif	to be thirsty
avoir sommeil	to be sleepy
avoir tort	to be wrong
changer d'avis	to change one's mind
donner du feu	to give a light
être malade	to be sick (serious illness)
être obligé de	to be obliged to

être souffrant	to be indisposed
être en train de	to be in the process of
faire attention	to watch out, be careful
faire chaud	to be warm (weather)
faire la connaissance de	to meet, make the acquaintance of
faire des courses	to go shopping
faire face à	to face
faire froid	to be warm (weather)
faire mal	to harm
faire la marché	to do the marketing
faire une promenade	to take a walk
faire le tour de	to go around
faire (rendre) une visite	to visit (people)
faire un voyage	to take a trip
jouer à	to play a game
jouer de	to play a musical instrument
ne servir à rien	to be of no use
prendre soin de	to take care of
se mettre à	to begin
s'occuper de	to take care of
se passer de	to do without
se rendre compte de	to realize
tenir à	to insist on, to be anxious to
valoir mieux	to be better
venir de	to have just
vouloir bien	to be willing
vouloir dire	to mean

"...il n'ont pas l'air de croire..."
(Fauré, "Clair de lune")

VERBS FREQUENTLY ENCOUNTERED IN MUSIC SCORES, TEXTS ON MUSIC, AND MUSICOLOGICAL ESSAYS

accorder	to tune
amortir	to mute (strings)
baisser	to lower a string
battre la mesure	to beat time
composer	to compose
déchanter	to lower the key in singing
démancher	to shift positions in string playing
détacher	to separate either notes or phrases
diriger	to conduct
diviser	to divide, as in string parts
doubler	to double, as in parts
donner le ton	to give the pitch
embellir	to ornament, embellish
étudier	to practice
exécuter	to perform
filer le son	messa di voce
ôter	to take off (an organ stop or string mutes)
pincer de	to pluck a musical instrument
préparer d'avance	to prepare in advance (organ stops)
ralentir	to slow down
renforcer	to reinforce, increase in loudness
ressortir	to emphasize
retenir	to hold back
s'accorder	to tune an orchestra
sonner	to sound
soutenir	to sustain a note
tirer	to play downbow; to draw an organ stop; to slow in tempo
toucher de	to play on a musical instrument
vocaliser	to vocalize

229

VERBS FREQUENTLY ENCOUNTERED
IN VOCAL LITERATURE

baiser[2]	to kiss
	(Paladilhe, "Psyché")
étinceler	to sparkle
	(Ravel, "Sainte")
harasser	to weary, tire out
	(Duparc, "Le Manoir de Rosemonde")
lutter	to wrestle, to struggle
	(Milhaud, "Les Malheurs d'Orphée: choeur des Métiers")
pleurer	to weep, cry
	(Fauré, "Le long du quai")
rajeunir	to restore to youth
	(Poulenc, "Paul et Virginie")
rayonner	to radiate
	(Fauré, "Après un rêve")
rougir	to redden, blush
	(Poulenc, "Une chanson de porcelaine")
sautiller	to hop, skip
	(Ravel, "Nicolette"—Trois chansons pour choeur)
soupirer	to sigh, to long
	(Debussy, "Nuit d'étoiles")
unir	to unite, join
	(Debussy, "La flûte,"—Trois chansons de Bilitis)
voler	to fly
	(Berlioz, "L'absence")

[2]This word is strictly literary in use, replaced by *embrasser* in conversation.

MUSICAL EXERCISES

1. Survey the texts of one of the following chanson groups by Maurice Ravel:

>Chansons Madécasses
>Don Quichotte à Dulcinée
>L'Enfant et les Sortilèges
>Shéhérazade
>Trois Poèmes de Mallarmé

a) List all verbs; translate each

b) Indicate the tense in which each is used

c) Indicate whether the verb is transitive/intransitive and regular/irregular.

2. Survey an aria from one of the following operas by Jean Philippe Rameau:

>Acanthe et Céphise
>Castor et Pollux
>Dardanus
>Les Fêtes d'Hébé
>Hippolyte et Aricie
>Les Indes Galantes
>Platée
>Zoroastre

a) List all verbs; translate each

b) Name the auxiliary verb

c) Cite the verb tense used.

Chapter Four

I. ADJECTIVES

An *adjective* is a word that describes or modifies a noun or pronoun and answers the question "which?", "which one?", or "what kind of?" a noun or pronoun.

A. Demonstrative Adjectives

Demonstrative adjectives point out or indicate the object spoken of; they do not describe. The forms of demonstrative adjectives in French are:

masculine: *ce* (*cet*)   this, that   *ces* these, those
feminine: *cette*   this, that   *ces* these, those

1. The demonstrative adjective *ce* [sə] is used before a masculine singular noun beginning with a consonant:

"...de *ce* silence profond..."
(Hahn, "En sourdine")

2. The demonstrative adjective *cet* [sɛt] is used before a masculine singular noun beginning with a vowel sound:

"...par *cet* après-midi..."
(Debussy, "Paysage sentimental")

3. The demonstrative adjective *cette* [sɛt] is used before a feminine singular noun beginning with a vowel or a consonant:

"...*cette* nuit, j'ai rêvé..."
(Debussy, "La chevelure")

"...*cette* fantaisie et *cette* raison!"
(Fauré, *La Bonne Chanson* - 9)

4. The demonstrative adjective *ces* [sez] is used before a masculine or feminine plural noun beginning with a vowel or a consonant:

"...dormir *ces* vaisseaux..."
(Duparc, "L'invitation au voyage")

"...dans *ces* ombres..."
(Fauré, "Dans les ruines d'une abbaye")

"...vois sur *ces* canaux..."
(Duparc, "L'Invitation au voyage")

"...et *ces* toiles sont tes yeux..."
(Debussy, "Nuit d'étoile")

Demonstrative adjectives must agree in gender and number with the noun modified.

5. In order to make demonstrative adjectives more emphatic, the suffix *-ci*, meaning "this" or "these" is hyphenated to the noun modified by the demonstrative adjective; the suffix *-là*, meaning "that" or "those", is hyphenated to the noun modified by the demonstrative adjective.

"...cette paisible rumeur-*là*..."
(Hahn, "Le ciel est, par-dessus le toit")

"...et ce jour-*là*..."
(Fauré, "Le long du quai")

B. Predicate Nominative

The *predicate nominative* in French consists of the demonstrative adjective *ce* used with the verb *être* followed by a noun that is equal to or describes the subject. The indefinite article (*un, une*) is not used before a *predicate adjective* or *predicate nominative* indicating nationality, religion, or profession.

"...c'est l'heure exquise..."
(Fauré, *La Bonne Chanson* - 3)

"...je suis le spectre d'une Rose..."
(Berlioz, "Le spectre d'une rose")

"...c'est l'histoire des oiseaux..."
(Fauré, "Dans les ruines d'une abbaye")

"...c'est l'extase langoureuse..."
(Debussy, "C'est l'extase")

"...cette rose, c'est ton haleine..."
(Debussy, "Nuit d'étoile")

C. Possessive Adjectives

Possessive adjectives indicate possession, or to whom something belongs; a possessive adjective must agree in gender and number with the noun modified. The forms of possessive adjectives in French are:

Singular

masculine	feminine		
mon [mõ]	ma [ma]	/mon [mõ]	my
ton [tõ]	ta [ta]	/ton [tõ]	your
son [sõ]	sa [sa]	/son [sõ]	his, her, its
notre [nɔtrə]	notre		our
votre [vɔtrə]	votre		your
leur [lœr]	leur		their

Plural

*masculine and
  feminine*

before a consonant	before a vowel	
mes [me]	mes [mez]	my
tes [te]	tes [tez]	your
ses [se]	ses [sez]	his, her, its
nos [no]	nos [nos]	our
vos [vo]	vos [vos]	your
leurs [lœr]	leurs [lœrz]	their

1. The possessive adjectives *ma*, *ta*, and *sa* are used before feminine singular nouns beginning with a consonant. The possessive adjectives *mon*, *ton*, *son* are used before all masculine singular nouns and before feminine singular nouns beginning with a vowel sound.

2. Note that the plural forms of possessive adjectives are pronounced according to the sound that follows (consonant or vowel) but are spelled the same for both forms.

> "...brillant à travers *leurs* larmes..."
> (Duparc, "L'Invitation au voyage")

> "...au fond de *mon* coeur..."
> (Debussy, "Nuit d'étoiles")

> "...sur *ses* genoux..."
> (Debussy, "La Flûte")

> "...*leur* vol léger..."
> (Fauré, "Les roses d'Ispahan")

3. A possessive adjective must agree with the noun indicating what is possessed, not with the possessor.

"...je sens...mon obstiné tourment..."
(Fauré, "Rencontre")

D. Adjective Word Order

In French, adjectives generally follow the nouns they modify. However, the following adjectives normally precede the noun they modify:

Singular		*Plural*		
m.	*f.*	*m.*	*f.*	
bon	bonne	bons	bonnes	good
mauvais	mauvaise	mauvais	mauvaises	bad
beau (bel)	belle	beaux	belles	beautiful
joli	jolie	jolis	jolies	pretty
grand	grande	grands	grandes	big, tall
gentil	gentille	gentils	gentilles	nice
petit	petite	petits	petites	small
long	longue	longs	longues	long
vieux (vieil)	vieille	vieux	vieilles	old
jeune	jeune	jeunes	jeunes	young
nouveau (nouvel)	nouvelle	nouveaux	nouvelles	new

"...les beaux jours..."
(Debussy, "Colloque sentimental")

1. The masculine forms *bel*, *vieil*, and *nouvel* are used only before masculine nouns beginning with a vowel sound.

2. Ordinal numbers also precede the noun modified.

3. The following are examples from music literature of adjectives which precede nouns:

Beau soir

La bonne chanson

Belle Ernelinde

Un jeune coeur

Première leçon

Viens, gentille Dame

a) Cite the composer of each.

E. Descriptive Adjectives

Descriptive adjectives are those adjectives that describe or tell "what kind of" about the noun modified; descriptive adjectives generally follow the noun and must agree in gender and number with the noun modified.

"...les riches plafonds...le splendeur orientale...sa douce langue..."
(Duparc, "L'Invitation au voyage")

"...l'âme évaporée et souffrante, l'âme douce, l'âme odorante..."
(Debussy, "Romance")

1. The feminine of most adjectives is formed by adding -*e* to the masculine form; the final consonant, which is normally silent in the masculine form, is pronounced in the feminine form:

bleu - bleue	blue
brun - brune	brown
français - française	French
grand - grande	big, tall
gris - grise	gray
vert - verte	green

2. If the masculine singular form of an adjective ends in -*e*, the feminine of the adjective is the same as the masculine form:

jaune	yellow
jeune	young
maigre	thin
noire	black
pâle	pale
rouge	red

a) Adjectives ending in -*er* in the masculine singular form become *ère* in the feminine.

3. The plural of most descriptive adjectives is formed by adding -*s* to the singular form; the final -*s* is pronounced only in linking (liason). If an adjective ends in -*s* in the masculine singular, its plural form is the same.

Most masculine plural adjectives are pronounced like the masculine singular form. Feminine adjectives are pronounced the same in the singular and plural.

joli - jolis

jolie - jolies

4. A few adjectives have slightly irregular forms:

Singular		*Plural*		
m.	*f.*	*m.*	*f.*	
actif	active	actifs	actives	active
neuf	neuve	neufs	neuves	new
heureux	heureuse	heureux	heureuses	happy
sérieux	sérieuse	sérieux	sérieuses	serious
doux	douce	doux	douces	gentle
gras	grasse	gras	grasses	fat
blanc	blanche	blancs	blanches	white
Italien	Italienne	Italiens	Italiennes	Italian

5. The names of all nationalities (Chapter Two) can also be used as adjectives and are declined according to the foregoing principles. Adjectives of nationality generally follow the noun modified; occasionally, however, these adjectives are placed before the noun modified for stylistic effect, special emphasis, or special meaning. Adjectives of nationality are capitalized and used without an article when used as a noun (predicate nominative) referring to a person:

Elle est Française.

Il est Américain.

"...de son beau pirate espagnol..."
(Debussy, "Fantoches")

MUSICAL EXERCISES

1. The following are examples from music literature of adjectives which follow nouns:

> Chansons madécasses
> Chansons populaires
> Chanson triste
> Cinq mélodies populaires grecques
> Colloque sentimental
> L'enfant prodigue
> Fêtes galantes
> Histoires naturelles
> Le parfum impérissable
> Paysage sentimental
> La vie antérieure

a) Cite the composer of each and identify the type of composition.

2. The following are adjectives in Shéhérazade (three poems for voice and orchestra) by Maurice Ravel:

a) Asie   "...vieux pays merveilleux...

ses voiles violettes...

un immense oiseau...

la mer perverse...

un vieux rythme...

des peaux jaunes...

au palais enchanté...

son grand sabre...

ma vieille tasse..."

b) La flûte enchantée "...un air...langoureux ou frivole...

mon amoureux chéri

un mystérieux baiser..."

c) l'Indifferent   "...la courbe fine...

ton beau visage...

une langue inconnue et charmante...

> une musique fausse...
>
> un dernier geste...
>
> ta démarche féminine et lasse..."

F. Past Participle

The *past participle* of a verb is used with an auxiliary verb to form compound tenses. The past participle of a verb may be used as an adjective; it agrees in gender and number with the noun modified:

> Ariettes oubliées
>
> Fleur jetée
>
> L'île inconnue

The past participle is frequently encountered in musical scores to describe the manner of interpretation:

abandonné	unrestrained, free
accusé	with emphasis
appuyé	emphasized
barré	barred: vibratory length of strings (guitar or lute) shortened by holding forefinger (or a bar) across them
bouché	stopped in horn playing
brisé	arpeggiated playing; detached bowing
cuivré	forced, harsh tone in playing, especially of the horn
détaché	detached bowing
empressé	hurried
étouffé	damped, muted (kettle drums, violins)
jeté	bow bounced on the string
marqué	marked, stressed
plaqué	indication for notes of a chord to be played simultaneously, as opposed to arpeggio
saccadé	abrupt, jerky
tiré	indication for downstroke of the bow, the drawing of organ stops, or slowing down of tempo

G. Present Participle

The *present participle* of verbs is formed by dropping the *-ons* of the first person plural form in the present tense and adding the ending *-ant*. The present participle is used occasionally as an adjective in French.

éclatant	brilliant, sparkling
son résultant	resulting tone
soupirant	sighing

"...le calme aimant..."
(Duparc, "Chanson triste")

H. Liaison

1. Liaison usually occurs

   a) Between an article and a noun

   b) Between an article and an adjective

   c) Between an adjective and a noun when the adjective precedes the noun

   d) Between a subject pronoun and a verb.

2. Liaison never occurs

   a) Before the numerals *un, huit, onze*

   b) Between the *t* or *et* and another word

   c) Before words which begin with an aspirate *h*

   d) Between a subject noun and its verb

   e) Between a singular noun and a following adjective.

II. COMPARATIVE AND SUPERLATIVE

The comparative and superlative of adjectives is formed in English either by adding *-er* and *-est* (louder, loudest) or by using the modifiers *more* and *most* (more interesting, most interesting).

A. Regular Adjectives

Regular adjectives and adverbs in French are made comparative according to the following pattern:

241

1. Superlative is expressed by *plus...que* (more...than).

> "*...plus* vite *que* le givre en fleurs, nos coeurs!"
> (Fauré, "Adieu")

> "*...plus* blanc *que* le lait..."
> (Fauré, "Lydia")

2. Equality is expressed by *aussi...que* (as...as).

3. Inferiority is expressed by *moins..que* (less.than).

> "...ont un parfum *moins* frais...
> ont une odeur *moins* douce...
> *que* ton souffle leger..."
> (Fauré, "Les roses d'Ispahan")

The final *s* of *moins* is pronounced before a vowel sound.

B. Superlative Construction

To express the superlative degree of adjectives, the appropriate definite article is inserted before the comparative form; the article and modifying adjective(s) must agree with the noun being modified.

> le (la, les) plus... the most

> le (la, les) moins... the least

> "...unis par *le plus* fort et *le plus* lien..."
> (Fauré, *La Bonne Chanson* - 8)

> "*...les plus* longs amours..."
> (Fauré, "Adieu")

> "...que ton *plus* beau sourire et ton meilleur baiser..."
> (Duparc, "Phidylé")

1. The superlative construction either precedes or follows the noun being modified, according to the usual position of the adjective in sentence structure.

> "...le coeur *le plus* triste..."
> (Fauré, *La Bonne Chanson* - 9)

When the superlative form of an adjective which follows the noun modified is used, the definite article is used twice, once before the noun, and again as part of the superlative form of the adjective.

III. ADVERBS

An *adverb* is a word that modifies a verb, an adjective, or another adverb. Adverbs answer the questions "How?", "Where?", "When?", "In what manner?", and are among the most important words in French for giving directions in music.

A. Forms

1. The superlative form of adverbs is similar to that of adjectives.

le plus -the most

le moins - the least

These expressions are adverbial and do not change to show agreement in gender or number.

B. Irregular Comparative and Superlative Forms

1. The adjective *bon* (good) is compared irregularly:

Positive	Comparative	Superlative
bon (good)	meilleur (better)	le meilleur (best)
bonne	meilleure	la meilleure
bons	meilleurs	les meilleurs
bonnes	meilleures	les meilleures

"...le jour...est *le meilleur*..."
(Fauré, "Lydia")

2. The adverb *bien* (well) is compared irregularly:

Positive	Comparative	Superlative
bien (well)	mieux (better)	le mieux (best)

   a) In English, the comparative and superlative of the adjective *good* (better, best) and the adverb *well* (better, best) are identical. In French, however, it is necessary to know whether the adjective or the adverb form is implied in order to use the correct form.

"...ton rire léger sonne *mieux* que l'eau...*mieux* que le vent..."
(Fauré, "Les Roses d'Ispahan")

C. Special Meanings

1. When the word *fort* is used as an adjective it agrees with the noun it modifies and means "strong"; when used as an adverb *fort* means "very".

"j'ai rêvé tellement *fort*..."
(Poulenc, "Dernier Poème")

2. When *même* is used as an adjective it means:

    a) "same"- before the noun or pronoun modified

    b) "self", "very"- after the noun or pronoun modified

"...tu t'écoules de *même*..."
(Fauré, "Le parfum impérissable")

"...l'air *même* que vous respirez..."
(Paladilhe, "Psyché")

    c) "even"- when used as an adverb

"...*même* ce Paris..."
(Fauré, *La Bonne Chanson* - 9)

3. For translation it is important to become familiar with the positive forms of all adjectives and be able to recognize the forms for comparative and superlative and adjectives and adverbs compared irregularly.

D. Adverbs Used in Music

The following are adverbs, some of which are also adjectives, frequently encountered in music literature:

1. Adverbs are often formed by adding *-ment* to the feminine form of adjectives; other adverbs already end in -ment.

alternativement	alternating
chevrotement[1]	unsteadily
croisement	crossing the hands in piano playing
doucement	sweetly
enchaînement	joining two movements without a break
vitement	quickly, fast
vivement	lively

2. The following adverbs and adverbial expressions are frequently used to give instruction in music literature:

assez	rather, enough, somewhat
brumeux	misty, veiled

---

[1]Some words such as *chevrotement, croisement, enchaînement* are nouns used in an adverbial sense (to tell how, in what manner) in giving directions in music.

244

en dehors	emphasized
douloureux	sorrowfully
élargissent	broadening in speed
éteint	barely audible
haut(e)	high
lourd	heavy
bien nourri	with a rich sound
à peine entendu	barely audible
un peu	a little
recueilli	meditative, contemplative
sourd	muffled, muted
vide[2]	empty
vif	lively
vite	fast, quickly
voilé	veiled, subdued

3. The following types of words generally indicate adjectives and adverbs in translation:

    a) The past participle of verbs ending in , *é*, *i*, and *u*

    b) The present participle of verbs ending in *-ant*

    c) The feminine form of adjectives with the ending *-ment*

RESEARCH QUESTIONS

1. Define the following terms, all of which contain an adjective:

             air gracieux

             air tendre

             basse fondementale

             chanson balladée

             chanson mesurée

             cinq pas

             drame lyrique

             fausse relation

---

[2]The term *vide* is used with its syllables *Vi-* and *-de* placed at separate places in the score, indicating an optional omission or cut in the music.

> formes fixes
> grand récitatif
> idée fixe
> La Jeune France
> musique concrète
> notes inégales
> la note soutenue
> opéra comique
> orgue expressif
> style brisé
> style galant
> vers mesuré

2. Define historically the *Paléographie Musicale*.

3. Describe the *Répertoire International des Sources musicales*.

4. Identify each of the following compositions (composer, form, etc.):

> Le carnaval Romain
> Le chasseur maudit
> Danse macabre
> L'homme armé
> Pierrot lunaire
> Variations symphoniques
> Valses nobles et sentimentales

5. Survey the *Symphonie fantastique* by Hector Berlioz:

   a) Write out in French the name and number of instruments used.

   b) Describe the literary influences portrayed in the *Symphonie fantastique*.

   c) Describe the unique unifying feature of the movements and the musical substance employed by Berlioz.

6. Describe the orchestra "Vingt-quatre Violons du Roi".

7. Survey a major organ composition by Olivier Messiaen.

   a) List all adjectives and adverbs in French that give direction in music; translate each.

8. Survey an opera by Giocomo Meyerbeer. List, in French

   a) Instrumentation-number and names of instruments

   b) all musical expressions in French and their translations.

9. Survey a tone poem by Claude Debussy for musical expressions; translate each.

MUSICAL VOCABULARY BUILDING

accolade	the bracket connecting two or more staves of a score (brace)
portée	staff
clef	clef
armure	key signature
oeuvre	opus
morceau	piece, composition
mouvement	movement, tempo
sujet, thème	subject
motif	motive
exposition	exposition
réexposition	recapitulation
contrepoint	counterpoint
fugue	fugue
divertissement	fugal episode
passacaille	passacaglia
polyphonie	polyphony
accord	chord
unison	interval of a first, unison
seconde	second
tierce	third
quatre	fourth
quinte	fifth
sixte	sixth
septième	seventh

octave	octave
neuvième	ninth
dixième	tenth
onzième	eleventh
douzième	twelfth
demi-ton	half-tone
ton	whole tone, as distinct from a half-tone
note de passage	passing tone
point d'orgue	pedal point
tierce de Picardie	Picardy third
renversement	inversion of intervals, chords, subjects
cadence	cadence
cadence rompue	deceptive cadence
pause, silence	rest
demi-pause	half-rest
pause	whole rest
soupir	quarter rest
demi-soupir	eighth rest
quart de soupir	sixteenth rest
huitième de soupir	thirty-second rest
seizième de soupir	sixty-fourth rest
carrée	double whole note
ronde	whole note
blanche	half note
noire	quarter note
croche	eighth note
double-croche	sixteenth note
triple-croche	thirty-second note
quadruple-croche	sixty-fourth note
queue	stem of a note
point	dot after a note; dot above a note to indicate staccato or portato
hauteur	pitch names

échelle, gamme	scale
gamme de physiciens	"natural" scale derived from just intonation
ton d'église	church mode
note sensible	leading tone
majeur	major
mineur	minor
bémol	flat sign
dièse	sharp sign
bécarre	natural sign
duolet	duplet
triolet	triplet
quartolet	quadruplet
quintolet	quintuplet
mesure	measure or meter
temps	beat
temps fort	strong beat
temps faible	weak beat
timbre	tone color
ton	pitch; key or mode
donner le ton	to give the pitch
diapason	tuning fork
double cadence	turn
doublé brisé	turn
mordant	mordent
basse chiffrée	thoroughbass, figured bass
concerto	concerto
piano à queue	grand piano
main droite	right hand
main gauche	left hand
à deux (quatre) mains	for two (four) hands
doigté	fingering

doigté fourchu	cross fingering
étouffoir	piano damper
table d'harmonie	soundboard
touche	key of the piano
prolongement	sostenuto pedal of the piano
réduction pour le piano	piano arrangement
réduction	arrangement
partition	score
conducteur	abridged orchestral score, usually a reduction for piano
répétition	rehearsal
répétition générale	dress rehearsal
chef d'orchestre	conductor
chef d'attaque	concertmaster
symphonie	symphony
orchestre	orchestra
unis	in orchestral music, unison
batterie	percussion section; a drumroll
baguette	drumstick; bowstick; baton
baguette de bois	wooden drumstick
baguette d'éponge	spongehead drumstick
les cuivres	brass instruments
piston	valve
coup de langue	tonguing
bocal	mouthpiece of a brass instrument
bouché	stopping in horn playing
vent	wind
instruments à vent	wind instruments
octavier	wind instruments with a conical bore that overblow at the octave
bois	the woodwinds
embouchure	proper position of the lips in playing of wind instruments

chalumeau	lowest register of the modern clarinet
pavillon	bell of wind instruments
bec	mouthpiece of the clarinet or recorder
anche	reed
anche battante	beating reed
anche double	double reed
anche libre	free reed
trio d'anches	trio for reed instruments
corde	string
corde à vide	open string
chevalet	bridge of string instruments
touche	fingerboard of stringed instruments
manche	neck of stringed instruments
cheviller	pegbox
cheville	peg of a stringed instruments
âme	sound post of stringed instruments
ouïe	sound hole
archet	bow
talon	nut of the bow
sourdine	mute
coup d'archet	bow stroke
poussé	up-bow
bariolage	special effect in string playing for broken-chord passages
louré	stroke used in bowing in slow tempo to separate slightly each of several notes taken in a slur
martelé	a "hammered" stroke in bowing
ondulé	an undulating movement of the bow
sautillé	a short bow stroke in rapid tempo in which the bow bounces slightly off the string
double corde	double stop
arraché	forceful pizzicato

quatour à cordes	string quartet
quintette	quintet
orgue	organ
plein-jeu	full organ
demi-jeu	half organ
orgue expressif	expressive organ
positif	choir organ
fonds d'orgue	foundation stops of the organ
fourniture	mixture stop of the organ
jeu	stop
jeu de fonds	foundation stop
jeu de mutation	mutation stop
jeu à bouche	flue stop
jeu d'anche	reed stop
anches	reed stops of the organ
pedalier	pedal board of the organ
voix	voice
voix de poitrine	chest voice
voix de tête	head voice
voix mixte	the middle register
demi-voix	half-voice
bouche fermée	singing with closed mouth
port de voix	portamento
roulade	vocal melisma or highly ornamented melody
récitative	recitative
opéra	opera
opéra bouffe	comic opera
regisseur	artistic stage director of an opera

ADJECTIVES AND ADVERBS ENCOUNTERED IN MUSIC

avec abandon	free, unrestrained
accélerant	becoming faster
accentué	accented, marked, stressed
en accompagnant	accompanying
accouplé	using a coupler
accusé	with emphasis
adoucissant	becoming gentler and smoother
aérien	light, airy
affaiblissez	becoming softer and weaker
affectueusement	fondly, tenderly
affirmatif	assertive, definite
affolé	distracted
agité	excited, restless
agressivement	forthright, bold
aigre	harsh, shrill
aigu	sharp, shrill
ailé	rapid and light
à la aise	comfortably, easily
ajoutez	add, interpolate
alangui	slowed down, weaker, softer
alenti	slowed down
alerte	lively, brisk
allant	lively
allègre	lively, gay
allez	go on, proceed
allonger	to slow down, to hold back, delay
alourdissez	make dull and heavy
amer	harsh, bitter
ample	broadly, with dignity
avec angoisse	with anguish
animé	animated

apaisé	calm, quiet
à peine	hardly, scarcely
appuyé	with emphasis
avec âpreté	harshly, violently
argentin	silver, clear
ârret	stop, halt
arrogamment	proudly
articulé	distinct, articulated
attendre	wait, pause
attendri	gently, tenderly
atténué	weaker, softer
en augmentant	becoming louder
autoritaire	commanding, decisive
avisée	carefully
à volonté	at will, freely
badin	playful
balancé	evenly
la basse marque	the bass part emphasized
belliqueux	martial
bizarre	strange, fanciful
bondissant	skipping, bounding
avec bonheur	happily
borrasque	angry, stormy
bousculeur	to hurry, become agitated
avec bravoure	bravely, gallantly
bref, brève	concise, brief
brillant	showy, brilliant
brusque	abrupt
caché	hidden, subtle
cadencé	measured, rhythmic
calme	calm, tranquil
capricieux	capriciously, playful
caressant	tenderly

avec chaleur	with warmth, fervently
avec charme	with charm, gracefully
chatoyant	brilliant, showy
chauffez	become faster, press on
chevrotant	quivering, trembling
chuchoté	whispered
cinglant	harsh
clair	clear, bright
avec colère	angrily, with passion
commodément	easily, comfortably
concentré	concentrated
confus	vague, indistinct
continu	continued
courante	running, rapid, flowing
court	short, brief, concise
dansant	dancing
début	beginning
décidé	firm, resolute
declamé	in a declamatory style
délicat	smoothly, delicately
discrètement	cautiously, with reserve
en disparaissant	disappearing, fading away
distinct	clear, distinct
dolent	mournful, plaintive
dynamique	energetic, vigorous
éplouissant	dazzling
effleuré	very light, gliding
également	uniformly
élargir	broaden and slow down
élegiaque	mournful
émouvant	moving, agitated
emporté	fiery, passionate
empressé	hurrying, rapid

ému	with feeling
enchaîner	connect, link together
énergique	vigorous, forceful
éveillé	brisk, animated
facile	free, easy, flowing
avec fantaisie	with fantasy
fermé	closed
fervent	fervently
avec feu	with fire, passionately
fluide	flowing, smooth
fondu	becoming softer, dying away
frais	fresh, brisk
fuyant	fleeing, fleeting, fading away
gai	merry, cheerful
gentiment	prettily
haletant	breathlessly
harmonieux	melodiously
hésitant	hesitating
avec humeur	with humor
impétueux	impetuously
implacable	constant
incisif	sharp, precise
indifférent	without emotion
indolemment	lazily
inflexible	firm, decisive
innocemment	simple, artless
inquiet	uneasy, agitated
irréel	imaginary, fanciful
joyeux	happy, joyfully
laissez	leave, leave alone
large	broad, full, fairly slow
léger	light, quick
lent	slow

libre	free, unrestrained
lié	tied, bound, legato
limpide	clear, transparent
loin	distant
lumineux	clear, luminous
lyrique	lyrically
majestueux	stately, majestic
marqué	marked, accented
mélancolique	sad, mournful
mélodique	melodious
modéré	at a moderate tempo
montant	becoming louder
en mourant	dying away, becoming faint
mouvementé	lively, animated
muet	silent, mute
murmuré	murmured, whispered
mystérieux	mysterious
ondoyant	undulating
palpitant	panting
passionné	passionate, fervently
pathétique	with great emotion
pénétrant	keen, acute, sharp
phrasé	phrased
plaintif	mournful, plaintive
en pleurant	weeping, lamenting
ponctué	punctuated, accented, marked
en pressant	hurrying
preste	very fast
puissant	forceful, loud
ralentir	slowing down
rapide	fast
avec ravissement	rapturously
renforcer	to reinforce or augment, grow louder

résonné	with full sound
retenant	holding back, slowing down
rigoreux	strict, precise
sec	dry, abrupt
serein	serenely
soigneusement	carefully, elegantly
sonore	resonant
souffrant	suffering
souple	flexible, smooth
soutenu	sustained, held
suivant	following
tendrement	tenderly
tenu	held, sustained
en torrent	pouring out
traîner	to drag, to hold back
tranquille	quiet, peaceful
tumultueux	stormy
uniforme	even, steady, regular
vibrant	vibrating, sounding
vigoureusement	energetic, forceful
à volonté	freely, at the performer's discretion

ADJECTIVES AND ADVERBS

d'abord	first, at first
absent	absent
absolument	absolutely
absurde	absurd
accidenté	hilly
accessible	accessible
actif, active	active
actuel	present

admirable	admirable
admirablement	admirably
adroit	skillful
aérien	aerial
affirmativement	affirmatively
agréable	pleasant
ailleurs	elsewhere
aimable	kind, nice
allumé	lighted
amusant	amusing
ancien	former, old
assez	enough, rather, fairly
attentivement	attentively
aucun, aucune	none
aujourd'hui	today
aussitôt	immediately
austère	severe
autrefois	formerly, once
aveugle	blind
barbare	barbarous
bas, basse	low
beaucoup	much, very much
bientôt	soon
blanc, blanche	white
bleu	blue
blond	blonde
bon, bonne	good
bondé	crowded
brave	good, worthy
brun, brune	brown
célèbre	well-known
certain	certain

certainement	certainly
certes	certainly
chacun, chacune	each, each one
chaque	each
chaud	warm
cher, chère	expensive, dear
chic	stylish
clair	clear; light-colored
commode	convenient
complet, complète	complete
complêtement	completely
compliqué	complicated
compréhensible	comprehensible
confortable	comfortable
content	glad
contraire	contrary
convenable	suitable
cosmopolite	cosmopolitan
coup, tout à coup	suddenly
couramment	fluently
courant	current, common
court	short
couvert	covered,cloudy
dangereux, dangereuse	dangerous
debout	standing
déçu	disappointed
dedans	inside
dehors	outside
déjà	already, before
delà	beyond
délicieux	delicious
demain	tomorrow
demi	half

dernier, dernière	last
derrière	behind
descriptif	descriptive
dessous	below
destiné	meant, intended
détruit	destroyed
dévoué	devoted
différent	different
difficile	difficult
directement	directly
distant	distant
documentaire	documentary
doré	gilded
doué	gifted
douloureux	painful
droit	straight, right
drôle	funny
durable	lasting
effrayant	frightful
égaré	lost
électricien	electrical
élégant	graceful
enchanté	delighted
énorme	enormous
ensuite	then, afterwards
entier, entière	entire, whole
entre	between, among
entr'ouvert	partly open
épais	thick
essoufflé	out of breath
établi	established, steeled
étonnant	astonishing
étonné	surprised

étranger, étrangère	foreign
étroit	narrow
européen, européenne	European
évidemment	evidently
exact	exact
excellent	excellent
exclusivement	exclusively
extraordinaire	extraordinary
fabriqué	made
en face de	opposite
fâché	sorry, angry
facile	easy
facilement	easily
tout à fait	quite, entirely
fatigué	tired
faux	false
favori, favorite	favorite
finalement	finally
foncé	dark-colored
forcé	forced
formidable	terrific
fort	very (adv); strong
fragmentaire	fragmentary
frais, fraîche	fresh, cool, cold
fréquent	frequent
fréquenté	popular (frequently visited)
frit	fried
froid	cold
gai	gay
gauche	left
gentil, gentille	nice
glissant	slippery
grand	tall, large, great

gras, grasse	fat
grave	serious
gris	gray
gros, grosse	big
groupé	grouped
habile	skillful
habilement	skillfully
heureux, heureuse	happy
historique	historical
horriblement	terribly
humble	humble
humide	humid
impair	odd (numbers)
imparfait	imperfect
impassible	impassive
impétueux	impetuous
imposant	imposing
impressionné	impressed
indéfini	indefinite
inoubliable	unforgettable
inquiet	worried
intelligent	intelligent
intéressant	interesting
ironique	ironical
jaloux, jalouse	jealous
jamais	never, ever
jaune	yellow
jeune	young
joli	pretty
juste	exactly, just
là-bas	there, over here
léger	light
lentement	slowly

libre	free
limité	limited
loin	far
lointain(e)	distant
long, longue	long
lorsque	when
lourd	heavy
lugubre	dismal, dreadful
magnifique	magnificent, splendid
maigre	thin
maintenant	now
majestueux, majestueuse	majestic
malade	sick
maladroit	clumsy, awkward
malheureusement	unfortunately
malheureux, malheureuse	unhappy
marine: bleu marine	navy blue
marron	brown
mauvais	bad, wrong
mécanique	mechanical
mécontent	dissatisfied
merveille: à merveille	marvelously
meublé	furnished
mieux	better
mince	thin
moindre(s)	lesser
moins	less
mondial	world-wide
monotone	monotonous
monumental	monumental
mouillé	wet
natal	native
national	national

naturel	natural
naturellement	naturally
négatif, négative	negative
négativement	negatively
neuf, neuve	new
noir	black
noirci	blackened
nombreux, nombreuse	numerous
nommé	named
nouveau	new
obligatoire	required
occupé	busy
ordinaire	ordinary
original	original, unusual
paisible	peaceful
par-dessous	under, beneath
parfait	perfect
parfaitement	perfectly
parfois	sometimes
parmi	among
particulièrement	particularly
partout	everywhere
pauvre	poor
pénétrant	penetrating
perdu	lost
petit	small, little
peu	little
pire	worse
pis	worse
pittoresque	picturesque
plein(e)	full
plusieurs	several
poétique	poetic

politique	political
possible	possible
précédant	preceding
précis	exact
préoccupé	worried
près	near, near by
presque	almost
prêt	ready
principal	principal
probable	probable
prochain(e)	next
prohibé	forbidden
propre	own; clean
prospère	prosperous
public, publique	public
puis	then
puisque	since
pur	pure
purement	purely
quand	when
quelquefois	sometimes
rafraîchissant	cooling
rare	rare
rarement	seldom
ravissant	ravishing, fantastic
reconnaissant	grateful
relativement	relatively
religieux	religious
responsable	responsible
rétabli	recovered
en retard	late
riche	rich

rouge	red
royal	royal
sain et sauf	safe and sound
saint	holy
sale	dirty
satisfait	satisfield, pleased
sauvage	wild
sensationnel	sensational, fantastic
serré	crowded
seul, seule	alone, single
seulement	only, but
silencieux, silencieuse	silent
simple	simple
simplement	simply, merely
situé	situated
sombre	dark
somptueux, somptueuse	sumptuous
souligné	underlined
sous	under
souterrain	underground
souvent	often
spécialement	especially
spécialité	specialty
spirituel	spiritual
spirituellement	mentally
suffisamment	enough
suivant	following
supplémentaire	supplementary
supportable	bearable, endurable
sûrement	surely, certainly
surtout	above all
sympathique	friendly, congenial
tard	late

tôt	soon
toujours	always, still
tout	all, every; quite, completely
traditionnel	traditional
tranquille	quiet
très	very, very much
triste	sad
trop	too, too much, too many
unique	unique
universel	universal
vaste	vast
véritablement	really
violent	violent
vite	fast
vivement	keenly
volontiers	willingly, gladly
vrai	true
vraiment	truly, really
zéro	zero

EXPRESSIONS

Bonjour	good morning, good afternoon, hello
Bonsoir	good evening
au revoir	good-bye
adieu	good-bye
merci	thank you
merci beaucoup	thank you very much
de rien	you're welcome
pardon	pardon me
ça va?	O.K.?
Comment allez-vous?	How are you?
à bientôt	see you soon
à demain	see you tomorrow

Chapter Five

I. SENTENCE STRUCTURE

The study of sentence structure in the next three chapters should substantially facilitate the translation of texts and augment understanding of the basic elements of grammatical construction.

Positive and Negative Forms

1. The word *oui* is the positive answer to a question and means "yes".

"...*oui*, je veux marcher droit et calme dans la vie..."
(Fauré, *Le Bonne Chanson* - 1)

2. The word *non* is the negative answer to a question and means "no". The adverb *si* is used to contradict negative statements.

"...toujours vois-tu mon âme en rêve?-*non*."
(Debussy, "Colloque sentimental")

3. The negative is formed in French by placing *ne* before the verb and *pas* after it. When the adverb *pas* appears in sentence structure in translating it indicates that the verb is negative.

a) The negative form of the *present tense* is:

je ne chant	pas	I do not sing
il ne joue	pas	he does not play
nous n'entendons	pas	we do not hear

"...le corps *ne* suit *pas*..."
(Berlioz, "L'absence")

Before a verb beginning with a vowel, *ne* becomes *n'*. When *pas* is followed by a consonant it is pronounced [pɑ]; *pas* may be pronounced [pɑ] or [pɑz] when followed by a vowel sound.

b) Compound verb tenses are made negative by negating the auxiliary verb and adding the past participle:
"...il n'a pas fait un hiver aussi terrible."
(Debussy, "Le tombeau des naïades")

c) The imperative is made negative by placing *ne* before the imperative verb form and *pas* after it.

"...mais n'espérez pas..."
(Fauré, *Poème d'un jour* - 2)

"...n'allez pas au bois d'Ormonde..."
(Ravel, "Trois Chansons pour choeur")

d) Reflexive verbs are made negative by placing *ne* after the subject before the reflexive pronoun and *pas* after the verb:

(1) Present tense: nous ne nous dépêchons pas

(2) In the negative form of the compound past tense of reflexive verbs, *ne* is placed before the reflexive pronoun, and *pas* stands between the form of *être* and the past participle: nous ne nous sommes pas dépêchés

4. The meaning "only" is expressed when *ne* precedes and *que* follows the verb.

"...tout n'est qu'ordre et beauté..."
(Duparc, "L'invitation au voyage")

"Ah! ne pouvoir que..."
(Duparc, "Soupir")

"...ainsi que deux lauriers n'ont souvent qu'une racine..."
(Debussy, "La chevelure")

5. The meaning "no, none, no one" is expressed when *ne* precedes and *aucun(e)* follows the verb: *aucun* is the masculine form, *aucune* the feminine form.

6. The following are other negative expressions with *ne* before the verb and another negative expression following the verb:

a) *ne...plus* = no more, no longer

"...ne fleurisse plus ton image!"
(Fauré, "Nell")

"...on n'entend plus rien..."
(Ravel, "Histoires naturelles - Le Grillon")

"...il n'est plus de parfum..."
(Fauré, "Les roses d'Ispahan")

b) *ne...jamais* = never

"...ma mère ne croira jamais..."
(Debussy, "La Flûte")

c) *ne...rien* = nothing

> "...nous n'avons rien à nous dire..."
> (Debussy, "La Flûte")

> "...il n'a rien..."
> (Ravel, "Histoires naturelles - Le Cygne")

> "...mais ne crains rien..."
> (Berlioz, "Le spectre de la rose")

d) *ne...ni...ni* = neither...nor

> "...je ne réclame ni messe ni De Profundis..."
> (Berlioz, "Le spectre de la rose")

e) *ne...pas du tout* = not at all

f) *ne...personne* = no one

(1) *Personne* or *rien* may be the subject or direct object of a sentence; in such cases, *ne* precedes the verb.

> "...il ne voit rien venir et personne ne répond..."
> (Ravel, "Histoires naturelles - Le Paon")

> "...rien n'a donc changé..."
> (Hahn, "Infidélité")

(2) When used in an interrogative sentence without *ne* before the verb, *jamais* and *personne* mean "ever", "anyone".

7. With the following verbs *ne* may be used without *pas* and still have full negative meaning:

> cesser - to cease
>
> oser - to dare
>
> pouvoir - to be able
>
> savoir - to know

8. The following should be noted for translation:

a) *pas* is seldom used in literary style when *ne* follows another negative expression, such as *non*, in the sentence.

b) *ne* is sometimes used redundantly and therefore has no negative meaning when it stands alone, and:

(1) after the verb *craindre* (to fear)

(2) after *à moins que* (unless)

(3) after *avant que* (before)

(4) after a comparative

II. PARTITIVE

When a noun refers to only a part of its whole, to *some* or *any*, it is in the *partitive* sense. The partitive sense in English is frequently expressed by the words *some* or *any*, often implied rather than stated. The partitive in French is always expressed in corresponding cases and is formed by combining the preposition *de* with the definite article *le, la, l', les*.

A. Partitive Forms

When nouns are used in a partitive sense in affirmative statements, commands, and questions, they are accompanied by one of the partitive forms:

1. *de* plus *le* = *du* [dy] is used before a masculine singular noun beginning with a consonant:

"...j'ai du plaisir..."
(Ravel, "d'Anne jouant de l'espinette")

2. *de la* [dəlɑ] is used before feminine singular nouns beginning with a consonant.

3. *de l'* [dəl] is used before a masculine or feminine noun beginning with a vowel sound.

4. *des* [de] is used before plural nouns beginning with a consonant.

"...voici des fruits, des fleurs, des feuilles et des branches..."
(Debussy, "Green")

"...qui me rafrachissaient le front avec des palmes..."
(Duparc, "La vie antérieure")

"...on effeuille des jasmines..."
(Fauré, "Dans les ruines d'une abbaye")

a) When *des* is used before plural nouns beginning with a vowel sound it is pronounced [dez].

"...je chanterai des airs ingénus..."
(Fauré, *La Bonne Chanson* - 2)

B. Use of the Partitive

1. The singular forms of the partitive "some" - *du, de la, de l'* - are used with non-countable nouns.

2. The plural form of the partitive "some" - *des* - is used before countable nouns.

3. The partitive is frequently used with verbs such as *vouloir, avoir, manger, commander, apporter* because only a part of the noun to which the partitive refers is generally desired.

4. The regular partitive (*du, de la, de l', des*) is used after *ne...que.*

C. Summary of Partitive Forms

de + le = du
de + la = de la
de + l'   = de l'
de + les = des

III. PREPOSITIONS

A *preposition* shows the grammatical relationship of a noun or pronoun to some other element in the sentence. The following are prepositions frequently encountered in French:

à	to, at, in
à travers	across
afin de	in order to
après	after, afterward
au-delà de	beyond
au-dessous de	under, below
au-dessus de	above
au-devant	towards
autour de	around
avant	before
avec	with
chez	at (to, in) the house (office) of
contre	against
au cours de	during

dans	into, in
de	of, about, from
dès que	as soon as
depuis	since, for
derrière	behind, back of
devant	in front of
en	in, to, by, while
entre	between, among
envers	towards
jusqu'à	until, up to, to
malgré	in spite of
par	by, through
parmi	among
pendant	during
pour	for, in order to, to
sans	without
selon	according to
suivant	according to, in accordance with
vers	toward
voici	here is, here are
voilà	there is, there are

Special Uses

1. The preposition *à* (to, in, at) is used before the name of a city: Je vais à Paris.

2. The preposition *en* (to, in, at) is used without an article before the names of continents or countries which are feminine; *en* is pronounced [an] before a vowel sound. The preposition *de* (from) is used without an article before the names of continents or countries which are feminine. Most names of countries that end in *-e* are feminine (Exception: Le Mexique).

Nous allons en France.

Ils viennent de Russie.

3. The preposition *à* (to, in, at) and *de* (from) are used in combination with the article before the names of countries that are masculine.

Je vais au Mexique.

Vous venez du Canada.

"...et j'arrive du paradis..."
(Berlioz, "Le spectre de la rose")

a) The preposition *aux* (to, at, in) is used before Etats-Unis: Elle est aux Etats-Unis.

4. Prepositions are frequently used with verbs in French.

a) The following verbs are used with prepositions in English but not in French:

> attendre - to wait for
> chercher - to look for
> demander - to ask for
> écouter - to listen to
> regarder - to look at

b) The following verbs are used with prepositions in French but not in English:

> changer de - to change
> demander à - to ask someone something
> entrer dans - to enter
> répondre à - to answer

c) The following prepositions may follow a conjugated verb that can take an infinitive:

(1) The preposition *à* follows these verbs before the infinitive:

> apprendre à - to learn
> aider à - to help
> avoir à - to have to
> commencer à - to begin
> continuer à - to continue
> inviter à - to invite
> se mettre à - to begin
> réussir à - to succeed

> "...il m'apprend à jouer..."
> (Debussy, "La Flûte")

275

(2) The preposition *de* follows these verbs before the infinitive:

conseiller de - to advise

craindre de - to fear

décider de - to decide

demander de - to ask

se dépêcher de - to hurry

dire de - to say

essayer de - to try

être de - to be

oublier de - to forget

permettre de - to permit

refuser de - to refuse

regretter de - to regret

"...vous me demandez de me taire...de fuir...de m'en aller..."
(Fauré, "Toujours")

"...demandez plutôt aux étoiles de tomber..."
(Fauré, "Toujours")

(3) A preposition is not required after the following verbs before an infinitive:

aimer

aller

devoir

faire

falloir

oser

pouvoir

savoir

sembler

suivre

venir

vouloir

"...le secret douloureux qui me faisait languir."
(Duparc, "La vie antérieure")

"...on peut l'épandre toute..."
(Fauré, "Le parfum impérissable")

"...nos chansons veulent se répondre..."
(Debussy, "La Flûte")

"...tu pourras suivre ma trace..."
(Duparc, "La manoir de Rosemonde")

"...un conseil...semble sortir...et monter..."
(Debussy, "Beau soir")

"...je ne veux vous voir..."
(Fauré, *La Bonne Chanson* - 5)

d) The verb infinitive may be used after these prepositions:

afin de - in order (to)

avant de - before

après - after

par - by

pour - for; in order to; so as to

sans - without

(1) When *pour* is used with an infinitive after the verb *aller* it means "for the express purpose of"; when followed by a noun or pronoun, *pour* means "for". When followed by an infinitive *pour* means "in order to".

"...c'est pour assouvir ton moindre désir..."
(Duparc, "L'invitation au voyage")

"...et pour fuir la vie importune..."
(Duparc, "Chanson triste")

(2) After *après* the perfect infinitive must be used:

après + infinitive + past participle

"...après m'avoir fui..."
(Fauré, *La Bonne Chanson* - 2)

(3) After the preposition *en* the present participle is used; when the present participle of a verb is used as a noun as the object of a preposition it is known as a *gerund*. The following verbs have irregular present participles:

avoir - ayant

être - étant

savoir - sachant

"...et je dis en quittant vos charmes..."
(Fauré, "Adieu")

"...il garde en se brisant..."
(Fauré, "Le parfum impérissable")

"...les houles, en roulant les images des cieux..."
(Duparc, "La vie antérieure")

"...la grenouille en nageant...l'hirondelle rase en passant..."
(Hahn, "Infidélité")

"...en suivant mon sang répandu..."
(Duparc, "Le manoir de Rosemonde")

5. The adverb *y* [i] replaces a preposition of place (à, dans, sur) and the object of the preposition. Although its meaning may vary depending upon the use of the preposition and noun which it replaces, *y* generally precedes the verb and means "there".

a) When a verb is used with an infinitive, *y* precedes the verb form to which it refers.

b) The expression *il y a* means:

(1) "there is", "there are"

(2) "ago"

(3) *il y a...que* - "for" - used with the present tense in French to describe an action begun in the past continuing to present time.

(a) The form in the imperfect tense is *il y avait...que*, referring to a continued action in past time.

(4) *il y a...que* means "ago" when used with the simple past or compound past tense (frequent in literary texts).

6. The preposition *pendant* (for) is used with the compound past tense before an expression of time to describe an action completed in the past. The preposition *depuis* (for) is used with the present tense before an expression of time to express an action that has begun in the past and continues through the present.

"...j'ai depuis un an le printemps dans l'âme..."
(Fauré, *La Bonne Chanson* - 9)

7. It is important to learn the exact meaning of prepositions for translation; these small words are critical in determining sentence meaning.

IV. CONJUNCTIONS

A *conjunction* is a word used to connect words, phrases, or clauses; a *clause* is a group of words containing a subject and a verb. A *main* (independent) clause can form a sentence in itself; a *subordinate* (dependent) clause can function only with an independent clause.

Uses

1. The following are conjunctions frequently encountered in French:

à moins que - unless

afin que - in order that, so that

après que - after

avant que - before

bien que - although

donc - then so

jusqu'à ce que - until

lorsque - when

parce que - because

de peur que - for fear that

pour que - so that

pourvu que - provided that

puisque - since

quand même - anyway

quoique - although

sans que - without

si - if, whether

tandis que - whereas

"...puisque vous reposez..."
(Debussy, "Green")

2. When the conjunctions "soit...soit...", "ou...ou..." appear in consecutive clauses or phrases they mean "either...or...".

3. The conjunctions "ni...ni..." mean "neither...nor..." (*ne* stands before the verb).

4. The conjunction *parce que* (because) may be followed by a clause; the prepositional expression *à cause de* (because of) is followed by a noun or pronoun and its modifiers.

5. After the conjunctions *quand* (when), *lorsque* (when), *aussitôt que* (as soon as), *dès que* (as soon as)

> a) the future tense is used in French when it is implied; the present tense is generally used in English instead of the future tense.

> b) the future perfect tense is used in French instead of the present perfect tense as in English.
> "...dès qu'il les flatte..."
> (Paladilhe, "Psyché")

"...dès que je pense être un peu aimé d'elle..."
(Ravel, "d'Anne jouant de l'espinette")

"...quand tout bas je soupire seul..."
(Debussy, "Nuit d'étoiles")

6. Note the similarities between conjunctions and prepositions:

Conjunctions	*Prepositions*
pendant que (while)	pendant (during, for)
pour que (in order that)	pour (for, in order to)
jusqu'à ce que (until)	jusqu'à (until)
afin que (in order that)	afin de (in order to)
avant que (before)	avant (before)
	avant de (before)
	devant (in front of)

Prepositions are used before nouns or infinitives; conjunctions are used before clauses.

> a) *avant* (before) is used before a noun phrase
>
> *avant de* (before) is used before infinitives
>
> *avant que* (before) precedes a clause
>
> b) *devant* (in front of) precedes an expression naming a place.

"...devant l'immensité..."
(Fauré, "Rencontre")

"...devant les meutes aux abois..."
(Duparc, "Phidylé")

V. ADDITIONAL PRONOUN FORMS

To this point, all nouns and pronouns have been in reference to the subject of the sentence. Additional pronoun forms describe the relationship in sentence structure of pronouns to other words. The French personal pronouns have two forms:

(1) *unstressed* form - used as the subject, direct object, and indirect object of verbs

(2) *stressed* form

A. Direct Object Pronouns

A *direct object* receives directly the action expressed by the verb. Direct object nouns follow the verb in French.

"...et j'entends l'âme de ma mie..."
(Debussy, "Nuit d'étoiles")

The *direct object pronouns* (unstressed) follow the subject of the sentence and precede the verb in French:

me (m')	me
te (t')	you
le (l')	him, it
la (l')	her, it
nous	us
vous	you
les	them

"...tu me pris..."
(Berlioz, "Le spectre de la rose")

"...et mon coeur te chérit sans te connaître bien..."
(Fauré, "Rencontre")

"...et il me regarda..."
(Debussy, "La chevelure")

"...peu soucieux qu'on nous ignore ou qu'on nous voie."
(Fauré, *La Bonne Chanson* - 8)

"...les rayons du soleil vous baisent..."
(Paladilhe, "Psyché")

"...je les caressais..."
(Debussy, "La chevelure")

1. The first, second, and third person singular forms are elided when followed by a vowel sound.

"...et peut l'appeler per son nom..."
(Fauré, "Au cimetière")

"...je veux que le matin l'ignore le nom que j'ai dit..."
(Fauré, "Le secret")

"...tu m'enveloppais..."
(Debussy, "Romance")

"...tu m'appelais...je t'appelle..."
(Fauré, "Après un rêve")

"...midi...rayonne, et t'invite au sommeil."
(Duparc, "Phidylé")

2. In compound verb tenses the direct object pronoun precedes the auxiliary verbs.

"...il m'a donné une syrinx..."
(Debussy, "La Flûte")

"...l'amour m'a mordu..."
(Duparc, "Le manoir de Rosemonde")

3. *Ne* precedes the direct object pronoun in a negative statement or negative imperative.

"...ne le déchirez pas..."
(Debussy, "Green")

4. When a verb is used with an infinitive, the direct object pronoun precedes the infinitive.

5. When the following verbs (normally conjugated with *être*) are used with a direct object, they are conjugated with the auxiliary verb *avoir*.

arriver

devenir

entrer

monter

mourir

naître

partir

passer

redevenir

rester

retourner

rentrer

revenir

sortir

tomber

6. Verbs conjugated with the auxiliary verb *avoir* are generally invariable in compound tenses; the past participle does not agree in gender and number with the subject. However, when the direct object precedes the past participle in sentence structure, the past participle must agree in gender and number with the preceding direct object. The past participle of a reflexive verb agrees in gender and number with the direct object pronoun when this object precedes the past participle.

7. The prepositional expressions *voici* (here is, here are) and *voilà* (there is, there are) follow the direct object pronouns.

8. It is important for translation to realize that some words have multiple grammatical functions. When *le, la,* and *les* are followed by a noun, these words are definite articles; when *le, la,* and *les* appear in sentence structure after the subject and before the verb they are direct object pronouns which replace the name of a person, place, or thing in the sentence. When *nous* and *vous* stand alone at the beginning of a sentence they are subject pronouns; when *nous* and *vous* stand after the subject and precede the verb in sentence structure, they are direct object pronouns. For translation it is important to learn to recognize what grammatical function words imply.

B. Indirect Object Pronouns

An *indirect object* indicates *to* or *for whom* the action of the verb is done. The *unstressed personal pronouns* in French used as the direct object of a verb refer only to persons:

me (m')	to me
te (t')	to you
lui	to him, to her
nous	to us
vous	to you
leur	to them

1. Note that *lui* and *leur* replace both masculine and feminine nouns.

> "...lui font de longs adieux..."
> (Fauré, "Au cimetière")

2. Note that *me* and *te* are elided when followed by a vowel sound.

3. Indirect object nouns are preceded by the preposition *à* (to) and follow the verb; indirect object *pronouns* precede the verb. In the compound past tense, indirect object pronouns precede the auxiliary verb.

> "...il m'a semblé..."
> (Debussy, "La chevelure")

4. When a verb is used with an infinitive, the indirect object pronoun precedes the infinitive.

5. In negative sentences, *ne* precedes the indirect object pronoun.

6. The pronoun *y* is the indirect object pronoun that refers to things only; note that *y* does not replace *à* plus an indirect object which is a person.

7. The partitive pronoun *en* is used to replace nouns used in a partitive sense, that is, the partitive article (de) plus its object, a noun naming a person or thing; *en* precedes the verb in sentence structure. When a verb is used with an infinitive, *en* precedes the infinitive.

> "...j'en murmure..."
> (Paladilhe, "Psyché")

The pronoun *en* replaces nouns modified by a number.

> Il a écrit cinq symphonies.

> Il en a cinq écrit.

a) The pronoun *en* must be used with the following expressions of quantity when the expression is the direct object of the verb:

> beaucoup
>
> pas
>
> un peu
>
> plusieurs
>
> quelques-uns (m. - some, a few)
>
> quelques-unes (f. - some, a few)

b) The pronoun *en* always stands last in sentence structure when another personal pronoun is the verb object.

> "...et qu'ainsi je m'en fus mourir..."
> (Duparc, "Le manoir de Rosemonde")

c) The pronoun *en* may replace prepositional phrases with *de* when the object is a thing, not a person.

> "...il en joue..."
> (Debussy, "La Flûte")

C. Pronoun Word Order

If both a direct object and an indirect object pronoun are used in sentence structure, they stand before the verb in the following order:

me			le			
te			la		lui	y en
se	precede		les		leur	
nous						
vous						

> "...toujours les lui tendre..."
> (Duparc, "Soupir")

1. When a finite verb is used with an infinitive, the pronoun objects precede the infinitive.

2. In negative sentences *ne* precedes the object pronouns. In the compound past tense, *pas* stands between the auxiliary verb and the past participle.

3. When used with imperative verbs in the affirmative, the pronoun objects are hyphenated to the verb.

a) The same direct and indirect object pronouns are used in the imperative as in other verb forms, except for *me* and *te*, which become *moi* and *toi* in the imperative.

"...ô nuit, rends-moi tes mensonges..."
(Fauré, "Après un rêve")

"...pardonnez-moi..."
(Fauré, *La Bonne Chanson* - 5)

"...ô dis-moi..."
(Fauré, "Rencontre")

b) If both the direct and indirect object pronouns are used after the imperative verb form, the direct object always comes first.

c) The pronoun *en* stands last when used with another pronoun object after the imperative. When followed by *en*, *moi* becomes *m'*; *toi* becomes *t'*.

d) In the imperative affirmative, word order for direct and indirect objects follows the pattern:

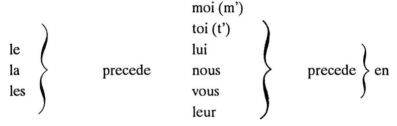

e) When the imperative is negative

(1) the pronoun objects precede the verb

(2) the unstressed forms of personal pronouns are used

(3) normal word order for pronoun objects in a declarative sentence is used (see p. 285).

VI. STRESSED FORMS OF PRONOUNS

The *stressed* form of personal pronouns differ from the unstressed in form and usage. The unstressed forms are generally used as the subject, direct object, and indirect object of verbs; the stressed forms of personal pronouns are generally used to refer to persons only:

moi	I, me
toi	you
lui	him, he
elle	her, she
nous	us, we
vous	you
eux	them, they
elles	them, they

The different forms for masculine and feminine *stressed* pronouns in the third person (Singular: lui, elle; Plural: eux, elles) should be noted. The third person of unstressed pronouns has only one form (lui) for the singular and one form (leur) for the plural.

Uses of Stressed Pronouns

1. Stressed forms of personal pronouns are used as the object of a preposition. (de, avec, sans, chez, pour, etc.)

"...il rentre chez lui et ferme sa porte..."
(Ravel, "Histoires naturelles - Le Grillon")

"...pour m'enfuir avec toi vers la lumière..."
(Fauré, "Après un rêve")

"...pour moi, mon âme, va tout droit..."
(Berlioz, "l'absence")

"...les délices...sortent de toi..."
(Fauré, "Lydia")

"...amour, qui m'emflammis pour elle!"
(Duparc, "Phidylé")

"...il en joue après moi..."
(Debussy, "La Flûte")

"...ou que tu entrais en moi..."
(Debussy, "La chevelure")

"...je pense être un peu aimé d'elle."
(Ravel, "d'Anne jouant de l'espinette")

"...cherchant jusqu'à toi..."
(Fauré, "Aurore")

"...guidé par vous...par toi conduit..."
(Fauré, *La Bonne Chanson* - 2)

"...à vous l'on se croyait fidèle..."
(Fauré, "Adieu")

"...déjâ m'enchaîne à toi..."
(Fauré, "Rencontre")

"...penche aussi vers moi..."
(Fauré, "Nell")

a) The stressed forms of personal pronouns generally refer to persons only.

(1) The pronoun *en* (of it, of them) replaces the preposition *de* plus a stressed form of the personal pronoun in reference to a thing.

2. Stressed pronoun forms are used after the comparative of an adjective.

3. Stressed pronouns are used to specify the persons indicated in a compound subject; it is standard practice in French to use the pronoun that sums up the subject parts after a compound subject.

4. Stressed pronouns are used after *c'est* and *ce sont* as predicate nominatives.

5. Stressed pronouns are used alone, as in a one-word answer.

6. Stressed pronouns are used for emphasis in addition to, or instead of, an unstressed pronoun form.

"...ô toi qui décore..."
(Fauré, *La Bonne Chanson* - 9)

7. Stressed pronouns may be hyphenated to *même*; the adjective *même* (self, same) agrees in number with the pronoun modified, and makes the stressed pronoun more emphatic.

moi-même	myself
toi-même	yourself
lui-même	himself

elle-même		herself
nous-mêmes		ourselves
vous-même(s)		yourself, yourselves
eux-mêmes		themselves
elles-mêmes		themselves

"...que je devenais toi-même..."
(Debussy, "La chevelure")

"...te mira blème toi-même..."
(Debussy, "L'ombre des arbres")

VII. POSSESSIVE PRONOUNS

Possessive adjectives modify nouns; *possessive pronouns* replace nouns modified by a possessive adjective.

Forms of Possessive Pronouns

Singular

masculine	feminine	
le mien	la mienne	mine
le tien	la tienne	yours
le sien	la sienne	his, hers, its
le nôtre	la nôtre	ours
le vôtre	la vôtre	yours
le leur	la leur	theirs

Plural

les miens	les miennes	mine
les tiens	les tiennes	yours
les siens	les siennes	his, hers, its
les nôtres	les nôtres	ours
les vôtres	les vôtres	yours
les leurs	les leurs	theirs

1. Possessive pronouns agree in gender and number with what is possessed (the possession).

> "...et c'étaient les miens..."
> (Debussy, "La chevelure")

> "...ta tristesse sauvage, à la mienne pareille..."
> (Fauré, "Rencontre")

> "...tout ce bonheur veut bien être le mien..."
> (Fauré, *La Bonne Chanson* - 2)

> "...c'est la nôtre, n'est-ce pas? la mienne, dis, et la tienne..."
> (Debussy, "C'est l'extase langoureuse")

2. When used with the preposition *à* the forms of the possessive pronouns are *au mien, à la mienne, aux miens, aux miennes*.

3. When used with the preposition *de* the forms of the possessive pronouns are *du mien, de la mienne, des miens, des miennes*.

VIII. DEMONSTRATIVE PRONOUNS

A *demonstrative pronoun* points out or indicates, and answers the question "which one(s)?".

Forms of Demonstrative Pronouns

Singular

masculine		*feminine*	
celui-ci	this one	celle-ci	this one
celui-là	that one	celle-là	that one

Plural

ceux-ci	these	celles-ci	these
ceux-là	those	celles-là	those

1. Demonstrative pronouns are used to distinguish between persons or things within a group.

2. Demonstrative pronouns must agree in gender and number with the nouns to which they refer.

3. The suffix *-ci* shows nearness to the object(s) named (this one, these).

4. The suffix *-là* connotes distance from the object(s) named (that one, those).

5. Demonstrative pronouns are used:

    a) To mean "former" and "latter". Demonstrative pronouns with *-ci* mean "former"; demonstrative pronouns with *-là* mean "latter".

    b) When *celui, celle, ceux,* and *celles* are followed by a phrase introduced by *de*, possession is indicated.

"...la trace...est celle d'un bouc..."
(Debussy, "Le tombeau des naïades")

    c) Unlike other demonstrative pronouns, *ceci* (this) and *cela* (*ça*) (that) refer to something pointed out but not specifically named, or to an idea, a statement, or a situation; these pronouns never refer to persons. *Cela* and *ça* have the same meaning; *ça* is used primarily in conversation.

PREPOSITIONS THAT GIVE DIRECTIONS IN MUSIC

avec le bois	with the wood of the bow
de la pointe	at the point of the bow
du talon	at the frog of the bow
près de la table	near the sounding board (harp)
sans sourdine	without mute
sur le chevalet	at (near) the bridge
sur la touche	on the fingerboard

ABBREVIATIONS

c.-à-d.	c'est à dire - that is to say
p. ex.	par example - for example
M.	Monsieur - Mr.
Mme	Madame - Mrs.
Mlle	Mademoiselle - Miss

Note that neither *Mme* nor *Mlle* require a period.

IDIOMATIC EXPRESSIONS

à côte	side by side
à votre service	at your service, don't mention it
au contraire	on the contrary
bien sûr	of course, certainly
cela ne fait rien	it doesn't matter
c'est-à- dire	that is to say
commi çi, comme ça	so-so
comme d'habitude	as usual
d'accord	in agreement
demain soir	tomorrow night
eh, bien	well
en effet	yes (indeed)
encore une fois	again
grâce à	thanks to
hier soir	yesterday evening
moi aussi	I too (so am I)
moi non plus	nor I (neither am I)
par contre	on the other hand
sans doute	probably, surely

PREPOSITION SUPPLEMENT

Time of Day

1. Quelle heure est-il? What time is it?
2. Il est onze heures. It is eleven o'clock.
3. The half hour is expressed

   Il est onze heures *et demie*. (11:30)
4. The quarter after the hour is expressed

   Il est onze heures *et quart*. (11:15)
5. The quarter before the hour is expressed

   Il est midi *moins le quart*. (11:45)

   (It is noon less a quarter of an hour.)

6. To express minutes between the hour and the half hour following, the number of minutes is added to the hour:

Il est quatre heures onze. (4:11)

7. To express minutes between the half hour and the following hour, the time is measured back from the next hour:

Il est cinq heures moins treize. (4:47)

8. *du matin* is used to express A.M.

de l'après-midi is used to express P.M. (afternoon)

du soir is used to express P.M. (evening)

9. Noon is expressed *midi*

Midnight is expressed *minuit*

10. The 24-hour system is used in official announcements, especially for travel, banks, theatres, offices, etc.; after noon 1:00 p.m. is 13.00 heures (treize heures), and so forth.

a) In this system, fractions of an hour are expressed in terms of minutes after the hour.

11. To express time passed, the expression *il y a* plus an expression of time may be used with the compound tense, meaning "ago".

a) The following words all mean "time" but are used in different contexts:

(1) *temps* (m.) refers to time in a general sense

(2) when used with the verb *faire*, *temps* refers to the weather

(3) *heure* (f.) is used in telling time

(4) *fois* (f.) is used in the following expressions:

une fois - one time, once

deux fois - two times, twice

plusieurs fois - several times

"...Oh! quelquefois sur tes genoux..."
(Duparc, "Chanson triste")

TRANSLATION EXERCISES

1. Translate the following from the article entitled "Quatuor" from the *Encyclopédie de la Musique*:

"Ce terme s'applique à toute oeuvre écrite à 4 parties harmoniques réelles: dans un sens large il designe l'ensemble de ses exécutants:...Sans avoir subi d'éclipse totale jusqu'à nos jours, il s'est effacé devant le quatuor instrumental, dont la forme suprème est la quatuor à cordes (2 viol., alto et vcelle), inconnu jusqu'au milieu du XVIIIᵉ siècle: à la Renaissance, la musique de chambre consistait surtout en chansons ou madrigaux à 4 ou 5 voix: ce répertoire céda la place, au XVIIIᵉ siècle, au trio instrumental (2 dessus et 1 basse), qui à son tour, disparut au milieu du XVIIIᵉ siècle devant le quatuor d'archets...en réalité, le quatuor à cordes provient des symphonies (ou sonates) à 4 - Sammartini, Vivaldi, Tartini, en Italie; Stamitz, Starzer, Hoffmann en Germanie; Guillemain, Gossec en France -, qui ouvrent la voie à Haydn et à Mozart. Beethoven porte le genre à son apogée;..."

2. Translate the following from the article entitled "Festivals" in the introduction to the *Encyclopédie de la Musique*:

"C'est le festival d'Aix-en-Provence (10-13 juillet), créé en 1947, qui est jusqu'ici le plus célèbre des festivals français; la ville, dans son genre, rivalise avec Salzbourg...et le soleil y est fidèle. Le théâtre en plein air improvisé dans la cour du palais de l'archevêché, magnifique édifice du XVIIᵉ siècle, forme un cadre idéal pour les représentations des opéras de Mozart, données par un ensemble international, avec concours de l'Orchestre de la Société des Concerts du Conservatoire de Paris, sous la direction de Hans Rosbaud. La musique contemporaine y a une place qui fait honneur autant aux organisateurs du festival qui ont pris l'initiative de la faire jouer, qu'au public qui a su l'apprécier."

3. Translate the following from the article "Droit du critique musical" by Jean Matthyssens in the introduction to the *Encyclopédie de la Musique*:

"Le critique a le droit d'informer ses lecteurs, de formuler ses appréciations sur l'opportunité des initiatives d'un compositeur, sur le mérite de ses oeuvres, mais il engage sa responsabilité, il commet un abus de son droit, s'il porte sur l'oeuvre un jugement excessif inspiré par la volonté de nuire.

Le critique commettrait une grave faute professionnelle en rendant compte d'un spectacle qu'il n'aurait pas vu."

Chapter Six

I. WORD ORDER IN SENTENCE STRUCTURE

A. Normal Word Order

1. Subject and its modifiers
2. Verb
3. Verbal modifiers

> "...je revois...tes regards..."
> (Debussy, "Nuit d'étoiles")

a) Short adverbs used with the compound past tense in French are usually placed between the auxiliary verb and the past participle.

B. Inverted Word Order

For stylistic variety or in order to emphasize a particular element, a sentence in French may begin with an element other than the subject; this is known as *inverted word order*.

1. Inverted word order is used in formal style after adverbs or adverbial phrases:

> à peine - scarcely
>
> aussi - therefore   (when used at the beginning of a sentence)
>
> peut-être - perhaps
>
> sans doute - without

2. When a clause is introduced by *que (qu')*, *comme*, or *où*, the subject may stand second in the sentence followed by the verb, as in normal word order, or the subject and verb may be inverted:

$$\left.\begin{array}{l} \text{que (qu')} \\ \text{comme} \\ \text{où} \end{array}\right\} \quad \text{verb} \quad \left.\right\} \quad \text{subject}$$

3. Another form of inverted word order is the *question*. Questions are formed in French in the following ways:

a) A declarative sentence may be made into a question by changing the punctuation from a period to a question mark.

b) A declarative sentence may be made into a question by using the interrogative phrase *est-ce que* (*est-ce qu'*) before the subject and verb in normal word order and adding a question mark.

c) A question may also be formed by adding the interrogative phrase *n'est-ce pas?* to a declarative statement, especially if an answer of confirmation is expected. The phrase *n'est-ce pas?* is translated "don't you think so?", "don't I?", "don't you?", "will you not?", "wouldn't you?", "didn't you?".

> "...n'est-ce pas? en dépit des sots et des méchants..."
> (Fauré, *La Bonne Chanson* - 8)

d) Questions are often formed in French by inverting the pronoun subject and the verb (the inverted verb-subject pronoun is hyphenated) and punctuating the inversion with a question mark; this form is known as a *direct question*.

> "...toujours vois-tu mon âme en rêve?"
> (Debussy, "Colloque sentimental")

> "...des tendresses du sang peut-on être jaloux?"
> (Paladilhe, "Psyché")

(1) When a verb and subject pronoun are inverted in the third person singular (il, elle), a *t* must be inserted between the inverted verb and the subject pronoun if the verb ends in a vowel.

> "...a-t-il fini? est-elle cassée?"
> (Ravel, "Histoires naturelles - Le Grillon")

(2) The subject pronoun *je* is not ordinarily used in inverted form (this form is encountered occasionally in literary texts). The interrogative *est-ce que* is used in forming a question with the subject pronoun *je*.

e) Subject-verb inversion and the use of *est-ce que* are frequently encountered forms of the question in French.

f) Word order of *object pronouns* in questions:

(1) The direct object pronoun precedes the verb both in subject-verb inversion and with *est-ce que*.

(2) The indirect object pronoun precedes the verb, both in subject-verb inversion and with *est-ce que*.

g) A question may be formed in French when the subject of the verb is a noun by using the noun subject and the inverted verb with the pronoun equivalent of the subject.

"...ton coeur bat-il toujours à mon seul nom?"
(Debussy, "Colloque sentimental")

h) The interrogative of the compound past tense of verbs is formed by inverting the form of the auxiliary verb and adding the past participle.

"Où donc les vents l'ont-ils chassée?"
(Debussy, "Romance")

Besides illustrating the interrogative of the compound past tense, this example illustrates several other points already mentioned. The main clause of the sentence is introduced by the interrogative adverb *où*. The subject stands second in the sentence; since the subject is a noun, the inverted verb also expresses the pronoun equivalent of the subject: ils = les vents. The direct object pronoun *l'* (l'âme, f.) precedes the verb; the past participle reflects the fact that the preceding direct object is feminine: chassé*e*.

i) When an interrogative adverb or adverbial expression is used to form a question, the interrogative word or expression generally stands first in the question.

à quelle heure? - at what time?

combien? - how much?

comment? - how?

où? - where?

quand? - when?

These interrogatives are followed by

(1) inverted word order: verb-subject pronoun

(2) *est-ce que?* plus normal word order

These adverbial expressions may be used with *noun* subjects in inverted word order if the subject is final in the sentence and the inverted verb does not thereby require the pronoun equivalent of the subject.

j) The adverb *pourquoi* (why?) requires the following word order when used with a noun subject in inversion:

pourquoi + noun subject + verb inverted with pronoun equivalent
"...pourquoi voulez-vous donc qu'il m'en souvienne?"
(Debussy, "Colloque sentimental")

k) A negative question is formed

(1) When *est-ce que* is used in a negative interrogative sentence the verb is made negative as in normal word order.

(2) When inversion is used in a negative interrogative sentence *ne* precedes the inverted form, *pas* or its negative equivalent follows the inverted form.

"...n'est-il plus un parfum...?"
(Debussy, "Romance")

(3) Interrogative adverbs and expressions precede the negative inversion.

l) In the interrogative form of reflexive verbs, the reflexive pronoun precedes the verb; the subject pronoun is hyphenated to the finite verb.

"Te souvient-il de notre extase ancienne?"
(Debussy, "Colloque sentimental")

II. INTERROGATIVE ADJECTIVES

Interrogative adjectives are used to modify nouns only.

Forms

The forms of interrogative adjectives are:

Singular		*Plural*	
m.	quel?	quels?	which? what?
f.	quelle?	quelles?	which? what?

1. An interrogative adjective modifies a noun; it agrees in gender and number with the noun it modifies.

2. The forms of *quel* may be separated from the noun modified by a form of the verb *être*.

"Quelle est cette langueur...?"
(Debussy, "Il pleure dans mon coeur")

III. INTERROGATIVE PRONOUNS

A. Subject

The following *interrogative pronouns* and phrases are used as the subject of a sentence:

Qui? } who?
Qui est-ce qui? }

qu'est-ce qui?　　　what?

1. The verb used with these pronoun forms is usually in the third person singular.

2. Normal word order is used with *qu'est-ce qui?* and *qui est-ce qui?*

B. Direct Object

The following interrogative pronouns are used as the *direct object* of a sentence:

qui? whom?
que? what?

1. When *qui?* or *que?* is used as a verb object or the object of a preposition, inverted word order (verb-subject) is used.

2. *Qui* is never elided before a word beginning with a vowel; *que* is elided before a word beginning with a vowel.

"Qu'a-t-elle donc?"
(Ravel, "Histoires naturelles - La Pintade")

"Dis, qu'as-tu fait...de ta jeunesse."
(Hahn, "Le ciel est, par-dessus le toit")

"Que cherches-tu?"
(Debussy, "Le tombeau des naïades")

3. *Qui?* and *que?* may be used with *est-ce que?*, in which case normal word order is used.

qui est-ce que? - whom?

qu'est-ce que - what?

"Mais qu'est-ce que je dis?"
(Ravel, "Histoires naturelles - Le Cygne")

301

C. Special Uses

1. These interrogative pronouns are used as the object of a preposition, and may be used in inversion or with *est-ce que*.

qui - whom

quoi- what

a) *quoi* may be used as an emphatic exclamation.

"Quoi! Nulle trahison?"

(Debussy, "Il pleure dans mon coeur")

2. *à qui?* (whose) is the interrogative form expressing possession which corresponds to the forms of the verb *être à* (to belong to).

3. The interrogative expression *Qu'est-ce que c'est que* is used to ask for a description or a definition.

4. The following interrogative pronouns are used to distinguish between two or more persons or things within a group.

Singular		*Plural*	
m.	lequel? which?	lesquels?	which ones?
f.	lequelle? which one?	lesquelles?	which ones?

a) These forms agree in gender and number with the nouns to which they refer.

b) The following contractions are made with the preposition *à*: *auquel, à laquelle, auxquels, auxquelles*

c) The following contractions are made with the preposition *de*: *duquel, de laquelle, desquels, desquelles*

IV. RELATIVE PRONOUNS

A *relative pronoun* is used to connect a dependent (relative) clause to a main clause; the relative pronoun refers to a noun in the main clause. Relative pronouns are a key to efficient translation.

Forms

English uses three relative pronouns: *who* refers to a person; *which, that* refer to a thing. The forms of relative pronouns in French are:

1. The relative pronoun *qui* (who, which, that) is used as the subject of a verb and may refer to persons or things. (The interrogative pronoun *qui?* refers only to persons).

a) The relative pronoun *qui* is never elided when followed by a vowel sound.

b) The verb which follows the relative pronoun *qui* agrees with the antecedent of *qui*, that is, the noun to which the relative pronoun *qui* refers.

> "...triste lyre, qui soupire..."
> (Debussy, "Nuit d'étoiles")

> "...le secret douloureux qui me faisait languir."
> (Duparc, "La vie antérieure")

> "...et lui diras une ballade qui semblera parler de nous..."
> (Duparc, "Chanson triste")

> "...au pays qui te ressemble!"
> (Duparc, "L'invitation au voyage")

> "...un parfum qui rest..."
> (Debussy, "Romance")

> "...l'orme qui balance son ombre..."
> (Hahn, "Infidélité")

> "...l'amie qui rendrait le bonheur..."
> (Fauré, "Rencontre")

> "...au vent qui frissonne!"
> (Fauré, "Dans les ruines d'une abbaye")

> "...cire qui est douce..."
> (Debussy, "La Flûte")

> "...le chant...qui commence avec la nuit..."
> (Debussy, "La Flûte")

2. The relative pronoun *qui* may be used as the object of a preposition (other than *de*); in this case *qui* refers only to persons.

3. The relative pronoun *que* (whom, which) is used as the direct object of a verb and may refer to either persons or things.

a) *que* is elided when followed by a vowel.

> "...tu sais bien qu'il compte les jours..."
> (Berlioz, "L'absence")

"...comme un essaim léger qu'à l'horizon...appelle un chant..."
(Fauré, "Aurore")

"...sous de vastes portiques, que les soleils...teignaient..."
(Duparc, "La vie antérieure")

"...des lys divins que j'ai cueillis..."
(Debussy, "Romance")

"...tant de baisers et de tendresses que peut-être je guérirai..."
(Duparc, "Chanson triste")

"...tu verras, que...j'ai parcouru ce triste monde..."
(Duparc, "Le manoir de Rosemonde")

"...le spectre...que tu portais hier au bal..."
(Berlioz, "Le spectre de la rose")

"...le printemps que Dieu sème!"
(Fauré, "Dans les ruines d'une abbaye")

"...dans la voie...que nous montre...l'Espoir..."
(Fauré, *La Bonne Chanson* - 8)

4. The relative pronoun *dont* (whose, of which, of whom) is used to replace the preposition *de* followed by a relative pronoun.

a) *dont* may refer to persons or things

b) *dont* is used only after an expressed antecedent

c) When *dont* means "whose", the definite article is used with the noun which follows.

"...dormir ces vaisseaux *dont* l'humeur est vagabonde..."
(Duparc, "L'invitation au voyage")

"...et *dont* l'unique soin était d'approfondir..."
(Duparc, "La vie antérieure")

"...*dont* le grenouille...trouble le miroir humide..."
(Hahn, "Infidélité")

"...le poète, *dont* les yeux sont pleins d'amour..."
(Fauré, *La Bonne Chanson* - 6)

5. The pronouns *lequel, laquelle, lesquels, lesquelles* are used as relative pronouns after prepositions such as *à, avec, dans, pour, sans*, to refer to things.

a) When used with the prepositions *à* and *de* the forms are *auquel, à laquelle, auxquels, auxquelles*; *duquel, de laquelle, desquels, desquelles*. These forms are used infrequently, since *dont* is the equivalent of a relative pronoun with the preposition *de*. These forms must be used instead of *dont*, however, with the following prepositional expressions:

à côté de - next to

au cours de - during

au-dessus de - above

autour de - around

près de - near to

6. Instead of the forms of *lequel* the adverb *où* may be used in relative clauses to indicate time and place (when, where).

"...l'immuable azur où rit mon amour..."
(Fauré, *La Bonne Chanson* - 9)

"...par où j'ai passé..."
(Duparc, "Le manoir de Rosemonde")

"...le bois où dort le silence..."
(Hahn, "Infidélité")

"...des jours où tu m'enveloppais..."
(Debussy, "Romance")

"...mais restons ici, où est leur tombeau..."
(Debussy, "Le tombeau des naïades")

"...la silhouette...où le vent pleure..."
(Fauré, *La Bonne Chanson* - 3)

V. INDIRECT INTERROGATIVE PRONOUNS

Uses

1. The relative pronoun *ce qui* (that which, what) corresponds to the interrogative pronoun *qu'est-ce qui*? (what?). In indirect interrogative phrases *ce qui* is used as the subject.

2. The relative pronoun *ce que* (that which, what) corresponds to the interrogative pronoun *qu'est-ce que*? (what?). In indirect interrogative phrases *ce que* is used as a direct object.

"...tout ce que contient la parole..."
(Fauré, *La Bonne Chanson* - 1)

"...sans nous préoccuper de ce que nous destine..."
(Fauré, *La Bonne Chanson* - 8)

3. The relative pronoun *ce que c'est que* is the indirect interrogative equivalent of the direct interrogative *qu'est-ce que c'est que*? (what is?).

VI. DEMONSTRATIVE PRONOUNS

Forms

The *demonstrative pronoun* forms *celui, celle* (the one), *ceux, celles* (the ones) are always modified by a relative clause or a prepositional phrase when independent of the suffixes *-ci* and *-là.*

1. The most frequently encountered forms of the demonstrative pronouns with relative pronouns are:

Singular		*Plural*	
m.	*f.*	*m.*	*f.*
celui qui	celle qui	ceux qui	celles qui
celui que	celle que	ceux que	celles que
celui dont	celle dont	ceux dont	celles dont
celui auquel	celle à laquelle	ceux auxquels	celles auxquelles

"...tous ceux qu'il a connus...sont ceux qui meurent à la mé..."
(Fauré, "Au cimetière")

"...l'âme...de ceux qui s'aiment..."
(Fauré, *La Bonne Chanson*-8)

VII. INDEFINITE ADJECTIVES AND PRONOUNS

Forms

An *indefinite* adjective or pronoun does not clearly define or designate the person or thing to which it refers. The following are used as indefinite adjectives and pronouns in French.

1. The most frequently encountered indefinite adjectives and pronouns which have the same form are:

tout, toute, tous, toutes	all, every
plusieurs	several
aucun, aucune	adjective: no, not
	pronoun: none, not a one
autre, autres	other
l'autre, les autres	another one, the other, others, other ones
même, mêmes	same
le même, la même, les mêmes	same one, same ones

a) When *aucun* is used with a verb, the verb must be preceded by *ne*; *pas* is not used.

b) *tous* is pronounced [tus] when used as a pronoun.

c) *d'autre(s)* may mean "other one(s)" or "else".

"...je ne veux pas d'autre paradis."
(Fauré, *La Bonne Chanson* - 2)

d) Used as an adjective *tout* means "all", "every", "whole".

"...chasse à jamais tout dessein..."
(Fauré, "En sourdine")

Used in the plural with the definite article *tout* means "all", "all the", "every".

"...tous les frissons des bois..."
(Debussy, "C'est l'extase langoureuse")

"...une rose que tous les rois vont jalouser..."
(Berlioz, "Le spectre de la rose")

"...tous les baisers..."
(Fauré, "Les roses d'Ispahan")

Used in the singular without the definite article *tout(e)* means "each", "every"; used in the singular with the definite article *tout(e)* means "the whole", "all".

"...de toute la nature..."
(Paladilhe, "Psyché")

"...toute la nuit..."
(Berlioz, "Le spectre de la rose")

307

e) The pronoun *tout* has no singular form; *tous* (*toutes*) means "all", "all of them".

f). The expression *avoir de tout* (to have everything) is idiomatic.

g) The expression *tout le monde* (everyone, everybody) is always conjugated with the third person singular verb.

2. The most frequently encountered indefinite adjectives and pronouns that have dissimilar forms are: *chaque* (adjective: each) and *chacun*, *chacune* (pronoun: each, each one).

> "...et chaque saison me sera charmante..."
> (Fauré, *La Bonne Chanson* - 9)

> "...de chaque branche..."
> (Fauré, *La Bonne Chanson* - 3)

> "...on s'embrasse à chaque instant..."
> (Fauré, "Dans les ruines d'une abbaye")

> "...chacun sur le bois noir peut voir..."
> (Fauré, "Au cimetière")

quelque, quelques	adjective: some, a few
quelqu'un, quelques-un(e)s	pronoun: somebody, someone, some, a few

a) Indefinite adjectives and pronouns agree in gender and number with the nouns to which they refer.

b) The final *-s* in *quelques* is pronounced when followed by a vowel sound.

c) Note that *quelqu'un* does not have a feminine form.

d) When *quelques-uns* (*-unes*) is used as a direct object, *en* is used after the subject in sentence structure to complete the meaning of the indefinite pronoun.

e) When the pronoun *quelque chose* (something) or *rien* (nothing) is followed by an adjective which describes the indefinite pronoun, the preposition *de* precedes the adjective.

3. The following indefinite pronouns have no corresponding indefinite adjectives:

l'un, l'une, les uns, les unes	the one, the ones
on	one, they, people, someone, anybody
personne	no one, nobody

a) The forms of *l'un* are always used in contrast to *l'autre.*
"...près l'un de l'autre..."
(Debussy, "La Flûte")

b) When *personne* is used with a verb, the verb is preceded by *ne*; *pas* is not used.

c) When the subject of a question is *on* or *quelqu'un*, the question is answered negatively with the pronoun *personne*. When the subject of a question is *quelque chose*, the negative response is *rien*.

d) The related expressions *les uns...les autres* (some...others) usually occur separately in sentence structure.

VIII. EXCEPTIONS TO PARTITIVE USAGE

After such negative expressions as *ne...pas*, *ne...plus* (no more, no longer) *de* (*d'*) is generally substituted for the partitive forms and the indefinite articles.

Forms

1. The partitive form is also *de* (*d'*) after expressions of quantity.

assez - enough

beaucoup - a lot, much, many

combien - how much, how many

tant - so much, so many

trop - too much, too many

un peu - a little

"...je boirai tant de baisers..."
(Duparc, "Chanson triste")

a) These expressions of quantity may be used with both countable and non-countable nouns. Exception: *un peu de* is used only with non-countable nouns.

2. Used to modify both masculine and feminine plural nouns, *plusieurs* (several) and *quelques* (a few) do not require the partitive forms; they are used only with countable nouns.

    a) The partitive *des* becomes *de* (*d'*) when an adjective precedes the noun it modifies.

> "...il prenait de grands morceaux froids..."
>
> (Debussy, "Le tombeau des naïades")

TRANSLATION EXAMPLE

The following guidelines suggest the systematic translation process of the article entitled "Trouvère" from the *Encyclopédie de la Musique*.

TROUVÈRE. C'est un poète lyrique de langue d'oïl, qui compose à la fois mus. et vers de ses chansons artistiques. L'activité des *t.* s'étend du milieu de XII^{e}s. à la fin du XIIIe. Les *t.*, comme les troubadours, se rencontrent des toutes les classes de la société (noblesse, clergés, roture), et le mot ne désigne en aucune façon un état social, comme le désigne ménestrel. Le *t.* est essentiellement chantre de l'idéal courtois, ce qui explique la répartition géographique des centres litt. où fut cultivée la poésie lyr. (cours de France, d'Angleterre, de Champagne, de Blois, de Flandres etc.). Cependant, les *t.* attachés à une cour princière sont assez rares, par le fait même que bon nombre d'entre eux étaient seigneurs. Ds certaines riches cités, telle Arras, les *t.* d'humble extraction pouvaient s'organiser en confréries musico-litt. et organiser de véritables tournois poétiques appelés *puys*, dont le vanqueur portait le titre de prince du puy. Env. 200 *t.* nous sont connus, parmi lesquels les plus reputés sont Adam de la Halle, Andrieu Contredit, Blondel de Nesles, Conon de Béthune, le Châtelain de Coucy, Colin Muset, Gace Brulé, Gautier de Dargies, Gautier de Coinci, Guillaume le Vinier, Guiot de Dijon, Jehan Bodel, Moniot d'Arras, Perrin d'Angicourt, Thibaut de Champagne, Rutebeuf, Thomas Hérier... Les sentiments exprimés sont souvent d'une justesse ou d'une émotion qui ne peut laisser indifferent. dep. la bonne humeur de Maître Adam et l'élégance racée de Thibaut de Champagne, jusqu'à la simplicité tragique de Jehan Bodel. Les genres sont très variables, la chanson occupant la 1re place. A l'exception d'Adam de la Halle (13 rondeaux à 3 v.) et d'un anonyme, les *t.* n'usent pas, de même que les troubadours, du style polyph. Le même Adam de la Halle organise de véritables spectacles en chansons avec ses jeux (*Robin et Marion, La feuillée*), en lesquels on a voulu voir les ancêtres des comédies en vaudevilles et op.-com. Toutes ces oeuvres nous ont été transmises par de grands chansonniers mss, copiés surtout aux XIIIᵉ-XIVᵉs., conservés notamment à Paris, Rome, Florence, Londres, Berne, Barcelone.

TROUVÈRE. The term is generally defined at the outset of such articles. *C'est un poète lyrique*: *C'* is a pronoun for the term "trouvère"; the predicate nominative construction with the verb *être* indicates that a *trouvère* is a *lyric poet* - note the use of the adjective following the noun modified. *de langue d'oïl*: the word *langue* is a cognate of the word "language"; it is necessary to refer to a dictionary to determine the meaning of the term *d'oïl*. Under the listing "oïl" it is explained that the term *langue d'oïl* is used to describe the language spoken north of the Loire (river); in the context of the sentence, a *trouvère is a lyric poet of the language spoken in northern France. qui compose à la fois mus. et vers de ses chansons artistiques*: *qui* is a relative pronoun that agrees in gender and number with the subject of the sentence (trouvère), *compose* is the present tense of the verb "composer"; *à la fois* is an idiomatic expression which means "at the same time". *mus.* is an abbreviation for the word *musique* (such abbreviations occur frequently in musicological texts); *et* means "and", *vers* is a cognate of the word "verses", *de* is the preposition meaning "for", used here possessivly to modify *ses chansons artistiques* - his artistic songs - note again the use of the adjective following the noun modified. This clause is translated in full "who composes at the same time music and verses for his artistic songs."

L'activité des t. s'étend: *L'activité* (the activity) is the subject of the sentence; *t.* is an abbreviation for *trouvères* (such an abbreviation will occur in an article every time reference is made to the main subject). The verb of the sentence, *s'étend* is the present tense of the reflexive verb "s'étendre" - to extend: *The activity of the trouvère extends du milieu du XIIᵉs. à la fin du XIIIᵉ*. Roman numerals are used in written texts to indicate centuries; the small *e* indicates that the century is an ordinal number: douzième. The abbreviation *s.* stands for the word *siècle* and is used each time the word "century" occurs. This prepositional phrase is translated "from the middle of the twelfth century to the end of the thirteenth". *Les t., comme les troubadours se rencontrent de toutes les classes de la société (nobless, clergé, roture)*: *Les t.* = the trouvères = subject of the sentence. *comme les troubadours* = like the troubadours, *se rencontrent* = present tense of the verb "se rencontrer" - to meet; *toutes les classes* = from all classes; *de la société* = of society (nobility, clergy, commoners). "The trouvères, like the troubadours, meet all classes of society (nobility, clergy, commoners)". *et le mot ne désigne en aucune façon un état social, comme le désigne ménestrel*: note the use of ne...aucune; "and the word (trouvère) designates in no way a social position, like the designation minstrel".

    1. Complete the translation of this passage in this form.

TRANSLATION EXERCISES

    1. Translate the following from the article entitled "Clavecin" from the *Encyclopédie de la Musique*:

> "CLAVECIN (clavicembalo, clavicymbalum, harpsichord). Instr. à cordes pincées considéré à tort comme l'ancêtre du piano, à cordes frappées, et à clavier, à registres et à combinaisons. Il fut précédé par le dulcimer, l'échiquier et l'épinette, se distingue de ce dernier par sa forme triangulaire ou pentagonale et par le fait qu'il repose sur des pieds. Ses parties essentielles sont la mécanique, les registres et le clavier..."

    2. Translate the following from "Remarques sur les Pièces de ce Livre, & sur les differens genres du Musique" (Nouvelles Suites de Pièces de Clavecin" - 1728) by Jean-Philippe Rameau:

> "...si la nouvelle tablature dont je me suis servi pour les Pièces de ce Livre a ses difficultés, elle a aussi des convenances qui, à ce que je crois, doivent en recompenser. De quelque côté que les mains se portent, les Clefs n'y changent jamais, et les Note qui doivent être touchées ensemble y sont arrangées de maniere a ne pouvoir s'y tromper. La seule difficulté consiste à savoir de quelle main toucher certaines parties du milieu: mais c'est ordinairement pour la main gauche que ces sortes de parties sont reservées, dés que la droite n'y peu suppléer aisément: au reste on doit en exempter, autant qu'il est possible, la main qui a quelques agrémens à faire, comme tremblement, pincé et port de voix."

    3. Translate the following from the *Encyclopédie de la Musique*:

> JONGLEUR. C'est un chanteur médiéval, de condition modeste, qui se déplaçait de château en château, exécutant son répertoire des les réunions courtoises, les foires ou les fêtes religieuses populaires. Les *j.* jouaient de la vièle, de la rote, instr. qu'ils portaient en sautoir, chantaient et dansaient selon des traditions souvent populaires. Ils vivaient essentiellement de la faveur des riches, célébrant les

généreux, dénigrant les pingres. Certains n'étaient que de simples bateleurs, équilibristes ou montreurs d'animaux, loin de la qualité du ménestrel, dont la situation était mieux établie. Qqs troubadours, trouvères et *Minnesänger* menèrent l'existence errante des *j.*, notamment Cercamon, dont le sobriquet est évocateur (<court-le-monde>). C'est en Espagne que le niveau des *j.* fut le plus élevé. Voir E. Faral, Les *j.* en France au m.-â., Paris 1910; J. Stosch, *Der Hofdienst d. Spielleute im deutschen* M.A., Berlin 1881; R. Menéndez Pidal, *Poesía juglaresca y juglares*, Madrid. J.Md.

4. Translate the following excerpt from the article entitled "Les Bibliothèques musicales françaises" by Vladimir Fédorov that appears in the introduction to the *Encyclopédie de la Musique*:

"La France est un pays fortement centralisé, et c'est à Paris que se trouvent ses plus importants dépôts publics de musique. La province n'y ajoute de son côté que quelques *unica* précieux, des collections isolées réunies un peu au hasard ou bien des curiosités locales.

Parisiens ou provinciaux, quels sont ces dépôts musicaux? que contiennent-ils? comment les utilise-t-on?

Nous ne connaissons qu'une seule grand bibliothèque musicale française: c'est le département de la musique de la Bibliothèque nationale. Il fut constitué en répartement en 1942 et comprend actuellement trois sections: les collections musicales de la Bibliothèque nationale elle-même; la bibliothèque du conservatoire national de musique de Paris; les bibliothèque de l'Opéra."

Chapter Seven

I. ADDITIONAL CHARACTERISTICS OF VERBS

Special Uses

1. A verb infinitive may be used in French as the subject of a sentence.

"...cueillir la pâquerette..."
(Ravel, "Trois chansons pour choeur")

"...aimer et mourir au pays qui te ressemble!"
(Duparc, "L'invitation au voyage")

2. The present tense of the verb *aller* plus an infinitive may be used to indicate an action which is to take place in the near future. When the infinitive of a reflexive verb follows the verb *aller*, the reflexive pronoun precedes the reflexive infinitive.

"...je vais avoir vingt huit ans..."
(Poulenc, "La souris")

"...tous les rois vont jalouser..."
(Berlioz, "Le spectre de la rose")

"...que je puisse mourir toujours!"
(Fauré, "Lydia")

3. The following verbs all mean "to take" or "to bring"; note the differences in meaning:

amener - to take, to bring (to bring - people)

conduire - to take, to drive (people, a vehicle)

emmener - to take (along)

emporter - to take (away - things)

porter - to take, to bring (to carry)

prendre - to take (to pick up)

suivre - to take, to follow (a class)

4. The verbs *savoir* and *connaître* both mean "to know", but can not be used interchangeably:

a) *savoir* - to know a fact

savoir plus an infinitive = to know how (to do something)

b) *connaître* - to know a person, places, etc.; to be acquainted with, to meet

5. Note the difference in meaning of the following verbs:

a) *dire* - to say, to tell - used to describe what has or will be said

parler - to speak, to talk - used to describe the act of speaking

parler de quelque chose - to tell about something

raconter - to tell - used in the sense of telling or relating a story, . event, tale, etc.

b) *vivre* - to live - in the sense of "to be alive"

habiter - to live - in the sense of "to inhabit"

demeurer - to live - in the sense of "to dwell"

c) When *devoir* (to have to, to owe) is followed by an infinitive, it implies obligation or probability.

d) When the verb *faire* is followed by an infinitive it means "to have something done", "to make", or "to cause" (something to be done). The verb *faire* plus an infinitive is termed *causative*, because the doer causes something to be done.

In causative sentence structure the word order is

subject > form of *faire* > infinitive > object

(1) If the direct object is a noun it follows the infinitive.

(2) If the direct object is a pronoun, it precedes the conjugated form of *faire*.

(3) A direct and an indirect object may be used with the causative construction of *faire*.

(a) A noun object follows the infinitive.

"...la note d'or que fait entendre un cor..."
(Fauré, *La Bonne Chanson* - 1)

"...puis fais luire ma pensées..."
(Fauré, *La Bonne Chanson* - 6)

(b) A pronoun object precedes the form of *faire*.

e) The verbs *laisser* (to let), *voir* (to see), *entendre* (to hear) may be used in sentence structure with an infinitive in the same form as the causative construction of *faire*. When these verbs are used with an infinitive and a noun object, the word order is

subject > conjugated verb > infinitive > object

(1) If the direct object is a pronoun, it precedes the conjugated verb form.

"...laissons-nous persuader..."
(Fauré, "En sourdine")

"...laissez rouler ma tête..."
(Debussy, "Green")

"...nous laissons fuir les chaleurs..."
(Hahn, "Infidélité")

"...laisse tes baisers...chanter..."
(Fauré, "Lydia")

f) Note the difference in meaning of the following verbs, which in general mean "to meet":

faire la connaissance de - to make the acquaintance of, to be introduced to

rencontrer to meet (someone) by chance

retrouver - to meet by previous arrangement

se retrouver - to meet (another person) by previous arrangement

g) *jouer à* + an object = to play a game or sport

jouer de + an object = to play a musical instrument
Ravel, "d'Anne jouant de l'espinette"

h) Note the difference in meaning of the following verbs, which in general mean "to leave":

laisser - to leave behind

quitter - to leave a place or person

s'en aller, partir - to leave, to go away

"...car nous nous en allons, comme s'en va cette onde..."
(Debussy, "Beau soir")

"...et de m'en aller..."
(Fauré, "Toujours")

sortir - to go out, to come out, to go out of a place, to go out with someone

i) The verb *manquer* has the following meanings:

   (1) to miss (a train)

   (2) to miss - a person or a place

   (3) to lack

j) The verb *penser de* (to think about) implies an opinion about someone or something. Stressed pronouns are used after *penser de* when referring to a person; when referring to a thing, *en* replaces *de* and the stressed pronoun.

k) The verb *penser à* (to think about) implies pondering, reflecting, or considering. Stressed pronouns are used after *penser à* when referring to a person; when referring to a thing, *y* replaces *à* and the stressed pronoun.

l) Note the following idiomatic uses:

   pouvoir - je peux - I can, I am able

   j'ai pu - I was able, I could (I succeeded)

   vouloir - je veux - I want

   je veux bien - I'm willing

   j'ai voulu - I tried

   je n'ai pas voulu - I refused

   savoir - je sais - I know how, I can

   j'ai su - I knew, I found out

m) The verb *être* is used to express possession by adding the preposition *à* and the name of the possessor, if a noun, or the stressed pronoun, if a pronoun, to the conjugated form of *être*.

n) The object of the verb *se souvenir* (to remember) is preceded by the preposition *de*.

   (1) The verb *se rappeler* (to remember) takes a direct object.

o) When used with the name of a person, *aimer* means "to love"; *aimer bien* means "to like".

6. An *impersonal verb* makes a general statement rather than referring to any particular person or thing. Impersonal verbs are conjugated solely with the "il" pronoun form, and can therefore be used only in the third person singular. The use of impersonal verbs is more frequent in French than in English.

   a) Those verbs which describe the weather are impersonal verbs: *pleuvoir* (to rain); *neiger* (to snow)

   b) The verbs *advenir* (to happen) and *falloir* (to be necessary) are both used impersonally in French. The conjugated forms of *falloir* (il faut, il a fallu) may be followed by an infinitive or a complete clause.
   "...il faut que le coeur le plus triste cède..."
   (Fauré, *La Bonne Chanson* - 9)

   "...car il faut que les femmes pleurent..."
   (Fauré, "Le long du quai")

7. The pronoun *il* is often used impersonally meaning "it", "there", "one". In the following expressions *il* is used impersonally:

il y a	there is, there are
il existe	there exist(s)
il est possible (de)	it's possible
il se peut	it's possible
il importe (de)	it's important
il s'agit de	it's a question of
il faut	it's necessary (one must)
il reste	there remains
il est certain	it's certain
il semble	it seems
il paraît	it appears
il est compréhensible	it's understandable

8. These frequently used expressions are derived from the verb *valoir*:
ça ne vaut pas la peine de - it's not worth the trouble
il vaut mieux - it is better
il vaudrait mieux - it would be better

319

These expressions may be followed by an infinitive or a complete clause.

9. As stated in Chapter Three, there are two voices of French verbs: active and passive. In the *active voice*, the subject performs some act; in the *passive voice*, the subject is acted upon. The meaning of a statement in either the active or the passive voice is generally the same; it is generally preferable and easier, however, to use the active voice. The passive voice is formed in French, as in English, by adding a past participle to the appropriate tense of the verb *être*; the past participle agrees with the subject.

II. SUBJUNCTIVE MOOD

It is most important to become familiar with the following information on the subjunctive and conditional moods in order to facilitate efficient translation.

Forms

The *subjunctive* is the mood (form of the verb showing the speaker's attitude toward what he says) which expresses conditions contrary to fact, wishes (a wish is not a factual statement because it contains an element of unreality), an opinion, doubts, or what is possible, rather than certain. The seven verb tenses studied in Chapter Three are all in the *indicative mood*, that is, all of these tenses express fact, rather than probability. Modern English has only a few genuine subjunctive forms and therefore uses substitute words like *may, let, should,* and *would*; French has distinct subjunctive forms which are used frequently. The subjunctive mood has the following characteristics:

1. Two frequently encountered tenses: present and compound past.

2. French verbs in the subjunctive mood (with the exception of *avoir* and *être*) all have the following endings in the *present tense*:

je   *-e*
tu   *-es*
il   *-e*
elle *-e*
nous *-ions*
vous *-iez*
ils   *-ent*
elles *-ent*

These endings are added to the stem of the first person plural of the present tense in the indicative mood:

Present tense

Indicative   nous *chant*-ons

Subjunctive   je chante

tu chantes

il, elle chante

nous chantions

vous chantiez

ils, elles chantent

a) Many verbs which are irregular in the present tense in the indicative mood are regular in the present tense in the subjunctive mood.

(1) Although all irregular verbs in the present tense of the subjunctive mood (except *avoir* and *être*) have the same endings as regular verbs, some irregular verbs have an irregular stem; the most frequently encountered irregular verbs that have an irregular stem in the present tense of the subjunctive mood are *faire* (fass-), *pouvoir* (puiss-) *savoir* (sach-).

être		avoir	
je sois		j'	aie
tu sois		tu	aies
il, elle soit	il, elle	ait
nous soyons	nous	ayons
vous soyez	vous	ayez
ils, elles soient	ils, elles	aient

(2) The following irregular verbs have one irregular stem for the first and second person plural forms and another stem for the other forms in the present tense subjunctive:

aller	j'	aille	nous	allions	vous	alliez
croire	je	croie	nous	croyions	vous	croyiez
prendre	je	prenne	nous	prenions	vous	preniez
venir	je	vienne	nous	venions	vous	veniez
voir	je	voie	nous	voyions	vous	voyiez
vouloir	je	veuille	nous	voulions	vous	vouliez

321

"...sans que tu puisses le chasser..."
(Berlioz, "Le spectre de la rose")

"...que je puisse mourir toujours!"
(Fauré, "Lydia")

"...avant qu'en mon coeur...ne fleurisse plus ton image!"
(Fauré, "Nell")

"...pourquoi voulez-vous donc qu'il m'en souvienne?"
(Debussy, "Colloque sentimental")

3. The present tense of the subjunctive mood is encountered frequently in texts and is used:

a) In subordinate clauses (a subordinate clause can function only with an independent clause) introduced by *que* when the principle clause expresses:

(1) a wish or a desire (aimer mieux, préférer, vouloir, désirer, souhaiter).

"...c'est pour assouvir ton moindre désir qu'il viennent...du monde..."
(Duparc, "L'invitation au voyage")

Note in this example that *que* (*qu'*) is actually a relative pronoun; because the word it modifies expresses *desire*, the subjunctive is used in the relative clause.

"...que vienne l'été! Que viennent encore l'automne et l'hiver!"
(Fauré, *La Bonne Chanson* - 9)

Note in this example that the conjunction *que* (that) is used with an exclamation point to express a wish, thus requiring the subjunctive.

The verb *espérer* (to hope) takes the present tense in the indicative mood rather than the present tense subjunctive when followed by a clause introduced by *que*.

(2) doubt or uncertainty (douter, croire)

(3) happiness, joy, state of well-being (être content, être heureux)

(4) regret or sorrow (regretter)

(5) necessity (falloir - il faut; valoir - il vaut mieux)[1]

(6) fear (craindre, avoir peur)

---

[1]If the dependent verb has no expressed subject, the infinitive is normally used instead of the subjunctive clause.

(a) affirmative verbs in the subjunctive mood which follow verbs of fearing in the main clause may be preceded by *ne*.

b) The present tense subjunctive may indicate either a present or a future action.

c) When the subject of the verb of the dependent clause is different from that of the main clause, the subjunctive mood is required; when the main verb and the subordinate verb have the same subject, the verb infinitive is used instead of the subjunctive clause.

d) The subjunctive mood is used in clauses introduced by the following conjunctions and conjunctive expressions:

> à moins que - unless
>
> afin que - in order that, so that
>
> avant que - before
>
> bien que - although
>
> jusqu'à ce que - until
>
> de peur que - for fear that
>
> pour que - so that
>
> quoique - although
>
> sans que - without

(1) A verb in the subjunctive mood which follows the conjunctions *à moins que*, *avant que*, *de peur que* may be preceded by *ne* and still be affirmative.

> "...avant que tu ne t'en ailles..."
> (Fauré, *La Bonne Chanson* - 6)

e) The subjunctive mood is used in clauses introduced by a relative pronoun when the pronoun antecedent is modified by a superlative or by the word *seul*.

f) Verbs which express belief, such as *croire, espérer, être sûr, penser*, do not always take the subjunctive mood.

(1) When doubt is not implied, these verbs are used in the indicative mood; these verbs are used in the subjunctive mood if doubt is implied.

> "...mais n'espérez pas que mon âme s'arrache..."
> (Fauré, "Toujours")

(2) The indicative mood is generally used after all forms of the verbs above in conversational French.

4. The *compound past tense* of the subjunctive mood consists of the present tense subjunctive of *avoir* or *être* plus the past participle of the verb.

chanter		être		avoir	
j' aie	chanté	j' aie	été	j' aie	eu
tu aies	chanté	tu aies	été	tu aies	eu
il ait	chanté	il ait	été	il ait	eu
elle ait	chanté	elle ait	été	elle ait	eu
nous ayons	chanté	nous ayons	été	nous ayons	eu
vous ayez	chanté	vous ayez	été	vous ayez	eu
ils aient	chanté	ils aient	été	ils aient	eu
elles aient	chanté	elles aient	été	elles aient	eu

The compound past tense of the subjunctive mood is generally used like the present tense of the subjunctive (governed by a main clause expressing a wish, fear, joy, or doubt):

a) after conjunctions such as *bien que* and *avant que*

b) to express actions that have already taken place
"...qu'il lui soit partonné, que mon mal soit béni!"
(Fauré, "Le parfum impérissable")

III. CONDITIONAL MOOD

The *conditional* mood is used to state what "would be" or "would have been". The fulfillment of the chain of actions is contingent on the occurrence of some basic action; the basic action is always a condition, expressed or understood. There are two tenses in the conditional mood: present and compound past.

A. Present Tense

The *present tense* of the conditional mood tells what "would (should) happen" and is formed by adding the following endings to the verb infinitive:

chanter - to sing

je chanter*ais*

tu chanter*ais*

il chanter*ait*

elle chanter*ait*

nous chanter*ions*

vous chanter*iez*

ils chanter*aient*

elles chanter*aient*

1. The final *-e* of verbs ending in *-re* is dropped before adding the present tense endings in the conditional mood.

2. Note that the endings for the present tense of the conditional mood are the same as those for the imperfect tense in the indicative mood; the conjugation of reflexive verbs in the conditional mood follows the usual pattern.

3. Those verbs with an irregular stem in the future tense of the indicative mood have the same stem for the present tense of the conditional mood:

être		avoir			
je serais	nous serions	j'	aurais	nous	aurions
tu serais	vous seriez	tu	aurais	vous	auriez
il serait	ils seraient	il	aurait	ils	auraient
elle serait	elles seraient	elle	aurait	elles	auraient

B. Uses

1. The conditional mood is used in the result clause of certain conditional sentences. In conditional sentences which describe *what would happen* if a certain condition were fulfilled, the conditional mood is used in the result clause; the verb in the "if "-clause should be in the imperfect tense (indicative mood).

"si" "if"-clause		*result clause*	
present tense	indicative mood	future tense	indicative mood
imperfect tense	indicative mood	present tense	conditional mood

"...et si mon corps avait une aile...j'irais d'un vol rapide..."
(Berlioz, "L'absence")

"...si mes vers avaient des ailes...ils voleraient...ils accourraient..."
(Hahn, "Si mes vers avaient des ailes")

2. The present tense in the conditional mood is often used even though the "if"-clause is omitted:

"...je voudrais m'en aller vers les îles de fleurs..."
(Ravel, "Shéhérazade")

"...des meubles luisants...décoreraient notre chambre..."
(Duparc, "L'invitation au voyage")

"...les fleuves et la mer inonderaient en vain..."
(Fauré, "Le parfum impérissable")

3. A statement or question is in *indirect discourse* when the statement or question is merely reported, but not in the exact words of the speaker or thinker. The present tense of the conditional mood is used in indirect discourse to express a future action which depends upon a verb in a past tense.

4. The conditional tense forms do not suggest obligation; the verb *devoir* is used to express "should" (obligation, ought to).

C. Compound Past Tense

The *compound past tense* of the conditional mood consists of the present tense conditional of *avoir* or *être* plus the past participle of the verb. The compound past tense of the conditional mood is used to express what "would have happened" and is used most often in conditional sentences in which the verb in the "if"-clause is in the pluperfect tense of the indicative mood.

"si" "if"-clause	*result clause*	
pluperfect indicative mood tense	compound past tense	conditional mood

If another action had taken place - what would have happend

être		avoir		chanter	
j' aurais	été	j' aurais	eu	j' aurais	chanté
tu aurais	été	tu aurais	eu	tu aurais	chanté
il aurait	été	il aurait	eu	il aurait	chanté
elle aurait	été	elle aurait	eu	elle aurait	chanté
nous aurions	été	nous aurions	eu	nous aurions	chanté

vous auriez	été	vous auriez	eu	vous auriez	chanté
ils auraient	été	ils auraient	eu	ils auraient	chanté
elles auraient	été	elles auraient	eu	elles auraient	chanté

"...plus d'un aurait donné sa vie..."
(Berlioz, "Le spectre de la rose")

TRANSLATION EXERCISES

1. Translate the following from the article "La presse musicologique" by François Lesure in the introduction to the *Encyclopédie de la Musique*:

"La liste ci-dessous - qui n'est qu'un choix - donne l'état présent de la presse musicologique dans le monde. Celle-ci s'est beaucoup développée ces dernières années: on le constatera déjà en notant les dates de création des périodiques cités. En fait, cette presse s'est développée plus rapidement que la musicologie elle-même, et les rédacteurs de beaucoup de ces revues éprouvent des difficultés à maintenir le niveau de leurs publications. A côté des noms des rédacteurs, il a paru indispensable de donner de brèves indications relatives au caractère général ou à la spécialisation de chaque périodique."

FRANCE: *Revue de musicologie* (depuis 1917), organe de la Société française de musicologie (comité de rédaction: A. Schaeffner, F. Lesure et A. Verchaly) donne chaque année une bibliographie étendue, particulièrement pour la France.

Annales musicologiques (depuis 1953), organe de la Société de Musique d'autrefois, spécialisé dans les études concernant le Moyen Age et la Renaissance (N. Bridgman, F. Lesure, L. Schrade et G. Thibault, rédacteurs.) Pas de comptes-rendus ni de bibliographie.

ALLEMAGNE: *Archiv für Musikwissenschaft (nouvelle série, depuis 1952), publie des études à l'exclusion de tout compte-rendu ou bibliographie (rédacteurs: W. Gurlitt, H. Besseler Gerstenberg et A. Schmitz).*

Die Musikforschung, (depuis 1948), organe de la Gesellschaft für Musikforschung (H. Albrecht, rédacteur), Comptes-rendus.

Kirchenmusikalisches Jahrbuch, (depuis 1886), spécialisé dans la musique religieuse (K. G. Fellerer, rédacteur).

The Music Review (depuis 1940), rédigé par G. Sharp, fait une place importante à la musique contemporaine.

The Galpin Society Journal (depuis 1948), spécialisé dans l'histoire de la facture instrumentale (T. Dart, puis A. Baines, rédacteur).

ÉTATS-UNIS: *The Musical Quarterly (depuis 1915), publié par Schirmer (rédacteur, P. H. Lang). Chronique périodique de musique contemporaine.*

Journal of the American Musicological Society (depuis 1948), organe de la dite société, dont le rédacteur change périodiquement.

Notes (depuis 1943), organe de la Music Library Association, qui s'adresse surtout aux bibliothécaires (R.S. Hill, rédacteur).

Musica Disciplina (depuis 1946), spécialisé dans les études concernant le Moyen-Age et la Renaissance. Bibliographie. Bien que dirigé par un américain (A. Carapetyan), a plutôt un caractère international.

ITALIE: *La Rassegna musicale (depuis 1928),* orienté plutôt vers l'esthétique, la musique moderne et contemporaine (G. Gatti, rédacteur).

2. Translate the following from the article "Un certain phénomène qu'on appelle musique" by Henri Michaux in the introduction to the *Encyclopédie de la Musique*:

"La musique, dans notre espèce humaine, propose un modèle de construction, et en construction, net, mais invisible. Un montage en l'air. Ce montage n'est pas à voir, ni même à concevoir ou à imaginer. Il est à parcourir.

Musique, art du comportement, quoique sans références au monde physique extérieur.

Musique, art qu'on recherche autant pour ses défauts que pour ses qualités, pour son eau tiède, pour ses accroche-coeur, pour sa densité insinuatrice et avilissante et pour tout ce qu'elle traîne à sa suite.

Musique, médicament de l'humeur, mais qui en est aussi le plus grand persécuteur, art enfin plus qu'aucun autre capable de donner le "Ah!" du pays et de l'époque."

ITALIAN

Italian is the logical sequel to French because of the similarities between vocabulary and grammatical construction. Historically and linguistically Italian is a direct descendant of Latin: as such, the Italian language has developed over centuries concurrent to many significant musical developments. Its emergence as a modern language can be directly traced to its significance in voice training; the methods of the "Old Italian School" are recognized and respected for proven results over several centuries. The sounds of the Italian language require a degree of vocal relaxation optimal for singing; thus Italian is often regarded as a language important only in the vocal art. However, a knowledge of Italian is equally important for the translation of many significant musicological treatises.

Chapter One

I. INTERNATIONAL PHONETIC ALPHABET

The value of a standardized set of symbols representing sounds becomes immediately apparent when the same alphabet letters used in a different sequence create a foreign language. It is thus necessary only to supplement the IPA symbols introduced in the foregoing study of English with those exclusive to Italian and explain the aural connatation of each symbol within the context of the Italian language. When the following guidelines are carefully followed, it should be possible to correctly pronounce most words in Italian.

A. General Principles of Pronunciation

1. There is only one stressed syllable in each word in Italian.

   a) Italian words are usually stressed on the *next-to-the-last* syllable: Cac*ci*ni, Gior*da*no

   b) Italian words that are stressed on the *last* syllable always have a grave accent(`) over the last vowel: Pietà

      (1) When there is no accent mark on the last syllable of a two-syllable word, the stress is on the first syllable: *Ro*sa

   c) Some Italian words are stressed on the third syllable (vowel) from the last: Ben*e*voli, C*o*ppola, Dallap*i*ccola

   d) A few Italian words are stressed on the fourth syllable (vowel) from the last.

      (1) The stressed syllable of words generally falls on the strong beat of musical texts composed in traditional styles.

      (2) When the stress of a word is not obvious from its structure or context, a standard dictionary should be consulted.

2. An apostrophe is generally used in Italian spelling to indicate that a final unstressed vowel has been dropped. The *elision* of an unstressed final vowel before the initial vowel of the following word occurs often in Italian conversation and in written texts: dall'Abaco, d'Astorga

3. The following words are not capitalized in Italian:

  a) the days of the week

  b) the months of the year

  c) adjectives of nationality

   (1) When a *noun* of nationality is plural, it is always capitalized.

  d)the titles   Mr.   - signor

               Mrs. - signora

               Miss - signorina

4. Syllabication

  a) Italian words are divided into syllables according to the following patterns:

   (1) A single consonant between two vowels *begins the syllable* of the following vowel: Bru-ni, Pa-ci-ni

   (2) The first of a double consonant belongs to the preceding syllable; the second of a double consonant begins the new syllable: Giovan-ni Bat-tista Bas-sani

   (3) When two consonants, the first of which is *l, m, n,* or *r*, occur together in a word, the two consonants belong to separate syllables: Al-berti, Ber-tali, Bian-cosi

   (4) Any other combination of two consonants belongs to the following syllable: Ario-*sti*, Cale-*st*ani, Ci-*fra*, To-*sti*

   (5) In a combination of three consonants, the first consonant (except when it is *s*) belongs to the preceding syllable: Bia*n-ch*i, Po*n-ch*ielli Exception: Bor-*sch*i, Fre-*sch*i

   (6) The combination of an unstressed *i* or *u* with another vowel is not divided: Casteln*uo*-vo, An*i*el-lo, Gabr*ie*-li

  b) The preceding guidelines for syllabication also apply to compound words, formed by the combination of two (or more) words, or by the addition of a prefix to form a new word. The syllable takes precedence over the word in Italian; compound words are therefore divided into syllables according to the spelling of the word as a whole, regardless of the compounded parts.

B. Specifics of Pronunciation

1. Vowels

The five vowel letters of the alphabet *a, e, i, o, u* represent seven vowel sounds in Italian. Italian is a language replete in vowel sounds; practically all words in Italian end with a vowel. In conversational Italian vowels are generally pronounced as short, pure sounds, devoid of any diphthonic inflection. A relaxed, somewhat extended tongue is a necessary prerequisite for correct vowel production in Italian.

a) The [ɑ] sound is produced with the jaw dropped comfortably, the lips relaxed and devoid of any tension, and with the tongue at rest on the floor of the mouth. The Italian [ɑ] is considered by many to be the cornerstone of correct vowel sounds in singing. The [ɑ] sound in Italian is spelled *a*; the letter *a* in Italian spelling always implies the [ɑ] sound: *A*lf*a*no, *A*ntoni*a*, C*a*ld*a*r*a*, C*a*t*a*l*a*ni, G*a*sp*a*rini

b) The [e] sound in Italian, often called "close *e*", is a pure vowel sound pronounced with no suggestion of diphthong. The [e] sound in Italian is spelled *e*. B*e*n*e*voli, L*e*o, L*e*oncavallo

c) The [ɛ] sound in Italian is often called "open *e*"; the term "open *e*", as opposed to "close *e*" ([e]), refers to the opening of the mouth. The [ɛ] sound in Italian is pronounced with no suggestion of diphthong and is spelled *e*: B*e*rti, Cl*e*menti, L*e*grenzi, P*e*ri, P*e*senti, Sanc*e*s, V*e*rdi

d) The [i] sound in Italian is a pure vowel sound devoid of diphthonic inflection. The [i] sound in Italian is spelled *i*. Cesar*i*ni, Car*i*ss*i*m*i*, Land*i*ni, Orland*i*ni, Pagan*i*ni

e) The [o] sound in Italian, often called "close *o*", is a pure vowel sound with no diphthonic inflection. The [o] sound is spelled in Italian *o*. Ag*o*stino, Bus*o*ni, L*o*nati, T*o*si

f) The [ɔ] sound in Italian is often called "open *o*"; the term "open *o*" refers to the wider mouth opening required for [ɔ] than for "close *o*" ([o]). The [ɔ] sound in Italian is spelled *o*. B*o*ssi, C*o*nti, C*o*relli, Fas*o*lo, Gast*o*ldi, G*o*ld*o*ni, L*o*tti

g) The [u] sound in Italian is a pure vowel sound produced with the lips rounder and more protruded than for the [u] sound in English.

The [u] sound in Italian is spelled *u*. D*u*rante, Gal*u*ppi, de L*u*ca, Mart*u*cci, Mar*u*lo, Petr*u*cci

2. Close and Open Vowels

Italian spelling does not indicate whether the pronunciation of the letters *e* and *o* is "close" or "open". Many Italian words are spelled identically but have different meanings, depending on whether the *e* or *o* is "close" or "open". It is therefore important to learn the following general principles for the correct pronunciation of "close" or "open" when the vowels *e* and *o* occur in spelling:

a) When a word in Italian has two meanings for the same spelling, depending on the pronunciation of *e* or *o*, the context in which the word is used will imply the correct pronunciation ("close" or "open").

b) Conversational Italian is generally spoken so rapidly that it is difficult to recognize whether *e* and *o* are "open" or "close" when *unstressed*. It is generally acceptable in singing to use the pronunciation [ɛ] and [ɔ], "open *e*" and "open *o*" when these vowels are unstressed. This practice is recognized as a principle of Italian lyric diction. The conversational practice for the pronunciation of *final* unstressed *e* and *o* varies widely; the practice of opening *e* and *o* when final and unstressed is considered acceptable. It is acceptable in singing for *final e* and *o* to be "open" [ɛ], [ɔ]. Cirill*o*, Marcell*o*, Pollarol*o*, Frescobald*o*, Nanin*o*

(1) In a word of more than one syllable, *e* and *o* are pronounced "open" when *unstressed*; this principle is always applicable in singing and varies only slightly in conversational Italian. L*o*gr*o*scin*o*, R*o*ssini, Sp*o*ntini

c) In words in which *e* and *o* occur, but are not final, or the unstressed vowel of a polysyllabic word, *e* and *o* may be pronounced either "close" or "open". There is unfortunately no standard in Italian for determining when *e* and *o* should be "close" or "open"; correct pronunciation may be verified in a standard dictionary or a knowledge of Latin might serve as a reliable reference.

d) Summary of the foregoing guidelines:

(1) There is a preponderance of "open" *e* and *o* in singing.

(2) The conversational pronunciation of *e* and *o* varies widely.

(3) When *e* and *o* are not final or unstressed, they may be pronounced either "close" or "open".

3. Diphthongs

Diphthongs in Italian are relatively few in number; diphthongs are always indicated in spelling by two letters which represent two vowel sounds. B*oi*to, de Cap*ua*, del L*eu*to, Tr*ae*tta, Matt*ei*s, Zandon*ai*

4. Consonants

The following are guidelines for the correct pronunciation of consonants; the respective consonant and vowel length is often the only means of distinguishing many words that are otherwise pronounced alike. A single consonant is short (in duration); the preceding vowel is long. A double consonant is long (in duration); the preceding vowel is short.

a) Voiceless consonants are those which are produced without vocalization and have no pitch. No expulsion of air should accompany the articulation of voiceless consonants in Italian. The slight aspiration heard after the voiceless consonants [p], [t], and [k] in English should not be articulated in Italian.

(1) The voiceless consonant sound [f] is spelled in Italian *f*, *ff*: *F*esta, *F*ranchetti, *F*rugoni, Ga*ff*i, Ste*ff*ani

(2) The voiceless consonant sound [k] is spoken farther forward in the mouth than [k] in English. The alphabet letter *k* appears in Italian only in words of foreign derivation; the [k] sound is spelled in Italian:

c (before *a*, *o*, *u*, *l*, *r*): Bian*c*osi, Bernas*c*oni, *C*asella, *C*avelli, Davi*c*o

ch (before *e*, *i*): Bros*ch*, *Ch*erubini, Mar*ch*etti

(3) The [kk] sound is implied when the following consonant combinations occur in spelling in Italian:

cc (before *a*, *o*, *u*): Corna*cc*uioli, Ro*cc*a

cq, *qq* *cch*: Bo*cch*erini, Co*cch*i, Pisto*cch*i, Se*cch*i, Ve*cch*i

(4) The voiceless consonant sound [p] is spelled in Italian *p*: *P*alestrina, *P*erti, *P*esenti, Por*p*ora, *P*uccini

(5) The voiceless consonant sound [s] is more intense than in English and is spelled in Italian *s*: Meta*s*ta*s*io, *S*acchini, *S*artorio. The [s] sound in Italian must always be voiceless:

(a) when in the initial position of a word and followed by a vowel: *S*arti

(b) when *s* precedes another voiceless consonant: *S*pontini, *S*tradella

(c) when *s* follows another consonant, either voiced or voiceless: Cal*s*abigi

(d) when doubled (*ss*): Schia*ss*i, Ro*ss*i

(e) when *s* is final: Sance*s*

(6) The voiceless consonant sound [t] is produced in Italian with the tip of the tongue touching the inside of the upper front teeth (rather than on the alveolar ridge as in English); the [t] sound is spelled in Italian *t*, *tt*: Bo*t*tegari, Busa*tt*i, Dapon*t*e, *T*ar*t*ini, *T*orelli. Note: final *t* does not occur in Italian.

(7) The voiceless consonant sound [ts] is spelled *z* in Italian; a dictionary should be consulted to determine when the letter *z* implies the voiceless [ts] sound rather than the voiced [dz] sound, also spelled *z*. Aga*zz*ari, Bu*zz*oleni, Man*z*ia, Proven*z*ale, *Z*amperelli, *Z*aneti

b) Voiced consonants are those which are produced with vocalization and have fractional initial pitch.

(1) The voiced consonant sound [b] is pronounced with full vocalization and is spelled in Italian *b*, *bb*: A*bb*atini, *B*ellini, *B*imboni, *B*ononcini

(2) The voiced consonant sound [d] is pronounced with full vocalization and with the tongue near the tip of the upper teeth; the [d] sound is spelled in Italian *d*, *dd*: Bor*d*oni, *D*onati, *D*onau*d*y, *D*onizetti, Stra*d*ivari

(3) The voiced consonant sound [g] is pronounced with full vocalization and is spelled in Italian:

g, *gg* (before *a, o, u, l, r*): Bra*g*a, *G*abrielli, *G*a*zz*aniga, *G*enerali

gh (before *e* or *i*): Dra*gh*i, Respi*gh*i, Ri*gh*ini

(4) The voiced consonant sound [r] is one of the phonetic sounds that distinguishes Italian linguistically. There are two varieties of the [r] sound in Italian: the *flipped r*, indicated by the IPA symbol [ɾ], and the *rolled r* [r].

The flipped *r* [ɾ] is produced when the tip of the tongue makes contact *once* with the inside gum ridge of the upper front teeth. The rolled *r* [r] is produced when the tip of the tongue makes contact with the gum ridge of the upper front teeth several times in rapid succession. The flipped *r* [ɾ] is used

> (a) when *r* occurs as a single consonant between two vowels: Ma*r*enzio

> (b) when *r* is the final letter of a word and is followed in context by a word beginning with a vowel.

The rolled *r* [r] is used

> (a) when *r* occurs in the initial position of a word: *R*ossi

> (b) when *r* precedes or follows another consonant: G*r*ossi, Piet*r*ag*r*ua, Za*r*lino

> (c) when *r* is doubled (*rr*): Sa*rr*i

> (d) when *r* is final in a word that has been shortened (frequently encountered in musical texts): Signor(a)

(5) The voiced consonant sound [v] is spelled in Italian *v*: Bre*v*i, Monte*v*erdi, *V*itali, *V*i*v*aldi

(6) The voiced consonant sound [z] in Italian is spelled *s*; the letter *s* implies the voiced consonant sound [z] (instead of [s]):

> (a) when *s* precedes a voiced consonant (before *b, d, g, l, m, n, v*): *S*mareglia

> (b) when *s* is a single consonant between two vowels: Ca*s*erta, Pero*s*i, Ro*s*a

(7) The voiced consonant sound [dz] is spelled *z* in Italian; a dictionary should be consulted to determine when the letter *z* implies the voiced [dz] sound rather than the voiceless [ts] sound, also spelled *z*. Cazzati, Mazzaferrata, Mazzoni, Pizzetti, Strozzi

c) Liquid consonants are those which are produced with vocalization and have full pitch.

(1) The liquid consonant sound [l] in Italian is produced with the tip of the tongue slightly touching the inside of the upper front teeth. The [l] sound is always short, regardless of its position in the word (initial, medial, final), and is spelled in Italian *l, ll*: A*l*binoni, Be*ll*i, Fede*ll*i, Ga*l*i*l*ei, *L*andi, *L*ati*ll*a, *L*ocate*ll*i, Petre*ll*a, Zampere*ll*i

(2) The liquid consonant sound [m] is spelled in Italian *m, mm*: *M*arazzoli, *M*azzocchi, *M*elani, *M*ontemezzi, Sa*mm*artini

(3) The liquid consonant sound [n] in Italian is produced with the tip of the tongue slightly touching the inside of the upper front teeth. The [n] sound (a single letter *n*) is always short, regardless of its position in the word and is spelled in Italian *n, nn*: *N*ani*n*o, Mercada*n*te

(4) The liquid consonant sound [ɲ], a sound also indigenous to French, is produced when the tongue moves in a single motion directly to the hard palate while the nasal passages are simultaneously opened. The liquid consonant sound [ɲ] is spelled in Italian *gn*: Ca*gn*oni, Masca*gn*i, Pi*gn*atta

(5) The liquid consonant sound [ŋ] occurs in Italian when an *n* is followed by a [k] or [g] sound. It is acceptable to substitute [n] for [ŋ] in singing because [n] is a more resonant sound; the [ŋ] sound is standard in conversation: Ba*n*chieri, Fra*n*chetti, Leo*n*cavallo, Zi*n*garelli

d) Semiconsonants are short, unstressed sounds that have the characteristics of both vowels and consonants.

(1) The semiconsonant [j] is pronounced [y] or [i] when used as a consonant; it is a short, transition sound spelled in Italian *i*: Aner*i*o, Cornaccu*i*oli, Falcon*i*eri, Grat*i*ana, Gemin*i*ani, Malip*i*ero, Pa*i*siello, Supr*i*ani, Z*i*ani

(2) The semiconsonant [w] is a short transition sound which implies phonetically the vowel sound [u]; the [w] sound in Italian is characterized by more lip-rounding than the [w] sound in English and is spelled in Italian *u*: G*u*arneri, L*u*aldi

e) The following consonant sounds are exclusive to Italian:

(1) The voiced sound [ʎ] does not exist in English; the [ʎ] sound in Italian is produced by articulating an [l] while the tip of the

tongue is in contact with the lower teeth and the tongue is against the front of the hard palate. The [ʎ] sound in Italian is spelled:

gl before *i, a, e, o, u*: Ga*gli*ano, Qua*gli*ati, Rospi*gli*oso, Tena*gli*a

(2) When the letter *g* is followed by *e* or *i*, it has the sound [dʒ]. When the combination *gi* is followed by *a, o*, or *u*, the *i* is not pronounced (unless stressed); the [dʒ] sound in Italian is spelled:

g before *i* or *e*: Bro*gi*, Calsabi*gi*, *G*eminiani

gi before *a, o, u*: *Gia*comelli

when *gg* precedes *e* or *i* it is pronounced [ddʒ] : Stri*ggi*o

(3) When the letter *c* is followed by *e* or *i*, it has the sound [tʃ]. When the combination *ci* is followed by *a, o*, or *u*, the *i* is not pronounced (unless stressed); the [tʃ] sound in Italian is spelled:

c before *e* or *i*: *C*esti, *C*imara, *C*imarosa, Man*c*ini, Pallavi*c*ino, Vera*c*ini, Vin*c*i

ci before *a, o, u*: Animu*ccia*

when *cc* precedes *e* or *i* it is pronounced [ttʃ] . Pi*cc*ini, Ri*cc*i

(4) The consonant combination *sc(h)* is pronounced [sk] when followed by *a, o, u, l, r*: *Sc*arlatti, Ma*sc*agni

(5) The consonant combination *sc* is pronounced [ʃ] when followed by *e* or *i*. Logro*sc*ino

(6) The consonant combination *sci* is pronounced [ʃ] when followed by *a, o*, or *u*.

(7) The letter *h* is always silent in Italian; it often indicates a hard pronunciation between other consonants: Bros*ch*i.

(8) The letter *j* was once used in spelling to indicate the semiconsonant [j], and may be encountered in translating older editions: De Ma*j*o, *J*ommelli. The letter *j* is not used in modern Italian spelling.

(9) The combination *qu* is pronounced [kw] in Italian: Pas*qu*ini, *Qu*agliati, Santoli*qu*ido

(10) The letters *w,x*, and *y* are not in the alphabet in Italian. When these letters are encountered in words of foreign derivation, they should be pronounced according to standard usage in the source language.

II. GUIDELINES FOR EFFICIENT PRONUNCIATION IN SYNTAX

A. Symbols Exclusive to Italian

1. The grave accent (`) is used in Italian to indicate stress on the final syllable of a polysyllabic word. The grave accent is also used with a few monosyllabic words to distinguish them from words that are spelled the same but which have a different meaning:

chè	for, because	che	who, etc. (relative pronoun)
dà	he gives	da	from
dì	day	di	of
è	he is	e	and
là	there	la	the, her, it
lì	there	li	them
nè	neither, nor	ne	of it, of them
sè	himself, herself	se	if
sì	yes	si	himself
tè	tea	te	you

2. Occasionally the acute accent (´) is encountered in texts to indicate a final "close e".

3. The grave or acute accent indicates the stressed syllable and thus the intended meaning of words which may have two meanings, according to the stress.

B. Cognates

Italian and English cognates include:

1. words that are spelled alike

2. words that are spelled differently but are easily recognizable

3. recognizable words which cannot be classified according to any system

4. scientific and technical terms

5. Not all words that look alike, however, are true cognates. Many words look alike in Italian and English but have widely different meanings; these words are known as false cognates.

MUSICAL EXERCISES

1. Look up the first name(s) of each composer cited in the pronunciation illustrations.

a) Write out the full names of each composer using IPA symbols.

b) List the birth and death dates of each composer.

SUPPLEMENTARY PRONUNCIATION EXERCISES

1. Just as the written symbol of each alphabet letter in English has a name (although the symbol may represent more than one sound), likewise in Italian each alphabet letter has a name and should be used when spelling any Italian word aloud.

ALPHABET

letters found only in foreign words

A	a	[ɑ]		K	k	[kɑppɑ]
B	b	[bi]		W	w	[doppjɔ vu]
C	c	[tʃi]		X	x	[iks, ikkesɛ]
D	d	[di]		Y	y	[ipsilɔn]
E	e	[ɛ]				
F	f	[ɛffe]				
G	g	[gi]				
H	h	[ɑkkɑ]				
I	i	[i]				
L	l	[ɛlle]				
M	m	[ɛmme]				
N	n	[ɛnne]				
O	o	[ɔ]				
P	p	[pi]				
Q	q	[ku]				
R	r	[ɛrre]				
S	s	[ɛsse]				
T	t	[ti]				
U	u	[u]				
V	v	[vu]				
Z	z	[tsɛtɑ]				

2. Just as alphabet lettes are used to spell words, so the same symbols are used to designate the pitch names of the modern diatonic scale. The following are the Italian letter names and pronunciation of each scale degree:

English	Italian	
C	do	[do]
C flat	do bemolle	[do bemɔllɛ]
C sharp	do diesis	[do djɛzis]
D	re	[re]
D flat	re bemolle	[re bemɔllɛ]
D sharp	re diesis	[re djɛzis]
E	mi	[mi]
E flat	mi bemolle	[mi bemɔllɛ]
E sharp	mi diesis	[mi djɛzis]
F	fa	[fɑ]
F flat	fa bemolle	[fɑ bemɔllɛ]
F sharp	fa diesis	[fɑ djɛzis]
G	sol	[sɔl]
G flat	sol bemolle	[sɔl bemɔllɛ]
G sharp	sol diesis	[sɔl djɛzis]
A	la	[lɑ]
A flat	la bemolle	[lɑ bemɔllɛ]
A sharp	la diesis	[lɑ djɛzis]
B	si	[si]
B flat	si bemolle	[si bemɔllɛ]
B sharp	si diesis	[si djɛzis]

♭♭ = doppio bemolle

𝄪 = doppio diesis

3. Opera titles in Italian

   a) Say each of the following opera titles aloud.

   b) Identify the composer of each work and cite the date of the first
      performance of each.

   c) Write out each title phonetically using IPA symbols.

Adelaide	La Battaglia di Legnano
Adelasia ed Aleramo	Battone alla porta
Adelina	Belfagor
Adriana Lecouvreur	Belkis
Aida	La Bohême
Alceste	La Buona figliuola
Allessandro nell'Indie	Cagliostro
Alessandro Severo	La campana sommersa
L'Amfiparnaso	Canti di liberazione
L'Amico Fritz	Canti di prigionia
L'amore dei tre rè	I Capricci di Callot
Andrea Chénier	La Catena d'Adone
Anna Bolena	Cavalleria rusticana
Antigona	La Cena delle beffe
Antonio e Cleopatra	La Cenerentola
Argia	Chi soffre, speri
Arianna	Le cinesi
Arlecchino	La Clemenza di Scipione
Armide	Il combattimento di Tancredi e
Aroldo	di Clorinda
Artaserse	Le Comte Ory
Assassinio nella cattedrale	Il convitato di pietra
Astianatte	Corispero
Attila	Il Corsaro
Attilio regolo	Cristoforo Colombo
Un Ballo in maschera	Dafne
Il Barbiere di Siviglia	Dal male il bene

Debora e Jaele

Dejanice

Demonfonnte

Diana schernita

Il dibuc

Didon

Didone

Didone abbandonata

Don Bucefalo

Don Carlos

Don Chisciotte

La Donna del lago

La donna à mobile

La donna serpente

Don Pasquale

La Dori

Il dottor Antonio

I due Foscari

Ecuba

Edgar

Egisto

Elda

Elisabetta regina d'inghilterra

L' Elisir d'amore

Eraclea

Ercole amante

Erminia sul Giordano

Ernani

Eteocle e Polinice

Eumelio

Euridice

Falstaff

La Fanciulla del West

Favola d'Orfeo

La Favorita

Fedora

Fedra

Le Feste d'Imeneo

La Fiamma

La figlia del rè

La figlia di Iorio

Il filosofo di campagna

La finta semplice

La flora

Floridoro

La forza d'amor paterno

La forza del destino

Fra due litiganti il terzo gode

Fra Gherardo

Francesca da Rimini

La gazza ladra

Germania

Gianni Schicchi

La Giara

Giasone

La Gioconda

Giovanna d'arco

Giulietta e Romeo

Giulio Cesare

Giulio Sabino

Il Giuoco della cieca

Il Giuramento

Il Giustino

Griselda

Guillaume Tell

Hamlet

Ifigenia

Ifigenie in Tauride

L'Incognita perseguitata

L'Incoronazione di Poppea

L'inganno felice

Ippolito ed Arice

Iris

L'Italiana in Algeri

Jone

King Lear

La leggenda di Sakuntala

I Lombardi alla prima crociata

Lucia di Lamermoor

Lucrezia Borgia

Luisa Miller

Macbeth

Madama Butterfly

Madonna Imperia

La Mandragola

Manon Lescaut

Maometto II

Marco Visconti

Maria di Rohan

Maria Egiziaca

I Masnadieri

Il matrimonio segreto

Il Medoro

Il mercato di Monfregoso

Merope

Minnie la candida

Mitridate Eupatore

La Molinara

Monarchia latina trionfante

Il mondo della luna

Montecchie Capuletti

La morte d'Orfeo

Mosè in Egitto

Nabucodonosor

La nave

Nina

Norma

Nozze istriane

Oberto

Oedipe à Colone

Oedipus Rex

Olimpiade

Olympie

L'Orfeide

Orfeo

Ormindo

Orontea

Orséolo

Otello

I Pagliacci

Il palazzo incantato

Il paride

La pietra del paragona

Il pirata

Il pomo d'oro

Il prigionero

La principessa fedele

I puritani di Scozia

Il rè pastore

Il rè Teodoro in Venezia

Rigoletto

Risurrezione

Il ritorno d'Ulisse in patria

La Rondine

La rosaura

Saffo

Sant'Alessio

La scala di seta

Schiava fortunata

Semiramide

Serse

La serva padrona

Servio Tullio

Simon Boccanegra

Socrate immaginario

Sofonisba

Il sogno di Scipione

La sonnambula

La statira

Stiffelio

La straniera

Le straniero

Suor Angelica

Il tabarro

La tancia

La Tancia, overo il podestà di
Colognole

Tancredi

La tapera

Tarare

Telemaco

Tigrane

I tintaridi

Tosca

La Traviata

Tre commedie goldoniane

Il trespolo tutore

Il trionfo dell'onore

Trionfo di Camilla

Il Trovatore

Turandot

L'ultimo Lord

L'uragano

Vanna Lupa

Venere prigionera

La vera constanza

La vestale

La vita humana

La Wally

Zaza

Chapter Two

In Chapter One Italian phonetics are so presented that it should now be possible to pronounce correctly most words in Italian. With this chapter begins the simplified grammatical approach to Italian which will ultimately enable musicians to read and translate for professional purposes, perform with understanding, and command the basic language skills of conversation and comprehension. When this is accomplished, Italian is indeed a practical modern language and a necessary tool for professional musicians.

I. NOUNS

A *noun* is the name of a person, place, or thing.

Specific Characteristics of Nouns in Italian

1. All nouns in Italian have a gender, with the grammatical designation of masculine or feminine. It is important to learn the gender of each noun in Italian along with the word meaning; the form of articles, adjectives, pronouns, and some verbs must conform to the gender of the noun to which they refer.

2. A *definite article* is a word modifying a noun that points out a particular person, place, or thing. In Italian, the definite article is repeated before each noun in sentence structure.

"...gli arboscelli, i fiori, l'erbe..."
(Respighi, "Pioggia")

In English the definite article used to distinguish nouns of all gender is *the*; in Italian there are seven forms of the definite article:

a) *l'* [l] is used before masculine or feminine singular nouns that begin with a vowel.

b) *la* [lɑ] is used before feminine singular nouns that begin with a consonant.

c) *lo* [lo] is used before masculine singular nouns that begin with *z* or *s* plus a consonant.

d) *il* [il] is used before masculine singular nouns that begin with any consonant other than *z*, or *s*[1] plus a consonant.

[1]When the consonant *s* is followed by a consonant it is called "*s* impure."

e) *gli* [ʎi] is used before masculine plural nouns that begin with a vowel, with *z*, or with *s* plus a consonant; *gli* is generally elided before a noun beginning with *i* (*gl'*).

f) *i* [i] is used before masculine plural nouns that begin with any consonant other than *z*, or *s* plus a consonant.

g) *le* [le] is used before all feminine plural nouns. The definite article *le* may be elided before a noun beginning with *e* (*l'*).

EXERCISES

1. Consult the pronunciation guide at the end of Chapter One; list all opera titles that contain the definite articles *l'*, *la*, *lo*, *il*, *gli*, *i*, *le*, and classify the modified nouns:

Masculine   *Feminine*

2. For further pronunciation practice, read the following list of instrument names aloud:

English		*Italian*
piccolo	il	flauto piccolo, l'ottavino
flute	il	flauto (traverso)
oboe	l'	oboe
English horn	il	corno inglese
clarinet	il	clarinetto
bass clarinet	il	clarinetto basso, il clarone
bassoon	il	fagotto
contrabassoon	il	contrafagotto
horn	il	corno
trumpet	la	tromba
trombone	il	trombone
tuba	la	tuba
timpani	il	timpano(i)
bass drum	la	gran cassa
cymbals	i	piatti, i cinelli

350

triangle	il	triangolo
tambourine	il	tamburino
snare drum	il	tamburo
tenor drum	la	cassa rullante
gong	il	tam-tam
castanets	le	castagnette, le nacchere
xylophone	il	silofono
glockenspiel	i	campanelli (campanette)
bells or chimes	le	campane
harp	l'	arpa
violin	il	violino
viola	la	viola
violoncello	il	violoncello
double bass	il	contrabasso

3. Identify the following instruments; note the gender of each:

alto	chitarra	cornetto	monacordo
arcicembalo	chitarrone	flautino	organo
arciorgano	chiterna	flautone	organetto
arpicordo	cialamello	flicorno	ottavino
bombarda	cimbasso	fortepiano	piffero
braccio	clavicembalo	ghironda	salterio
calescione	cornamusa	gravicembalo	storta
cetera, cetra	cornetta	liuto	

3. It should be clear from the foregoing exercises that nouns in Italian posses a gender, which is generally indicated by the preceding article.

As in English, there also exists in Italian the *indefinite article*, a word modifying a noun that does not indicate a *particular* person, place, or thing. The indefinite articles in English are *a* and *an*; in Italian the indefinite articles are:

a) *un* [un] is used with masculine singular nouns.

b) *uno* [uno] is used before masculine singular nouns that begin with a *z*, or *s* plus a consonant.

c) *una* [unɑ] is used with feminine singular nouns.

d) *un'* [un] is used before feminine singular nouns that begin with a vowel.

EXERCISES

1. Substitute the correct indefinite article for the definite article in the preceding list of instrument names; write out each name phonetically.

2. Identify the following compositions (composer, style, etc.); the titles are all nouns:

Il	bacio	La	pastorella
Il	bove	I	pastori
La	danza	Le	pecorelle
L'	eco	O	primavera
La	farfaletta	La	speranza
L'	infinito	La	violetta
La	najade	La	zingara

3. Identify the following musical terms; indicate whether each noun is masculine or feminine.

affetti	brindisi	capotasto	continuo
aggizunione	buffo	capriccio	contradanza
alta	burla, burlesca	cascarda	coranto
andamento	burrasca	castrato	durezza
aria	cabaletta	cavatina	echegiatta
arietta	caccia	chiamata	elevazione
ballata	cambiata	chiavette	epitalamio
ballo	camerata	ciaccona	espressione
band	cantata	coda	falsobordone
barcarola	cantino	coloratura	fanfara
barzelletta	canto	commiato	farsa
bassadanza	canzona, canzone	concertante	finale
bombo	concertato	folia
brando	canzonet, canzonetta	conservatorio	frottola

352

gagliarda	maggiolata	pasticcio	serenata
giro	maniera	recercada	solfeggio
gorgia	marcia	ricerata	sparta
groppo	messa	ricercar(e)	stravaganza
gruppetto	minuetto	ritornello	strisciando
gruppo	minuta	romanza	tastar
imbroglio	mutazione	scampata	tedesca
incatenura	obbligato	scrittura	tirata
intrada	parte	segno	trio
lamento	passamezzo	senario	verismo

4. The primary difference between nouns in English and Italian, then, is the characteristic of gender. In English

the music

the piano

must be learned in Italian as

la musica

le pianoforte[2]

a) Because nouns in Italian do not exist independently of their gender, it is necessary to learn the gender of each noun with the meaning of the word and thereby associate the appropriate definite or indefinite article with each word. Although nouns sometimes occur in Italian, especially in musical titles, without a definite or indefinite article to indicate the gender, it is essential to learn noun genders for the purpose of accurate translating and reading in Italian and most especially for effective conversation, as much of Italian grammar is founded upon noun genders.

---

[2]In Italian a distinction is made between an upright piano, *piano verticale*, and a grand piano, *piano a coda.*

5. The gender of many nouns can be determined by the word meaning or ending; the following general rules are applicable:

a) A singular noun that ends in *-o* is generally masculine:

il ballo

il buffo

lo strisciando

b) A singular noun that ends in *-a* is generally feminine.

l' aria

la bassadanza

la cavatina

la messa

c) Nouns that end in *-e* in the singular may be masculine or feminine; the gender of nouns that end in *-e* should be memorized.

la canzone   (f.)

l' elevazione (f.)

l' espressione (f.)

il finale   (m.)

d) The gender of those nouns that refer to persons usually corresponds to their sex.

6. Just as nouns in English have a plural form designating more than one person, place, or thing, nouns in Italian may also be pluralized.

a) The plural of most nouns in Italian is distinguished by the article used:

Singular: l', lo, il, la

Plural *gli, i, le*

b) When a singular noun in Italian ends in *-o* or *-e*, the plural form of the noun is formed by changing the final *-o* or *-e* to *i*.

aggizunion*e* - aggizunioni

brand*o* - brandi

cant*o* - canti

gir*o* - giri

partiment*o* - partimenti

c) When a singular noun in Italian ends in -*a*, the plural form of the noun is formed by changing the final -*a* to -*e*.

ariett*a* - ariett*e*

cantat*a* - cantat*e*

fanfar*a* - fanfar*e*

romanz*a* - romanz*e*

(1) Masculine nouns ending in -*a* (infrequent) form the plural by changing -*a* to -*i*: il poeta - i poeti

d) Feminine singular nouns (and adjectives) that end in -*ca* and -*ga* are pluralized by inserting an *h* after the final consonant and changing the final -*a* to -*e*.

burles*ca* - burles*che*

burras*ca* - burras*che*

tedes*ca* - tedes*che*

e) Feminine nouns (and adjectives) that end in -*cia* and -*gia* are pluralized by changing the final -*a* to -*e* and dropping the -*i*.

caccia - cac*ce*

gorgia - gor*ge*

marcia - mar*ce*

(1) When *i* is stressed in the singular form of the noun (or adjective) it is *not* dropped in the plural form.

f) Masculine nouns (and adjectives) that end in -*go* are pluralized by inserting an *h* after the final consonant to retain the [g] sound, and by changing the final -*o* to -*i*.

il catalogo - i catalo*ghi*

g) When a masculine noun (or adjective) ends in -*co* and the stress falls on the preceding syllable, the plural is formed by inserting an *h* after the final consonant in order to retain the [k] sound, and by changing the final -*o* to -*i*.

bianco - bian*chi*

h) When a masculine noun (or adjective) ends in -*co* and the stress is *not* on the preceding syllable, the plural is formed simply by changing the final -*o* to -*i*.

il medico - i medi*ci*

355

Frequently encountered exceptions:

amico - ami*ci*

nemico - nemi*ci*

greco - gre*ci*

i) Masculine nouns (and adjectives) that end in unstressed *-io* have only one *-i* in the plural.

capriccio - capric*ci*

pasticcio - pastic*ci*

j) Nouns that usually refer to professions end in *-ista* in the singular. When the noun refers to a man it is masculine and is pluralized by changing the final *-a* to *-i*; when the noun refers to a woman it is feminine and is plualized by changing the final *-a* to *-e*.

il violinista - i violinist*i*

la violinista - le violinist*e*

k) The following nouns are the same in the plural form as in the singular:

(1) Nouns ending in an accented vowel:

il rè - i rè

il tè - i tè

(2) Nouns ending in a consonant: band, tastar

(3) Nouns ending in *-ie*: la serie - le serie

EXCEPTION: la moglie - le mogli

(4) Nouns ending in *-i*: affett*i*, brindis*i*

(5) Some single words: il soprano - i soprano

l) Some masculine nouns that end in *-o* have an irregular feminine plural in *-a* and are accompanied by the feminine article *le*. The most frequently encountered include:

Singular	*Plural*	
il braccio	le braccia	arm
il centinaio	le centinaia	hundred
il ciglio	le ciglia	eyelash

il	dito	le	dita	finger
Singular		*Plural*		
il	ginocchio	le	ginocchia	knee
il	labbro	le	labbra	lip
le	membro	le	membra	member
il	migliaio	le	migliaia	thousand
il	miglio	le	miglia	mile
l'	osso	le	ossa	bone
il	paio	le	paia	pair
l'	uovo	le	uova	egg

m) Other irregular plural forms include:

il	bue	i	buoi	ox
il	dio	gli	dei	God
l'	uomo	gli	uòmini	person

EXERCISES

1. Practice the pronunciation of the following country names, inhabitants and languages:

America	l'	America	l'	americano	l'	inglese(f)
			l'	americana		
Germany	la	Germania	il	tedesco	il	tedesco
			la	tedesca		
England	l'	Inghilterra (f)	l'	inglese	l'	inglese
			l'	inglese		
France	la	Francia	il	francese	il	francese
			la	francese		
Greece	la	Grecia	il	greco	il	greco
			la	greca		
Italy	l'	Italia (f)	l'	italiano	l'	italiano (m)
			l'	italiana		
Austria	l'	Austria	l'	austriaco	il	tedesco
			l'	austrica		

Russia	la Russia	il	russo	il russo
		la	russa	
Switzerland	la Svizzera	le	svizzero	il tedesco
		la	svizzera	il francese
Spain	la Spagna	lo	spagnolo	lo spagnolo
		la	spagnola	

2. As with alphabet letters, the written symbols that represent numbers have names for spoken use in Italian. The cardinal numbers (a numeral that answers the question "how many?") are:

0 - zero		30 - trenta	
1 - uno, una		33 - trentatrè	
2 - due		40 - quaranta	
3 - tre		44 - quarantaquattro	
4 - quattro		50 - cinquanta	
5 - cinque		55 - cinquantacinque	
6 - sei		60 - sessanta	
7 - sette		66 - sessantasei	
8 - otto		70 - settanta	
9 - nove		77 - settantasette	
10 - dieci		80 - ottanta	
11 - undici		88 - ottantotto	
12 - dódici		90 - novanta	
13 - trédici		99 - novantanove	
14 - quattòrdici		100 - cento	
15 - quìndici		105 - centocinque	
16 - sédici		285 - duecento ottanta cinque	
17 - diciassette		500 - cinquecento	
18 - diciotto		1000 - mille	
19 - diciannove		2000 - duemila	
20 - venti		100,000 - centomila	
21 - ventuno		1,000,000 - un milione	
22 - ventidue			

a) The numbers *venti, trenta, quaranta, cinquanta, sessanta, settanta, ottanta,* and *novanta* drop the final vowel when combined with *uno* or *otto.*

(1) When a noun follows a number that ends in *-uno,* the final *-o* is dropped.

b) When *-tre* is suffixed to the above numbers it requires an accent (*-trè*).

c) *cento* (one hundred) and *mille* (one thousand) do not require *uno* or *une* (one); the plural of *mille* is *mila.*

d) Compound numbers are always broken down into thousands and hundreds in Italian:

3900 (thirty-nine hundred)	- tre mila novecento
1100 (eleven hundred)	- mille cento
1700 (seventeen hundred)	- mille settecento
2400 (twenty-four hundred)	- due mila quattrocento

3. The ordinal numbers (a numeral expressing the order of a number in a series) are:

1st	primo	16th	sédicèsimo
2nd	secondo	17th	settedicèsimo
3rd	terzo	18th	ottodicèsimo
4th	quarto	19th	novedicèsimo
5th	quinto	20th	ventèsimo
6th	sesto	30th	trentèsimo
7th	settimo	40th	quarantèsimo
8th	ottavo	50th	cinquantèsimo
9th	nono	60th	sessantèsimo
10th	dècimo	70th	settantèsimo
11th	undicèsimo	80th	ottantèsimo
12th	dodicèsimo	90th	novantèsimo
13th	tredicèsimo	100th	centèsimo
14th	quattordicèsimo	1,000th	millèsimo
15th	quindicèsimo	1,000,000th	milionèsimo

a) All ordinal numbers after 10 are formed by dropping the final
vowel of the cardinal number and adding the suffix *-èsimo*. If a
cardinal number ends in *-trè*, the final *-e* is retained.

b) For translation note that the following forms (especially in reference to literature and art) are used to refer to centuries from the
thirteenth on:

il Duecento	the thirteenth century
il Trecento	the fourteenth century
il Quattrocento	the fifteenth century
il Cinquecento	the sixteenth century
il Seicento	the seventeenth century
il Settecento	the eighteenth century
l' Ottocento	the nineteenth century
il Novecento	the twentieth century

c) Identify the composition entitled *Tre Canzone Trecentesche*.

4. Names of the days of the week:

Sunday	domenica
Monday	lunedì
Tuesday	martedì
Wednesday	mercoledì
Thursday	giovedì
Friday	venerdì
Saturday	sàbato

5. Names of the months of the year

January	gennaio
February	febbraio
March	marzo
April	aprile
May	maggio

June	guigno
July	luglio
August	agosto
September	settembre
October	ottobre
November	novembre
December	dicembre

6. Names of directions:

north	il nord
south	il sud
east	l'est (m)
west	l'ovest (m)

7. Names of the seasons of the year (la stagione):

winter	l'inverno (m)
spring	la primavera
summer	l'estate (f)
autumn	l'autunno (m)

8. The following are nouns frequently encountered in vocal literature:

l' acqua (f)	water
l' alba (f)	dawn, daybreak
l' alma (f)	soul
l' amante	lover
l' amore (m)	love
l' ansia (f)	anxiety
l' arboscello (m)	shrub, sapling
l' ardore (m)	ardor, warmth
l' aria (f)	air
l' augello (m)	bird
l' aurora (f)	dawn

la bellezza	beauty, charm
la beltà	beauty
il bene	good
il bosco	wood, forest
la cara	beloved
la carezza	caress
il cielo	sky, heaven
il cor(e)	heart
il cuore	heart, love
il desiro(e)	desire
il dì	day
il disinganno	disenchantment
la doglia	ache, pain
la dolcezza	sweetness
il dolore	sorrow, pain, grief
il duolo	grief, sorrow, pain
l' erba (f)	grass, herb
la fiamma	flame
la finestra	window
il fiore	flower, blossom, bloom
il fiume	river, stream
la foglia	leaf, leaves
il fonte	spring, fountain
la forza	force, strength
il fuoco (foco)	fire, burning
il gelo	frost, ice, cold
la gelosia	jealousy
il giardino	garden
la gioia	joy
il giorno	day
il giovanetto	young boy
la goccia	drop
il guardo	look

l' incanto (m)	enchantment, charm
il labbro	lip; border, edge
la lacrima	tear
la libertà	liberty, freedom
il litorale	coastline
la lontananza	distance
la luce	light
il lume	light
il mare	sea, ocean
la marina	sea, seashore
la miseria	misery, distress
il monte	mountain, hill
la morte	death
la nebbia	fog
la notte	night
l' occhio (m)	eye, sight, view
l' ombra (f)	shade, shadow, darkness
la pietà	pity, compassion, mercy
la pioggia	rain
il prato	meadow
la preghiera	prayer, request
la querela	complaint
la quiete	quiet, calm
i rai	rays of the sun
il rio	brook, stream
il sangue	blood
il sasso	stone
la selva	wood, forest
la sete	thirst
lo sguardo	look, glance
il sogno	dream
il sole	sun, sunshine
la speranza	hope, trust

lo	spirto	spirit
la	stella	star
la	storia	story, tale
il	traditore	traitor
la	tenebra	darkness
la	terra	earth
il	tesoro	darling, treasure
il	tormento	worry, torment, pain, grief
il	tronco	tree trunk
il	tumulto	tumult
la	vallata	valley
la	via	way, route
la	voce	voice
la	vollutà	lust, pleasure

a) For each noun substitute the correct indefinite article for the definite article.

b) Form the plural of each noun.

II. PRONOUNS

A *pronoun* is a word used in place of a noun. The following are the *subject pronouns* in Italian:

Singular

io		[io]	I
tu		[tu]	you
lui	(egli)	[lui]	he
	(esso)		
lei	(ella)	[lei]	she
	(essa)		
Lei		[lei]	you

Plural

noi		[nɔi]	we
voi		[vɔi]	you
loro	(essi)	[lorɔ]	they (m)
loro	(esse)	[lorɔ]	they (f)
Loro		[lorɔ]	you

Pronoun Substitution

When a pronoun is substituted in sentence structure for the name of a person, place, or thing, it must agree in gender (masculine or feminine) and number (singular or plural) with the noun it replaces.

1. The pronoun *Lei* is the singular polite or conventional form of "you"; *Loro* is the plural polite form of "you". *Lei* and *Loro* replace the names of persons in Italian addressed as "signor" (Mr.), "signora" (Mrs.), or "signorina" (Miss). When addressing a person in conversational Italian, the pronoun *Lei* or *Loro* is used unless it is a family member, an intimate friend, or a child, in which case the familiar forms *tu* and *voi* are used. The use of the *tu* and *voi* forms has become more common in Italian usage, especially among young people; however, the *tu* and *voi* forms should never be used in speaking to an Italian person unless it has already been used in direct address.

2. The polite forms *Lei* and *Loro* are always capitalized.

3. The third person subject pronouns have two forms;

    a) *lui, lei, loro* are used almost exclusively in conversation.

    b) *egli, ella, esso, essa, essi, esse* are used almost exclusively in written Italian, a fact important for translation. These pronouns may be used in conversation, but even then primarily only in highly cultured speech.

"...sculta...ella è qui..."
(Bellini, *La Sonnambula*, "Ah! non credea mirarti")

"...elle ne appresta l'altare..."
(Verdi, *Il Trovatore*, "Il balen del suo sorriso")

"...ch'ella i languidi lumi..."
(Monteverdi, "In un fiorito prato")

4. *lui*, *lei* are used to refer to persons or things that have already been definitly identified in sentence context; when a subject pronoun is substituted for a noun, *lui* must replace a masculine singular noun, *lei* must replace a feminine singular noun.

III. PREPOSITIONS

A *preposition* shows the grammatical relationship of a noun or pronoun to some other element in the sentence. The following are the most frequently encountered contractions of prepositions with the definite article in Italian:

	-il	-i	-lo	-l'	-la	-gli	-le
a (to, at)	al	ai	allo	all'	alla	agli	alle
da (from, by)	dal	dai	dallo	dall'	dalla	dagli	dalle
di (of)	del	dei	dello	dell'	della	degli	delle
in (in)	nel	nei	nello	nell'	nella	negli	nelle
su (on)	sul	sui	sullo	sull'	sulla	sugli	sulle
con (with)	col	coi					
per (for)	pel	pei					

Peri - Nel puro ardor

Paesiello - Nel cor più non mi sento

Galuppi - La pastorella al prato

da Capua - Nell'orro di notte oscura

Santoliquido - Nel giardino

Caccini - Al fonte, al prato

Caccini - Sfogava con le stelle

Caldara - Alma nel core

Frescobaldi - A piè della gran croce

"...dal giardin..."
(Respighi, "Pioggia")

"...su l'ascose miserie, su l'ebbrezze perdute, sui muti sogni..."
(Respighi, "Notte")

Respighi - Pioggia   "...dal cielo sul davanzal...

          e nell'angoscia dell'ardor...

          sotto il vel delle gocciole implorate...

          s'acchetava il tumulto dei colori...

          la pioggia sui capelli...

          e intorno ai pioppi ai frassini agli allori."

Pizzetti - I Pastori   "...i pascoli dei monti...

          e vanno pel tratturo antico...

          su le vertigia degli antichi padri..."

Special Uses of the Definite and Indefinite Article

1. The prepositions *con* (with) and *per* (for) are seldom combined with the definite article.

2. Possession is expressed by the preposition *di* (of) before a noun; *di* may be contracted to *d'* before a vowel.

"...fresche forlate d'erbe risorte..."

(Respighi, "Pioggia")

a) Identify the following:

      Fontane di Roma

      Pini di Roma

      Toccata di durezza e ligature

      Fatto per la notte di natale

      Canto di primavera

      viola di bordone

      Il volo di notte

      Il campanello di notte

      corno d'amore

      corno di bassetto

      corno di caccia

      tono di combinazione

      oboe d'amore

      viola d'amore

3. The definite article is required in Italian before a noun used in a general or abstract sense.

4. The definite article is required in Italian before the name of a continent, country, region, or large island. L'Italia, L'Europa

5. The definite article is not required when the name of an unmodified *feminine* continent, country, region, or large island is preceded by the preposition *in* (in, to). in Europa, in Francia

6. The definite article is generally used when the name of a masculine country, region, or island is preceded by the preposition *in*. nel Messico

7. The definite article is required before a title, except in direct address. il signor Porpora

> a) Titles ending in *-ore* (masculine singular) drop the final *-e* before a proper noun.

> b) Titles are often preceded by *signor*, *signora*, or *signorina* in Italian. signor professore

MUSICAL EXERCISES

1. Define the following terms:

alla breve	con moto
alla mente	con sordino(i)
al fine	sul ponticello
al talone	sul tasto
col arco	sulla tastiera
coll'ottava	

2. Identify each of the following:

a) Teatro alla moda

b) Dramma per musica

c) Regola dell'ottava

d) Dialogo dell musica antica e della moderna

e) Rappresentazione di anima e di corpo

f) Congregazione dell'oratorio

g) Commedia dell'arte

3. Define the following terms, all of which are nouns:

acciaccature	inno
appoggiatura	ligatura
balletto	melodramma
battaglia	notturno
calata	oratorio
cantilena	partimento
capitolo	ribattuta
chiarenzana	ripieno
concertino	rubato
divertimento	salmo
eco	solfegietto
fantasia	spartita
fioritura	trillo
glissando	volta

4. Define historically the *Micrologus*.

5. Compare and contrast the terms *sonata da chiesa* and *sonata da camera*.

6. Describe in detail the composition *Le Stagione* by Antonio Vivaldi, including historical background, instrumentation, etc.

7. Identify the composition *Il Tramonto* by Ottorino Respighi.

8. Identify the following compositions:

> Giovane bella, luce del mio core
>
> Fuor de la bella gaiba
>
> Amante sono, vaghiccia di voi

Chapter Three

I. VERBS

The following study of verbs demonstrates how the theory of noun construction (noun genders, plurals, and article forms) is transformed into practical knowledge, especially as it relates to text translation.

A *verb* is that part of speech which expresses an action or state of being. Italian verbs appear complicated because of the number of different forms and the seemingly complex word order in sentence structure; it is therefore desirable to reduce the study of verbs to its simplest and most practical form in order to facilitate translation, comprehension, and conversation.

A. Terminology

The terminology used in reference to verbs should be defined before actually beginning with Italian verbs; although other terms will be subsequently defined, an understanding of these terms is essential:

1. *Tense* is the form of the verb showing the time of an action or of a state or condition. The two forms of tense are:

    a) *Simple* - verb form that requires no auxiliary verb to express the time

    b) *Compound* - verb form that requires an auxiliary verb to express the time

2. *Conjugation* - the inflections or changes of form in verbs showing:

    a) *Tense* - simple or compound

    b) *Mood* - the form of the verb showing the speaker's attitude toward what he says (indicative, subjunctive, conditional)

        (1) *Attitudes* - ability, permission, compulsion, desire, obligation

    c) *Voice* - the form of the verb indicating whether the subject acts (Active Voice) or is acted upon (Passive Voice)

    d) *Person*

    e) *Number* - the form of a verb indicating one (singular) or more than one (plural)

3. *Auxiliary verb* - a verb that helps in the conjugation of another verb

4. *Principle parts* - verb forms from which tenses are formed

   a) *Infinitive* - verb form which expresses general meaning without the distinction of grammatical person or number: cantare - *to* sing

   b) *Present participle* - the verb form ending in *-ando* (*-endo*) equivalent to verb forms in English ending in *-ing*: cant*ando* - sing*ing*

   c) *Past participle* - the verb form used as part of a compound tense. The word *compound* implies more than one part; a compound verb structure requires some form of an auxiliary verb plus the past participle of the verb.

It is desirable to learn the principle parts of Italian verbs because they are the basis of verb structure; it is practical for this study to be able to recognize verb forms in texts.

B. Categories of Verbs

Before explaining Italian verb tenses, it should be noted that certain large groups of verbs are conjugated in the same way. The two categories of verbs in Italian are:

1. *Regular verbs* - Verbs that follow the pattern of a particular conjugation group are regular verbs; all forms of regular verbs can be derived from certain key verb forms.

   a) The following are verbs that refer specifically to music:

   cantare - to sing

   suonare - to play, sound

   accordare - to tune

The infinitive of the foregoing Italian verbs ends in *-are*. In order to conjugate verbs, that is, assign person and number, a common denominator derived from the verb infinitive known as the *verb stem* is necessary. The verb stem of the group of Italian verbs known as *regular "-are" verbs* (first conjugation) is obtained by dropping the final *-are* of the infinitive. This is by far the largest group of Italian verbs.

   cantare (cant-) - to sing

   suonare (suon-) - to play

   accordare (accord-) - to tune

In conjugating verbs in Italian (assigning person and number) it is necessary to add an ending to the verb stem. In the *present tense* only the third person singular form in English has an ending; in Italian, the verb has an ending for *each* person in the present tense. The following endings are added to the verb stem to form the present tense of *regular "-are" verbs* in Italian:

cantare - to sing

Singular		*Plural*	
io cant*o*		noi	cant*iamo*
tu cant*i*		voi	cant*ate*
lui cant*a*		loro	cant*ano*
lei cant*a*		loro	cant*ano*
Lei cant*a*		Loro	cant*ano*

b) When the verb stem ends in *-i* (cominciare - to begin; studiare - to study), there is only one *i* in the second person singular and the first person plural: cominci; studiamo

c) Since the endings of verb forms in Italian indicate the person and number of a tense, the subject pronouns may be omitted in Italian except when necessary for clarity or when emphasis or contrast is desired.

"...protesa io gli arboscelli..."
(Respighi, "Pioggia")

d) Depending on the context, the present tense in Italian may be equivalent in English to:

(1) the simple verb form: io canto - I sing (all the time, as a habit)

(2) the progressive form: io canto - I am singing (right now)

(3) the emphatic form: io canto - I do sing

(4) When the present tense verb form is followed by the preposition *da*, the present tense expresses an action, state of being, or condition which began in the past and is still going on in the present.

e) The second group of regular Italian verbs are those known as *regular "-ere" verbs* (second conjugation). The verb stem of *regular "-ere" verbs* is obtained by dropping the final *-ere* of the infinitive. The following endings are added to the verb stem to form the present tense of *regular "-ere" verbs* in Italian:

battere - to beat

Singular	*Plural*
batt*o*	batt*iamo*
batt*i*	batt*ete*
batt*e*	batt*ono*

f) The third group of regular Italian verbs are those known as *regular "-ire" verbs* (third conjugation); relatively few common verbs belong to this group. The verb stem of *regular "-ire" verbs* is obtained by dropping the final *-ire* of the infinitive. The following endings are added to the verb stem to form the present tense of *regular "-ire" verbs* in Italian:

applaudire - to applaude

applaud*o*	applaud*iamo*
applaud*i*	applaud*ite*
applaud*e*	applaud*ono*

Some *-ire* verbs insert *isc* between the stem and the ending of all forms of the singular and the third person plural:

capire - to understand

cap*isc*o	capiamo
cap*isc*i	capite
cap*isc*e	cap*isc*ono

2. *Irregular verbs* - those verbs which are dissimilar to other groups of verbs and which do not follow an established pattern of conjugation are known as *irregular verbs*.

a) The present tense of irregular verbs is almost always irregular. Irregular verbs may have two spellings of the verb stem, one for the first and second persons plural, another for the other persons.

b) Irregular verbs that end in *-are* generally have the following endings in the *present tense*:

andare - to go

vad*o*	and*iamo*
v*ai*	and*ate*
v*a*	v*anno*

stare - to stay

Singular	*Plural*
st*o*	st*iamo*
st*ai*	st*ate*
st*a*	st*anno*

"...lascian gli stazzi e vanno verso il mare: scendono all'Adriatico..."
(Pizzetti, "I Pastori")

c) Five groups of irregular verbs end in *-ere*:

(1) Those which are regular in the present tense:

leggere - to read

leggo	leggiamo
leggi	leggete
legge	leggono

mettere - to put

metto	mettiamo
metti	mettete
mette	mettono

chiudere	to close
conoscere	to know
nascere	to be born
prendere	to take
ridere	to laugh
rispondere	to answer
scendere	to go down
scrivere	to write
spendere	to spend
vedere	to see
vivere	to live

(2) Those which have regular endings but an irregular stem:

bere - to drink

bevo	beviamo
bevi	bevete
beve	bevono

375

(3) those which have a different stem spelling in the first and second persons plural:

sedere - to sit down

Singular	*Plural*
siedo	sediamo
siedi	sedete
siede	siedono

(4) Those which have a different stem spelling in the first person singular and/or plural and in the third person plural:

piacere - to be pleasing

piac*c*io	piac*c*iamo
piaci	piacete
piace	piac*c*iono

rimanere - to remain

rimango	rimaniamo
rimani	rimanete
rimane	rimangono

scegliere - to choose

sce*l*go	scegliamo
scegli	scegliete
sceglie	sce*l*gono

(5) Those which have more than two stem spellings:

dovere - to have to, must

devo	dobbiamo
devi	dovete
deve	devono

potere - to be able

posso	possiamo
puoi	potete
può	possono

sapere - to know

Singular	Plural
so	sappiamo
sai	sapete
sa	sanno

tenere - to keep

tengo	teniamo
tieni	tenete
tiene	tengono

volere - to want

voglio	vogliamo
vuoi	volete
vuole	vogliono

d) Two important irregular verbs in Italian are:

essere - to be

avoir - to have

Besides being independent verbs, these two verbs are the auxiliary verbs in Italian; one is always present in the conjugation of verbs in compound tenses. These two verbs are conjugated in the *present tense*:

essere - to be

sono	siamo
sei	siete
è	sono

avere - to have

ho[1]	abbiamo
hai	avete
ha	hanno

e) Since the spelling changes in the stems of irregular verbs follow no regular pattern, the various forms, especially for the purpose of conversation, should be systematically learned. For translation it is necessary to identify verbs as regular or irregular, indicated by the stem spelling and/or the past participle ending.

---

[1]Note the silent letter *h*.

C. Imperative

The *imperative* is the mood of a verb expressing a command. Direct commands may be given to persons addressed as *tu, Lei, noi, voi,* and *Loro.* The command, or imperative form of Italian verbs is always expressed without the subject pronoun. The imperative forms of *regular verbs* are:

-are verbs		*-ere verbs*	
cantare - to sing		battere - to beat	
(tu) cant*a*	sing	batt*i*	beat
(Lei) cant*i*	sing	batt*a*	beat
(noi) cant*iamo*	let us sing	batt*iamo*	let us beat
(voi) cant*ate*	sing	batt*ete*	beat
(Loro) cant*ino*	sing	batt*ano*	beat

-ire verbs		*-ire verbs*	
applaudire - to applaude		capire - to understand	
applaudi	applaude	capisci	understand
applauda	applaude	capisca	understand
applaudiamo	let us applaude	capiamo	let us understand
applaudite	applaude	capite	understand
applaudano	applaude	capiscano	understand

Udite amanti   - Caccini

Note that the *noi* and *voi* forms are the same as the present tense forms. The imperative of *essere* and *avere* are irregular:

avere - to have		essere - to be	
abbi	have	sii	be
abbia	have	sia	be
abbiamo	let us have	siamo	let us be
abbiate	have	siate	be
abbiano	have	siano	be

Other irregular imperatives include:

fare - to do		venire - to come		andare - to go	
fa'	do	vieni	come	va'	go
faccia	do	venga	come	vada	go
facciamo	let us do	veniamo	let us come	andiamo	let us go
fate	do	venite	come	andate	go
facciano	do	vengano	come	vadano	go

"...settembre, andiamo..."
(Pizzetti, "I Pastori")

"...vieni, è buia la vallata..."
(Respighi, "Nebbie")

Some musical terms which give a command are:

> alzati - remove the mutes
>
> attacca - attack suddenly; continue without a pause
>
> cambiano, cambia - change instruments or tuning (orchestral score)
>
> divisi - divide into two groups
>
> marcata - mark, emphasize

D. Compound Past Tense

The *compound past tense*, or *passato prossimo* is composed of the present tense of the appropriate auxiliary verb (*avere* or *essere*) plus the past participle of the verb. The compound past tense in Italian is used to express an event completed in the past or a condition that existed in the past, and corresponds in meaning to the present perfect tense and the simple past tense in English.

1. The compound past tense of most Italian verbs consists of the present tense of the auxiliary verb *avere* and the past participle of the verb; most Italian verbs that take *avere* as the auxiliary verb are *transitive* (active) verbs, that is, they can take a direct object. The verb *essere* is used as the auxiliary verb in compound tenses of *intransitive* (passive) verbs, that is, verbs expressing an action, change of position, or state of being which do not require a direct object. In order to determine whether a verb is transitive or intransitive, the question "Who or what does the action of

the verb affect?" should be asked. If the question can be answered, the verb is transitive, or the action is performed upon the direct object; if the question can not be answered, the verb is intransitive or passive. Determining whether a verb is transitive or intransitive simplifies forming compound tenses; most transitive verbs take *avere* as the auxiliary verb, most intransitive verbs take *essere* as the auxiliary verb.

2. The past participle of regular verbs is formed:

a) For *regular "-are" verbs*: by adding *-ato* to the verb stem:

cantare - to sing

io ho	cantato	noi abbiamo	cantato
tu hai	cantato	voi avete	cantato
lui ha	cantato	loro hanno	cantato
lei ha	cantato		
Lei ha	cantato	Loro hanno	cantato

"...rinnovato hanno verga d'avellano..."
(Pizzetti, "I Pastori")

b) For *regular "-ere" verbs*: by adding *-uto* to the verb stem:

battere - to beat

ho	battuto	abbiamo	battuto
hai	battuto	avete	battuto
ha	battuto	hanno	battuto

c) For *regular "-ire" verbs*: by adding *-ito* to the verb stem:

applaudire - to applaude

ho	applaudito	abbiamo	applaudito
hai	applaudito	avete	applaudito
ha	applaudito	hanno	applaudito

capire - to understand

ho	capito	abbiamo	capito
hai	capito	avete	capito
ha	capito	hanno	capito

3. The past participle of many irregular verbs is formed by adding the endings *-ato, -uto, -ito* to the verb stem.

380

4. The auxiliary verbs are conjugated in the compound past tense.

essere			avere		
io sono	stato(a)		io	ho	avuto
tu sei	stato(a)		tu	hai	avuto
lui è	stato		lui	ha	avuto
lei è	stato		lei	ha	avuto
Lei è	stato(a)		Lei	ha	avuto
noi siamo	stati(e)		noi	abbiamo	avuto
voi siete	stati(e)		voi	avete	avuto
loro sono	stati(e)		loro	hanno	avuto
Loro sono	stati(e)		Loro	hanno	avuto

5. When *essere* is used as the auxiliary verb in a compound tense, the past participle must always agree in gender and number with the subject.

6. The study of structure is the obvious tool of translation; the following guidelines for efficient translation should be cultivated:

a) Determine the subject of the sentence: who or what performs the action expressed by the verb, or on whom the action is performed, in the case of intransitive verbs.

b) Determine the verb meaning by dissecting the form. When one of the verbs that can be used as an auxiliary verb is encountered, this should indicate the possibility of a compound verb structure; the past participle is distinguished in Italian by its ending. Having determined the verb meaning from the past participle, it should be possible to translate the tense of the verb form. It is of primary importance in translating to develop the practice of first determining the verb meaning and tense.

c) Determine the direct object and/or the indirect object.

E. Reflexive Verbs

A *reflexive verb* is a verb whose subject reflects or reacts upon itself; its object is always a pronoun corresponding to the subject. In reflexive verb construction, a *reflexive pronoun* is placed before the verb. The infinitive of all reflexive verbs ends in *-si*; when the verb is conjugated, *-si* is replaced by the appropriate reflexive pronoun, which is placed

The reflexive pronouns in Italian used accordingly are:

io- *mi*	myself	
tu- *ti*	yourself	
lui, lei, Lei- *si*	himself, herself, itself, yourself	
noi- *ci*	ourselves	
voi- *vi*	yourselves	
loro, Loro- *si*	themselves, yourselves	

The pronouns *mi, ti, si, vi* are contracted to *m', t', s', v'* before words beginning with a vowel or a mute *h. Ci* is contracted to *c'* only before *i* or *e*. The reflexive pronoun must agree in gender and number with its corresponding subject. Among the most frequently encountered reflexive verbs in Italian are:

accomodarsi	to make oneself comfortable
addormentarsi	to fall asleep
alzarsi	to get up, rise
avviarsi	to start out
avvicinarsi (a)	to come near, to approach
chiamarsi	to be named, be called
divertirsi	to amuse oneself, have a good time
farsi coraggio	to take courage, cheer up
fermarsi	to stop
laurearsi	to graduate
lavarsi	to wash oneself
levarsi	to rise, to get up; to take off
portarsi dietro	to carry around
raccomandarsi	to beg
sbrigarsi	to hurry
scusarsi	to excuse oneself, apologize
sdraiarsi	to lie down, stretch out
sedersi	to sit down
stabilirsi	to settle (down)
trattarsi di	to be a matter of

trovarsi	to get along (in a place; be located)
tuffarsi	to dive
vertirsi	to dress oneself

1. Reflexive verbs are conjugated according to the type of verb (regular or irregular); the verb endings agree in number and gender with the subject and reflexive pronoun.

2. All reflexive verbs in Italian are conjugated with the auxiliary verb *essere*; accordingly, the past participle of all compound tenses must agree in gender and number with the subject.

3. The imperative of reflexive verbs is formed regularly according to the type of verb (see p. 378); the reflexive pronoun precedes the inflected verb form in a command:

Se levano i sordini - take off the mutes

(Note that the present tense form (levano) is substituted for the true imperative (levino) in this command; this construction is encountered occasionally with *-are* verbs).

levarsi - to take off (mutes); to rise, get up

Present tense

Singular				*Plural*		
io	mi	levaro	noi	ci		levariamo
tu	ti	levari	voi	vi		levarate
lui	si	levara	loro	si		levarano
Lei	si	levara	Loro	si		levarano

Compound past tense

io	mi sono	levarto(a)	noi	ci	siamo	levarti(e)
tu	ti sei	levarto(a)	voi	vi	siete	levarti(e)
lui	s' è	levarto	loro	si	sono	levarti(e)
lei	s' è	levarta				
Lei	s' è	levarto(a)	Loro	si	sono	levarti(e)

F. Verb Spellings

1. In conjugating verbs with infinitives ending in -*care* and -*gare*, an *h* is added before *e* or *i*.

cercare - to look for

cerco	cer*ch*iamo
cer*ch*i	cercate
cerca	cercano

spiegare - to explain

spiego	spie*gh*iamo
spie*gh*i	spiegate
spiega	spiegano

2. In conjugating verbs with infinitives ending in -*ciare* and -*giare*, the *i* is dropped before an *e* or *i*:

assag*giare* - to taste	incomin*ciare* - to begin
assaggio	incomincio
assaggi	incominci
assaggia	incomincia
assaggiamo	incominciamo
assaggiate	incominciate
assaggiano	incominciano

3. In conjugating verbs with infinitives ending in -*cere* and -*scere* an *i* is added before the -*uto* of the past participle:

conoscere - conosciuto

nascere - nasciuto

piacere - piaciuto

riconoscere - riconosciuto

II. INDICATIVE MOOD

There are seven tenses in the *indicative mood* (the mood of a verb expressing a fact) in Italian:

A. Present Tense

B. Compound Past Tense (passato prossimo)

C. Simple Past Tense (passato remoto)

The names *passato prossimo* (compound past) and *passato remoto* (simple, absolute, or literary past) are used to distinguish two tenses which generally have the same meaning; both tenses are used to express simple past actions. The compound past tense in Italian is most frequently used in conversation to express an action completed in the recent past; the *simple past tense* is used in conversation only in reference to historical events in the distant past, or in relating or narrating an event or story far in the past. The simple past tense is used almost exclusively in literary narrative style to indicate an action completed in the distant past. This is especially important for translation; it is advisable that the musician interested in Italian translation become familiar with the simple past tense form, which is otherwise of relatively minor importance. The simple past tense is formed according to the following pattern:

1. The following endings are added to the verb stem of regular verbs to form the simple past tense:

    a) Regular "-are" verbs

cantare - to sing

cant*ai*	cant*ammo*
cant*asti*	cant*aste*
cant*o*	cant*arono*

    b) Regular "-ere" verbs

battere - to beat

batt*ei*	batt*emmo*
batt*esti*	batt*este*
batt*è*	batt*erono*

c) Regular "-ire" verbs

capire - to understand

cap*ii*	cap*immo*
cap*isti*	cap*iste*
cap*ì*	cap*irono*

d) The simple past tense of the auxiliary verbs is formed irregularly:

essere - to be	avere - to have
fui	ebbi
fosti	avesti
fu	ebbe
fummo	abemmo
foste	aveste
furono	ebbero

"...già v'ebbe un uomo..."
(Respighi, "Il Tramonto")

e) The simple past tense of irregular verbs follows no predictable pattern; the verb stem is often spelled differently from the infinitive and the past participle. However, irregular verbs generally have the following endings in the simple past tense (variations are noted in parentheses):

dovere - to have to, must

dov*ei*	(-ai, i, ì)
dov*esti*	(-asti)
dov*è*	(ò, -e)
dov*emmo*	(-ammo, -immo)
dov*este*	(-aste, -iste)
dov*erono*	(-arono, -ero, -irono)

f) The simple past tense forms of the verb *nascere* (to be born) are used only in historical reference.

lui, lei nacque

loro nacquero

Lotti - Pur dicesti, o bocca bella

"...che allor solo conobbe l'abbandono pieno..."
(Respighi, "Il Tramonto")

"...anno per anno visse ancora..."
(Respighi, "Il Tramonto")

D. Imperfect Tense

The *imperfect tense* in Italian generally expresses habitual actions in the past, a state of affairs in the past, or continuous past action. The imperfect tense is used to tell what used to be done, what was done in the past, or the way things were in the past.

compound past tense: what happened - completed action

imperfect tense: circumstances or state of affairs at a past time

The imperfect tense is formed by adding the following endings to the verb stem:

cantare	battere	capire
cant*avo*	batt*evo*	cap*ivo*
cant*avi*	batt*evi*	cap*ivi*
cant*ava*	batt*eva*	cap*iva*
cant*avamo*	batt*evamo*	cap*ivamo*
cant*avate*	batt*evate*	cap*ivate*
cant*avano*	batt*evano*	cap*ivano*

"...regnava nel silenzio alta la notte e bruna..."
(Donizetti, *Lucia di Lammermoor*)

"...(pensavo)..."
(Respighi, "Pioggia")

"...quando vivevo..."
(Salieri, "In questa tomba oscura")

"...beveano ingorde le zolle assertate..."
(Respighi, "Pioggia")

1. The imperfect tense of the auxiliary verbs is formed irregularly:

essere	avere
ero	avevo
eri	avevi
era	aveva
eravamo	avevamo
eravate	avevate
erano	avevano

"...e tanto era in quel guardo..."
(Donizetti, *Don Pasquale*, "So anch'io la virtù magica")

2. Except for an irregular stem spelling, the imperfect tense of irregular verbs is generally formed with regular endings.

3. The imperfect tense is used most frequently:

a) to describe an habitual action in the past

b) to describe what was going on when an action took place

c) to describe a situation that existed in the past

d) to descibe one's impression, feelings, or appearance in the past

e) to express time of day in the past

4. When the imperfect tense verb form is followed by the preposition *da*, the imperfect tense implies that an action, state of being, or condition that had begun in the past was still going on at a certain time.

E. Future Tense

The *future tense* in Italian is used to denote futurity. To form the future tense in Italian the final *-e* of the infinitive is dropped and the following endings are added: *regular "-are" verbs* change the *a* of the infinitive ending to *-e*:

cantare	battere	applaudire
canterò	batterò	applaudirò
canterai	batterai	applaudirai
canterà	batterà	applaudirà
canteremo	batteremo	applaudiremo
canterete	batterete	applaudirete
canteranno	batteranno	aplaudiranno

"...vedrai la forte..."
(Cimarosa, *Don Calandrino*)

"...il tutor ricuserò, io l'ingegno aguzzerò,
alla fin s'accheterà, e contenta io resterò,

Sì, Lindoro mio sarà, lo giurai, la vincerò."
(Rossini, *Il barbiere di Siviglia*, "Una voce poco fa")

"...io pregherò per te..."
(Donizetti, *Lucia di Lammermoor*, "Regnava nel silenzio")

"...e se pur lo trovarete, mentre un bacio
gli darete, cangierà tosta il rigor..."
(Torelli, "Ricercate, o mie speranze")

The future tense of *essere* and *avere* is irregular:

essere	avere
sarò	avrò
sarai	avrai
sarà	avrà
saremo	avremo
sarete	avrete
saranno	avranno

1. Other verbs also form the future tense using irregular stems; in translating, the letter *r* before a future ending should signal the future tense.

    a) When the sentence context denotes futurity rather than motion the future tense is used in Italian with the meaning "to go".

    b) The future tense is used idiomatically in Italian to express conjecture or probability in the present.

F. Future Perfect Tense

The *future perfect tense* is used to express an action that will take place in the future before another future action takes place, or to express probability in the past. When the future perfect tense is used in a clause in sentence structure, the verb in the other clause is always in the future tense. The future perfect tense consists of the future tense of the auxiliary verb *avere* or *essere* and the past participle of the finite verb.

cantare

avrò	cantato	I	will have sung
avrai	cantato	you	will have sung
avrà	cantato	he, she, you	will have sung
avremo	cantato	we	will have sung
avrete	cantato	you	will have sung
avranno	cantato	they, you	will have sung

battere		andare	
avrò	battuto	sarò	andato(a)
avrai	battuto	sarai	andato(a)
avrà	battuto	sarà	andato(a)
avremo	battuto	saremo	andati(e)
avrete	battuto	sarete	andati(e)
avranno	battuto	saranno	andati(e)

avere		essere	
avrò	avuto	sarò	stato(a)
avrai	avuto	sarai	stato(a)
avrà	avuto	sarà	stato(a)
avremo	avuto	saremo	stati(e)
avrete	avuto	sarete	stati(e)
avranno	avuto	saranno	stati(e)

G. Past Perfect Tense

The *past perfect tense* expresses an action that had already taken place when another past action took place. There are two forms of the past perfect tense in Italian:

1. The *trapassato prossimo* consists of the imperfect tense of the auxiliary verb *avere* or *essere* and the past participle of the finite verb:

cantare			andare		
avevo	cantato	I had sung	ero	andato(a)	I had gone
avevi	cantato		eri	andato(a)	
aveva	cantato		era	andato(a)	
avevamo	cantato		eravamo	andati(e)	

avevate	cantato		eravate	andati(e)
avevano	cantato		erano	andati(e)

2. The *trapassato remoto* consists of the simple past tense of the auxiliary verb and the past participle of the finite verb:

cantare			andare	
ebbi	cantato	I had sung	fui	andato(a) I had gone
avesti	cantato		fosti	andato(a)
ebbe	cantato		fu	andato(a)
avemmo	cantato		fummo	andati(e)
aveste	cantato		foste	andati(e)
ebbero	cantato		furono	andati(e)

The *trapassato prossimo* may be used in a main clause or in a subordinate clause in a sentence when the verb in the main clause is in the imperfect tense. The *trapassato remoto* is used *only* in subordinate clauses when the verb in the main clause is in the simple past tense.

III. PREFIXES

Two additional points should be made before examining a large number of verbs:

A. Forms

A number of Italian verbs begin with a prefix that is attached to a simple verb; such verbs are conjugated like the root verb without the prefix. In the listing of verbs that follows, when a new verb originates from a basic verb, the basic verb within the new verb is underlined. Although the prefix generally does not suggest the meaning of the new verb, the following generalities may assist in translating verbs to which a prefix has been added.

1. The prefix *de-* generally has a negative connotation approximately equivalent to the English prefix *un-*:

> decentrare - to decentralize
>
> decolorare - to discolor
>
> decrescere - to decrease

2. The prefix *dis-* is often equivalent to the prefix *dis-* in English:

disabbellire - to disfigure

disabituare - to disaccustom

disaccordare - to disagree

3. The prefix *pre-* is often equivalent to the prefix *pre-* in English:

preaccennare - to indicate in advance

precedere - to precede

precipitare - to precipitate

4. The prefix *ri-* generally indicates a repetition of an action:

prendere - to take	riprendere - to take again	
portare - to carry, take	riportare - to take back	
vedere - to see	rivedere - to see again	
suonare - to sound	risuonare - to resound	

B. Cognates

An important principle in translating verb meanings is that some Italian verbs have English cognates, that is, counterparts that sound and/or are spelled alike. It is an asset to efficient translation to recognize the basic verb and rely on the knowledge of the basic verb form for correct grammatical structure.

IV. SUMMARY

A. Categories of Verbs

All verbs in Italian are either

1. Regular

2. Irregular

Regular and irregular verbs are either

1. Transitive - takes a direct object

2. Intransitive - does not take a direct object

B. Auxiliary Verbs

All verbs in Italian have an auxiliary verb.

1. All reflexive verbs take the auxiliary verb *essere*.

C. Stem Spelling

Some irregular verbs have more than one stem spelling in conjugation.

D. Indicative Mood

There are seven tenses in Italian in the *Indicative Mood* (the mood of a verb expressing a fact):

1. Present tense
2. Compound past tense
3. Simple (literary) past tense
4. Imperfect tense
5. Future tense
6. Future perfect tense
7. Past perfect tense

   a) trapassato prossimo

   b) trapassato remoto

E. Tenses

The seven tenses are formed:

1. Present tense = verb stem + endings
2. Simple past tense = verb stem + endings
3. Imperfect tense = verb stem + endings
4. Future tense = infinitive (final -*e* dropped) + endings
5. Compound past tense = present tense of auxiliary verb + past participle
6. Future perfect tense = future tense of auxiliary verb + past participle
7. Past perfect tense

   a) trapassato prossimo = imperfect tense of auxiliary verb + past participle

   b) trapassato remoto = simple past tense of auxiliary verb + past participle

PRINCIPLE PARTS OF REGULAR AND
IRREGULAR VERBS

R = Regular
I = Irregular
a = avere:auxiliary
e = essere:auxiliary

infinitive	first person simple past tense	past participle		
abborrire	abborrii	abborrito	(a-R)	to abhor
abitare		abitato	(a-R)	to live, dwell
accendere	accesi	acceso	(a-I)	to light, kindle
accludere	acclusi	accluso	(a-I)	to include
accompagnare		accompagnato	(a-R)	to accompany
adempire	adempii	adempito	(a-R)	to fulfill
affliggere	afflissi	afflitto	(a-I)	to afflict
aggiu*stare*			(a-I)	to adjust
aiutare		aiutato	(a-R)	to help, aid
alludere	allusi	alluso	(e-I)	to allude
alzare		alzato	(a-R)	to lift, raise
andare	andai	andato	(e-I)	to go
annettere	annessi	annesso	(a-I)	to annex
annunziare		annunziato	(a-R)	to announce, call
apparire	apparii	apparso	(a-I)	to appear
appendere	appesi	appeso	(a-I)	to hang up
ap*plaudire*			(a-R)	to applaud
ap*prendere*			(a-I)	to learn
aprire	aprii	aperto	(a-I)	to open
ardere	arsi	arso	(e-I)	to burn
arrivare		arrivato	(e-R)	to arrive
arrossire		arrossito	(e-R)	to blush
a*scendere*			(e-I)	to ascend
asciugare		asciugato	(a-R)	to dry
ascoltare		ascoltato	(a-R)	to listen
ascondere	ascosi	ascosto	(a-I)	to hide

aspergere	aspersi	asperso	(a-I)	to sprinkle
aspettare		aspettato	(a-R)	to wait
assaggiare		assaggiato	(a-R)	to taste
assistere	assistetti assistei	assistito	(a-I)	to assist
assolvere	assolsi assolvei	assolto	(a-I)	to absolve
assorbire		assorbito	(a-R)	to absorb
assumere	assuni	assunto	(a-I)	to assume
attendere	attesi	atteso	(a-I)	to wait
attingere	attinsi	attinto	(a-I)	to attain
avere	ebbi	avuto	(a-I)	to have
avvertire	avertii	avvertito	(a-R)	to warn
ballare		ballato	(e-R)	to dance
bastare		bastato	(e-R)	to be enough
bere	bevvi	bevuto	(a-I)	to drink
bruciare		bruciato	(a-R)	to burn
bussare		bussato	(a-R)	to knock
cadere	caddi	caduto	(e-I)	to fail
cambiare		cambiato	(a-R)	to change
camminare		camminato	(e-R)	to walk
cantare		cantato	(a-R)	to sing
capire	capii	capito	(a-R)	to understand
cedere	cessi cedei	cesso (ceduto)	(a-I)	to yield
cercare		cercato	(a-R)	to look for
chiamare		chiamato	(a-R)	to call (on)
chiedere	chiedi chiedei	chiesto	(a-I)	to ask
chiudere	chiusi	chiuso	(a-I)	to close
cogliere	colsi	colto	(a-I)	to gather
compartire	compartii	compiendo	(a-R)	to distribute
compire	compii	compito	(a-R)	to finish

comprare		comprato	(a-R) to buy
com*prendere*			(e-I) to comprehend
comprimere	compressi	compresso	(a-I) to compress
coincidere	coincisi	coinciso	(e-I) to coincide
concedere	concessi concedei	concesso (conceduto)	(a-I) to concede
connettere	connessi	connesso	(a-I) to connect
conoscere	conobbi	conosciuto	(a-I) to know
conseguire	conseguii	conseguito	(a-R) to obtain
con*sentire*			(a-R) to consent
consistere		consistito	(a-R) to consist
contare		contato	(a-R) to plan to
continuare		continuato	(a-R) to continue
conversare		conversato	(a-R) to converse
convertire	convertii	convertito	(a-R) to convert
correre	corsi	corso	(e-I) to run
cor*rispondere*			(a-R) to correspond
costare		costato	(e-R) to cost
costruire		costruito	(a-R) to build
credere	credei	creduto	(a-R) to believe
crescere	crebbi	cresciuto	(e-I) to grow
cuocere	cossi	cotto	(a-I) to cook
dare	diedi detti	dato	(a-I) to give
decidere		deciduto	(a-R) to decide
desiderare		desiderato	(a-R) to wish, desire
difendere	difesi	difeso	(a-I) to defend
dimenticare		dimenticato	(a-R) to forget
dipingere	dipinsi	dipinto	(a-I) to depict
dire	dissi	detto	(a-I) to say
dirigere	dirigetti diressi	diretto	(a-I) to conduct
dis*piacere*			(e-I) to displease

dissuadere	dissuasi	dissuaso	(a-I)	to dissuade
distinguere	distinsi	distinto	(a-I)	to distinguish
dividere	divisi	diviso	(a-I)	to divide
divertire	divertii	divertito	(a-I)	to amuse
dolere	dolsi	doluto	(e-I)	to ache
domandare		domandato	(a-R)	to ask
dormire	dormii	dormito	(e-R)	to sleep
dovere	dovei	dovuto	(a-I)	to be obliged to
	dovetti			
durare		durato	(e-R)	to last
eccedere	eccedei	ecceduto	(a-I)	to exceed
elidere	elisi	eliso	(a-I)	to elide
eludere	elusi	eluso	(a-I)	to elude
emergere	emersi	emerso	(e-I)	to emerge
emulgere	emulsi	emulso	(a-I)	to soften
entrare		entrato	(e-R)	to enter
ergere	ersi	erto	(a-I)	to stand upright
erigere	eressi	eretto	(a-I)	to erect
escludere	esclusi	escludendo	(a-I)	to exclude
esigere	esigei	esatto	(a-I)	to exact
esistere	esistei	esistito	(a-I)	to exist
espellere	espulsi	espulso	(a-I)	to expel
esplodere	esplosi	esploso	(a-I)	to explode
essere	fui	stato	(e-I)	to be
estinguere	estinsi	estinto	(a-I)	to extinguish
evadere	evasi	evaso	(a-I)	to evade
fare	feci	fatto	(a-I)	to do
fendere	fendei	fesso (fenduto)	(a-I)	to split
	fendetti			
festeggiare		festeggiato	(a-R)	to celebrate
figgere	fissi	fitto	(a-I)	to fix
fingere	finsi	finto	(a-I)	to feign
finire	finii	finendo	(a-R)	to finish

fondere	fusi	fuso	(a-I)	to cast, mould
fuggire	fuggii	fuggito	(e-R)	to flee
gettare		gettato	(a-R)	to throw
giacere	giacqui	giaciuto	(e-I)	to lie down
giocare		giocato	(a-R)	to play
giungere	giunsi	giunto	(e-I)	to arrive
godere		goduto	(a-R)	to enjoy
gridare		gridato	(e-R)	to shout
guardare		guardato	(a-R)	to look, look at
illudere	illusi	illuso	(a-I)	to deceive
immergere	immersi	immerso	(a-I)	to emerge
imparare		imparato	(a-R)	to learn
impellere	impulsi	impulso	(a-I)	to impel
importare		importato	(e-R)	to matter
impostare		impostato	(a-R)	to mail
imprimere	impressi	impresso	(a-I)	to print
incominciare		incominciato	(a-R)	to begin
incontrare		incontrato	(a-R)	to meet
indulgere	indulsi	indulto	(a-I)	to indulge
inflettere	inflettei	inflettendo	(a-I)	to inflect
infliggere	inflissi	inflitto	(a-I)	to inflict
infrangere	infransi	infranto	(a-I)	to break
insegnare		insegnato	(a-R)	to teach
interessare		interessato	(a-R)	to interest
intrudere	intrusi	intruso	(a-I)	to intrude
invadere	invasi	invaso	(a-I)	to invade
invitare		invitato	(a-R)	to invite
istruire	istruii	istruito	(a-I)	to instruct
languire	languii	languito	(e-R)	to languish
lasciare		lasciato	(a-R)	to leave, let
leggere	lessi	letto	(a-I)	to read
mancare		mancato	(a-R)	to lack
mandare		mandato	(a-R)	to send

mangiare		mangiato	(a-R)	to eat
mentire	mentii	mentito	(a-R)	to lie
mettere	misi	metto	(a-I)	to put
mordere	morsi	morso	(a-I)	to bite
morire		morito	(e-R)	to die
muovere	mossi	mosso	(a-I)	to move
nascere	nacqui	nato	(e-I)	to be born
nascondere	nascosi	nascosto	(a-I)	to hide
negligere	neglessi	negletto	(a-I)	to neglect
nevicare		nevicato	(e-R)	to snow
notare		notato	(a-R)	to note
numerare		numerato	(a-R)	to number
nuocere	nocqui	nociuto	(a-I)	to injure
nuotare		nuotato	(e-R)	to swim
offendere	offesi	offeso	(a-I)	to offend
offrire		offrito	(a-R)	to offer
opprimere	oppressi	oppresso	(a-I)	to oppress
ordinare		ordinato	(a-R)	to order
pagare		pagato	(a-R)	to pay
parere	parvi	parso	(e-I)	to seem
	parsi			
parlare		parlato	(a-R)	to speak
partire		partito	(e-R)	to leave
passare		passato	(e-R)	to pass, go by
percuotere	percossi	percosso	(a-I)	to strike
perdere	perdei	perduto (perso)	(a-I)	to lose
	persi			
persuader	persuasi	persuaso	(a-I)	to persuade
piacere	piacqui	piaciuto	(e-I)	to please
piangere	piansi	pianto	(a-I)	to weep
pingere	pinsi	pinto	(a-I)	to depict
piovere	piovve	piovuto	(e-I)	to rain
plaudire	plaudii	plaudito	(e-R)	to applaude

porgere	porsi	porto	(a-I)	to offer
porre	posi	posto	(a-I)	to put
portare		portato	(a-R)	to carry
potere	potei	potuto	(e-I)	to be able
pranzare		pranzato	(e-R)	to dine
preferire		preferito	(a-R)	to prefer
prendere	presi	preso	(a-I)	to take
preparare		preparato	(a-R)	to prepare
presentare		presentato	(a-R)	to present
presumere	presunsi	presunto	(e-I)	to presume
pro*seguire*			(a-R)	to continue
proteggere	protessi	protetto	(a-I)	to protect
pulire		pulito	(a-R)	to clean
rag*giungere*			(a-I)	to join, reach
rappresentare		rappresentato	(a-R)	to represent
recidere	recisi	reciso	(a-I)	to cut off
redigere	redassi	redatto	(a-I)	to draw up
redimere	redensi	redento	(a-I)	to redeem
reggere	ressi	retto	(a-I)	to govern
rendere	resi	reso	(a-I)	to give back
repellere	repulsi	repulso	(a-I)	to repel
rescindere	rescissi	rescisso	(a-I)	to rescind
restare		restato	(e-R)	to stay
ricevere		ricevuto	(a-R)	to receive
ri*chiedere*			(a-I)	to require
ri*conoscere*			(a-I)	to recognize
ricordare		ricordato	(a-R)	to remember
ridere	risi	riso	(e-I)	to laugh
riempire		riempito	(a-R)	to fill
riflettere	riflessi	riflettuto	(a-I)	to reflect
	riflettei	(riflesso)		
rimanere	rimasi	rimasto	(a-I)	to remain
ringraziare		ringraziato	(a-R)	to thank

ripetere		ripetuto	(a-R)	to repeat
ri*portare*			(a-R)	to take back
riposare		riposato	(e-R)	to rest
ri*prendere*			(a-I)	to take again
riscuotere		riscuotuto	(a-R)	to cash
rispondere	risposi	risposto	(a-I)	to respond
ritornare		ritornato	(e-R)	to return
riuscire		riuscito	(e-R)	to succeed
ri*vedere*			(a-I)	to see again
rompere	ruppi	rotto	(a-I)	to break
rovinare		rovinato	(a-R)	to ruin
salire	salii	salito	(e-I)	to go forth
salutare		salutato	(a-R)	to greet
sapere	seppi	saputo	(a-I)	to know
scegliere	scelsi	scelto	(a-I)	to choose
scendere	scesi	sceso	(e-I)	to descend
scernere	scernei	scernuto	(a-I)	to discern
scherzare		scherzato	(e-R)	to joke
sciare		sciato	(e-R)	to ski
scindere	scissi	scisso	(a-I)	to separate
scrivere	scrissi	scritto	(a-I)	to write
scuotere	scossi	scosso	(a-I)	to shake
sedere	sedei	seduto	(e-I)	to sit
seguire	seguii	seguito	(a-R)	to follow
sembrare		sembrato	(e-R)	to seem
sentire	sentii	sentito	(e-R)	to feel
separare		separato	(a-R)	to separate
servire	servii	servito	(a-R)	to serve
sfogliare		sfogliato	(a-R)	to leaf through
significare		significato	(a-R)	to signify
sognare		sognato	(e-R)	to dream
solere		solito	(e-I)	to be in the habit of

solvere	solvei	solto	(a-I)	to solve
sorgere	sorsi	sorto	(e-I)	to rise
sor*ridere*			(e-I)	to smile
sortire	sortii	sortito	(e-R)	to go out
sospirare		sospirato	(a-R)	to sigh
spandere	spansi	spanto	(a-I)	to spread
spargere	sparsi	sparso	(a-I)	to disperse
s*partire*			(a-R)	to divide
spegnere	spensi	spento	(a-I)	to extinguish
spendere	spesi	speso	(a-I)	to spend
sperare		sperato	(a-R)	to hope
spiegare		spiegato	(a-R)	to explain
spingere	spinsi	spinto	(a-I)	to push
splendere		splenduto	(e-R)	to shine
stare	stetti	stato	(e-I)	to stand
stringere	strinsi	stretto	(a-I)	to press
struggere	strussi	strutto	(a-I)	to destroy
studiare		studiato	(a-R)	to study
suonare		suonato	(a-R)	to sound
tacere	tacqui	taciuto	(a-I)	to be silent
telefonare		telefonato	(a-R)	to telephone
tendere	tesi	teso	(a-I)	to stretch
tenere	tenni	tenuto	(a-I)	to hold
tergere	tersi	terso	(a-I)	to wipe
togliere	tolsi	tolto	(a-I)	to take away
trarre	trassi	tratto	(a-I)	to draw
traversare		traversato	(a-R)	to cross
travestire	travestii	travestito	(a-R)	to disguise
trovare		trovato	(a-R)	to find
uccidere	uccisi	ucciso	(a-I)	to kill
udire	udii	udito	(a-I)	to hear
usare		usato	(a-R)	to use
uscire	uscii	uscito	(e-I)	to go out

valere	valsi	valso (valuto)	(e-I)	to be worth
vedere	vidi	visto (veduto)	(a-I)	to see
venire	venni	venuto	(e-I)	to come
vestire	vestii	vestito	(a-R)	to dress
viaggiare		viaggiato	(e-R)	to travel
vincere	vinsi	vinto	(a-I)	to vanquish
visitare		visitato	(a-R)	to visit
vivere	vissi	vissuto	(e-I)	to live
	vivei			
volare		volato	(e-R)	to fly
volere	volli	voluto	(e-I)	to be willing
volgere	volsi	volto	(e-I)	to turn around

REFLEXIVE VERBS

abituarsi	to accustom oneself to
accomodarsi	to make oneself comfortable
accorgersi	to perceive
addormentarsi	to fall asleep
alzarsi	to get up, rise
astenersi	to abstain
avviarsi	to start out
avvicinarsi	to come near, to approach
chiamarsi	to be named, be called
contentarsi	to be satisfied, pleased
divertirsi	to amuse oneself, have a good time
dolersi	to complain
fermarsi	to stop
incontrarsi	to meet
interessarsi	to interest oneself in
lagnarsi	to complain
lamentarsi	to complain
laurearsi	to graduate
lavarsi	to wash oneself

levarsi	to rise, get up, take off
liberarsi	to get rid of
mettarsi	to begin
pentersi	to repent
raccomandarsi	to recommend oneself; to beg
ricordarsi	to remember
riposarsi	to rest
sbarazzarsi	to get rid of
sbrigarsi	to hurry
scusarsi	to excuse oneself
sdraiarsi	to lie down, stretch out
sedersi	to sit down
servirsi	to use
sforzarsi	to endeavor
sovvenirsi	to remember
stabilirsi	to settle
svegliarsi	to wake up
trattarsi	to be a matter of
trovarsi	to get along - in a place; be located
tuffarsi	to dive
unirsi	to unite
vestirsi	to dress oneself

IDIOMATIC VERBS

andare in giro	to wander
avere...anni	to be...years old
avere bisogno di	to need
avere fame	to be hungry
avere freddo	to be cold (person)
avere fretta	to be in a hurry
avere luogo	to take place
avere paura	to be afraid

avere sete	to be thirsty
avere sonno	to be sleepy
cercare di	to try
dare la mano	to shake hands with
domandare	to ask of (a person)
essere nato	to be born
essere in ritardo	to be late
fare colazione	to have lunch, breakfast
fare la conoscenza	to make the acquaintance of
fare il conto	to add up (the total)
fare freddo	to be cold (weather)
fare fresco	to be cool (weather)
fare il giro	to make the tour, the rounds
fare un giro	to go around, make a tour
fare male	to hurt, ache
fare una passeggiata	to take a walk
fare una sorpresa	to surprise
fare le spese	to shop
fare lo spiritoso	to try to be funny
fare una telefonata	to make a call
fare le valige	to pack
fare vedere	to show
fare un viaggio	to take a trip
riprendere il cammino	to continue on one's way
sentire parlare di	to hear about
stare per	to be about
tirare vento	to be windy
volere dire	to mean, signify

VERBS FREQUENTLY ENCOUNTERED IN MUSIC SCORES, TEXTS ON MUSIC, AND MUSICOLOGICAL ESSAYS

abbellire	to ornament, embellish
accentuare	to emphasize, accent
accordare	to tune
battere	to beat (a drum or other percussion instrument)
comporre	to compose
dirigere	to conduct
dividere (divisi)	to divide, as in string parts
eseguire	to perform
essertarsi	to practice
forzare	to force, strain
frenare	to restrain, hold back
lasciare vibrare	to let sound (continue to sound)
levare	to take off (organ stops, mutes)
mettere la sordina	to mute
pizzicare	to pluck a musical instrument
placare	to grow calm
raddoppiare	to double, usually at the lower octave
raggiungere	to reach, to attain (a speed)
rallentare	to slow down
riprendere	to take up (the original tempo)
risuonare	1) to resound, echo, continue sounding
	2) to repeat
segnare il tempo	to beat time
sostenere	to sustain
sparire	to fade away

staccare; separare	to detach, separate either notes or phrases
suonare	to sound
suonare a fantasia	to improvise
tacere	to be silent
tirare	to draw (organ stops, slides, etc.)
vocalizzare	to vocalize

VERBS FREQUENTLY ENCOUNTERED IN VOCAL LITERATURE

bagnare	to wet, dip, moisten; bathe (Salieri, "In questa tomba oscura")
celare	to conceal, hide (Bononcini, *Mario Fuggitivo*, Dalinda's aria)
consolare	to console, comfort (Steffani, *Enrico Leone*, Errea's aria)
consumare	to wear out, use up, consume (Bononcini, "Cara, si, tu mi consumi")
imbiondire	to become fair (hair); to ripen (grain) (Pizzetti, "I Pastori")
innamorarsi	to fall in love with (A. Scarlatti, *La donna ancora è fedele*, Alidoro's aria)
parere	to seem, to look (D. Gabrielli, *Flavio Cuniberto*, Emilia's aria)
penare	to suffer, to be in pain (Gaffi, "Lungi dal ben, ch'adoro")
respirare	to breathe; inhale (Cesti, *I casti amori d'Orontea*, Recitative of Orontea)
ricercare	to seek for, to seek out

	(Torelli, "Ricercate, o mie speranze")
soffrire	to suffer (Respighi, "Nebbie")
sparire	to disappear; to vanish (Pasquini, *Erminia in riva del Giordano*, Erminia's aria)
tradire	to betray (Cesarini, "Fuggite, amanti")

MUSICAL EXERCISES

1. Identify the following compositions (composer, style, etc.):

   a) "Chi vuole innamorarsi"

   b) "Mi parto"

   c) "Sentirsi dire"

2. Survey the text of the Lamento d'Arianna by Monteverdi.

   a) List all verbs

   b) Translate each

   c) Indicate the tense in which each is used

   d) Indicate whether the verb is transitive/intransitive and regular/irregular.

3. Survey an area from one of the following operas by Giacomo Puccini:

   La Bohême
   La fanciulla del West
   Gianni Schicci
   Madama Butterfly
   Manon Lescaut
   Suor Angelica
   Il tabarro
   Tosca
   Turandot

a) List each verb

b) Name the auxiliary verb

c) Cite the tense used

Chapter Four

I. ADJECTIVES

An *adjective* is a word that describes or modifies a noun or pronoun and answers the question "which?", "which one?", "what kind of?" a noun or pronoun.

A. Demonstrative Adjectives

Demonstrative adjectives point out or indicate the object spoken of; they do not describe. The forms of demonstrative adjectives in Italian are:

Singular				*Plural*	
Masculine: *questo*	this	*quello*	that	*questi*	these, those
Feminine: *questa*	this	*quella*	that	*queste*	these, those

> "...in questa tomba oscura..."
> (Salieri, "In questa tomba oscura")

> "...questa vaga del mio tormento..."
> (Falconieri, "Segui, segui, dolente core")

> "...leggete queste note credete a questa carta..."
> (Monteverdi, "Se i languidi miei sguardi")

1. Before a vowel *questo* and *questa* may be contracted to *quest'*; this elision occurs only in the singular form.

> "...sì da quest'isola deserta..."
> (Ponchielli, *La Gioconda*, "Pescator, affonda l'esca")

2. The forms of *quello* are similar to the forms of the definite article combined with *di* (Chapter Two); these forms always precede the noun modified.

> quel + il *quel* (del)
> quel + i *quei* (dei)
> quel + lo *quello* (dello)
> quel + l' *quell'* (dell')
> quel + la *quella* (della)
> quel + gli *quegli* (degli)
> quel + le *quelle* (delle)

"...a quella tregua..."
(Respighi, "Pioggia")

"...quel guardo, il cavaliere..."
(Donizetti, *Don Pasquale*, Act I)

"...quella crudel beltà..."
(Verdi, *Falstaff*, Act II)

3. Demonstrative adjectives must agree in gender and number with the noun modified.

B. Predicate Nominative

The *predicate nominative* in Italian consists of the demonstrative adjective *quest'* used with the verb *essere* followed by a noun that is equal to or describes the subject. The indefinite article (*un, uno, una, un'*) is not used before an unmodified *predicate adjective* or *predicate nominative* indicating nationality, religion, or profession. Some examples of the predicate nominative in music literature are:

"...quest'è la pace..."
(Verdi, *Don Carlos*, Act I)

"...quest'è una ragna..."
(Verdi, *Otello*, Act III)

"...questo è un martire questo è un dolore..."
(Vinci, "Sentirsi dire")

"...Io sono docile, son rispettosa, sono obbediente, dolce, amorosa..."
(Rossini, *Il barbiere di Siviglia*, " Una voce poco fa")

Respighi	- Io sono la madre
Busatti	- Morto son io
Perti	- Io son zittella
Rossi	- Fanciulla son io
Scarlatti	- La fortuna è un pronto ardir

C. Possessive Adjectives

Possessive adjectives indicate possession, or to whom something belongs; a possessive adjective must agree in gender and number with the noun modified. The forms of possessive adjectives are:

Singular

Masculine	*Feminine*	
il mio	la mia	my, mine
il tuo	la tua	your, yours
il suo	la sua	his, her, hers
il Suo	la Sua	your, yours
il nostro	ma nostra	our, ours
il vostro	la vostra	your, yours
il loro	la loro	their, theirs
il Loro	la Loro	your, yours

Plural

i miei	le mie	my, mine
i tuoi	le tue	your, yours
i suoi	le sue	his, her, hers
i Suoi	le Sue	your, yours
i nostri	le nostre	our, ours
i vostri	le vostre	your, yours
i loro	le loro	their, theirs
i Loro	le Loro	your, yours

1. Possessive adjectives are usually preceded by the definite article.

"...il mio tesoro..."
(Mozart, *Don Giovanni*)

"...la notte le sue lagrime piange..."
(Respighi, "Notte")

"...i miei pastori..."
(Pizzetti, *I Pastori*)

"...e la mia voluttà..."
(Tosti, "L'alba separa dalla luce l'ombra")

Marcello - Il mio bel foco

Busatti - E tornato il mio ben

Paesiello - Il mio ben quando verrà

Carissimi - La mia fede altrai giurata

Quagliati - Apra il suo verde seno

A. Scarlatti - La tua gradita fé

413

2. The definite article is omitted in direct address and before a singular, *unmodified* noun denoting a family relation.

Calestani	- Ferma, Dorinda mia
A. Scarlatti	- Siete estinte, o mia speranza
Zaneti	- Avvezzati, mio core
A. Scarlatti	- Speranze mie
Sarti	- Mia speranza io pur vorrei
Peri	- O miei giorni fugaci
Da Gagliano	- Mie speranze
Cimarosa	- Voi avete, o mia signora
Cimarosa	- Resta in pace, idolo mio
Cimarosa	- Perdonate signor mio
Cimarosa	- Mio signor
Carissimi	- Vittoria, mio core

3. The definite article is never omitted with the possessive adjective *loro*.

4. A possessive adjective must agree with the noun indicating what is possessed, not with the possessor.

5. Possessive adjectives are generally repeated before each noun to which they refer.

a) In order to avoid ambiguity in the third person singular forms (his, her, hers)

il sue pianoforte - his, her piano

may be expressed

il pianoforte di lui - his piano

il pianoforte di lei - her piano
"...nome di lui si amato..."
(Verdi, *Rigoletto*, "Caro nome")

6. Possessive adjectives may be placed after the noun modified for emphasis; it agrees with the noun as in regular word order.

Monteverdi	- Se i languidi miei sguardi
Leo	- Ah! che la pena mia
Cesti	- Intorno all'idol mio
Carissimi	- Sventura, cuor mio

Bianchi - Tu seconda il voti miei

Leo - Dirti, ben mio, vorrei

7. When a possessive adjective follows a preposition, the definite article of the possessive adjective is contracted with the preposition.

"...o felice dei loro amori!"
(Verdi, *Un ballo in maschera,* "Volta la terrea")

"...per amor del mio sogno..."
(Tosti, "L'alba sepàra dalla luce l'ombra")

"...nel tuo sen materno..."
(Tosti, "L'alba sepàra dalla luce l'ombra")

"...dal mio desire..."
(Tosti, "L'alba sepàra dalla luce l'ombra")

Peri - Gioite al canto mio

Paradies - M'ha preso alla sua sagna

Monteverdi - Dal mio permesso amato

Cherubini - Ah! che forse ai miei di

A. Scarlatti - Se tu della mia morte

D. Adjective Word Order

In Italian adjectives generally follow the nouns they modify. The following adjectives, however, normally precede the noun they modify.

Singular		*Plural*		
m.	*f.*	*m.*	*f.*	
bello	bella	belli	belle	beautiful
bravo	brava	bravi	brave	good, able
brutto	brutta	brutti	brutte	ugly
buono	buona	buoni	buone	good
grande	grande	grandi	grandi	large, great
lungo	lunga	lunghi	lunghi	long
nuovo	nuova	nuovi	nuove	new
piccolo	piccola	piccoli	piccole	small, little
cattivo	cattiva	cattivi	cattive	bad
giovane	giovane	giovani	giovani	young
stesso	stessa	stessi	stesse	same
vecchio	vecchia	vecchi	vecchie	old

Pasquini   - Bella bocco

Falconieri   - Bella fanciulla

Cimara   - Vecchia chitarra

Caccini   - Belle rose purpurine

1. These adjectives must *follow* the noun modified

  a) when used for emphasis or contrast

  b) when modified by an adverb or a suffix.

Demonstrative and possessive adjectives and ordinal numbers precede the noun modified.

Pergolesi - Tre giorni

2. The following are examples from music literature of adjectives which precede nouns:

Le nuove musiche - Caccini

Il primo libro di Capricci - Frescobaldi

Alberti bass

altra volta

bel canto

cinque passi

Florentine camerata

ombra scene

prima donna

prima vista

Ruggiero bass

secconda prattica

  a) Identify each of the above works/terms; describe the historical significance of each.

3. Identify each of the following compositions (composer, style, etc.):

Caldi sospiri

Caro volto

Il clefta prigione

Nudo arciero

Povera pellegrina

L'ultima canzone

E. Descriptive Adjectives

Descriptive adjectives are those adjectives that describe or tell "what kind of" about the noun modified; descriptive adjectives generally follow the noun and must agree in gender and number with the noun modified.

d'Astorga	- Auretta vezzosa
Cimara	- Melodia autumnale
Malipiero	- Rose spinose
Respighi	- Canto funebre
d'Astorga	- Fiore ingrato
Caccini	- Occhi immortali
Caldare	- Selve amiche
Cimarosa	- Fanciulla Sventura
Rosa	- Star vicino
A. Scarlatti	- Marmi adorati e cari
Vivaldi	- Amato ben

There are two groups of descriptive adjectives in Italian:

1. Adjectives ending in *-o* have four form endings:

	Singular	*Plural*
m.	-o	-i
f.	-a	-e

nero	- black
giallo	- yellow
rosso	- red
azzurro	- blue
bruno	- brown
Brogi	- Gotine gialla

2. Adjectives ending in *-e* are the same in the masculine and feminine singular forms; in the plural form the *-e* changes to *-i*. verde - verdi

3. An adjective takes the masculine form when modifying two nouns of different gender.

4. Some irregular adjective plurals are formed:

    a) Feminine adjectives that end in *-ca* and *-ga* are pluralized by inserting an *h* after the ending consonant and changing the final *-a* to *-e*. lunga - lunghe

    b) Feminine adjectives that end in *-cia* and *-gia* are pluralized by dropping the *-i* and changing the final *-a* to *-e*. grigia - grige

        (1) When *-i* is stressed in the singular form of the adjective it is not dropped in the plural form.

    c) Masculine adjectives that end in *-go* are pluralized by inserting an *h* after the *g* in order to retain the [g] sound, and by changing the final *-o* to *-i*. lungo - lunghi

    d) When a masculine adjective ends in *-co* and the stress falls on the preceding syllable, the plural is formed by inserting an *h* after the *c* in order to retain the [k] sound, and by changing the final *-e* to *-i*. bianco - bianchi

        Donaudy - Freschi luoghi

    e) When a masculine adjective ends in *-co* and the stress is not on the preceding syllable, the plural is formed simply by changing the final *-o* to *-i*. magnifico - magnifici

    f) Masculine adjectives that end in unstressed *-io* have only one *-i* in the plural: arancio - aranci; vecchio - vecchi

5. The names of all nationalities (Chapter Two) can also be used as adjectives and are declined according to the foregoing principles. Adjectives of nationality generally follow the noun modified; occasionally, however, these adjectives are placed before the noun modified for stylistic effect, special emphasis, or a special meaning.

        Rossini - La regata Veneziana

Adjectives of nationality are used without an article when used as a noun with *essere* as a predicate nominative referring to a person.

        è italiano.

        è americana.

MUSICAL EXERCISES

1. The following are examples from music of adjectives which follow nouns:

banchetto musicale	salterio tedesco
balletti galiarde	festa teatrale
ottava bassa	trillo caprino
bocca chiusa	stile lombardo
bocca ridente	accompanimento obbligato
chitarra battente	sinfonia concertante
concerto grosso	soggetto cavato
coro spezzato	viola paradon
danza tedesca	viola pomposa

   a) Identify each term; describe the historical significance of each.

2. Identify the following words:

   Cento concerti ecclesiastici

   Madrigali a note nere

   Madrigali guerrieri ed amorosi

   Fiori musicali

   Il primo libro de madregali cromatici a cinque

   Dialogo dell musica antica e della moderna

   a) Identify the composer/author of each.

   b) Describe each work historically.

3. Define historically the term *musica reservata*.

4. Define historically the term *stile rappresentativo*.

F. Past Participle

The past participle of a verb is used with an auxiliary verb to form compound tenses. The *past participle* of a verb may also be used as an adjective; it agrees in gender and number with the noun modified.

        Malipiero - Cacio stillato

        Traetta - Didone abbandonata

        Anfossi - L'incognita perseguitata

        Rossi - Il Palazzo incantato

        Galuppi - Prigioniera, abbandonata

The past participle is frequently encountered in musical scores to describe the manner of interpretation:

accentato	accented
agitato	excited, restless
animato	animated, lively
arcato	bowed
cadenzato	measured; in a regular rhythm
concertato	conducted; scored, orchestrated
distaccato	detached, separated
marcato	marked, emphasized
parlato	spoken
pizzicato	plucked
puntato	dotted, staccato
ridotto	reduced, arranged
ritenuto	held back
scucito	unconnected; non legato
separato	detached
spezzato	split, broken
tenuto	held, sustained

G. Present Participle

The *present participle* of verbs is formed by adding *-ando* to the stem of *"-are"* verbs, and -endo to *"-ere"* and *"-ire"* verbs. The present participle is frequently encountered in music as an adjective:

accelerando	becoming faster
accompagnando	accompanying
affrettando	hurrying, rushed
allargando	slowing down, becoming broader
arpeggiando	playing broken chords
aumentando	becoming louder
camminando	"walking", pushing on
crescendo	becoming louder
decrescendo	becoming softer
diminuendo	becoming softer

espirando	fading away
improvisando	improvising
languendo	languishing
largando	becoming broader
lontanando	fading into the distance
morendo	fading away
parlando	in an expressive, declamatory style
portando la voce	carrying the voice over
rallentando	becoming slower
ritardando	becoming slower
scherzando	jokingly
smorendo	dying away
smorzando	fading away
sospirando	sighing
stringendo	pressing on, hurrying

II. COMPARATIVE AND SUPERLATIVE

The comparative and superlative of adjectives is formed in English either by adding *-er* and *-est* (louder, loudest) or by using the modifiers *more* and *most* (more musical, most musical).

A. Regular Adjectives

Regular adjectives in Italian are made comparative according to the following pattern:

1. Superlative is expressed by *più...di* (more...than).
2. Equality is expressed by *così...come*, *tanto...quanto* (as (so)...as).
3. Inferiority is expressed by *meno...di* (less...than).

    a) *che* is also used to express "than" when two objects being compared are both related to the same verb.

    b) *di quel che* is used to express "than" before an inflected verb.

B. Relative Superlative

To express the relative superlative degree of adjectives, the appropriate definite article is inserted before the comparative form.

il (la, i, le) più...

> the most (-est).

le (la, i, le) meno..

> the least..

1. The articles and adjectives must agree with the noun modified. If the adjective normally follows the noun, the superlative construction also follows the noun; if the adjective normally precedes the noun, the superlative construction also precedes the noun. When the superlative construction follows the noun, the definite article is omitted.

C. Irregular Forms

The most frequently encountered adjectives which have irregular comparative and relative superlative forms include:

Adjective		*Comparative*		*Relative Superlative*	
buono	good	migliore	better	il migliore	the best
cattivo	bad	peggiore	worse	il peggiore	the worst
grande	large	maggiore	larger	il maggiore	the largest
piccolo	small	minore	smaller	il minore	the smallest
alto	higher	superiore	high	il superiore	the highest
basso	low	inferiore	lower	l' inferiore	the lowest

Irregular forms are generally figurative in meaning.

1. *maggiore* and *minore* are often used with the meaning "older, oldest," and "younger, youngest" when referring to relatives.

2. The forms of the irregular adjective *buono* (*buon, buona, buon', buono*) are used like the indefinite article *un, una, un', uno*.

3. The irregular adjectives *grande* (large) and *santo* (saint) are shortened to *gran* and *san* before a masculine noun beginning with a consonant (except *z*, and *s* plus a consonant); *grande* and *santo* are contracted to *grand'* and *sant'* before any noun beginning with a vowel.

> Cavalli - Gran pazzia (Eritrea)

> "...gran Dio, non mirar il mio pianto..."
> (Bellini, *La Sonnambula*, "Ah! non credea mirarti")

4. When the adjective *bello* (beautiful) precedes a noun, it takes the following forms, similar to those of *quello*:

bel	(quel)
bei	(quei)
bello	(quello)
bell'	(quell')
bella	(quella)
begli	(quegli)
belle	(quelle)

Perti   - Begli occhi, io non mi pento

5. For translation it is important to become familiar with the positive forms of all adjectives and be able to recognize the forms for comparative and superlative and adjectives and adverbs compared irregularly.

6. The absolute superlative of adjectives in Italian is translated in English by such adverbs as *very, extremely* etc. plus the adjective. The following forms are used to express the absolute superlative of adjectives in Italian:

a) The Italian equivalent of the adverb *molto, assai* (very), *estremamente* (extremely) plus the adjective: molto adagio

b) The final vowel of the adjective is dropped and the ending *-issimo* (-a, -i, -e) is added:

> prestissimo - very quickly
>
> adagissimo - very adagio
>
> pianissimo - very softly
>
> fortissimo - very loudly

> "...sul bellissimo cinabro..."
> (Falconieri, "Bella porta di rubini")

> "...fortunatissimo per verità!"
> (Rossini, *Il barbiere di Siviglia*, "Largo al factotum")

> Scarlatti - O dolcissima speranza
>
> Falconeri - O bellissimi capelli

(1) Adjectives that end in *-co* and *-go* add an *h* to the stem before adding *-issimo*.

(2) Adjectives that end in *-cio* and *-gio* drop the *i* before adding *-issimo*.

c) The adjectives *buono* and *cattivo* have a regular and an irregular absolute superlative:

buono	good	buonissimo	very good
		òttimo	
cattivo	bad	cattivissimo	very bad
		pèssimo	

III. ADVERBS

An *adverb* is a word that modifies a verb, an adjective, or another adverb. Adverbs answer the questions "How?", "Where?", "When?", "In what manner?", and are among the most important words in Italian for giving directions in music. The following adverbial expressions, some of which are also adjectives, are frequently encountered in music literature:

largo

larghetto

adagio

adagietto

andante

andantino

moderato

allegro

allegretto

presto

A. Forms

Most Italian adverbs are formed by adding *-mente* (equivalent to *-ly* in English) to the feminine singular adjective form. If the last syllable of the feminine adjective is *-le* or *-re*, and it is preceded by a vowel, the final *-e* is dropped before *-mente* is added: facile - facil-mente

agiatamente	easily, comfortably
allegramente	cheerfully, gaily
ampiamente	broadly
arditamente	boldly
chiaramente	clearly, brightly

424

deliberamente	deliberately
duramente	harshly
gentilmente	gently
lentamente	slowly
liberamente	freely
pianamente	smoothly, evenly
sordamente	mutedly
strasciamente	draggingly
ugualmente	equally

B. Irregular Comparative and Superlative Forms

Adverbs which form the comparative and the relative superlative irregularly include:

Adverb		Comparative		Relative Superlative	
bene	well	meglio	better	il meglio	the best
male	badly	peggio	worse	il peggio	the worst
poco	little	meno	less	il meno	the least
				(pochissimo)	
molto	much	più	more	il più	the most
				(moltìssimo)	

C. Adverbs Used in Music

The following are adverbs and adverbial expressions frequently used to give instruction in music literature:

più	rather
assai	much, very
più tosto	more quickly; rather, somewhat
ben, bene	well, quite
breve	brief, concise
come	how, like, as
corta, corto	short, brief, concise
di nuovo	again, anew
dopo	after, beyond
doppio	twice, double, twofold

doppio	twice, double, twofold
eguale	even, smoothly
grande	broadly
meno	less
la metà	half
mezza	medium, half
mòsso	moved, agitated
ogni	every
piena	full
pièno	fully
poco	little, a bit
poco a poco	little by little
poco meno	a little less
quanto	much, how much, as much
quasi	almost, as if
sempre	always, continually, throughout
sotto	under, below
subito	suddenly, immediately, at once
tanto	much, so much, as much
troppo	too, too much
tutto	all, total
via	away
vicino	nearby, close
piano	softly
forte	loudly
mezzo forte	medium loud
mezzo piano	medium soft

"...tu non sai quanto soffrì..."
(Verdi, *La Traviata*, "Di provenza il mer")

D. Suffixes

There are many suffixes in Italian which alter word meaning when added to a noun, an adjective, or an adverb (after the final vowel has been dropped). The most frequently encountered suffixes in Italian are:

426

-ina, ino		denotes smallness and, but not
-ello, -etta, -etto		necessarily, affection
	Falconieri	- Occhietti amati
	Albinoni	- Rusceletto limpidetto
-uccia, -uccio		denotes smallness and insignificance (also affection)
-otto, -one(a)		implies largeness
-astro, -accia, -accio		indicates worthlessness, scorn

In general a noun modified by a suffix retains its original gender; however, a feminine noun may be made masculine by the addition of a suffix.

E. Special Uses

1. The adverb *come* (how) is used before an adjective as an exclamation:

"...come ho freddo!..."
(Respighi, " Nebbie")

2. The adverbs *che* and *quanto* and the adjectives *quel* and *qual* may be used to introduce an idiomatic exclamation:

Cimarosa	- Che terrore, che paura (I finti nobili)
Cesti	- Che angoscia, che affanno (Il pomo d'oro)
Caccini	- O che felice giorno
Legrenzi	- Che fiero costume
Leo	- Ah, che la pena mia
Cimarosa	- Quel soave e bel diletto
Abbatini	- Quanto è bello il mio diletto
Pasquini	- Quanto è folle quell' amante
D. Scarlatti	- Qual farfaletta amante

3. The following types of words generally indicate adjectives and adverbs in translation:

a) The past participle of verbs ending in *-ato*, *-uto*, *-ito*.

b) The present participle of verbs ending in *-ando* and *-endo*.

c) The feminine form of adjectives with the ending *-mente*.

427

RESEARCH QUESTIONS

1. Define the following terms, all of which contain an adjective:

> basso ostinato
>
> basso continuo
>
> basso ripieno
>
> basso seguente
>
> dramma giocoso
>
> dramma lirico
>
> opera buffa
>
> opera seria
>
> opera semiseria
>
> stile recitativo
>
> stile antico
>
> stile concitato
>
> stile moderna

2. Identify the *Biblioteca di rarità musicali.*

3. Define historically *I classici della musica italiana.*

4. Identify each of the following compositions (composer, form, etc.):

> Musica sacra, ricercari e canzoni
>
> Primo e secondo libro di toccate
>
> La pazza senile
>
> I fidi amanti
>
> Feste romane

5. Define the term *Florentine camerata*, including a description of its activities, its members, etc.

6. Define the term *La scuola musicale di Napoli* including:

   a) the characteristics of this school of composition

   b) its exponents, indicating the area(s) of composition

   c) the periods of the Neapolitan school

7. Define the term *La scuola musicale Bolognesa* including:

   a) the characteristics of this school of composition

   b) its exponents, indicating the area of composition

   c) the significant instrumental forms that developed through the Bologna school

8. Define neo-classicism in the context of keyboard compositions by Ferrucio Busoni.

   a) Examine one of the following compositions; list all terms or phrases in Italian that give direction and translate each:

Una festa di villaggio, sei pezzi caratteristici

(1) preparazione alla festa

(2) marcia trionfale

(3) in chiesa

(4) la fiera

(5) danza

(6) notte

Danza antiche

Racconti fantastici

Danza notturna

Macchiette medioevali

Fantasia contrappuntistica (three versions)

9. Identify the following compositions:

Sinfonie musicali a otto voci

Sonate concertate in stilo moderno

Concerti ecclesiastici

Concerti musicali a 4

La regata Veneziana

MUSICAL VOCABULARY BUILDING

rigo	staff
chiave	clef
pezzo	piece, composition
movimento	movement
tema	theme, subject
motivo	motive, motif

svolgimento	development
melodia	melody
frase	musical phrase
contrappunto	counterpoint
fuga	fugue
fughetta	a short fugue
guida	subject of a fugue
proposta	subject of a fugue
divertimento	fugal episode
risposta	answer of a fugue
stretta, stretto	in a fugue, the imitation of the subject in close succession, with the answer entering before the subject is completed
presa	a sign(s) used in canons to indicate the place where the imitating voice(s) enter
rovescio	retrograde motion or inversion
riverso, rivolto	retrograde motion
recte et retro	retrograde motion
passacaglia	passacaglia
preludio	prelude
intermedio	intermezzo
variazione	variation
partita	variation
polifonia	polyphony
accordo	chord
arpeggio	notes of a chord played consecutively rather than simultaneously
prima	unison
seconda	interval of a second
terza	third
quarta	fourth
quinta	fifth
sesta	sixth
settima	seventh

ottava	octave
nona	ninth
decima	tenth
undicesima	eleventh
duldecima	twelfth
nota di passaggio	passing tone
pedale	pedal point
fermata	pedal point
riverso, rivolto	inversion
cadenza	cadence
inganno	deceptive cadence
pausa	rest
silenzio	silence, a rest
pausa di semibreve	whole rest
pausa di bianca	half rest
pausa di nera	quarter rest
pausa di croma	eighth rest
pausa di semicroma	sixteenth rest
pausa di biscroma	thirty-second rest
pausa di semibiscroma	sixty-fourth rest
battuta d'aspetto	one-measure rest
punto d'organo	the pause and its sign
semibreve	whole rest
bianca	half note
nera	quarter note
croma	eighth note
semicroma	sixteenth note
biscroma	thirty-second note
semibiscroma	sixty-fourth note
punto	a dot (1) after a note; (2) above a note to indicate staccato or portato
intonazione	pitch
scala	scale

maggiore	major key
minore	minor key
bemolle	flat sign
diesis	sharp sign
bequandro	natural sign
acuto	top note
cromatico	chromatic
passaggio	transition, modulation
terzina	triplet
misura	measure, beat
battuta	beat, strong beat at the beginning of a measure
sincopa	syncopation
battuta in aria	upbeat
battuta in terra	downbeat
tempo	speed of a composition
istesso tempo	indication that the duration of the beat remains unaltered even though the meter changes
medisimo tempo	the same tempo
ritmo	rhythm
timbro	tone color
tono (tuono)	tone
suono	musical sound
modo	manner, style
stile	style
mordente	mordent
fioritura	turn (ornamentation)
corona	the pause, the sign for which resembles a crown
fermata	hold - corona
fin' al segno	"as far as the sign" - indicates repetition from the beginning to the sign
fine	end, close

principio	beginning
dal principio al fine	from beginning to end
come in principio	as at the beginning
portato	a manner of performance that combines legato and staccato
ottava alto	one octave higher
ottava bassa	one octave lower
prima volta, seconda volta	the different endings for the first and second performances of a repeated section
ripetizione	a repeat
corista	orchestral pitch
corista di camera	chamber pitch
corista	tuning fork
guida	an abbreviated orchestral score
partitura	score
riduzione	arrangement
principale	chief part, solo
in due	in two voice parts; with two beats
sinfonia	a small symphony, usually also for a smaller orchestra
tutti	in orchestral works, particularly concertos, indication for the parts for the whole orchestra as distinct from those for the soloist
senza ripieni	the first player of each section only
violino primo	concertmaster
violino da spalla	concertmaster
stromenti a corde	stringed instruments
corda	string
corda vuota	open string
tasto	fingerboard of stringed instruments
manico	fingerboard of stringed instruments
ponticello	bridge of stringed instruments

occhi	sound hole
anima	sound post
archetto, arco	bow of stringed instruments
legno	wood (of the bow stick)
col legno	in stringed playing, striking the strings with the bow stick
sordino	mute
scordatura	abnormal tuning of a stringed instrument in order to obtain unusual chords
arcata in giù	down-bow
arcata in su	up-bow
col arco	with the bow after pizzicato
colpo d'arco	stroke of the bow
a punto d'arco	with the point of the bow
spiccato	bow is dropped on the string and is lifted again after each note
tremolo	in stringed instruments, the quick reiteration of the same tone, produced by a rapid up-and-down motion of the bow
ondeggiando	ondulating tremolo in string playing
martellato	in bowing, heavy, detached strokes
saltato, saltando	a short stroke played in rapid tempo in the middle of the bow so that the bow bounces slightly off the string
flautando	in bowing, a tone produced by bowing gently but fast over the fingerboard; producing harmonics on stringed instruments
manica	shift of position in string playing
stromenti da fiato	wind instruments
stromenti di legno	woodwind instruments
legni	the woodwind section
scialumo	chalumeau - the lowest register of the modern clarinet
ancia	reed

ancia battente	beating reed
ancia doppia	double reed
bocchino, bochetta	mouthpiece
stromenti d'ottone	brass instruments
ottoni	brass section
padiglione	the bell of a wind instrument
pistone	valve
colpo di lingua	tonguing
aperto	open notes in horn playing
chiuso	stopped in horn playing
stromenti a percossa	percussion instruments
percussione	percussion section
timpani coperti	kettledrums muted by being covered with a cloth
muta	indication for a change of tuning in timpani parts
panno	a piece of cloth used to muffle a drum
bacchetta	drumstick
bacchetta di legno	wooden drumstick
bacchetta di spugna	spongeheaded drumstick
spazzole	brushes used with percussion instruments
bisbigliando	a special effect in harp playing obtained by a quickly reiterated motion of the finger, resulting in a soft tremolo
stromenti da tasto	keyboard instruments
tasto	key of a keyboard
tastiera	keyboard
tavola armonica	soundboard
pedale	pedal
sordino	piano damper
pedale celeste	damper pedal
pedale del forte	sustaining pedal
pedale doppio	double (the part) on the pedal
aperto	depress damper pedal

435

una corda	depress soft pedal
tutte le corde	release soft pedal
tre corde	release soft pedal
diteggiatura, tocca	fingering
colla sinistra	with the left hand
martellato	in piano playing a forceful, detached effect in which the hands act like hammers, usually in rapidly alternating octaves
quatro mani	four hands
volteggiando	crossing the hands in piano playing
concerto	concerto
cadenza	a cadenza - florid passage
acuta	in organs, a mixture stop that includes a rank of pipes sounding a third higher than the keys played
amorosa (flauto amabile)	in organs, a hybrid flute stop
aperto	open pipes of an organ
buccina	in organs, a chorus reed stop
celestina	in organs, a very small-scaled open flute stop
contra bombarde	in organs, a deep-toned chorus reed stop
contra bourdon	in organs, the principal stopped bass stop, with a big, intense tone
contra dulciana	in organs, a very soft foundation stop
contra gamba	in organs, a low-pitched string stop
contra posaune	in organs, a low-pitched, loud chorus reed stop
contra viola	in organs, a string stop
contra violone	in organs, a bass string stop
corno d'amore	in organs, a solo reed stop
corno di bassetto	in organs, an 8-foot manual reed stop whose tone is similar to that of a basset horn
corno di caccia	in organs, a reed stop designed to sound like a hunting horn

gran coro (organo pieno)	full organ
dulciana	in organs, a soft stop similar to the diapasons in quality
flautada	in organs, a loud low-pitched foundation stop
flautino	in organs, an open flute stop
flauto d'amore	in organs, a soft solo flute stop
flauto dolce	in organs, a very soft open flute stop
flauto mirabilis	in organs, a loud open flute stop with brilliant tone
flauto traverso	in organs, an important open flute stop designed to imitate the tone of the orchestral flute
fugara	in organs, a fairly loud string stop
manubrio	the knobs and handles of the organ stops
oboe d'amore	in organs, a soft 8-foot manual reed stop
registro di mutazione	mutation stop of an organ
pedale	in organ music, indication to use pedals only
ripieno	in organs, a mixture stop
tromba	in organs, a chorus reed stop
tuba	in organs, a name for various chorus reed stops with a firmer tone quality than the trompette or trumpet stops
tuba mirabilis	in organs, a very loud and intensely brass-like 8-foot tuba stop
tuba magna	in organs, a loud, brilliant chorus reed stop
violetta	in organs, a loud, brilliant string stop
vox humana	in organs, an important reed stop
duetto	duet
quartetto di corde	string quartet
quintetto	quintet
sestetto	sextet

ottetto	octet
nonetto	nonet
coro	choir, chorus
corale	chorale
parte	voice-part
esercizio	exercise, etude
vocalizzo	vocalization
tessitura	the general range of a vocal part
alto (contralto)	a female voice of low range
bassista	a bass singer
basso profondo	a bass singer with low range, powerful voice, and solemn character
basso cantate	lyrical bass
basso buffo	comical, agile bass
quattro voci	four voices
falsetto (quillio)	falsetto
respiro	breath
fiato	breath
filar il tuono	messa di voce
fila la voce	in vocal music, prolong a note with crescendo and decrescendo
inflessione	inflection, vocal inflection; flexibility
messa di voce	vocal technique in which a sustained note is crescendoed and decrescendoed
mezza voce	with "half" voice; restrained volume
metallo	vocal timbre, tone
portamento	manner of singing in which the voice glides gradually from one pitch to the next
opera	opera
libretto	the text of an opera, oratorio, etc.
recitativo accompagnato	dramatic, accompanied recitative
recitativo secco	"dry" recitative, characterized by a lack of expressiveness

ADJECTIVES AND ADVERBS ENCOUNTERED IN MUSIC

con abbandono	unrestrained, free, passionate
abbastanza	enough, rather
abbruciante	fiery
accanito, accanitamente	frenzied, furious
accarezzevole	caressing, soothing, affectionate
accelerando	becoming faster
accentato	accented, emphasized, stressed
acceso	sparkling, brilliant
acciaccato	pounded, hammered
accompagnando	accompanying
accorato	sad, melancholy
come accordando	as if in unison
accordo	sustain the chords
d'accordo	in tune
acuto	high-pitched, shrill, sharp
adagio	slower than andante
addolcito	softer, sometimes also slower
adirato	enraged, angry
aereo	light, graceful, airy
affabile	gentle, pleasing
affannato	breathless, hurried, agitated
affettuoso	tenderly, with feeling
con affezione	tenderly, with feeling
affrettando	hurrying, rushed, pressing on
agevole	easy, smooth, fluent
aggressivo	bold, forthright
agiatamente	with ease, unhurried, comfortably
con agilatà, agilmente	nimbly, lightly
agitato	excited, restless
alato	eloquent, lofty
alcuna	some, certain
aleggiare	fluttering, quivering

439

allargando	slowing down, becoming broader/louder
allegramente	cheerfully, gaily
allegretto	moderately quick - slower than allegro
allegro	in a fast, lively tempo
allentando	slowing down
con alterezza	proudly
alzando	rising, becoming louder
amabile	sweet, loving
amaramente	harshly, sharply
con amore	fondly, with love, with warm feeling
ampiamente	broadly
ancora	again
andante	moderately slow - faster than adagio
andantino	slightly faster than andante
con angoscia, angoscioso	sorrowful, grieving, anguished
animato	lively, animated, spirited
ansante	breathless, panting, gasping
ansioso	eagerly, longingly, impatiently
aperto	open; obvious, clear
appena	scarcely, very slightly
appessantendo	becoming heavier and broader
appoggiando	emphasized, reinforced; supporting
appressando	approaching, coming closer, becoming louder
appuntato	sharply, precisely
arcato	bowed
ardente	passionate, fervent, impetuous
ardito, arditamente	bold
con ardore	with great warmth, fervently
arioso	melodic, singing
armonioso	tuneful, harmonious
arpeggiando	playing broken chords
articolando	pronouncing clearly and distinctly

aspro	harsh, rough, sharp
assai	much, very
assordire	very loud
attaca	continue without a pause
aumentando	becoming louder
con avvilimento	dejected, discouraged
avvivando	becoming livelier
con azione	with action, staged
con baldanza	boldly, confidently
ballabile	dancelike
balzando	bouncy, springy
barbaro	fierce, savage
ben, bene	well, quite
ben sentito	warmly, strongly
bestiale	brutal, cruel
bizarro	unusual, capricious
blandamente	gently, softly
con bonarietà	with good nature, aimably
con bravura	with great technical skill
breve	brief, concise
alla breve	twice as fast
brillante	sparkling, spirited
con brio, brioso	vigorously, with fire
brusco	sharply, curtly, abruptly
burra, buffo	comic, clownish
alla burla	playful, joking
burlesco	jesting, light
cadendo	becoming softer
cadenzato	in a regular rhythm, measured
calando	becoming softer and slower
calcando	forcefully, pressing on
caldo	heated, passionate
calmando	quieting down, subsiding

con calore	with warmth; fervent, impetuous
cantabile	in a singing style, lyrical
cantilena	melodious
capriccioso	fanciful, freely
in carattere	in character, typical, appropriate
carezzando	loving, affectionate
caricato	heightened, intensified, exaggerated
caricaturale	caricatured, over-exaggerated
cedendo	yielding, slowing down
celere	swift, rapid
al centro	at the center
cheto	quiet, hushed
chiaro, chiaramente	clear, bright, distinct
chiusa, chiuso	closed
circa	about, approximately
col, colla, colle	with the
come	how, like, as
comodo	comfortable, easy, unhurried
completo	wholly, entirely
con	with
concentrando	concentrating, condensing, becoming faster
concertato	conducted; scored, orchestrated
concitato	excited, agitated
contemplativo	dreamy, meditative
coperto	covered, muted
corrente	rapid, flowing
senza correre	without hurrying
corta, corto	short, brief, concise
crescendo	becoming louder
cristallino	clear, bright, pure
cupo	gloomy, deep
decisivo	decisive, firm

442

deciso	bold, forceful
declamato	recited, spoken
decrescendo	becoming softer
deliberamente	deliberately, ponderously
delicatamente	daintily, elegantly
delirando	raving, wild
con derisione	mockingly
desiderato	desired, welcome
desolato	sorrowful, disconsolate
devoto	dedicated, sincere
con dignità	with dignity, gravely
diminuendo	becoming softer
di nuovo	again, anew
disinvolto	freely, easily, deftly
con disperazione	wildly, despairingly, despondently
distaccato	detached, separated
disteso	extended, broad
distinto	clear, distinct, separate
diventando	becoming, changing to
dolce	sweet, smooth, gentle
dolcissimo	as sweet and gentle as possible
dolente	sorrowful, mournful
doloroso	lamenting, grieving
dopo	after, beyond
doppio	double, twofold, twice
drammatico	dramatically, somewhat exaggerated
duramente	harshly, severely
con ebbrezza	with elation, enraptured, blissful
eccitando	becoming excited or agitated
con effetto	dramatically, forcefully
con effusione	pouring out, emotional
eguale	even, smooth
elegante	graceful

elegiaco	mournful, lamenting
con eloquenza	with eloquence
energico	with vigor, powerfully
enfatico	exaggerated, pompous
con entusiasmo	vigorously, enthusiastically
eroico	heroic, dramatic
esaltatissimo	very excited, elated
esatto	precise, exact
esitando	hesitant, wavering
espansive	expansive, broad
espirando	fading away
espressivo	with expression, with feeling
estando	becoming broader, and usually louder
estatico	ecstatically, rapturously
estinto	very soft, barely audible
estremamente	very, exceedingly
esubarante	lively and loud
evidente	in evidence, present, audible
evvivando	becoming loud, cheering
facile	free, easy, flowing
con fantasia	freely, with imagination
fantastico	fanciful, irregular
felice	happy, glad, exultant
fermamente	steadily, unwaveringly
fervido	ardent, impassioned
con fervore	with vehemence, ardently
festivamente	joyfully, cheerfully
festoso	merry, gay
fieramente, fiero	vehemently, boldly
con finezza	with refinement, elegant
fisso	steady, firm
fitto	firmly
flessibile	agile, flexible

fluente	flowing, pulsating, wave-like
fortepiano	loud, then soft
fortissimo	very loud
con forza	powerful, forceful, loud
fragile	weak, soft
freddo	cold, without emotion
fremente	raging
frenetico	frenzied, wild
funero (funebre)	sad, mournful
con fuoco	with fire, passionately, excited
furioso	wild, passionate
gagliardo	robust, powerful, vigorous
gaio	gay, joyful
gentilmente	gently, with refinement
giocoso	jocose, humorous
gioioso	joyous, cheerful
giusto	just, right, appropriate
glorioso	glorious, splendid
con gradazione	by degrees, subtly shading
grande	broadly
grandendo	becoming broader
con grandezza	with grandeur, stately
grave	solemn, serious, slow
con gravità	dignified, serious
con grazio	with grace
grazioso	graceful and easy
alla guerra	in a martial style
con gusto	with style, with zest
imitando	imitating, echoing
immobile	motionless
con impeto	rushing in, impetuous
impetuoso	violent, impetuous
improvisando	improvising

incisivo	incisive, clear-cut
indifferente	indifferently
indolente	listless, indolent
iniziale	original, initial
coma una innodia	hymnlike
inquieto	restless, uneasy
con insistenza	persistent
intensificando	intensifying, becoming louder
intenso	intense, violent
con intenzione	purposeful, deliberate
intimement	intimately, confidentially, quietly
intrepido	fearless, undaunted
irato	furious, enraged
ironico	ironical
irresoluto	uncertain, tentative
irritato	irritated, annoyed
l'istesso tempo	at the same tempo
lacrimoso	mournful
con lamento	mournful, plaintive
con lancio	with verve
languendo	weak, faint, languishing
largamente	broadly
largando	becoming broader, slowing down
larghetto	in a slow tempo
largo	slow, solemn, sustained
legato	smooth, even with no break between notes
con leggerezza, leggèro	lightly, nimbly
lentamente	slowly
lento	in a slow tempo
lento epico	slow and stately
libero, liberamente	freely
a libro aperto	at sight

con licenza	freely, at the performer's discretion
lieve	light, easy
lirico	lyrical, poetic
lontanando	fading into the distance
lontano	far-off, remote
luminoso	bright, shining, clear
lunga, lungo	long, sustained
lusinghiero, lusingando	flattering, pleasing, caressing
maestoso	with dignity, nobly
malincònico	melancholy, gloomy
marcado, marcato	marked, pronounced; accented, stressed
marciale	marchlike, martial
massiccio	solid, heavy
meccanico	mechanical, without expressing emotion
medismo	the same
meditando	thoughtful, reflective
melodico	melodic, tuneful
meno	less
mèsto	sad, mournful
la metà	half
a metà strada	halfway between
mezzo, mezza	medium, half
misterioso	mysterious
misurato	measured, moderate, in strict time
mite	gentle, moderate
mobile	changeable, capricious
moderato	in a moderate tempo, neither fast nor slow
senza modificazioni	without changes; as written
molle	soft, languid
con mollezza	delicately
monotamente	very evenly, without much expression
morbido	soft, delicate
morboso	morbid

447

mordente	biting
morendo	fading away
mormorando	murmuring, whispering
mòsso	moved, agitated
con moto	somewhat lively, not too slowly
movendo	moving along
muovere un poco	keep going, keep moving
mutamento	change, alteration
narrante	recounting, telling
nervoso	restless, agitated
netto	clearly, plainly, distinctly
niente	nothing
nobilmente	dignified, stately
normale	return to normal tuning
occore	as needed
ogni	every
ondeggiando	gently rocking
ondulando	ondulating
oppure	or else, indicating an alternative version
oramai	from now on
ordinario	as usual, customary
oscuro	dark, unclear
ossia	or, or else
ovvero	or else, indicating an alternative version
pacato	calm, tranquil
palpitante	pulsating
parlando	in an expressive, declamatory style
parlato	spoken
passionato, con passione	impassioned
pastorale	in a pastoral style
patètico	with great emotion
penetrante	acute, penetrating
pensieroso	thoughtful, serious, solemn

perdendo	dying away
perpetuo	constant, perpetual
pesante	weighty, dull
piacevole	pleasing, agreeable, graceful
pianissimo	very soft
piano	soft
pieghevole	flexible, accommodating
piena	full
pièno	full
pietoso	loving, devoted
più	more
piu tosto	more quickly; rather, somewhat
pizzicato	plucked
placabile	soothing, mild
placido	calm, tranquil
poco	little, a bit
poco a poco	little by little
poco meno	a little less
poetico	poetic, lyrical
pomposo	stately, majestic
preciso	exact, very accurate, precise
prestissimo	as fast as possible
presto	fast, faster than allegro
prima, primo	first, principle, original
profondo	profound, deep
pronto	promptly, swiftly
pronunziato	enunciated
puntato	dotted, staccato
quanto	much, how much, as much
quasi	almost, as if
quieto	quiet, hushed
rallentando	becoming slower
rapidamento, rapido	quickly

rappresentativo	expressive, illustrative, typical
ravvivando	quickening, brightening
recitando	singing
ridendo	laughing
rigido de movimento	in strict time
rigoroso	strictly, in strict time
rinforzando	a sudden accent
risoluto	boldly, decisively
risonante	resounding, ringing, sonorous
ritardando	becoming slower
ritenuto	immediately slower, held back
ritmico	rhythmic, in strict time
ritornando	returning
scandendo	ascending
ben scandito	pronounced distinctly, well articulated
scherzando	playfully, jestingly
scherzo	lively and brisk
sciolto	easy, fluent
scolpito	clear and distinct
scordato	out of tune
secco	plain, simple, unadorned
segue	continue without pausing
semplice	simple, unaffected
sempre	always, continually, throughout
sensibile	sensitive, tender
con sentimento	with feeling
sentito	heard; expressive, heartfelt, warm
senza	without
separato	detached
sforzando	with a strong accent
sforzata	forced
con sicurezza	with assurance
simile	similarly, in like manner

sine	without
sino	up to, until
sinuoso	smooth, curving
smorendo	dying away
smorzando	fading away
soave	gentle, sweet, delicate
soffice	light, gentle, soft
sognando	dreaming, musing
solo	single, alone
sonabile	sonorous, ringing, resonant
sonoro	resonant, full-toned
sopra	over, above
sordamente	muted, very soft
sospirando	sighing, plaintive
sostenuto	sustained
sotto	under, below
sotto voce	softly, in a low voice
senza speranza	without hope, lacking confidence
spiegato	with full voice and becoming louder
spietato	ruthless, cruel
spiritoso	spirited, lively
con spirito	with spirit
staccato	detached, with each note separated
steso	slow, broad
stesso	same
strasciando, strascicamente	dragging
alla stretta	faster
stretto	accelerated, faster
stringendo	pressing on, hurrying, speeding up
subito	suddenly, immediately, at once
svelto	brisk, light, lively
tanto	much, so much, as much
tardo	slow, serious; late, delayed

tempestoso	stormy, violent
tenebroso	gloomy, somber
tenuto	held, sustained
tetro	gloomy, dark, sad
tornando	returning
tragico	tragic
tranquillo	quiet, peaceful, soft
trattenuto	held, sustained, slowed down
tremolando	quivering, trembling, rippling
trepidamente	anxious, fearful, trembling
trionfale	exultant, victorious
tronco	cut short, abrupt
troppo	too, too much
tutta, tutte, tutti	all, total
udibile	audible
uguale	equal, uniform, regular
ugualmente	equally, just the same as
ultima, ultimo	the last
con umore	with humor
unisono	in unison
con vaghezza	with charm, gracefully
vago	vague, uncertain
velato	veiled, subdued
veloce	quite fast
via	away, remove
vibrante	forceful, vigorous
vibratissimo	trembling, very agitated
vicino	nearby, close
vigoroso	vigorously, energetically
colla violenza	vehemently, with force
virtuoso	brilliant, technically very difficult
più vita	livelier, more animated
vivace	in a lively tempo, faster than allegro

con vivezza	lively, brisk, animated
con voglia	longingly, eagerly
volando	flying, rapidly
volante	rushing, rapid
con volgare	in the vernacular
vuota	open
zeffiroso	very light and airy

ADJECTIVES AND ADVERBS

abbastanza	enough
adesso	now
affollato	crowded
agitato	excited, nervous
alcuni	some, a few
allora	then
alto	tall, high
altro	other
ancora	yet, still
antico	ancient, old
aperto	open
appena	just, as soon as
artificiale	artificial
artistico	artistic
assolutamente	absolutely
attento	attentive
attivo	active
attraverso	across
avanti	ahead
azzurro	blue
basso	below
basta	enough
bene	well
bello	beautiful

benissimo	very well, fine
bianco	white
bionda	blonde
bravo	fine, good, skillful
breve	short, brief
bruna	brunette
brutto	ugly
buono	good
caldo	warm
carino	pretty
caro	dear
cattivo	bad
centro	center
certamente	certainly
certo	certain, sure
certo (che)	certainly, of course
chiaro	clear
chiuso	closed
ci	here, there
circondato	surrounded
classico	classic
come	how, as, like
commerciale	commercial
commodo	comfortable
contento	glad, satisfied
coperto	covered
cordiale	cordial, polite
dappertutto	everywhere
davvero	truly
decorato	decorated
delizioso	delicious
destro	right
difficile	difficult, hard

diverso	different
diversi	various, several
dolce	sweet
domani	tomorrow
dove	where
due	two
eccellente	excellent
esaurito	sold out, finished, exhausted
fa	ago
facile	easy
facilmente	easily
famoso	famous
favorevole	favorable
felice	happy
finalmente	finally
forte	strong, loudly
freddo	cold
fresco	cool
gentile	kind, polite, friendly
giallo	yellow
giovane	young
gran, grande	large, big, great
ieri	yesterday
impertinente	impertinent
importante	important
impossibile	impossible
incantevole	enchanting
indimenticabile	unforgettable
insieme	together
interessante	interesting
interno	interior
inutile	useless
invernale	winter

iscritto	enrolled
là	there
leggiero	light
lì	there
lontano	far, far away
lungo	long; along
maggiore	greater, greatest, older, oldest
magnifico	magnificent
mai	never, ever
male	badly
mattinata	morning
medioevale	medieval
meglio	better, best
meno	less
meraviglioso	wonderful, marvelous
mezzo	middle
mica	at all
migliore	better, best
minore	smaller, smallest, younger, youngest
moderno	modern
molto	much; very
morto	dead
naturalmente	naturally
nazionale	national
neanche	not even
necessario	necessary
nemmeno	not even
nero	black
non	not
nulla	nothing
nuovo	new
occupato	busy
oggi	today

ogni	each, every
ora	now
originale	original
ormai	now, by now
ottimo	excellent, very good
peggio	worse, worst
peggiore	worse, worst
pendente	leaning
perchè	why, because
personalmente	personally
pessimo	very bad
piano	slowly
piccolo	small, little
pieno	full
più	more
piuttosto	rather
poco	little
poi	after, then
povero	poor
preciso	precise, exactly, on the dot
preferito	favorite
presente	present
preso	taken
presso	near, among; in care of
presto	early, soon
prima	before, first
primo	first
pronto	ready
proprio	really, indeed, truly
purchè	provided
qua	here
qualche	some, a few, any
quando	when

quanto	how much
quasi	almost
qui	here
raccomandato	registered
raramente	rarely
regolare	regular
religioso	religious
risposto	answered
rosso	red
santo	saint, holy
scorso	last
scritto	written
seduto	seated
seguente	following
semplice	simple
sempre	always
sepolto	buried
sicuro	sure, safe
simpatico	charming, pleasant
sinistro	left
solamente	only
solito: di solito	usually
solo	alone, only
speciale	special
specialmente	especially
spesso	often
spiritoso	witty
squisito	exquisite
stamani	this morning
stanco	tired
stasera	this evening, tonight
stesso	same
strano	strange, peculiar

subito	immediately
sveglio	awake
tanto	much, so much
tardi	late
terribile	terrible
triste	sad
troppo	too, too much
tutto	all, everything
ultimo	last, latest
unico	only, single
utile	useful
vecchio	old
veloce	fast
velocemente	rapidly, fast
veramente	truly, as a matter of fact
verde	green
vero	true
vi	there
vicino	near
lì vicino	near there
qui vicino	near here, nearby
volentieri	willingly, gladly
vuoto	empty

EXPRESSIONS

buon giorno	good morning (good day)
buona sera	good afternoon (good evening)
buona notte	good night
ciao	hello, good-bye (colloquial)
grazie	thank you
grazie lo stesso	thank you just the same
scusi	excuse me
per favore	if you please

prego	you're welcome
Come sta Lei?	How are you?
bene	well
Sto bene, grazie	I am well, thank you
qui	here
là	there
a destra	to the right
a sinistra	to the left
diritto	straight ahead

Chapter Five

I. SENTENCE STRUCTURE

The study of sentence structure in the next three chapters should substantially facilitate the translation of texts and augment understanding of the basic elements of grammatical construction.

Negative Forms

1. The word *sì* is the positive answer to a question and means "yes".

2. The word *no* is the negative answer to a question and means "no".

"...rispondi: no o sì!"
(D. Gabrielli, *Flavio Cuniberto*, "Emilia's aria")

3. The negative is formed in Italian by placing *non* before the verb. Whenever the adverb *non* appears in sentence structure in translating, it indicates that the verb is negative.

a) The negative form of the present tense is:

cantare - to sing

non canti	non cantiamo
non canti	non cantate
non canta	non cantano

J.C. Bach - Non è ver

Sarri - Non ha ragione ingrato

Carissimi - Ma no, non fuggir

Legrenzi - Non mi dir di palesar

Caccini - Non piango e non sospiro

Buzzoleno - Non fuggirai

Compound tenses are made negative by placing *non* before the auxiliary verb; the auxiliary verb is never separated from the past participle in Italian.

b) The imperative is made negative by placing *non* before the imperative verb form. Exception: the negative imperative of the second person singular (tu) is the infinitive.

"...e non bagnar mie ceneri..."
(Salieri, "In questa tomba oscura")

c) Reflexive verbs are made negative by placing *non* before the reflexive pronoun.

Carissimi - No, no, non si speri

4. The following negative expressions generally follow the verb in Italian and require *non* before the verb. When used for emphasis, these words precede the verb; *non* is not required.

mai - never (ever)

niente, nulla - nothing (anything)

nemmeno, neanche - not even

nessuno - no one

nè...nè - neither...nor

non più - no more

Carissimi - Filli, non t'amo più

Falconieri - Non più d'amore

"...ma nulla valse ai lassa..."
(Monteverdi, "In un fiorito prato")

"...e nessun rifà il mio danno..."
(Vinci, "Vedovella afflitta e sola")

"Nessuno mai m'amò, nessuno ho amato, nessuna cosa mai di diè piacere!"

(Puccini, *La fanciulla del West*, "Minnie, dalla mia casa")

II. PARTITIVE

When a noun refers to only a part of its whole, to *some* or *any*, it is in the *partitive* sense. The partitive sense in English is frequently expressed by the words *some* or *any*, often implied rather than stated.

Partitive Forms

1. The partitive is expressed in Italian by the preposition *di* plus the definite article. The partitive meaning "any" is generally not expressed in interrogative and negative sentences in Italian.

2. The partitive may be expressed by *alcuni(-e)* plus the noun modified; *alcuni(-e)* may also be used as a partitive pronoun when the partitive sense (some, any) implies "several" or "a few."

3. The partitive may be expressed by *qualche* plus the singular form of the noun modified when the partitive sense (some, any) implies "several" or "a few".

4. The partitive may be expressed by *un po' di* when the partitive sense (some, any) means "a little", "a bit of"; the partitive *un po'* may also be used as a partitive pronoun.

5. The partitive is frequently used with verbs such as *volere, avere, mangiare, ordinare, portare* because only a part of the noun to which the partitive refers is generally desired.

III. PREPOSITIONS

A *preposition* shows the grammatical relationship of a noun or pronoun to some other element in the sentence. The following are prepositions frequently encountered in Italian:

a	at, in, to
attraverso	across
avanti	before, forward
circa	about
con	with
da	from, by since
davanti	before, in front of
di	of, than, from
dopo	after, afterwards
durante	during
eccetto	except
fino, fin	until, as long as, as far as
fra	between, among, within
fuori	out, outside
in	in, into, within
per	for, in order to; through
presso	near, among; in care of

senza	without
sopra	on, above, upon
sotto	under, beneath
su	on, upon, concerning
verso	toward, about
secondo	according to
contro	against

"...sotto alla pia a la dolcissima del tuo sospir..."
(Ponchielli, *Il figliuol prodigo*, "Roccogli e calma")

"...sovra il mar degli anni, cui l'onda batte..."
(Verdi, *Ernani*, "Oh! de'verd'anni miei")

Algara - Saggio sopra l'opera in musica

Special Uses

1. The preposition *a* means "in, to" when used before the name of a city.

2. The preposition *a* follows these verbs before an infinitive: *andare, continuare, imparare, incominciare, venire*

"...vieni a consolar il pianto mio..."
(Mozart, *Don Giovanni*, "Deh, vieni alla finestra")

Respighi - Venitelo a vedere

3. The preposition *di* follows these verbs before an infinitive:

bramare

cercare

cessare

dire

domandare

finire

permettere

promettere

pregare

sperare

Cimarosa - Bramar di perdere - (Artaserse)

Scarlatti - O cessate di piagarmi

464

4. A preposition is not required after the following verbs before an infinitive:

desiderare

dovere

fare

potere

preferire

sapere

sentire

vedere

volere

Perti - Sperar io non dovrei

Manzia - Voglio farti dire il vero

de Luca - Non posso disperar

Bononcini - Più non ti voglio credere

Carissimi - Non posso vivere

5. The preposition *da* is used

a) before an infinitive that depends on *qualcosa, niente (nulla), molto, poco, tanto*.

b) to express *purpose, use* or *manner* when used before a noun.

c) to indicate "at somebody's office (place)", "at the house of", etc., when used before a name, a pronoun, or before a noun which refers to a person.

6. It is important to learn the exact meaning of prepositions for translation; these small words are critical in determining sentence meaning.

IV. CONJUNCTIONS

A *conjunction* is a word used to connect words, phrases, or clauses; a *clause* is a group of words containing a subject and a verb. A *main* (independent) clause can form a sentence in itself; a *subordinate* (dependent) clause can function only with an independent clause. The following are conjunctions frequently encountered in Italian:

a meno che...non	unless
almeno	at least
anche, altresì	also
avanti che	before
dopo che	since
dunque	then
e, ed	and
finchè, fino a	until
inoltre	besides, moreover
ma	but
mentre	while
nemmeno	not even
o, od	or
perchè	because
perciò	therefore
però	but, however
poichè	since
pure	anyway, also
se	if

"...forse - perché una pioggia di soavi rugiade...cade.-"
(Respighi, "Notte")

Piccini - Se il ciel mi divide

Monteverdi - Se i languidi miei sguardi

Scarlatti - Se Florinde è fedele

A. Coordinating Conjunctions

Coordinating conjunctions connect expressions of equal value and are used:

1. to connect affirmative and negative sentences:

e, ed	and
anche, altresì	also
per di più, inoltre	besides, moreover
pure	also, yet
neanche, neppure	not even

2. to express two or more possibilities:

o, od	or
ovvero	or, or also
oppure, ossia	or, or else

3. to express contrast or opposition:

ma, però	but
tuttavia	however, nevertheless
anzi	on the contrary
eppure	and yet, still
nondimeno	nevertheless

4. to express a result:

dunque	then
quindi	therefore
perciò	therefore

5. to express a mutual relationship:

e...e	not only...but also
(non) nè...nè	neither...nor
così...come	as well as
tanto...quanto	as well as
o...o	either...or
sia...sia	be it...be it
non solo...ma anche	not only...but also

a) The expression "either...or" may be expressed by using *o...o*, or by using *nè...nè* with *non* before the verb.

6. to introduce an explanation:

infatti, invero	in fact

B. Subordinating Conjunctions

Subordinating conjunctions introduce dependent clauses and connect them to main clauses, and are used:

1. to express a time concept:

quando, allorchè	when
appena che, tostochè	as soon as
fino a che	as long as
mentre	during, while
dopo che	since
prima che	before
finchè	until, as long as

2. to state a reason:

perchè	because
giacchè, poichè, siccome	because
visto che, dal moment che	since, because

3. to express a purpose:

affinchè, acciocchè, perchè	therewith

4. to express a condition

se	if, whether
nel caso che	in case
a condizione che	under the condition that
a meno che	except when
supposto che	assuming that

5. to express an admission or allowance:

benchè, sebbene	although

6. to express a comparison

come se	as though

7. to denote a result or sequence:

cosicchè, di modo che	so that

V. INTERJECTIONS

An *interjection* is an exclamation in sentence structure; the most frequently encountered interjection in Italian is *Deh*! (ah!, oh!)

VI. ADDITIONAL PRONOUN FORMS

To this point all nouns and pronouns have been in reference to the subject of the sentence. Additional pronoun forms describe the relationship in sentence structure of pronouns to other words. The Italian personal pronouns have two forms: (1) *conjunctive pronouns* - used as the subject or object in direct conjunction with verbs, and (2) *disjunctive pronouns* - used as objects, but not necessarily as the object of a verb.

A. Direct Object Pronouns

A *direct object* receives directly the action expressed by the verb. *Direct object pronouns* are conjunctive pronouns because they are used in conjunction with a verb. Direct object pronouns generally precede the verb in Italian:

Singular		*Plural*	
mi	me	ci	us
ti	you	vi	you
lo	him, it	li	them (m)
la	her, it	le	them (f)
La	you	Li	you (m)
		Le	you (f)

1. The forms *mi, ti, lo, la, vi* are generally contracted to *m', t', l', v',* before a vowel or mute *h*.

"...mi battea la pioggia..."
(Respighi, "Pioggia")

"...un più divino amor dal ciel vi sgombra..."
(Tosti, "L'alba separa dalla luce l'ombra")

"...Oscar lo sa, ma nol dirà..."
(Verdi, *Un ballo in maschera*, "Saper vorreste")

Note the contraction here
nol = non + lo

"...Lindoro...lo giurai, la vincerò..."
(Rossini, *Il barbiere di Siviglia*, "Una voce poco fa")

Malipiero - Se tu m'ami

Torelli - Tu lo sai

Caldara - Si t'intendo

2. *ci* is contracted to *c'* only before *i* or *e*.

3. When *La, Li, Le* are capitalized, they always mean "you" (polite form).

4. When the pronoun refers to a group of masculine and feminine members, the masculine forms *li, Li* are used.

5. In a negative sentence the direct object pronoun is placed between *non* and the conjugated verb.

Tosti - Non m'ama più

6. When the verb form is a compound tense, the direct object pronoun precedes the auxiliary verb; the past participle must accordingly agree in gender and number.

"...Ah! l'ho perduto..."
(Bellini, *La Sonnambula*, "Ah! non credea mirarti")

B. Indirect Object Pronouns

An *indirect object* indicates *to* or *for whom* the action of the verb is done. Like direct object pronouns, the *indirect object pronouns* are conjunctive pronouns because they are used in conjunction with a verb. Indirect object pronouns generally precede the verb in Italian:

Singular		*Plural*	
mi	to me	ci	to us
ti	to you	vi	to you
gli	to him, to it	loro	to them (m and f)
le	to her, to it		
Le	to you	Loro	to you (m and f)

"...e mi repete..."
(Respighi, "Nebbie")

d'Astorga - Ti parlo

Bononcini - Se ti piace

1. The forms *mi, ti, vi* are generally contracted to *m', t', v'* before a vowel or mute *h*.

2. *Ci* is contracted to *c'* only before *i* or *e*.

3. The indirect object pronoun *loro* (*Loro*) always follows the verb in Italian.

C. Position of Conjunctive Pronouns

1. Conjunctive pronouns precede all forms of the negative imperative and the affirmative imperative forms of *Lei* and *Loro*.

2. Conjunctive pronouns follow the affirmative imperative of *tu, noi, voi* and are attached directly to the verb.

Buzzoleni - Volgimi, o cara filli

Respighi - Venitelo a vedere

Carissimi - Soccorretemi

Monteverdi - Illustratevi, o cieli

Monteverdi - Lasciatemi morire

Provenzale - Deh, Rendetemi

Rossi - Ah, Rendimi

Carissimi - Deh contentatevi

"...chiudimi, o notte...spegnetevi incorrotte!..."
(Tosti, "L'alba sepàra dalla luce l'ombra")

"...lasciami riposar..."
(Salieri, "In questa tomba oscura")

a) *loro* is not attached to the verb.

3. The initial consonant of the conjunctive pronoun is doubled (Exception: *gli*) when attached to a monosyllable imperative (generally the *tu* form).

Pizzetti - Levommi il mio pensier

4. Conjunctive pronouns always follow and are directly attached to the infinitive. The final *-e* of the infinitive is dropped before the conjunctive pronoun is attached.

Bononcini - Per la gloria d'adorarvi

Cesti - Tu mancavi a tormentarti

Cimarosa - Nel lasciarti

A. Scarlatti - Sono unite a tormentarmi

"...e sai spiegarle..."
(Caccini, "Ch'hai le penne, amore")

"...sapranno i labbri miei scoprirgli il tuo desio..."
(Traetta, "Dirò che fida sei")

"...O betta diglielo..."
(Traetta, "Ma che vi costa, signor tuttore")

    a) *Loro* (*loro*) is never attached to the infinitive.

5. If both a direct and an indirect object pronoun are used in sentence structure in Italian, the indirect object precedes the direct object; both either precede or follow the verb according to the foregoing principles.

    a) The indirect object pronouns *mi, ti, si, ci, vi* change the final -*i* to -*e* and become *me, te, se, ce, ve* when followed by the direct object pronouns *lo, la, li, le, ne*.

    b) When the indirect object pronouns *gli* and *le* are followed by the direct object pronouns *lo, la, li, le, ne*, the indirect object pronoun becomes *glie* and combines with the following pronouns: *glielo, gliela, glieli, gliele, gliene*.

    c) The indirect object pronoun *Loro* (to you, to them) always follows the verb.

6. The past participle of verbs conjugated with *avere* agrees with the direct object (preceding the verb) when it refers to a person; agreement is optional if the direct object does not refer to a person.

7. The conjunctive pronoun *ne* refers to a noun modified by the preposition *di* plus an article, or by the preposition *di* alone. According to the meaning of the antecedent, *ne* means "of it", "of him", "of her", "of them", "some of it", "some of them", "any", "a few", etc.

    a) The Italian equivalent of *ne* must always be expressed.

    b) The position of *ne* in the sentence is the same as that of any other conjunctive pronoun. When *ne* is used in place of a direct object in a compound tense, the past participle of the verb agrees with *ne* in gender and number.

8. The adverb *ecco* (here is, here are; there is, there are) is used as an exclamatory expression in Italian; the conjunctive pronouns are always attached to *ecco*.

VII. DISJUNCTIVE FORM

The *disjunctive* form of personal pronouns differs from the conjunctive in form and usage. The conjunctive forms are generally used as the subject, direct object, and indirect object of verbs; the disjunctive forms of personal pronouns are generally used to refer to persons only:

Singular		*Plural*	
me	me	noi	us
te	you	voi	you
lui	him	loro	them
lei	her		
Lei	you	Loro	you
sè	himself, itself	sè	themselves, yourselves
	herself, yourself		

Uses of Disjunctive Pronouns

1. Disjunctive forms of personal pronouns are used as the object of a preposition (con, fra, per, di, da, etc.).

"...la vita è il nulla senza di te!"
(Ponchielli, *Il figliuol prodiga*, "Raccogli e calma")

"...a poco parlando con me..."
(Sartorio, "Oh, che umore stravagante")

"...ch'a noi, al bosco, al prato..."
(Provenzale, "Deh! riedi, riedi omai")

2. Disjunctive forms of personal pronouns are used in place of object (conjunctive) pronouns for emphasis or contrast. When the verb has two or more objects the disjunctive pronoun forms follow the verb.

VIII. POSSESSIVE PRONOUNS

Possessive adjectives modify nouns; *possessive pronouns* replace nouns modified by a possessive adjective.

Forms of Possessive Pronouns

Singular		*Plural*		
m.	f.	m.	f.	
il mio	la mia	i miei	le mie	my, mine
il tuo	la tua	i tuoi	le tue	your, yours
il suo	la sua	i suoi	le sue	his, her, hers
il Suo	la Sua	i Suoi	le Sue	your, yours
il nostro	la nostra	i nostri	le nostre	our, ours
il vostro	la vostra	i vostri	le vostre	your, yours
il loro	la loro	i loro	le loro	their, theirs
il Loro	la Loro	i Loro	le Loro	your, yours

1. Note that the forms of the possessive pronouns are the same as those of the possessive adjectives (Chapter Four).

a) The definite article usually precedes a possessive pronoun.

b) Possessive pronouns agree in gender and number with what is possessed (the possession).

IX. DEMONSTRATIVE PRONOUNS

A *demonstrative pronoun* points out or indicates, and answers the question "which one(s)?".

Forms of Demonstrative Pronouns

Singular			*Plural*	
m.	questo	this one	questi	these
	quello	that one	quelli	those
f.	questa	this one	queste	these
	quella	that one	quelle	those

1. Demonstrative pronouns are used to distinguish between persons or things within a group.

2. Demonstrative pronouns must agree in gender and number with the nouns to which they refer.

3. In contrast to the demonstrative adjective forms, the demonstrative pronouns *questo* and *quello* replace rather than modify nouns.

"...da questa apprende nel dubbio cor..."
(Verdi, *Un ballo in maschera*, "Volta la terrea")

"Madamina! I catalogo è questo..."
(Mozart, *Don Giovanni*)

"...questa o quella..."
(Verdi, *Rigoletto*, Act I)

4. *Quello* is also translated "the one of" (one's).

5. The adverbs *qui* (*qua*) "here" and *lì* (*là*, "there" correspond to the demonstrative adjective and pronoun forms *questo* and *quello*; *ci* and *vi* are used as unstressed adverbs of place meaning "there", "here". These forms are used to refer to a place already mentioned in the sentence, and precede or follow the verb in the same pattern as conjunctive pronouns.

"...Figaro qua, Figaro là, Figaro su, Figaro giù..."
(Rossini, *Il barbiere di Siviglia*, "Largo al factotum")

"...tantin, tantino - venite qua."
(Traetta, "Ma che vi costa, signor tutore")

PREPOSITIONS THAT GIVE DIRECTIONS IN MUSIC

a due	in two parts
a tempo	return to normal speed
a tre voce	in three parts
a voce piena	with full voice
al fine	to the end
col legno	with the wood of the bow
con sordino(i)	with mute(s)
senza sordino	without mute
sul ponticello	at (near) the bridge
sul tasto	on the fingerboard
sulla tastiera	on the fingerboard

PREPOSITION SUPPLEMENT

A. Time of Day

1. Che ora è? Che ore sono? - What time is it?

2. È l'una. It is one o'clock.

   È mezzogiorno. It is noon.

   È mezzanotte. It is midnight.

   Sono le due. It is two o'clock.

   Sono le cinque. It is five o'clock.

3. The word *ora* (singular) *ore* (plural) is implied but not expressed in giving the time of day.

4. The half hour is expressed:

   Sono le cinque *e mezzo(a)*. It is 5:30.

5. The quarter after the hour is expressed:

   Sono le cinque *e un quarto*. It is 5:15. (quarter past five)

6. The quarter to the hour is expressed:

   Sono le cinque *meno un quarto*. It is a quarter to five.

   Manca un quarto alle cinque. It is a quarter to five.

7. To express minutes between the hour and the half hour the number of minutes is added to the hour.

   È l'una e dieci. (1:10)

8. To express minutes between the half hour and the following hour, the time is measured back from the next hour:

   Sono le cinque *meno* dodici. It is 4:48.

   Mancano dodici minuti alle cinque. It is 4:48.

9. *in punto* is used to mean "exactly"

   mezzogiorno - noon

   mezzanotte - midnight

   di mattina is used to express A.M.

   del pomeriggio is used to express early P.M. (afternoon)

   di sera is used to express late P.M. (evening)

10. The 24-hour system is used in official announcements, especially for travel, banks, theatres, offices, etc.; after noon 1:00 is 13.00 (le tredici), and so forth.

    a) In this system, fractions of an hour are expressed in terms of minutes after the hour.

B. Dates

1. In Italian, a date is expressed in the order *day, month* year.

2. The first day of the month is *il primo*.

3. The other days of the month are expressed by the cardinal numbers.

    a) The definite article is used to express "on".

4. The answer(s) to the question "Quanti ne abbiamo oggi?" (What is today's date?) is "Oggi è il tre.".

ABBREVIATIONS FOUND IN MUSIC

m.s.	- mano sinistra	left hand
c.s.	- colla sinistra	with the left hand
c.d.	- colla destra	with the right hand
c.b.	- col basso	with the bass
div.	- divisi	divided
loc.	- loco	used to indicate return to the normal octave after all'ottava or similar designations
pp	pianissimo	very soft
p	piano	piano
mp	mezzopiano	medium soft
mf	mezzoforte	medium loud
f	forte	loud
ff	fortissimo	very loud
sfz	sforzato	loud then suddenly soft
D.C.	da capo	from the beginning
D.S.	dal segno	repetition from the sign

TRANSLATION EXERCISES

1. Translate the following article "Musica d'oggi" from the *Dizionario Ricordi della musica e dei musicisti.*[1]

> Musica d'oggi - periodico della casa Ricordi, fondato nel 1919 da Carlo Clausetti e Renzo Valcarenghi. Trimestrale nel 1919, divenne mensile nel 1920 e continuò le pubblicazioni fino a tutto il 1942. Interrotto dalla guerra, fu sostituito da "Ricordiana" nel 1951, diretto da Pietro Montani, al quale venne affiancato come redattore Riccardo Allorto nel 1955. Nel 1958 ne ha assunto la direzione Guido Valcarenghi (Redattore R. Allorto), e la rivista ha ripreso la testata primitiva (Nuova Serie). Svolge un programma informativo e critico, con dichiarata fedeltà alla tradizione italiana, ma senza pregiudizi.

2. The following guidelines suggest the systematic translation process of the article entitled "Musicologia" from the *Dizionario Ricordi.*

> *Musicologia*. E' l'applicazione del metodo scientifico di ricerca e di studio al fenomeno musicale in tutta la sua estensione e in tutte le sue manifestazioni. Necessita quindi di solida e vasta preparazione culturale generale e tecnica specifica (dall'acustica alla paleografia, dalla storia all psicologia, dalla teoria mus. all'estetica e via dicendo). E'scienza modernamente coltivata nelle nazioni culturalmente più avanzate. In Italia vi contribuiscono solamente alcuni musicologi isolati. per iniziativa personale, poichè l'istruzione statale non prepara sufficientemente a questo genere di studi.

> *musicologia*: *musicology* - the term is generally defined at the outset of such articles. *è l'applicazione del metodo scientifico* - the predicate nominative construction with the verb *essere* indicates that *musicology is the application of the scientific method*; note the use of the adjective *scientifico* following the noun modified. *di ricerca e di studio*: *of research and study* - note the repetition of the preposition *di* (of) before *studio*, which is not translated into English. *al fenomeno musicale*: *to the musical phenomenon* - note the contraction *al = a + il* and the use of the adjective following

---

[1] *Dizionario Ricordi della musica e dei musicisti*, (Milano: G. Ricordi and C., 1959).

the noun modified. *in tutta la sua estensione e in tutte le sue manifestazioni*: the word *estensione* is a cognate of the English word *extension*; *estensione* is singular and is modified accordingly by the possessive adjective form *la sua*.

manifestazioni, "manifestations" is plural and is modified by the possessive adjective form *le sue*. The adverb forms *tutta*, *tutte* are used in the prepositional sense to mean "all of". Translation of the first sentence: "Musicology is the application of the scientific method of research and study to the musical phenomenon in all of its extension and in all of its manifestations."

Necessita quindi di solida e vasta preparazione: *necessita* is the third person singular form (present tense) of the verb *necessitare*, "to necessitate", translated "it necessitates"; "it" refers to *musicology*. *quindi* is an adverb meaning "hence, therefore, then". The preposition *di* is used in an indefinite partitive sense, and is not translated into English; *solida* (solid) *e vasta* (broad) are adjectives preceding the noun modified - *preparazione*, "preparation". *culturale generale e tecnica specifica*: *culturale* is an adjective modifying *preparazione*: *generale* is an adjective modifying *culturale*; *tecnica* is an adjective modifying *preparazione*; *specifica* is an adjective modifying *tecnica*; these adjectives all follow the noun modified. Translation in context: "it necessitates, therefore, a solid and broad general cultural and specific technical preparation..." (*dall'acustica alla paleografia, dalla storia alla psicologia, dalla teoria mus. all'estetica e via dicendo*): ("from acoustics to paleography, from history to psychology, from music(al) theory to aesthetics, by way of example.") Note the use of the contracted forms of the prepositions *da* and *a* with the definite article for the contrast between extremes. The present participle of the verb *dire - dicendo -* is used here idiomatically.

a) Complete the translation of this passage, using this form.

Chapter Six

I. WORD ORDER IN SENTENCE STRUCTURE

A. Normal Word Order

1. Subject and its modifiers
2. Verb
3. Verbal modifiers

   a) Since the personal endings of verb forms indicate the person and number of a tense, subject pronouns may be omitted in sentence structure in Italian except when necessary for clarity, or when emphasis or contrast is desired.

B. Inverted Word Order

For stylistic variety or in order to emphasize a particular element, a sentence in Italian may begin with an element other than the subject; this is known as *inverted word order*.

   1. The most frequently encountered form of inverted word order is the *question*. Questions are formed in Italian in the following ways:

   a) A declarative sentence may be made into a question by changing the punctuation from a period to a question mark.
   "Dimmi s'è ver che m'ami?"
   (Bellini , *I Puritani*, "Son vergin vezzosa")

   b) Questions are often formed in Italian by inverting the subject and verb.
   Bassani - Dormi, bella, dormi tu?

   c) When an interrogative adverb or adverbial expression is used to form a question, the interrogative word or expression generally stands first in the question.
   quanto? - how much?

   dove? - where?

   perchè? - why?

   "...ah perchè non son io co' miei pastori?"
   (Pizzetti , "I Pastori")

   Paesiello - Dove, ahi dove son io?

   Pergolesi - L'amico dov'è?

481

II. INTERROGATIVE ADJECTIVES AND PRO-NOUNS

A. Forms of Interrogative Adjectives

quale? - which?

che, che cosa, cosa? - what?

"Qual uom qual Dio a questa febbre del mio desio ti può rapir?"
(Ponchielli, *Il figliuol predigo*, "Roccogli e calmi")

"Che siete voi?"
(Verdi, *Ernani*, "Oh! de' verd'anni miei")

"Qual destino ti furò al natio fulgente sol?"
(Verdi, *La Traviata*, "Di provenza il mar")

"Dimmi, o caro infedel, che t'ho fatt'io?"
(A. Scarlatti, "Se delitto è l'adorarti")

1. An interrogative adjective modifies a noun or pronoun; it agrees in gender and number with the noun it modifies.

B. Interrogative Pronouns

1. The following *interrogative pronouns* are used as the subject of a sentence: chi? - who?; che? - what?

Paesiello - Chi vuol la zingarella?

Jommelli - Chi vuol comprar la bella calandrina?

"Chi mi nomasti?"
(Donizetti, *Lucia de Lammermoor*, "Regnava nel silenzio")

"Che chiedi?"
(Donizetti, *Lucia di Lammermoor*, "Regnava nel silenzio")

a) The verb used with these pronouns is usually in the third person singular.

2. The following *interrogative pronouns* are used as the direct or indirect object of a sentence:

Direct	*Indirect*
chi? whom?	a chi? to whom?
che? what?	a che? to what?

482

3. The interrogative pronoun *di chi?* (whose) is the interrogative form expressing possession which corresponds to the prepositional possessive *di.*

4. The forms of the interrogative pronoun *quale?* are used to distinguish between two or more persons or things within a group. These forms agree in gender and number with the nouns to which they refer.

Singular	*Plural*
m. quale? which?	quali? which ones?
f. quale? which one?	quali? which ones?

III. RELATIVE PRONOUNS

Forms

A *relative pronoun* is used to connect a dependent (relative) clause to a main clause; the relative pronoun refers to a noun in the main clause. Relative pronouns are a key to efficient translations.

1. English uses three relative pronouns: *who* refers to a person; *that, which* refer to a thing. The forms of relative pronouns in Italian are:

a) The relative pronoun *che* (who, whom, that, which) is invariable; *che* is never used with prepositions, and may refer to persons or things. (The interrogative pronoun *che?* refers only to things.)

(1) The relative pronoun *che* is contracted to *ch'* before a vowel.

(2) The verb which follows the relative pronoun *che* agrees with the antecedent of *che*, that is the noun to which the relative pronoun *che* refers:

Mancini - Dir ch'io t'ami

Aniello - Lo so che pria mi moro

Pizzetti - Quel rosignuol che si suave piagne

Cimarosa - Pria che spunti in cielo

Cimarosa - È vero che in casa io sono padrone

Cimarosa - È ver che le villane

"Caro nome che il mio cor festi primo palpitar..."
(Verdi, *Rigoletto*, "Caro nome")

"...dite alla cruda ch'io l'amo e l'adoro..."
(Rontani, "Caldi sospiri")

> "...lascia che l'ombre ignude..."
> (Salieri, "In questa tomba oscura")

b) The relative pronoun *cui* (whom, which) is invariable; *cui* is generally used only after a preposition.

> "...nel cui tenue spirto..."
> (Respighi, "Il Tramonto")

> "...ho chiome odorose cui cinser tue rose..."
> (Bellini, *I Puritani*, "Son vergin vezzosa")

c) The relative pronoun *quale* (who, whom, that which) is variable; *quale* is always preceded by the definite article. This form is infrequent; it is occasionally used instead of *che* after a preposition for clarity.

Singular	*Plural*
m. il quale	i quali
f. la quale	le quali

d) The relative pronoun *chi* is translated "he who", "the one who".

> "...qual di chi parla..."
> (Donizetti, *Lucia di Lammermoor* , "Regnava nel silenzio")

> "...chi non piange d'amar non si dia vanto..."
> (Carissimi, "Piangete, ohimè, piangete")

e) The relative pronoun *quello che* (quel che) means "what" when it implies "that which". The form *ciò che* can also mean "that which".

IV. INDEFINITE ADJECTIVES AND PRONOUNS

An *indefinite* adjective or pronoun does not clearly define or designate the person or thing to which it refers. The following are indefinite adjectives and pronouns in Italian:

A. Indefinite Adjectives

altrettanto	as much as
certo	certain
differente, diverso	different
ogni	every
qualche	some, a few, any
qualsìasi	whichever, whatever; any
qualunque	whatever; each, any
tanto	so much, very much

B. Indefinite Pronouns

altri...altri...	the one...the other
altrui	others, of others
certuno, taluno	someone
certuni, taluni	many
chiunque	whoever, anybody
niente, nulla	nothing
ognuno	everybody
qualche cosa, qualcosa	something
qualcheduno, qualcuno	someone
uno	one, someone

C. Indefinite Adjectives or Pronouns

altro	someone, anyone; other
alcuno	some, someone, anyone
ambedue	both
ciascheduno, ciascuno	every
medisimo, stesso	same
molto	much
nessuno	no, nothing

parecchio	several
poco	a few
tale	such
troppo	too much
tutto	all, whole

"...tutti mi chiedono, tutti mi vogliono..."
(Rossini, *Il barbiere di Siviglia*, "Largo al factotum")

EXERCISE

1. Translate the following from the article "Pianoforte" from the *Dizionario Ricordi*.

> PIANOFORTE. (fr. e sp. piano; ingl. pianoforte; ted. Klavier, Flügel). Strumento della famiglia dei cordofoni, nel quale le corde vengono percosse da martelletti azionati da una tastiera. Dopo l'organo è le str. che ha la maggior estensione, comprendendo dalla nota più bassa alla più acuta l'estensione di tutta l'orch. sinfonica. Attualmente la tastiera del P. ha l'estensione LA_1-do_7; qualche rarissimo P. da concerto si estende di altre 4 note verso il basso (fino al FA1) e di 5 note verso l'acuto (fina al fa_7). D'altra parte molti P. verticali non arrivano verso l'acuto fino al do7 ma solo al la6.

TRANSLATION EXERCISES

1. Translate the following article from the *Dizionario Ricordi*.

Chapter Seven

I. ADDITIONAL CHARACTERISTICS OF VERBS

Special Uses

1. A verb infinitive may be used in Italian as a noun (subject, direct object); when used as the subject of the sentence the infinitive may take the masculine definite article.

> "...esser pianta, esser foglia, esser stello..."
> (Respighi, "Pioggia")

2. The verbs *dovere*, *potere*, *volere*, *sapere* are sometimes used as modal auxiliary verbs with a verb infinitive. These verbs describe a state of mind or mood and help convey the idea expressed by the complementary infinitive. These verbs are conjugated with either *essere* or *avere*, depending on the auxiliary verb of the dependent infinitive. Conjunctive pronouns may precede the conjugated verb or follow the infinitive.

> "...morir debbo..."
> (Tosti, "L'alba separa dalla luce l'ombra")

3. Note the difference in meaning of the following verbs:

a) The verbs *sapere* and *conoscere* both mean "to know", but can not be used interchangeably:

(1) *sapere* - to know a fact, to know how (to do something)

(2) *conoscere* - to know a person, place, etc.; to be acquainted with, to meet

b) *dire* and *parlare*

(1) *dire* - to tell, say - used to describe what has or will be said

(2) *parlare* - to speak, to talk - used to describe the actual act of speaking

c) *vivere* and *abitare*

(1) *vivere* - "to live" in the sense of "to be alive"

(2) *abitare* - "to live" in the sense of "to inhabit"

d) When the verb *fare* is followed by an infinitive it means "to have something done", "to make", or "to cause" (something to be done). The verb *fare* plus an infinitive is termed *causative*, because the doer

487

causes something to be done. In causative sentence structure the word order is

fare + infinitive + noun

(1) *fare* plus an infinitive also translates "to have someone do something"; in this construction, the "something" is the direct object, the "someone" the indirect object. If both objects are nouns the word order is: infinitive + direct object + indirect object. If the objects are pronouns, they precede *fare*. (Exception: *loro* always follows the infinitive).

"...il ciel l'ha fatta nascere..."
(Donizetti, *Don Pasquale*, "Bella siccome un angelo")

"...che il destin me fe' soffrir..."
(Donizetti, *Don Sebastiano*, "O Lisbona, alfin ti miro")

Cavalli - Affè mi fate ridere

e) When the verb *piacere*. (to be pleasing) is used idiomatically meaning "to like" the subject of the sentence is an indirect object.

4. An *impersonal verb* makes a general statement rather than referring to any particular person or thing. Impersonal verbs are conjugated solely with the *lui* form, and can therefore be used only in the third person singular. The use of impersonal verbs is more common in Italian than in English.

a) The most obvious group of impersonal verbs are those which describe the weather:

piovere - to rain

nevicare - to snow

tirare vento - to be windy

"...piovea; perle finestre spalancate..."
(Respighi, "Piogga")   ·

5. The pronoun *si* is often used impersonally to mean "one", "they", "people", etc. The third person singular of the verb is used when the indefinite subject is *si*. If the indefinite subject has a *plural* direct object, the third person *plural* of the active verb should be used with *si*; if the verb is reflexive, *ci* is substituted for *si* in the third person.

6. The present participle (gerund) in Italian, formed by adding *-ando* or *-endo* to the verb stem, is used to translate the English participle in *-ing*, and with the verb *stare* to express an action in progress.

"...offron, pregando, i bronchi nudi..."
(Respighi, "Nebbie")

a) Conjunctive and reflexive pronouns follow the present participle and are attached to it. (Exception: *Loro*)

b) The past form of the gerund consists of the present participle of *avere* or *essere* (avendo, essendo) plus the past participle of the finite verb; the past participle may conform to the principles of agreement.

7. In the *active voice* the subject performs some act; in the *passive voice*, the subject is acted upon. The meaning of a statement in either the active or the passive voice is generally the same; it is generally preferable and easier, however, to use the active voice. The passive voice is formed in Italian, as in English, by adding a past participle to the appropriate tense of the verb *essere*; the past participle agrees with the subject.

II. SUBJUNCTIVE MOOD

It is most important to become familiar with the following information on the subjunctive and conditional moods in order to facilitate efficient translation.

Forms

The *subjunctive* is the mood (form of the verb showing the speaker's attitude toward what he says) which expresses conditions contrary to fact, wishes (a wish is not a factual statement because it contains an element of unreality), an opinion, doubts, or what is possible, rather than certain. The seven verb tenses studied in Chapter Three are all in the *indicative mood*, that is, all of these tenses express fact, rather than probability. Modern English has only a few genuine subjunctive forms and therefore uses substitute words like *may*, *let*, *should* and *would*; Italian has distinct subjunctive forms which are used frequently. The subjunctive mood has the following characteristics:

1. Four frequently encountered tenses: present, imperfect, compound past, past perfect.

2. Italian verbs in the subjunctive mood have the following endings in the *present tense*:

cantare	applaudire	battere	capire	avere	essere
canti	applauda	batta	capisca	abbia	sia
canti	batta	applauda	capisca	abbia	sia
canti	batta	applauda	capisca	abbia	sia
cantiamo	battiamo	applaudiamo	capiamo	abbiamo	siamo
cantiate	battiate	applaudiate	capiate	abbiate	siate
cantino	battano	applaudano	capiscano	abbiano	siano

"...Oh! che il mio epitaffio, che io tuo sia "Pace!"..."
(Respighi, "Il Tramonto")

"...le doglie e l'asprezze sian nuove dolcezze..."
(Cesti, "I casti amori d'Orontea")

a) The subject pronoun is usually used with the first, second, and third person singular forms for clarity.

b) Many verbs which are irregular in the present tense of the indicative mood are regular in the present tense of the subjunctive mood.

(1) Although all irregular verbs in the present tense of the subjunctive mood (except *avere* and *essere*) have the same endings as regular verbs, some irregular verbs have an irregular stem; the most frequently encountered irregular verbs that have an irregular stem in the present tense of the subjunctive mood are:

andare: vad-

dare: di-

dire: dic-

dovere: dev-; dobb-

fare: facc-

potere: poss-

stare: sti-

tenere: teng-

venire: veng-

volere: vogl-

Note that *dovere* has one irregular stem for the first, second, and third persons singular and the third person plural, another stem for the other forms in the present tense of the subjunctive mood.

3. The present tense of the subjunctive mood is encountered frequently in texts and is used:

    a) in subordinate clauses (a subordinate clause can function only with an independent clause) introduced by *che* when the principle clause expresses:

        (1) a wish or a desire - desiderare, volere

        (2) doubt or uncertainty - dubitare

        (3) ignorance - non sapere

        (4) belief - credere, pensare

        (5) fear - avere paura

        (6) hope - sperare

    b) If the verb in the dependent clause expresses a future idea or action, the future tense in the indicative mood may be used instead of the present tense in the subjunctive mood (especially after *se* and *quando*). Verbs expressing a wish or command are in the subjunctive mood even when a future idea or action is expressed.

    c) The subjunctive is used in a subordinate clause after an impersonal expression or verb implying doubt, necessity, possibility, desire, or emotion.

        (1) Impersonal expressions which are positive assertions do not require the subjunctive.

        (2) If the subordinate clause has no subject, the infinitive form of the verb is used instead of the subjunctive mood.

    d) The subjunctive mood is required after the relative superlative or the adjectives *unico, solo* when the subordinate clause is introduced by *che*.

    e) The following conjunctions and conjunctive expressions are used frequently to introduce clauses in the subjunctive mood:

affinchè	so that, in order that
a meno che...non	unless
benchè	although
sebbene	although
perchè	in order that
prima che	before
purchè	provided that
senza che	without

f) The subjunctive mood is used in a main clause introduced by *che* to express wishes and exhortations.

4. The *compound past tense* of the subjunctive mood consists of the present tense subjunctive of *avere* or *essere* plus the past participle of the verb.

cantare			andare		
abbia	cantato	I (may) have sung	sia	andato(a)	I (may) have gone
abbia	cantato		sia	andato(a)	
abbia	cantato		sia	andato(a)	
abbiamo	cantato		siamo	antadi(e)	
abbiate	cantato		siate	andati(e)	
abbiano	cantato		siano	andati(e)	

The compound past tense of the subjunctive mood is generally used like the present tense of the subjunctive (governed by a main clause expressing a wish, fear, joy, or doubt) to express actions that have already taken place.

a) If the verb of the main clause is in the present or future tense of the indicative mood or is an imperative, the present or compound past tense in the subjunctive mood is used in the subordinate clause.

5. The *imperfect tense* in the subjunctive mood (governed by a main clause expressing a wish, fear, joy, or doubt) is used to express habitual actions in the past, a state of affairs in the past, or continuous past action that might be. The endings for the imperfect tense in the subjunctive mood are:

past tense in the subjunctive mood is used in the subordinate clause.

5. The *imperfect tense* in the subjunctive mood (governed by a main clause expressing a wish, fear, joy, or doubt) is used to express habitual actions in the past, a state of affairs in the past, or continuous past action that might be. The endings for the imperfect tense in the subjunctive mood are:

cant*are*		batt*ere*	applaud*ire*
cant*assi*	I sang, I might sing	batt*essi*	applaud*issi*
cant*assi*		batt*essi*	applaud*issi*
cant*asse*		batt*esse*	applaud*isse*
cant*assimo*		batt*essimo*	applaud*issimo*
cant*aste*		batt*este*	applaud*iste*
cant*assero*		batt*essero*	applaud*issero*
avere		essere	
avessi	I had, I might have	fossi	I was, I might be
avessi		fossi	
avesse		fosse	
avessimo		fossimo	
aveste		foste	
avessero		fossero	

"Oh! se una volta sola rivederlo io potessi anzi che all'ara altra sposa
ei guidasse!"
(Bellini, *La Sonnambula*, "Ah! non credea mirarti")

6. The *past perfect tense* (trapassato prossimo) in the subjunctive mood (governed by a main clause expressing a wish, fear, joy, or doubt) is used to express an action that might have already taken place if another past action had taken place, and consists of the imperfect tense in the subjunctive mood of the auxiliary verb (*avere* or *essere*) plus the past participle.

cantare		andare	
avessi	cantato I might have sung	fossi	andato(a) I might have gone
avessi	cantato	fossi	andato(a)

III. CONDITIONAL MOOD

The *conditional mood* is used to state what "would be" or "would have been". The fulfillment of the chain of actions is contingent on the occurrence of some basic action; the basic action is always a condition, expressed or understood. There are two tenses in the conditional mood: present and compound past.

A. Present Tense

The *present tense* of the conditional mood tells what "would (should) happen" and is formed by adding the following endings to the verb stem used for the future tense in the indicative mood:

cantare		battere	applaudire
cant*erei*	I would (should) sing	batt*erei*	applaud*irrei*
cant*eresti*		batt*eresti*	applaud*iresti*
cant*erebbe*		batt*erebbe*	applaud*irebbe*
cant*eremmo*		batt*eremmo*	applaud*iremmo*
cant*ereste*		batt*ereste*	applaud*ireste*
cant*erebbero*		batt*erebbero*	applaud*irebbero*

"...saper vorreste di che si veste..."
(Verdi, *Un ballo in maschera*)
Stradella - Col mio sangue comprenderei

avere		essere	
avrei	I would have	sarei	I would (should) be
avresti		saresti	
avrebbe		sarebbe	
avremmo		saremmo	
avreste		sareste	
avrebbero		sarebbero	

1. Verbs in *-are* change the *a* of the infinitive ending to *e*.

2. Note that the endings are identical for all verb conjugations.

3. Verbs with irregular stems in the future tense of the indicative mood have the same stem for the present tense of the conditional mood.

B. Compound Past Tense

The *compound past tense* of the conditional mood consists of the present tense of the conditional mood of *avere* or *essere* plus the past participle of the verb. The compound past tense of the conditional mood is used to express what "would have happened".

cantare		andare		
avrei	cantato I would have sung	sarei	andato(a)	I would have gone
avresti	cantato	saresti	andato(a)	
avrebbe	cantato	sarebbe	andato(a)	
avremmo	cantato	saremmo	andati(e)	
avreste	cantato	sareste	andati(e)	
avrebbero	cantato	sarebbero	andati(e)	

C. Uses

1. In the result clause of certain conditional sentences. In conditional sentences which describe *what would happen* if a certain condition were fulfilled, the present or compound past tense of the conditional mood is used in the main or result clause; the verb in the "if"-clause (*se*) should be in the imperfect or past perfect tense in the subjunctive mood, depending on the time to which the sentence refers.

2. In all other conditional sentences the appropriate tense in the indicative mood is used in both clauses.

"...se il padre s'adira, io volo a mia stanza..."
(Bellini, *I Puritani*, "Son vergin vezzosa")

"Se Florinda è fedele, io m'innamorerò."
(A. Scarlatti, *La donna ancora fedele*, "Alidoro's aria")

3. If the verb of the main clause is in a past tense or in the conditional mood, the imperfect or past perfect tense in the subjunctive mood is used in the subordinate clause.

4. The conditional tense forms do not suggest obligation; to express "should" (obligation, ought to) the verb *dovere* is used. The present tense of *dovere* in the conditional mood denotes obligation and is translated "should", "ought to"; the present tense of *potere* in the conditional mood is translated "could", or "might". The compound past tense of *dovere* in

the conditional mood is translated "ought to have", "should have"; the compound past tense of *potere* in the conditional mood is translated "could have", "might have".

TRANSLATION EXERCISES

1. Translate the following article from the *Dizionario Ricordi*.

QUARTETTO *(fr. quatuor;* ingl. *quartet:* ted. *Quartett: sp. cuarteto)*. Composizione per 4 strumenti o 4 voci, e per estensione nome dato al complesso degli esecutori.

La più importante e classica delle combinazioni quartettistiche è quella di 4 str. ad arco (Q. d'archi: fr. *quatuor cordes;* ingl. *string quartet*; ted. *Streichquartett*) formato da 1° e 2° vl., viola e vc., che risale alla seconda metà del sec. XVII. Tuttavia il Q. d'archi raggiunse la sua totale autonomia costituendo un complesso omogeneo e inscindibile solo nella seconda metà delll '700, con Haydn e Mozart. Dal punto di vista formale il quartetto d'archi classico è composto come una sonata o una sinfonia, ma può talora anche essere formato da diversi pezzi in forma di suite ecc.

Un'altra formazione usuale del Q. è quella di 3 archi (vl., viola e vc.) e pf. usata da Mozart, Beethoven, Schumann, Mendelssohn, Brahms ecc. (ingl. *piano quartet*; ted. *Klavierquartett*). Tuttavia nessun limite si pone alla fantasia del comp. nella combinazione strumentale di un Q., sì che si possono trovare gli accostamenti più vari: 4 tromboni (*Equali* di Beethoven); 4 corni (*Sonata* di Hindemith); vl., cl., sxf. e pf. (*Q.* di Webern); fl., viola, chitarra e vc. (Schubert); vl., viola, vc. e chitarra (Paganini); ob., vl., viola e fg. (Malipiero), ecc.

Il Q. vocale solistico si trova soprattutto nelle opere italiane già nel sec. XVII, ma fu più tardi introdotto anche nella MdC da Mozart, Schumann e Brahms.

LETT. - W. Altmann, *Handbuch für Streichquartettspieler*, Berlino 1928; P. Schülter, *Die Anfänge des modernen Streichquartetts*, Bleicherode 1939; U. Lehmann, *Deutsche und italienische Streichquartette*, Dissertation, Berlino 1939; M. Pincherle, *Les instruments du quatuor*, Parigi 1948.

2. Translate the following from the article "Sinfonia" from the *Dizionario Ricordi*.

Sinfonia. 1) I greci, intendendo il termine nello stretto significato etimologico, indicavano con esso la consonanza degli intervalli, contrapponendola a *diaphonia*, e l'unisono contrapponendolo a *paraphonia* e a *antophonia* (quinta e ottava).

2) Nel medioevo il termin indica le consonanze di ottava, quarta, quinta e doppia ottava e viene applicato a comps. basate su questi principi. È spesso sinonimo di canto e di melodia in genere e con S. si indicano anche alcuni strumenti (più precisamente *symphonia*): la *ghironda*, il *tamburo* e un particolare tipo di clavicordo.

3) Il primitivo uso del termine, come sinonimo di pezzo strumentale, va ricercato forse già nel sec. XV dove appare in un ms. conservato a Lipsia e contenente una S. per "tuba e altri strumenti armonici", ma organicamente il concetto è sviluppato da L. Marenzio con alcuni intermedi orchestrali del 1589 già definiti come S.; più tardi le usarono S. Rossi (*Primo libro delle S.* 1607) e A. Banchieri (*Eclesiastiche S. dette Canzoni* op. 16, 1607). Ma già in queste prime accezioni il termine S. andava sempre più distinguendosi dalla sonata, per indicare un brano in forma bipartita con riprese, e tale precisazione chiaramente avvertibile nelle S. di S. Rossi (1613) e nella *Sinfonia breve* contenuta negli *Affetti musicali* op. 1 di B. Marini (1617). La destinazione del termine a comps. strumentali prive del concorso delle voci è poi riconfermata dal Praetorius (syntagma musicum).

La prima definizione formale della S. va ricercata in quella comps. definita verso la fine del sec. XVII e indicata come *ouverture all'italiana* (o *sinfonia avanti l'opera*) costituita da tre tempo di movimento contrastante (Allegro-Adagio-Allegro), dove il tempo centrale ha carattere di transizione e si collega con il precedente e il conseguente su una cadenza imperfetta, che permette una concezione continua della comps. e non una netta separazione tra gli elementi della comps. stessa.

Tornando alla S. come concezione strumentale, dobbiamo ricordare l'importanta sviluppo dato agli inizi del sec. XVIII dalle scuole tedesche al concetto di bitematismo, principalmente a Vienna...

THE AUTHOR

JULIE YARBROUGH, a native of Dallas, Texas, holds the B.M. in voice (magna cum laude, 1970), the B.M.E. (magna cum laude, 1970) and the M.M. in voice (1971) from Texas Christian University in Fort Worth, Texas.

She studied at the Staatliche Hochschule für Musik in Freiburg, Germany and received the artist diploma from that institution in 1974.

From 1976–1980 she was engaged for leading mezzo-soprano roles at the Stadttheater in Regensburg, Germany and performed widely throughout Germany as a concert singer specializing in the repertory of J. S. Bach.